# A HISTORY OF THE BILDUNGSR

The Bildungsroman has been one of the most significant genres in Western literature since the eighteenth century. This volume, comprising eleven chapters by leading experts in the field, offers original insights into how the novel of formation developed a strong tradition in Germany, France, Britain, Russia and the USA. In demonstrating how the genre has been adopted and adapted in innovative forms of fiction, this volume also shows how a genre traditionally associated with the young white man has been used to give expression to the formative experiences of women, LGBTQ people and postcolonial populations. Exploring the genre's emergence and evolution in numerous countries and across more than two hundred years, this volume provides unprecedented historical and geographical coverage and demonstrates that the Bildungsroman has a rich heritage and a bright future.

DR SARAH GRAHAM is Lecturer in American Literature at the University of Leicester.

# A HISTORY OF THE BILDUNGSROMAN

EDITED BY

SARAH GRAHAM

*University of Leicester*

CAMBRIDGE UNIVERSITY PRESS

# CAMBRIDGE
## UNIVERSITY PRESS

University Printing House, Cambridge CB2 8BS, United Kingdom

One Liberty Plaza, 20th Floor, New York, NY 10006, USA

477 Williamstown Road, Port Melbourne, VIC 3207, Australia

314-321, 3rd Floor, Plot 3, Splendor Forum, Jasola District Centre, New Delhi - 110025, India

79 Anson Road, #06-04/06, Singapore 079906

Cambridge University Press is part of the University of Cambridge.

It furthers the University's mission by disseminating knowledge in the pursuit of education, learning and research at the highest international levels of excellence.

www.cambridge.org
Information on this title: www.cambridge.org/9781316501870
DOI: 10.1017/9781316479926

First published 2019
First paperback edition 2021

*A catalogue record for this publication is available from the British Library*

ISBN 978-1-107-13653-3 Hardback
ISBN 978-1-316-50187-0 Paperback

Cambridge University Press has no responsibility for the persistence or accuracy of URLs for external or third-party internet websites referred to in this publication, and does not guarantee that any content on such websites is, or will remain, accurate or appropriate.

# Contents

# Notes on Contributors

GREGORY CASTLE is Professor of British and Irish literature at Arizona State University, USA. In addition to essays on W. B. Yeats, John M. Synge, James Joyce, Bram Stoker, Oscar Wilde, George Moore, Emily Lawless and other Irish writers, he has published *Modernism and the Celtic Revival* (Cambridge), *Reading the Modernist Bildungsroman* and the *Literary Theory Handbook*. He has edited the *Encyclopedia of Literary and Cultural Theory*, vol. 1 and the *History of the Modernist Novel* (Cambridge). With Patrick Bixby, he has edited Standish O'Grady's *Cuchulain: A Critical Edition*, and is currently editing *A History of Irish Modernism* (Cambridge). He continues to work on the Bildungsroman and the temporalities of Irish Revival.

ALISON FINCH is Professor Emerita of French Literature, University of Cambridge, UK, and a Fellow of Churchill College, Cambridge. She has published widely on French literature, with a particular emphasis on the nineteenth century. Her books include *Proust's Additions: The Making of 'A la recherche du temps perdu'* (Cambridge, 1977); *Stendhal: La Chartreuse de Parme* (1984); *Women's Writing in Nineteenth-Century France* (Cambridge, 2000); and *French Literature: A Cultural History* (2010).

IAN GORDON is Professor of American History at the National University of Singapore. His books include *Comic Strips and Consumer Culture* (1998); *Superman: The Persistence of an American Icon* (2017); and *Kid Comic Strips: A Genre Across Four Countries* (2016); the edited volumes *Ben Katchor: Conversations* (2018); *The Comics of Charles Schulz: The Good Grief of Modern Life* (2017); and *Film and Comic Books* (2007). He is an International Contributing Editor to the *Journal of American History* and on the editorial board of several journals including the *Journal of Graphic Novels and Comics; Popular Communication; Studies in Comics; Inks*; and *ImageText*.

SARAH GRAHAM is Lecturer in American Literature at the University of Leicester, UK. Her research area is North American writing from the modernist period to the contemporary. Her publications to date have focused on the work of H. D. (Hilda Doolittle), J. D. Salinger, and contemporary fiction, including: Editor, *J. D. Salinger's The Catcher in the Rye* (2007); Author, *Salinger's The Catcher in the Rye* (2007); chapters in *The Cambridge Companion to H. D.* (2011) and *The Cambridge Companion to American Novelists* (2013). Her current projects include a monograph, *Reading J. D. Salinger's Short Fiction* (2019), while ongoing research in twentieth- and twenty-first-century American novels and short stories considers the evolution of the Bildungsroman in America; representations of adolescence and the family; and gender and sexuality.

ERICKA HOAGLAND is Associate Professor of English at Stephen F. Austin State University, USA. Her work focuses on the African Bildungsroman, including a 2014 presentation on the postcolonial Bildungsroman for the 10th International Janheinz Jahn Symposium on African Literature, as well as intersections between science fiction and empire. Her publications include *Science Fiction, Imperialism, and the Third World* (2010); an essay, 'Colonial Ambiguity and Ambivalence in Gwyneth Jones' Aleutian Trilogy' for *The New Centennial Review* (Fall 2013); and an essay, 'Mothering the Universe on Star Trek' for *To Boldly Go: Essays on Gender and Sexuality in the Star Trek Universe* (2017).

MARY (MAROULA) JOANNOU is Professor Emerita at Anglia Ruskin University, Cambridge, UK, and has published some forty book chapters and essays in peer-reviewed journals. Her publications include *'Ladies, Please Don't Smash These Windows': Women's Writing, Feminism and Social Change, 1918–1938* (1995) and *Women's Writing, Englishness and National and Cultural Identity: The Mobile Woman and the Migrant Voice, 1938–1962* (2012). She has edited *Women's Writing of the 1930s: Gender Politics and History* (1998) and volume eight (1920–45) of *The Palgrave History of British Women's Writing* (2012).

TODD KONTJE is Distinguished Professor of German and Comparative Literature at the University of California, San Diego, USA. He is the author of *Private Lives in the Public Sphere: The German Bildungsroman as Metafiction* (1992) and *The German Bildungsroman: History of a National Genre* (1993), as well as books on German women writers, German Orientalism and Thomas Mann. His most recent book is

*Imperial Fictions: German Literature Before and Beyond the Nation-State* (2018).

FIONA MCCULLOCH was Lynn Wood Neag Distinguished Visiting Professor of British Literature at University of Connecticut in 2015, and is currently an independent scholar. As well as publishing several peer-reviewed articles, her books include *Contemporary British Children's Fiction and Cosmopolitanism* (2017); *Cosmopolitanism in Contemporary British Fiction: Imagined Identities* (2012); *Children's Literature in Context* (2011); and *The Fictional Role of Childhood in Victorian and Early Twentieth-Century Children's Literature* (2004).

MEREDITH MILLER is Lecturer in English at Cardiff University, UK. Her DPhil (University of Sussex) focused on lesbian novels and readership in the mid-twentieth century, and she has published widely on gender, sexuality and popular fiction. Her most recent monograph is *Feminine Subjects in Masculine Fiction: Modernity, Will and Desire, 1870–1910* (2013). Two recent book chapters focus on masculine identity and the aesthetics of nation and empire in the nineteenth-century novel. She is also the author of two published novels, with a third forthcoming.

RICHARD SALMON is Senior Lecturer at the University of Leeds, UK, where he teaches nineteenth- and early twentieth-century literature. His main research interests are in the Victorian novel, nineteenth-century print culture and professional authorship, and the work of Henry James. Book publications include, most recently, *The Formation of the Victorian Literary Profession* (Cambridge, 2013); *Thackeray in Time: History, Memory, and Modernity* (co-edited with Alice Crossley, 2016); and a scholarly edition of *The Reverberator* for *The Cambridge Edition of the Complete Fiction of Henry James* (2018). He has previously written on the nineteenth-century English Bildungsroman for a volume of *The Oxford History of the Novel* (2012) and in relation to Victorian narratives of the literary profession.

LINA STEINER is Senior Lecturer in Philosophy at the University of Bonn, Germany. Her publications include a monograph on the history of the Russian Bildungsroman, *For Humanity's Sake: The Bildungsroman in Russian Culture* (2011), and numerous articles on Russian and German literary history and theory. She is currently editing *The Palgrave Handbook to Russian Thought* and is working on a new monograph entitled *The Russian Prometheus: Lev Tolstoy and Enlightenment*.

# Acknowledgements

I would like to thank the contributors, who have been wonderful to work with. My editors at Cambridge University Press, Linda Bree and Bethany Thomas, have offered support and advice at every stage of the project. Thanks to the University of Leicester for research leave that enabled me to complete this book. And, finally, special thanks to Emma Parker for her invaluable insight and encouragement.

# Introduction

## Sarah Graham

Anyone who reads fiction will eventually encounter a Bildungsroman –
a novel about a young person facing the challenges of growing up – because
it is one of the most popular and enduring genres in literary history.
Depicting the journey from youth to maturity, a classic Bildungsroman
concentrates on a protagonist striving to reconcile individual aspirations
with the demands of social conformity. The narrative offers privileged
access to the psychological development of a central character whose sense
of self is in flux, paralleling personal concerns with prevailing values.
The Bildungsroman's ability to explore the relationship between self and
society accounts for its lasting global appeal.

*A History of the Bildungsroman* is the first comprehensive study of the
genre and the broadest in terms of historical and geographical scope to
date. Its sweeping perspective reveals the remarkable adaptability and
diversity of the genre. By exploring its emergence and endurance in multiple locations over more than two hundred years, rather than focusing solely
on national or historical literary traditions or the influence of identity
politics, the volume investigates the genre in a new way. The chapters range
widely in terms of place and time, and offer a variety of approaches to the
subject. Firstly, there is discussion of the genre's evolution in the countries
that have most fully embraced it: Germany, France, Britain, Russia and the
Soviet Union, and the United States of America, all of which have
substantial Bildungsroman traditions. Secondly, there is analysis of how
the genre, historically associated with the realism, was adopted and adapted
in innovative forms of fiction, such as Modernist novels at the beginning of
the twentieth century and contemporary graphic fiction. Thirdly, consideration is paid to the ways in which the Bildungsroman, originally concerned with young, white, privileged, heterosexual men, came to give
expression to the marginalised and silenced, in writing about the formative
experiences of women, LGBTQ people, and postcolonial populations.
The chapters, written by prominent critics in Bildungsroman studies,

discuss canonical and less familiar texts, forming an original analysis of how
the genre has been adapted to the concerns of various times and places.
The volume as a whole conveys that the Bildungsroman has not only
survived but thrived while other traditional forms, like the epistolary
novel, the picaresque, and the allegory, have all but disappeared.
*A History of the Bildungsroman* thus explores the principal aspects of the
genre – its themes, ideologies, implications and effects – to show why it has
been, and remains, an integral part of literary culture.

*A History of the Bildungsroman* enriches debates about a genre that has
inspired little critical consensus. While there is agreement that
'Bildungsroman' is a German word, every other aspect of the genre has
been debated, from when it first appeared to whether it exists at all.[1] Tobias
Boes credits Karl Morgenstern with first defining the genre in a lecture
titled 'On the Nature of the Bildungsroman' (1819), although he acknowledges that Wilhelm Dilthey popularised the term in his study, *Poetry and
Experience* (1906).[2] 'Bildungsroman' has been widely adopted untranslated,
which could suggest shared understanding of its meaning, though for
Jeffrey L. Sammons the word 'lurks about in non-German usage because
it resists easy translation'.[3] That 'roman' means 'novel' is commonly
accepted, but 'bildung' could be rendered in English as 'formation',
'development', 'growth', or 'education'. Marc Redfield contends that the
'word *Bildung* is untranslatably rich. *Bild* means "image," "painting,"
"figure," or "trope," and *Bildung* thus commands a range of aesthetic
associations'.[4] Additional complications arise with the variant terms that
are near-synonyms for Bildungsroman, such as Entwicklungsroman,
Erziehungsroman, and the more commonly used Künstlerroman.[5]
Antibildungsroman and Metabildungsroman add to the variety of terms
available, indicating the range of narratives that can be understood to be
part of the tradition of the genre.[6]

Like one of its protagonists, the Bildungsroman has an origin story, but
there is ongoing disagreement on its key points. Several critics assert that
Johann Wolfgang von Goethe's multi-volume novel, *Wilhelm Meisters
Lehjahre* (*Wilhelm Meister's Apprenticeship*, 1795–6), is the urtext, while
others make that claim for *Geschichte des Agathon* (*The Story of Agathon*,
1766–7) by Christoph Martin Wieland.[7] Either way, the genre's birth
seems deeply implicated with the German Enlightenment. In his
renowned study of the genre, *The Way of the World* (1987), Franco
Moretti argues that the Bildungsroman arises in the late eighteenth century
because it allows writers and readers to navigate the rapid pace of social
change in Europe. 'Youth is … modernity's "essence"', argues Moretti,

underscoring the connection between the progress of a young person and the transformation of European culture.[8] Because of its association with the German Enlightenment, it has been argued that only a German novel of the era of Goethe and Wieland that depicts the transition from youth to maturity can be truly considered a Bildungsroman. In 1916, for instance, Thomas Mann defined the genre as 'a variety of the novel that is German, typically German, legitimately national'.[9] Kelsey Bennett avers that 'many view bildung as a summation of the eighteenth century's impossibly utopian Enlightenment ideals', suggesting that the genre has strict boundaries.[10] These critical assessments call into question the capacity of the Bildungsroman to integrate itself into the literature of other nations while maintaining a distinct identity as a genre.

The chapters collected in this volume contest the notion that the Bildungsroman is exclusively German. Equally, they resist Michael Beddow's claim that, once outside the context of German studies, 'any novel which depicts the development of a single hero or heroine' might be labelled a Bildungsroman, a definition that risks becoming meaningless because it is too wide.[11] As *A History of the Bildungsroman* shows, although it rarely presents the intense philosophical debates often seen in its early German incarnation, 'Bildungsroman' is much more than a bland synonym for any story of personal formation. Though adaptable, the genre retains fundamental characteristics that render it distinct. Thus, the Bildungsroman is recognisable wherever it appears. Although responsive to culture, history, and society, Martin Swales asserts that '[a]s long as the model of the genre is intimated as a sustained and sustaining presence in the work in question, then the genre retains its validity as a structuring principle within the palpable stuff of an individual literary creation'.[12] In Mikhail Bakhtin's formulation, what is vital about the genre is that at its heart is a person in the process of becoming, someone who 'emerges *along with the world* and [who] reflects the historical emergence of the world itself'.[13] However, for Michael Minden, trial and failure are far more important than becoming: 'the *Bildungsroman* makes the shortcomings of the individual . . . the driving force of its narratives'.[14] Minden's emphasis on failure challenges the traditional view that the Bildungsroman traces its protagonist's journey to social integration and success.

Despite the specifics of its birth in eighteenth-century Germany and attempts to control its form and meaning, the Bildungsroman has proved, as Bennett observes, 'fully capable of resonating with meaning in a number of widely divergent quarters'.[15] All the chapters in this study refer to the key aspects of the Bildungsroman identified in its German manifestation, but also show how and why other national literatures have embraced it for their own purposes, typically using it to communicate concerns that extend beyond the literary sphere to wider society. As Moretti argues, the Bildungsroman is crucial 'not only in the history of the novel, but in our entire cultural legacy', because it 'depicts and re-enacts as we read it, a relationship with the social totality' (23). As several chapters in this volume show, the Bildungsroman is profoundly concerned with what it means to be an individual and to participate in the life of a nation.

According to Moretti, the different eras of the Bildungsroman cannot be traced in a rigid, linear manner. He suggests, '[w]e need a different geometrical pattern here – not a straight line but a tree, with plenty of bifurcations for genres to branch off from each other' (234). Progression in the Bildungsroman since the publication of *The Way of the World* might be considered new branches of the genre's genealogical 'tree'. However, Moretti's metaphor of roots and shoots implies that varieties of Bildungsroman subsequent to the German original are marginal and inferior. An alternative metaphor for the genre's growth might be the rhizome. In *A Thousand Plateaus* (1980), Gilles Deleuze and Félix Guattari adopt the rhizome, a term taken from botany, as an image of thought. In contrast to the tree, the rhizome is a tangled network of interwoven roots, a structure without origin or end. As John Marks explains, 'the model of the tree is hierarchical and centralized whereas the rhizome is proliferating and serial, functioning by means of the principles of connection and heterogeneity'.[16] Embracing Deleuze and Guattari's concept to reconceive the tradition of the Bildungsroman, the chapters in this book together demonstrate that the expansion of the genre is less arboreal than rhizomatic.

In Chapter One, 'The German Tradition of the Bildungsroman', Todd Kontje challenges theorists who claim that the genre 'expresses the mysterious essence of the German soul', proposing that it has been employed to critique rather than simply articulate national identity. For Kontje, this makes the German Bildungsroman a highly political form. His analysis of texts such as Goethe's *Wilhelm Meister's Apprenticeship*, Gottfried Keller's *Green Heinrich* (1854–5), Thomas Mann's *Magic Mountain* (1924) and Günter Grass's *The Tin Drum* (1959) counters the traditional view of the German bildungsroman as an intellectual and philosophical investigation of personal identity. Instead, Kontje proposes that the genre comments critically on the complex history of the German nation.

In Chapter Two, Alison Finch explores 'The French Bildungsroman'. She highlights ambivalence towards the genre, reflected in the absence of both 'Bildungsroman' and its equivalent, 'roman de formation', from the French language prior to the 1960s. As Finch observes, this does not mean that there are no Bildungsromane in French literature. On the contrary, the genre existed before the publication of *Wilhelm Meisters Lehjahre*: the anonymously authored *The Princesse de Clèves* (1678) and Françoise de Graffigny's *Letters of a Peruvian Woman* (1747) may in fact have influenced Goethe. When it is adopted, it is often with irony, as seen in the hero's journey from kind-heartedness to egocentricity in Stendhal's *Red & Black* (1830). Though out of fashion by the end of the nineteenth century, Proust's *À la recherche du temps perdu* (1913) brought the genre back to life. While French literature may not have adopted the traditional Bildungsroman unequivocally, it has produced some of the influential examples of the genre.

In Chapter Three, Richard Salmon acknowledges the irrefutable significance of *Wilhelm Meister* to nineteenth-century British fiction. He argues that all the major authors of the era were familiar with Goethe's text and that innumerable novels, both famous and obscure, show its influence. Salmon contends that a cohesive body of work that responds to the German Bildungsroman emerges across the period. Thomas Carlyle's *Sartor Resartus* (1833–4) is a novel of formation and his translation of Goethe has been credited with establishing the genre in English literature. Salmon assigns equal significance to relatively unfamiliar novels such as Edward Bulwer-Lytton's *Ernest Maltravers* (1837) and George Meredith's *Beauchamp's Career* (1876) and renowned texts like Charles Dickens's *David Copperfield* (1849–50) and George Eliot's *Daniel Deronda* (1876). He suggests that the popularity of the genre lies in its capacity to combine ostensibly oppositional Victorian values.

In Chapter Four, 'The Bildungsroman in Imperial Russia and the Soviet Union', Lina Steiner makes a case not only for the importance of Russian writers and literary theorists in the evolution of the genre, but also for its significance in Russian culture. Bakhtin's consideration of the Bildungsroman is still cited widely today. Through the Bildungsroman, artists and intellectuals connected with European thought and modernity. Alexander Pushkin's *The Captain's Daughter* (1836), Lev Tolstoy's *War and Peace* (1869) and Fyodor Dostoevsky's major works all underscore the importance of self-development in the nineteenth century, the era of Russia's cultural ascendancy. Although the social changes brought by the Bolshevik Revolution of 1917 placed restrictions on the intelligentsia, Steiner argues that certain post-revolutionary novels, such as Mikhail

Bulgakov's *The Master and Margarita* (1940) and Boris Pasternak's *Doctor Zhivago* (1957), express scepticism about Soviet ideology.

In Chapter Five, 'The American Bildungsroman', I argue that the genre expresses the USA's unique sense of youth and potential through young protagonists on a formative journey. The chapter proposes that there are two distinct strands of American Bildungsroman. One, exemplified by the work of Horatio Alger, celebrates the nation's promise of life, liberty and happiness (enshrined in the Declaration of Independence) as well as the American Dream that promises success and prosperity to all. The second reveals that the nation's assurances do not hold for many young Americans. The chapter focuses on this second strand and analyses representations of white working-class boys and girls of all classes, whose stories reveal the hollowness of America's pledges to its citizens. It also discusses coming-of-age novels depicting social groups typically marginalised and dispossessed in the USA, including African and Native Americans. It concludes by showing that even a privileged white boy like Holden Caulfield in *The Catcher in the Rye* (1951) is unimpressed by American ideals and definitions of success.

Many Bildungsromane, especially those of the nineteenth century, are realist novels, but in Chapter Six, 'The Modernist Bildungsroman', Gregory Castle shows that the genre is evident in more experimental fictions, too. In particular, the Künstlerroman plays a significant role in modernism, Castle argues, because it offers a way of expressing the creativity and dynamism of the protagonist's interior world that the classical version of the genre does not permit. Castle analyses representations of the artist in Walter Pater's *Imaginary Portraits* (1888), Oscar Wilde's *The Picture of Dorian Gray* (1890) and James Joyce's *A Portrait of the Artist as Young Man* (1916). He also examines 'portraits of aesthetic life' in E. M. Forster's *A Room with a View* (1908), Virginia Woolf's *The Voyage Out* (1915), and Dorothy Richardson's *Pilgrimage* (beginning in 1915). These texts, and fiction of the 1920s by H. D. and Elizabeth Bowen, all 'blur the line between the artists and the subject of the portrait' through their formal experiments. Ultimately, an aesthetic life, Castle argues, shapes an individual's relationship with the world. In this way, modernist portraits of the artist show protagonists interwoven with their milieu, connecting inner and outer worlds.

While many novels of formation are written by and for adults, some are aimed at younger readers, conveying to an audience still in the process of maturation how they might attain adulthood. In Chapter Seven, 'Bildungsromane for Children and Young Adults', Fiona McCulloch explores examples of such narratives and considers how they might shape the expectations of younger readers as they connect the adventures depicted in fiction with their own futures. McCulloch observes that novels for younger readers that are didactic capitalise on children's simultaneous desire for and terror of the unknown to encourage 'compliant and productive citizen[s] who [have] internalised society's hegemonic values'. However, McCulloch argues that literature for children and young adults can present childhood 'as a contested and dynamic rather than settled space'. Her discussion of a range of fiction for younger readers, from Victorian classics to contemporary dystopias, conveys the genre's potential to empower its audience rather than inculcate compliance.

In Chapter Eight, 'The Female Bildungsroman in the Twentieth Century', Maroula Joannou questions the primacy of *Wilhelm Meisters Lehrjahre* by noting the earlier publication of Eliza Haywood's *The History of Miss Betty Thoughtless* (1751). Like Finch's identification of *The Princesse de Clèves* (1678) as a foundational text of the genre in France, Joannou also stresses the significance of Haywood's novel being a female narrative. Although the genre is traditionally male-dominated and conservative, presenting social integration as an ideal, Joannou shows that writers from Charlotte Brontë and George Eliot to Sarah Waters and Zadie Smith have used it to interrogate and subvert white, heteronormative patriarchy, undermining the supposed universality of male experience through woman-centred accounts of female maturation. In a reading of texts as varied as George Eliot's *The Mill on the Floss* (1860), Radclyffe Hall's *The Unlit Lamp* (1924) and Meera Syal's *Anita and Me* (1996), Joannou shows how women writers challenge the conventions of the classic Bildungsroman.

Ericka A. Hoagland's analysis of 'The Postcolonial Bildungsroman' in Chapter Nine highlights a process of appropriation and adaptation of the genre by writers dealing with the legacy of colonialism. Despite the genre's Eurocentrism, postcolonial writers utilise it to respond to the trauma of colonialism and neo-colonialism, conveying the difficulties of maturing in a racially oppressive context. Like many of the novels discussed in Chapter Five on the American Bildungsroman and in Chapter Eight on female Bildungsromane, Hoagland sees a departure from European tradition in novels from Africa. As with other forms of the genre that represent marginalised people, the postcolonial Bildungsroman has been integral to the emergence of the postcolonial subject. Hoagland argues that postcolonial literature reinvents the master narrative of the Bildungsroman as a 'political act of counter-colonisation'.

Like Hoagland, Meredith Miller explores how the Bildungsroman has been appropriated and repurposed by those traditionally left out of the genre. In Chapter Ten on 'Lesbian, Gay and Trans Bildungsromane', she contends that just as sexual dissidence poses a threat to normative social structures, so lesbian, gay and transgender narratives take issue with the conservatism of the classic novel of formation and rework the traditional structure to interrogate the relationship between sexuality and life narratives. Texts such as Audre Lorde's *Zami: A New Spelling of My Name* (1982) and Jeanette Winterson's *Oranges Are Not the Only Fruit* (1985) position their protagonists 'as emerging into meaning against the national historical'. According to Miller, 'the Bildungsroman is the inevitable form for queer subcultural articulation' and the twenty-first century is 'the Bildungsroman's queer moment'.

In the final chapter, 'Bildungsromane and Graphic Narratives', Ian Gordon examines comics and graphic novels. Depicting the hero's transition from child to young adult is a feature of numerous comics, including *The Amazing Spider-Man* and *Archie*, but it is graphic novels since the publication of Art Spiegelman's *Maus* (1986) that most clearly show what visual art brings to the genre: a new way of representing memory and time. Gordon analyses a selection of graphic Bildungsromane, both fiction and memoir, to show how they convey 'what it means to move through time, or be stuck in it, and the implications of those two experiences for a sense of coming of age'. Acclaimed texts like *Maus* and Alison Bechdel's *Fun Home* (2006) simultaneously comment on their younger and adult selves in a way that can only be presented clearly through the artwork. As Gordon explains, graphic narratives make a unique contribution to the Bildungsroman by offering 'not simply a story told but a story revealed'.

As these chapters show, the significance of the journey to adulthood is recognised all over the world. However, the volume illustrates that teenage experience is inflected in different ways in different places. Youth is a powerful symbol of a nation or an era, full of vitality and potential. The progress to maturity can celebrate a young character's time and place or reveal its flaws. Youths understand the implications of social norms for the first time, and structural inequalities are exposed through the trials they face in maturation. As protagonists weigh the pressure to conform against the desire to be themselves, the true extent of their freedom is brought sharply into focus. As Colin Wilson notes in *The Outsider* (1967), the Bildungsroman is 'a sort of laboratory in which the hero conducts an experiment in living'.[17] *A History of the Bildungsroman* highlights how experimentation defines the genre in terms of theme and form.

The chapters examine its formation and continuing evolution. Like its protagonists, the Bildungsroman has places to go: relatively new research in the fields of disability, the post-human, critical animal studies and eco-criticism are beginning to explore the genre in fascinating and productive ways.[18] *A History of the Bildungsroman* leaves no doubt that the novel of development has a rich heritage and a bright future.

CHAPTER I

# The German Tradition of the Bildungsroman

## Todd Kontje

In the late eighteenth century a new type of novel arose in Germany, and shortly thereafter an otherwise obscure professor in East Prussia (today's Estonia) coined a name for the genre: the Bildungsroman.[1] Since that time two traditions have emerged, one literary, the other critical, that stand in an often uncomfortable relation to one another. On the one hand, we find a series of German novels that depict a young protagonist's development towards personal maturity and social integration. On the other, we find some critics who identify the Bildungsroman as a specifically German contribution to the history of the novel, others who extend the term to different national literatures, and still others who deny the existence of the genre altogether. The purpose of this chapter is to explore the specificities of one national tradition in a critical and historical context. My goal is not to add my voice to those who have claimed that the Bildungsroman expresses the mysterious essence of the German soul, but rather to view it as a response to the specific conditions of German history. The German-speaking lands of Central Europe have a long history of political fragmen-tation (viewed negatively) or participation in larger confederations (viewed more positively) that extend from the Holy Roman Empire to today's European Union. More often than not, the tenuous sense of linguistic and cultural unity among members of the German nation did not develop within the boundaries of a single political state. The German Bildungsroman can be used to explore many themes – individual psycho-logical development, changing gender roles, the value of labour in a capitalist society, the importance of religion in a secular age – but my focus in this chapter will be primarily on the ways in which several prominent authors reflect in their works on the question of German national identity, broadly construed. Far from being the genre best suited to a 'nonpolitical' nation of poets and thinkers (*Dichter und Denker*), I will argue that the German Bildungsroman is an intrinsically political genre that explores in various ways the relation between the cultural nation (*Kulturnation*) and the political state.

As a genre devoted to the depiction of individual maturation, the Bildungsroman would seem at first glance to have an almost unlimited range: everyone grows up and learns to fit more or less successfully into a given society. Two factors delimit the genre to a considerably narrower focus from the outset, however: first, as the name of the genre indicates, the Bildungsroman is a 'Roman', a vernacular prose novel of the sort that arose in early modern Europe and became widely popular only in the course of the eighteenth century. Second, the personal development of the individual takes place against the backdrop of a world that is changing as well. As Mikhail Bakhtin puts it, the 'human emergence' of the protagonist in a modern Bildungsroman 'is inseparably linked to historical emergence ... He emerges *along with the world* and he reflects the historical emergence of the world itself.'[2] The fate of a Baroque hero may rise and fall, but the wheel of fortune remains in place as it turns; the modern hero, in contrast, matures in a world engaged in an open-ended process of development. Thus, Franco Moretti concludes that the modern Bildungsroman should be viewed as 'the "symbolic form" of modernity'.[3]

The European Bildungsroman, therefore, is a form of the novel that emerges together with historical consciousness towards the end of the eighteenth century. Considerations of social class and gender further delimit the scope of the genre. The protagonists of the Bildungsroman typically belong to the middle class, as opposed to the aristocracy and lower classes of the Old Regime or the industrial proletariat that emerged in the course of the nineteenth century. As Norbert Elias explains in his classic study of court society, aristocrats lead a performative existence.[4] That is, they are defined by who they are, rather than by what they can do, by their title rather than their profession. Within the closed world of court society there is no distinction between public and private; the aristocrat is always 'on stage', constantly performing his or her identity. As a result, there is no advantage to baring one's soul in public and little room for personal development. The courtiers depicted in such novels as Madame de la Fayette's *Princesse de Clèves* (1678) or Chaderlos de Laclos's *Liaisons Dangereuses* (1782) are involved in an intricate and sometimes deadly game of sexual politics within a closely circumscribed social hierarchy. The protagonists of the Bildungsroman, in contrast, venture out into the world to encounter experiences, often with members of different social classes, which leave a lasting mark on their evolving sense of self that is deepened by a series of retrospective reflections. As Rousseau famously put it in the opening page of his *Confessions*, 'I am unlike any one I have ever met; I will even venture to say that I am like no one in the world. I may be no better, but at least I am different.'[5]

While membership in the upper echelons of European court society was restricted to a narrow elite, the vast majority of eighteenth-century subjects were illiterate peasants with neither the leisure nor the ability to participate in the public sphere. This realm was reserved for the growing and increasingly self-conscious members of the middle class. The proverbial 'rise of the novel' went hand in hand with the 'structural transformation of the public sphere'.[6] As newspapers evolved into moral weeklies, letter-writing gave birth to epistolary fiction, and taverns, coffee houses and Masonic lodges became part of popular culture, new venues emerged for the cultivation of middle-class consciousness. Print culture played a key role in disseminating new ideas about romantic intimacy, gender roles, and the family, while sowing the seeds of potential political revolution and forging the 'imagined communities' of the modern nation state.[7]

The Bildungsroman arises in tandem with the bourgeois public sphere. Its protagonists are reading heroes, shaped by the literature that they read and in turn influencing the readers who identify with their experiences.[8] In this regard they differ from characters depicted in the adventure novels and epics of earlier generations. Odysseus does not read, and he does not change; in the words of Erich Auerbach, 'the Homeric heroes . . . have no development, and their life-histories are clearly set forth once and for all . . . Odysseus on his return is exactly the same as he was when he left Ithaca two decades earlier.'[9] Don Quixote is defined by his reading experiences, but once the basic premise of the novel is set up, it remains in place: Quixote's desire to emulate chivalric heroes of yore serves as the motor for a series of picaresque adventures in which he plays much the same role. In Defoe's *Robinson Crusoe* (1719) we find the beginnings of a new subjectivity in the novel, as the protagonist experiences a religious crisis on his desert island and keeps a fragmentary autobiography, yet he remains untroubled by sexual desire and re-enters European society with no psychological scars, despite more than two decades of solitude. The protagonist of Goethe's *Wilhelm Meister's Apprenticeship* (*Wilhelm Meisters Lehrjahre*, 1795–6), in contrast, develops from a callow youth in the raptures of his first love to a young man on the cusp of marriage; his life experiences have left an indelible mark on his psyche. Eighteenth-century religious autobiographies and the epistolary novels of Richardson, Rousseau, and the young Goethe had already displayed an increasing interest in psychological depth and developed language to express the inner life.[10] The Bildungsroman continues the exploration of the protagonists' subjectivity while adding worldly experiences that influence character development. Thus, the Bildungsroman is often described as a 'rendering inward' (*Verinnerlichung*) of the adventure novel and a secularisation of the religious autobiography.[11]

Don Quixote identifies with Amadis of Gaul, a paragon of knightly virtue who serves as the absolute standard for the latter-day hidalgo.[12] Wilhelm Meister, in contrast, identifies with Shakespeare's Hamlet, the quintessentially troubled soul caught up in what Freud would term the Oedipus complex. Freud describes his central psychological concept as if it were an unchanging feature of human development, but social historians would argue that he in fact describes the dynamics of the nuclear family that emerged in the course of the eighteenth century. The constriction of the extended family into a more intimate unit with correspondingly intensified emotional bonds helped to solidify the class consciousness of the emerging bourgeoisie. Couples married for love, remained monogamous, and doted on their children in a way that distinguished them from the aristocratic libertines who preyed with impunity on the virtuous daughters of the lower social classes. Whereas aristocratic women had played active roles in court society, middle-class women were expected to remain in the domestic sphere, devoting themselves to their duties as wives, mothers, and managers of the household economy. At least in theory, therefore, they were excluded from the public sphere that played such a crucial role in the formation of middle-class male identity. When the French revolutionaries rose up against their aristocratic masters, women were not welcome on the barricades or in the government. Thus, Joan Landes concludes that 'the revolt against the father was also a revolt against women as free and equal public and private beings ... the Republic was constructed against women, not just without them.'[13]

In practice it was not always possible to exclude women from political action or the public sphere. For every Charlotte Corday, there were dozens of women who wrote novels and thousands who read them. The bourgeois ethos nevertheless militated against the open-ended exploration of new experiences that was so important for male development and the literary genre of the Bildungsroman, and thus the very concept of a female Bildungsroman has sometimes been rejected as a contradiction in terms.[14] Others have explored the possibilities of female development in nineteenth-century fiction: Franco Moretti groups *Pride and Prejudice* (1813) together with *Wilhelm Meister's Apprenticeship* as an example of the classical Bildungsroman, and Jeannine Blackwell has written a pioneering analysis of female protagonists in literature by German women.[15] The basic parameters for male and female development were nevertheless quite different: while the young men typically experience a series of sexual adventures on the way to a marriage that marks the beginning of a public career, the women remain virgins until they find their Mr Darcy in a plotline that leads to a happy ending of the novel and also the end of any career ambitions. The popular German writer E. Marlitt specialised in fiction of this sort, featuring resourceful women who are quite capable of holding their own in public, but then surrender all ambition when they find their future husbands.[16]

Thus described, both the male and female variants of the genre sound precariously close to pulp fiction.[17] In Hegel's mocking description, the hero of the Bildungsroman 'usually gets his girl and some sort of job, marries, and becomes a Philistine like everybody else'.[18] There is much to be said for the appeal of generic convention: we know that tragedies end in death and comedies culminate in marriage and we are drawn to them because of, not despite, the fact that they fulfil expectations. Still, a paradigm repeated to the point that it becomes a hackneyed cliché can become tiresome, and in fact most if not all of the canonical German Bildungsromane are considerably more complex and far less upbeat than fairy tale romances and Horatio Alger success stories. As a result, there is a long critical tradition that questions whether less-than-formulaic novels should be considered examples of the Bildungsroman, and even if the genre itself might be largely 'missing' or a 'phantom' of the critical imagination.[19]

Using a simplistic definition of the genre to highlight the complexity of a given text can serve as a useful critical strategy, but when novel after novel is deemed unworthy of the generic distinction to which it allegedly aspires, one begins to wonder if there is any point to the critical detour through a category that is introduced only to be cast aside in the end.[20] Two possible responses suggest themselves: we can follow this train of thought to its logical conclusion and retire the term from the critical vocabulary, focusing instead on other subgenres of the novel (picaresque, epistolary, gothic, historical, detective, etc.) that more accurately reflect the actual literary production of a given era, or we can revise our understanding of the genre to allow for more variation than Hegel's parodic definition permits.[21] To take a parallel example, Northrop Frye once viewed the descent into the mine depicted in the opening chapters of Émile Zola's *Germinal* (1885) as an archetypal journey to the underworld that repeats the pattern found in Virgil and Dante, dismissing the historically specific details as so much window dressing to be pushed aside to reveal the mythic substructure of a superficially realistic text.[22] Hegel does much the same for the

Bildungsroman, albeit in a derogatory fashion, highlighting the dreary repetitiveness of a pattern in popular fiction with no regard for the variations on a theme that might make a particular work stand out from its more predictable counterparts. Archetypal critics reduce complexity to discover structural similarities; cultural critics highlight significant differences to reveal ways in which a given literary text responds to a specific historical situation. From this perspective, a protagonist's inability to resolve all problems into a happy ending may open a window onto the irresolvable conflicts of a given society or reveal the sacrifices required for social integration. If the genre of the Bildungsroman is to be retained as a useful category of critical analysis, in other words, it must be conceived in a flexible enough way to include the possibility of parody, compromise, and disappointment within a pattern that theoretically leads to personal maturation and social affirmation.

### A German Genre?

Is the Bildungsroman a specifically German genre? The name suggests as much. Although terms such as the *novel of formation* or the *novel of education* are sometimes used, the genre is typically labelled with its German name, sometimes capitalised and italicised to indicate its status as a foreign word, sometimes written lower case without italics as a loan word, and sometimes capitalised but not italicised, as in this chapter, to indicate its awkward position between languages as a half-assimilated, half-foreign term.[23] Critical discourse on the genre reflects a similar uncertainty. As Tobias Boes argues in his incisive study of the genre, critics tend to fall 'between the Scylla of national essentialism and the Charybdis of an empty universalism'.[24] Among the latter we find the previously cited Mikhail Bakhtin and Franco Moretti, each of whom links the genre to the emergence of modernism in general, while the former include any number of German writers and critics who insist that the Bildungsroman has a special place within German literature.[25] One of the most prominent of these was Thomas Mann: 'There is however one variant of the novel that is German, typically German, legitimately national, and this is the autobiographically charged *Bildungs-* and *Entwicklungsroman*.'[26]

Mann wrote these words in 1916, at a time when he styled himself as the proud keeper of Germany's 'non-political' tradition against the loathed forces of Western liberal democracy.[27] According to this view, the Germans were a nation of profound philosophers and romantic souls unwilling to sully themselves in the rough and tumble of political strife.

A complementary nationalist myth cast the Germans as a Faustian nation, willing to plunge into action with reckless abandon and fight to the bitter end, even for a lost cause.[28] These constructions of German national identity have been used to explain the fatal course of twentieth-century history, as a nation of otherworldly dreamers allowed themselves to be led astray by their Faustian leaders. The problem with such myths, however, is that they are by their nature not historically accurate. 'Of all the myths of German history that have been mobilised to account for the coming of the Third Reich in 1933,' notes Richard J. Evans, 'none is less convincing than that of the "nonpolitical German".'[29] Although Mann's turn to democracy in the early 1920s and his subsequent critique of German National Socialism are well known, he remains in his literary works uncomfortably close to the sort of national essentialism that Boes rightly criticises. His allegorical Bildungsroman, *Doctor Faustus* (1947), uses the protagonist's pursuit of artistic innovation as a metaphor for Germany's pact with the devil of fascist ideology, but as critics have often noted and Mann himself conceded, the novel makes use of the nationalist myths that it would expose and refute, thus inadvertently lending an aura of tragic grandeur to the criminal deeds of the Third Reich.[30]

A more productive line of inquiry in seeking to define the German tradition of the Bildungsroman is to view it as the product of historical circumstances, rather than an upwelling from the immutable depths of the German psyche. Wilhelm Dilthey follows just this path in his influential definition of the genre. Although he was not the first to coin the term Bildungsroman, Dilthey did more than anyone else to introduce it into critical discourse. His description of a genre that depicts young men who struggle to find themselves and their place in the world is frequently cited without noting that he consigns the genre to the past, to a time when 'the power of the state administration and the military in Germany's small and mid-sized principalities stood apart from the young writers as an alien force.' When we pick up these novels today, writes Dilthey in 1906, 'the faint breath of a bygone world wafts up from the old pages', evoking 'the dark, dreamy, still veiled power of ideals in young German souls who were at that time so ready to take up the battle with this outmoded world in all its life forms, and so incapable of winning.'[31]

As I will argue, the German Bildungsromane of the late eighteenth and nineteenth centuries were not as politically disinterested as has often been claimed, nor did the literary genre disappear at the end of the nineteenth century. To understand the specificities of the German literary tradition, we must turn briefly to the nation's historical development. As is well known, Germany was not unified as a discrete nation state until 1871, and even then the German Empire was more of a confederation of semi-autonomous principalities than a homogeneous nation state.[32] For more than a thousand years, the German-speaking territories of Central Europe were under the aegis of the Holy Roman Empire, an institution whose sense of sovereignty differed fundamentally from that of the modern nation. As James J. Sheehan explains, 'the Reich came from a historical world in which nationality had no political meaning and states did not command total sovereignty. Unlike nations and states, the Reich did not insist upon pre-eminent authority and unquestioning allegiance. Its goal was not to clarify and dominate but rather to order and balance fragmented institutions and multiple loyalties.'[33] Change began to occur in the course of the eighteenth century, as local governments grew and a new generation of 'non-noble elites' were educated to fill the new positions. Sovereignty shifted from the personal authority of the local lord (*Herrschaft*) to the impersonal mechanism of the state administration (*Verwaltung*) (24–41). Reinhart Koselleck observes that the absolutist state cared little for the emotional life of its subjects, as long as they obeyed the law.[34] Thus the public sphere arose as the venue for the exploration and articulation of bourgeois subjectivity that was so important for the birth of the Bildungsroman. What was true for the individual was also true for the collective: the public sphere also served as a venue for the formation of the 'imagined community' of the modern nation. The state imposed its order from the top down; nationalism arose from the bottom up. The state was to function as an efficient machine; the nation mobilised collective passions. The absolutist state left the feudal order intact; modern nationalism was implicitly egalitarian and revolutionary, replacing the old vertical hierarchies with 'a deep, horizontal comradeship'.[35]

The French revolutionaries sought to combine the efficiency of the modern, centralised state administration with the passions of modern nationalism. In Germany, however, there was no revolution, and the aspirations of the liberal nationalists who rose up against Napoleon's armies in 1813 were quickly thwarted by the reactionary policies of the Restoration governments. As a result, the politically fragmented German-speaking territories of Central Europe were united only in the realm of culture. Goethe and Schiller's 'Xenia', or two-line poem titled 'Deutschland', succinctly formulates the concept of the German *Kulturnation*:

Deutschland? Aber wo liegt es? Ich weiß das Land nicht zu finden,
Wo das gelehrte beginnt, hört das politische auf.

Germany? But where is it? I can't find the country;
Where the intellectual realm begins, the political realm stops.[36]

The German Bildungsroman, therefore, becomes the genre that explores
individual development and national identity in a politically fragmented
state. In the second half of this chapter I will focus on a few examples of the
ways in which representative authors seek to come to terms in their works
with the emergence of modern individualism in a political context that had
more in common with the hierarchical heterogeneity of the Holy Roman
Empire than the egalitarian homogeneity of the centralised nation state.

## Goethe, *Wilhelm Meister's Apprenticeship*

We begin, inevitably, with Johann Wolfgang von Goethe's *Wilhelm
Meister's Apprenticeship* – inevitably, because it was identified early on as
the paradigmatic example of the German Bildungsroman and retained its
reputation even when critics challenged the assumption that it provides an
unambiguously successful model of personal development within an
affirmed social order. The novel begins with the familiar Romantic opposition between the artist and the Philistine: Wilhelm Meister is a sensitive
soul who seeks adventures, erotic and otherwise, in the realm of the theatre,
while Werner, his friend and future brother-in-law, wants only to advance
the family business. A secondary opposition arises as a result of the first:
Werner is content to remain within the boundaries of his social class,
whereas Wilhelm seeks the freedom for self-expression previously reserved
for the nobility. Acting becomes the means to the end of a kind of ersatz
nobility, as he aspires to a model of social grace outlined in Castiglione's
*Book of the Courtier* and similar treatises. Wilhelm Meister also hopes to
establish a national theatre that will unite his fellow Germans in the realm
of culture, even if they remain divided in the realm of politics.

Multiple ironies qualify Meister's quest for personal fulfilment and
national improvement. The reality of life as an itinerant actor in
Germany proves far more difficult than he originally imagined: constant
bickering and petty jealousies mar the miniature society of the acting
troupe that suffers financial woes from a fickle public and is subject to
the arbitrary whims of a decadent aristocracy. Before Meister leaves home
he encounters a kindred spirit who fell in love with an actress and ran off to
join the theatre, but this young man wants nothing more than to return to

the safety of his middle-class origins; Meister, too, will abandon the theatre after a single performance of *Hamlet*. His mission to establish a national theatre is not realised; instead, he is severely wounded when he and his companions blunder into a local conflict within the confines of the German territories. Meister does attain social graces that make him seem superior to Werner, who re-enters the action looking careworn and prematurely aged, but Meister's sense of personal autonomy is soon revealed to be an illusion, as he has been manipulated from beginning to end by a secret society of aristocrats. This is not to say that Goethe rejects Wilhelm Meister's 'theatrical mission' as fundamentally misguided or that he abandoned the cultural aspirations of Weimar Classicism. It does suggest, however, that Goethe was painfully aware of the factors that militated against the fulfilment of such ideals and unwilling to write a utopian novel that obscured the obstacles to them.

Instead, Goethe depicts a model of social reform in the final segments of *Wilhelm Meister's Apprenticeship* that offers an implicit alternative to the French Revolution. Years before, Wilhelm's grandfather had invested the profits of the successful family business in an extensive art collection; his father later sold the collection to pay for an ostentatious new home. Now Werner, who has married Wilhelm's sister and taken over the business that Wilhelm neglected, decides to sell the house and invest the profits in land speculation. Both grandfather and father aspired to the quasi-aristocratic status of a patrician class that used art or, more crassly, the large home, as an expression of social rank, whereas Werner pursues the stripped-down functionalism of modern capitalism. He is met halfway in his goals by Lothario, a liberal aristocrat who has just returned to Germany after fighting in support of the American Revolution. Lothario decides to do away with what he terms the 'hocus-pocus' of the fee entail on his ancestral estates, whereby property was passed down from one generation of an aristocratic family to the next. In rejecting this age-old custom, Lothario turns his land into a commodity that can circulate on the open market. He joins with Werner in a capital venture that Wilhelm resists in the name of his poetic aspirations.

As a result, the dichotomies that structure the opening pages of *Wilhelm Meister's Apprenticeship* become something quite different towards the end: aristocrat and bourgeois unite, not in the imaginary world of the theatre, but rather in the economic reality of land speculation. A newly mobile form of capitalism revitalises the old economy, without, however, leading to the radical egalitarianism of the French Revolution. The art that graced the old regime resurfaces in the new: it turns out that Lothario and his aristocratic friends were the ones who purchased the art collected by Wilhelm's grandfather. Thus, the paintings that once reflected the social aspirations of the patrician class now grace the halls of the liberal aristocrats willing to join forces with the modern bourgeoisie. *Wilhelm Meister's Apprenticeship* ends with a series of marriages across class lines and an argument for the liberation of land and its servants from feudal restraints.

Thus, *Wilhelm Meister's Apprenticeship* suggests two complementary, equally qualified, responses to German particularism in the era of the French Revolution. The first views the theatre as a compensatory realm for the kind of personal development otherwise restricted to the nobility and the national integration denied by Germany's political fragmentation. The second lays out a programme of economic reform that could be called progressive conservatism, transforming land into dynamic capital in a way that revitalises rather than destroys the old regime.[37] As Schiller explains in his letters *On the Aesthetic Education of Man* (*Über die ästhetische Erziehung des Menschen*, 1794–5), artisans and politicians face analogous tasks under different circumstances: 'When the mechanic has the works of a clock to repair, he lets the wheels run down; but the living clockwork of the State must be repaired while it is in motion, and here it is a case of changing the wheels as they revolve.'[38] Once again, Goethe stops short of an unqualified endorsement of the new proposal: the members of the Tower Society manipulate Wilhelm Meister in ways that he experiences as oppressively authoritarian, and Lothario remains a lothario, a reckless libertine who leaves a trail of broken hearts behind him even as he aspires to import American ideals into Europe.

## Wilhelm Meister's Legacy

Goethe's novel inspired a rich legacy of literary offspring, or 'brothers', to introduce the metaphors of kinship that play a prominent role in many histories of the Bildungsroman.[39] As is well known, Friedrich von Hardenberg (Novalis) expressed bitter disappointment at what he felt was the increasingly prosaic nature of *Wilhelm Meister's Apprenticeship*. As he put it, the protagonist's theatrical mission devolved into a mere 'pilgrimage toward a patent of nobility' (*Wahlfahrt nach dem Adelsdiplom*).[40] His fragmentary *Heinrich von Ofterdingen* (1800) initiated a series of Romantic Bildungsromane that sought to remain true to the artistic spirit that Goethe allegedly betrayed. Thus, Heinrich von Ofterdingen sets off on a mystical quest to unite the universe in poetic harmony in a work that infuses Christian millennialism with philosophical idealism. Ludwig Tieck's slightly earlier *Franz Sternbald's Wanderings* (*Franz Sternbalds Wanderungen*, 1798) follows the fortunes of a young student of Albrecht Dürer who discovers sensual pleasure and spiritual renewal in Renaissance Italy. More frequent, however, are those Bildungsromane of the Romantic era that expose the difficulties of life in the German territories. Friedrich Hölderlin's *Hyperion* (1797–9), an epistolary novel set mainly in modern Greece, culminates in a harsh denunciation of German society. Jean Paul's *Titan* (1800–3) and *Adolescent Years* (*Flegeljahre*, 1804–5) bring sensitive souls into contact with the unpleasant realities of life in provincial Germany. The aristocratic hero of Eichendorff's *Presence and Presentiment* (*Ahnung und Gegenwart*, 1815) fights against Napoleonic rule in Austria, only to renounce the world in melancholy resignation. E. T. A. Hoffmann's *Tomcat Murr's Perspectives on Life* (*Lebensansichten des Kater Murrs*, 1820/22), finally, parodies the Bildungsroman in the autobiography of a complacent cat in a work that simultaneously offers a biting critique of arbitrary rule in one of Germany's petty provinces.

The tendency either to avoid or expose the political reality of the German-speaking regions of Central Europe continues in the work of the next generation. At one extreme we find Adalbert Stifter's *Indian Summer* (*Nachsommer*, 1857), an Austrian novel in which the young son of a businessman is initiated into a stylised aesthetic realm that represses all passion and leaves practicality behind; at the other we find Gustav Freytag's *Debit and Credit* (*Soll und Haben*, 1855), an unabashed glorification of the business world in which the hero rises from humble origins to find financial rewards and marital bliss. *Debit and Credit* was one of the bestselling German novels of its time, a popular success that lasted well into the twentieth century, no doubt because it provided a flattering image of the German national identity even as it told an emotionally satisfying story of personal happiness. From today's perspective, however, *Debit and Credit* has disturbing elements. Freytag sets his novel on the Prussian-Polish border, a decision that plays a defining role in the political dimension of the novel. The personal maturation of the protagonist, Anton Wohlfahrt, becomes a paradigmatic example of the virtues of the Protestant Prussian middle class, defined in opposition to decadent aristocrats, slovenly Poles, and conniving Jews.

The setting of *Debit and Credit* in the border zone between Germanic and Slavic peoples distinguishes Freytag's popular Bildungsroman from its contemporary French counterparts. The primary geopolitical opposition in the novels of Stendhal, Balzac, and Flaubert is between Paris and the

provinces. Thus, Julien Sorel pursues a course of ruthless ambition in
*The Red and the Black* (*Le rouge et le noir*, 1830) that leads him from his
humble origins in the town of Verrières to the Hôtel de la Mole in Paris.
In *Le Père Goriot* (1835), Eugène de Rastignac exploits his provincial family
to get ahead in Paris and Lucien de Rubempre does the same in *Lost
Illusions* (*Illusions perdues*, 1837–43). Frédéric Moreau's sentimental education also begins when he leaves Normandy for Paris. Anton Wohlfahrt, in
contrast, can only move between the border town of Breslau and the Polish
wilderness; in 1855 there was no German equivalent to Paris or London.
'In the novels taking place in France, Britain, Russia, and Spain (that is, in
long-established nation-states), the hero's trajectory towards the capital
city is usually very direct,' summarises Franco Moretti; 'in the German,
Swiss, and Italian texts, the lack of a clear national center produces by
contrast a sort of irresolute wandering.'[41] That may be true of Wilhelm
Meister, but there is nothing irresolute about Anton Wohlfahrt's wandering: his foray into Polish territory solidifies his sense of German national
identity and paves the way for his success in business. Rather than embracing the hybridity of the border zone in a way that might seem appealing to
today's transnational subjects or postcolonial theorists, he uses the border
as a way to draw sharp lines between what he considers essentially German
and its alien others.

   We find a very different use of the border in Gottfried Keller's *Green
Heinrich* (*Der grüne Heinrich*, 1854–5; second substantially revised version
1879–80).[42] Keller was a native of Zurich and thus Swiss, but he also spent
several of his formative years in Germany and considered himself part of
the larger German-language cultural realm. For this reason he resisted the
trend among some of his contemporary Swiss writers, including Jeremias
Gotthelf, to write in dialect, opting instead, like Freytag, for the standard
High German of Goethe and Schiller. Unlike the Prussian chauvinist,
however, Keller was a liberal republican who was proud of Switzerland's
democratic traditions. His semi-autobiographical Bildungsroman takes as
one of its central themes the relationship between German conservativism
and Swiss liberalism, contrasting the backward-looking veneration of the
Holy Roman Empire in nineteenth-century Germany with the progressive
democracy of the federated Swiss cantons.

   The first version of *Green Heinrich* begins with a border crossing, as the
young Swiss protagonist, Heinrich Lee, leaves Zurich on his way to
Germany, where he hopes to become a successful landscape painter. He
grows excited as he approaches the Rhine, as it marks the boundary of
a nation that stands in his imagination for linguistic purity, the beloved

folk tales collected by the Grimm brothers and other Romantics, and the common Alemannic ancestors of the Southern Germans and the Swiss. He receives a brusque welcome in Bavaria, however, as the customs officials threaten to open fire on the boat suspected of entering German territory illegally. The police then accost the Swiss democrat for his failure to display the appropriate deference to royal authority. The scene sets the stage for the ongoing investigation of German-Swiss relations in the novel. Heinrich settles in an unnamed city that is clearly modelled on Munich, where Keller had lived in the early 1840s. There the aspiring artist makes friends from other peripheral regions of the German-speaking realm: one is Dutch and the other is from the German-Danish border zone. Ironically, the three artists from the edges of the German-speaking regions in Europe seem more typically German than those at its centre: 'Each of them came from a home where, in distinctive and ancient festivals, the German character still lived in customs, linguistic usage, and a personal sense of independence,' and all three are alienated by the hypocritical combination of superficial politeness with deep-seated hostility that they encounter on a daily basis in Bavaria.[43]

The tension between the Bavarian monarchy and Swiss democracy finds its fullest expression in the depiction of two popular festivals. Towards the end of his stay in Munich, Heinrich takes part in a Mardi Gras celebration of Germany's early modern past. The city puts on an elaborate pageant in which individuals portray such figures as Emperor Maximilian, Hans Sachs, and Albrecht Dürer. The Swiss counter with an amateur performance of Schiller's *Wilhelm Tell*, a drama that celebrates the founding moment of Swiss democracy, when representatives of the medieval Swiss cantons formed an alliance to resist the encroachment of the Austrian Empire. The opposition seems clear: the Bavarians use the past to glorify an anachronistic feudal order in a way that recalls Richard Wagner's *Meistersinger von Nuremberg*, whereas the Swiss commemorate the first step towards the future republic. They do so, however, by reciting lines written by a German author, Friedrich Schiller, or, more precisely, a Swabian living in Weimar who had never set foot in Switzerland. And yet the Swiss villagers who put on Schiller's play do not experience the work as an alien import; instead, they embrace it as an ennobled version of their own national heritage. The Swiss performance of Schiller's play thus suggests a utopian fusion of German culture with Swiss politics. As a young man Keller wrote a poem in which he expressed his sense of dual identity as both Swiss and German; late in life he stirred up controversy by suggesting the possibility, perhaps in the distant future, of a Central European state that would preserve Swiss democracy within a larger pan-German confederation.[44] In this regard the performance of *Wilhelm Tell* stands not only as a marker of national difference that distinguishes liberal Switzerland from conservative Germany, but also as an adumbration of a future federation that could unite Switzerland's progressive politics with the cultural achievements of the larger German-speaking lands.

## The Modern German Bildungsroman

It is often said that the German Bildungsroman was a product of the 'Age of Goethe', exuding an optimistic faith in the human potential for growth into an affirmed society that became increasingly difficult to sustain as the nineteenth century wore on. According to this view, any residual hope for successful Bildung died on the battlefields of the First World War. If the genre were to survive at all, as Thomas Mann argued in the fall of 1916, then it could only continue as a parody.[45] Mann made his remarks while introducing a public reading from his *Confessions of Felix Krull, Confidence Man* (*Bekenntnisse des Hochstaplers Felix Krull*), a novel that is indeed a brilliant parody of the classical genre.[46] He returned to the problem of parody in a tragic vein in *Doctor Faustus* (1947), whose protagonist, Adrian Leverkühn, makes a symbolic pact with the devil in an effort to move beyond the stale conventions of traditional music to an art that recaptures the raw power of cultic rituals. Leverkühn's breakthrough to a new form of artistic expression comes at a high price, however, for his music refutes the hope for universal human brotherhood voiced in the final chorus of Beethoven's Ninth Symphony and serves as an unwitting parallel to the Nazi embrace of a new political barbarism that leaves the niceties of faith, hope, and love far behind. Oskar Matzerath evokes Saint Paul's words with rhythmic insistency in one of the most powerful chapters of *The Tin Drum* (*Die Blechtrommel*, 1959), in which Günter Grass exposes the Nazis' utter perversion of the humanist tradition. The protagonist of this Bildungsroman literally stops growing, preferring to remain a child-sized outsider in a society that has become thoroughly corrupt.

Can one even use the term 'Bildungsroman' to describe Grass's novel? And the same could be asked of *Doctor Faustus*, which ends with references to the apocalypse as its protagonist succumbs to insanity caused by a syphilitic infection. Certainly, we are far from the unexpected happiness that overwhelms Wilhelm Meister at the end of Goethe's novel, the utopian promise glimpsed by Heinrich von Ofterdingen, or the cheerful embrace of bourgeois respectability in *Debit and Credit*. Thus, Gerhart

Mayer introduces the term *Antibildungsroman* to characterise works that invoke the optimistic premises of the genre only to reject them in the end.[47] In making a neat distinction between the Bildungsroman and the Antibildungsroman, however, Mayer risks using an overly simplistic understanding of the primary genre in order to underscore the problematic aspects of its negative counterpart. In other words, he forgets or downplays the fact that Wilhelm Meister is as much overwhelmed as he is overjoyed by the Tower Society's intervention into his life, and that the happiness granted him is not extended to other characters in the novel. 'Far from being mankind's coming of age,' concludes Franco Moretti, 'the classical *Bildungsroman* is illuminated by a meaning that is *octroyé*: benignly granted to the "pliant" subject, not forcibly seized and built by the free citizen.' More succinctly, 'meaning, in the classical *Bildungsroman*, has its price. And this price is freedom.'[48]

Thus, rather than distinguishing between the genre of the Bildungsroman and its dialectical opposite at any given time, or tracing a narrative of decline that falls from Goethean heights to Grassian depths, I prefer to consider the ongoing permutations of an inherently problematic genre in socio-political context. My focus in this chapter has been on ways in which German novels of personal formation also engage with political issues, or, more specifically, how a genre that has close ties to the emergence of modern nationalism fared in a land that had a sense of linguistic and cultural unity, but also a long history of political fragmentation and authoritarian rule. I turn in conclusion, therefore, to two German Bildungsromane of the twentieth century, *The Magic Mountain* (*Der Zauberberg*, 1924) and *The Tin Drum*.

Mann referred to *The Magic Mountain* as a Bildungsroman, but it hardly fits the pattern caricatured by Hegel in his brief remarks on the genre.[49] The protagonist, Hans Castorp, is about to begin work as a ship's engineer in Hamburg when he decides to visit his ailing cousin at a Swiss sanatorium. Castorp is soon diagnosed with a touch of tuberculosis and ends up spending seven years on the mountain, abandoning his career plans and losing all contact with the 'flatlands' until he is drafted into the army at the beginning of the First World War. We last see him on the battlefield as he stumbles towards near-certain death. Very little has happened in those seven years, at least in relation to the length of the thousand-page novel: Castorp flirts with a Russian woman who reminds him of a boy he once knew at school, but she leaves the sanatorium immediately after their one night together. Castorp's cousin dies, and he is left to listen to long debates between two mentor figures, Ludovico Settembrini and Leo Naphta. He

later falls under the spell of Mynheer Peeperkorn, a ravaged Dutch planta-
tion owner from the island of Java. Both Peeperkorn and Naphta commit
suicide, the social order of the sanatorium disintegrates, and chaos reigns as
the novel concludes.

*The Magic Mountain* inverts the premises of the nineteenth-century
Bildungsroman in that it seduces its protagonist away from practical
activity in the world, but it also fulfils them, in that the years at the
sanatorium allow Hans Castorp to explore ideas that would not have
interested him had he pursued his original plan to become an engineer.
Even though he abandons his career and leaves the mountain only when he
heads off to war, Castorp has experienced dramatic intellectual growth
during his seven years on the mountain. Thus, one of the novel's earliest
and most perceptive critics, Hermann Weigand, refers to *The Magic
Mountain* as a Bildungsroman that depicts 'the transformation of [a]
simple young man into a genius'.[50] From another perspective, however,
Castorp serves less as a traditional hero whose adventures are of central
importance to the novel than as a passive receptacle for the ideas of others.
In this regard he continues a tradition established by Goethe's *Wilhelm
Meister's Apprenticeship*. As Schiller put it in a letter to Goethe, 'Wilhelm
Meister is to be sure the most necessary, but not the most important
character. Just this is one of the peculiar features of your novel: it neither
has nor needs a single most important character. Everything happens *to*
him and *around* him, but not really *for his sake*.'[51] Friedrich Schlegel echoes
Schiller's thoughts in his review of Goethe's novel when he notes that the
narrator 'almost never mentions the hero without irony', because it is not
one of those conventional novels 'in which characters and events are of
ultimate importance', but rather a work that foregrounds 'the loftiest
ideas'.[52] Mann subordinates action to ideas to an even greater extent than
Goethe, making *The Magic Mountain* a prime example of the trend
towards what David Luft has termed *philosophical essayism* in modern
German and Austrian novels.[53] Together with works such as Hermann
Broch's *The Sleepwalkers* (*Die Schlafwandler*, 1931–2), Robert Musil's
*The Man Without Qualities* (*Der Mann ohne Eigenschaften*, 1933–43) and
Hermann Hesse's *The Glass Bead Game* (*Glasperlenspiel*, 1943), *The Magic
Mountain* blurs the boundary between fiction and non-fiction. It combines
an engaging story of a young man's formative experiences with disquisi-
tions on the nature of time, the virtues of the European Enlightenment and
the fate of empires on the eve of the First World War.

Castorp comes to the mountain in the summer of 1907 and leaves it in
1914, but the novel was not published until 1924. Thus, Mann begins his

work with a preface in which he notes that the story to be told took place in the past which, objectively speaking, was not very long ago, but which, from the post-war perspective, seemed infinitely far away. The First World War had not only unleashed the power of mechanised warfare that left a generation of young men dead, maimed, or shell-shocked, but it also marked cataclysmic political changes that included the Russian Revolution and the collapse of the German and Austrian empires. The post-war years witnessed the founding of the fragile Weimar Republic and the first stirrings of a fascist movement that would soon sweep into power in both Italy and Germany. Thomas Mann, who had insisted in his *Reflections of a Nonpolitical Man* that he was a typical German artist who had little concern for political affairs, was in fact extremely concerned by the turmoil that surrounded him as he completed *The Magic Mountain*, and the debates between Naphta and Settembrini reflect those concerns.

The arguments turn on the question of finding an appropriate form for the states of modern Europe. They take place on the eve of the First World War within the context of the novel, but they raise issues that preoccupied Mann and his contemporaries in its immediate aftermath. Settembrini is an Italian patriot and supporter of the French Revolution who champions the virtues of the modern nation state; Naphta prefers forms of government that preceded and might eventually supersede the nation. Thus, he defends the otherwise contradictory combination of medieval Catholicism and modern Communism, as both are based on a world order that transcends the boundaries of discrete nations. Settembrini looks back approvingly to the time when 'a sense of national honor began to solidify against hierarchical pretension;' Naphta rejects his 'nationalist mania' for 'the world-conquering cosmopolitanism of the Church'.[54] Settembrini attacks the Austro-Hungarian Empire as 'a mummified version of the Holy Roman Empire' (374) and an enemy of Italy; Naphta derides the capitalist economy of the nation state. He shares the medieval rejection of usury and welcomes the idea that 'these economic principles and standards have been resurrected in the modern movement of communism' (396). Settembrini insists on the supremacy of civilisation over barbarism, the West over the East, enlightenment over obscurantism, and democracy over tyranny; Naphta argues for the primacy of the community over the individual, faith over reason, 'discipline and sacrifice, renunciation of the ego and coercion of the personality'. As Settembrini becomes increasingly agitated, Naphta drives home his point: 'What our age needs, what it demands, what it will create for itself, is – terror' (393).

Hans Castorp listens attentively to the two men, absorbing their ideas and parroting them back, but without committing firmly to either position. Rather than using his protagonist to declare a clear-cut winner in the debate, Mann employs him as a sounding board for ideas expressed by the two older men. Given Mann's unexpected decision in 1922 to come out in public support of the Weimar Republic, it would seem that his sympathies lie with Settembrini, and he is indeed the more appealing character. Settembrini may be a slightly ludicrous organ grinder, as Castorp dubs him, who repeats the same optimistic tune again and again, but he is a well-meaning mentor with genuine affection for the young German, whereas Naphta is both physically repellent and personally abrasive. And yet Naphta's vision of a cosmopolitan world order that transcends the limitations of the modern nation state was also appealing to Mann, who speculated in his post-war diaries about the possibility of establishing a pan-German confederation in Central Europe that might recapture in modern form the spirit of the old Holy Roman Empire.[55] Naphta's defence of social hierarchies also held some appeal to the patrician's son from Lübeck who was suspicious of popular democracy and shared Nietzsche's distaste for the unwashed masses. Yet Naphta's advocacy of violence and blind obedience to authority already seemed untenable in the early 1920s, when paramilitary bands known as the Freikorps were committing atrocities in the name of the nation, and Mann correctly sensed that worse was soon to come. Against this ominous historical backdrop, Settembrini's advocacy of enlightened reason and liberal democracy had begun to seem more appealing to Mann than it had a decade earlier, and yet he stops short of an unqualified endorsement of Settembrini's position for two reasons: first, Settembrini lacks the appreciation of the irrational forces that were central to the world view of a writer steeped in the spirit of Schopenhauer's blind will, Nietzsche's nihilistic vitalism, and Wagner's hypnotic music. Second, Mann was acutely aware that the modern nation state had given rise not only to liberal democracy, but also to bellicose nationalism and imperial aggression of the sort that provoked the First World War.

By staging *The Magic Mountain* as a historical novel of the recent past, Mann does not offer clear-cut solutions to the present crisis, but rather a diagnosis of ideas that led to the catastrophic conflict. To his post-war readers he offers only tentative alternatives to the self-undermining ideological positions staked out by Settembrini and Naphta. When Hans Castorp is lost in the snow, he has an allegorical vision that ends in the insight that he should acknowledge the Dionysian forces that have us in their grasp without succumbing entirely to their power: '*For the sake of goodness and love, man shall grant death no dominion over his thoughts.*'[56] Castorp's vision is fleeting and the lesson soon forgotten, but it does gesture towards a synthesis that moves beyond the stalemate reached by Naphta and Settembrini. This episode is followed immediately by the death of his cousin, Joachim Ziemssen, a moving scene in which compassion and love temporarily silence the bickering of the warring ideologues. Mynheer Peeperkorn has a similar effect on the two intellectuals, and he impresses Castorp with his commanding presence and gargantuan appetites, but the inarticulate, alcoholic, impotent, and ultimately suicidal man can hardly serve as an unqualified positive role model. We are left in the end with the plaintive voice of the narrator, who, in summoning up the chaos of the battlefield, can only express the hope that 'love someday [will] rise up out of this . . . festival of death' (706).

That hope was not fulfilled. Things went from bad to worse in the years after Mann published *The Magic Mountain*, until by 1945 Germany had been reduced to rubble and exposed to shame for committing unspeakable crimes against humanity. Günter Grass was a seventeen-year-old member of the Waffen-SS when the war ended, and although he did not reveal this embarrassing detail until late in life, he was always open about the fact that he had believed to the bitter end that Germany would and should win the war. Only after the defeat did the thoroughly indoctrinated teenager begin to realise the extent of Germany's guilt, and he spent the rest of his life urging his fellow Germans to do the same. *The Tin Drum* was the first and perhaps most important step in this direction, as it showed how the Nazi ideology infiltrated the lives of ordinary Germans, described the turmoil of the war years, and revealed the refusal on the part of many post-war Germans to acknowledge their complicity in the Nazi era. In writing a novel that follows a young man from birth to his thirtieth birthday, Grass taps into the legacy of the German Bildungsroman, although, as noted, he inverts the genre's optimistic premises. In the place of a protagonist who seeks to develop his full potential and find a place in an affirmed society, we find Oskar Matzerath, who deliberately stunts his growth and records the sordid details of his life in the Third Reich. Wilhelm Meister wants to found a national theatre; Oskar entertains Nazi officers on the Western Front. Meister plans to become a medical doctor; Oskar ends up in prison.

Like Thomas Mann, Grass uses his fiction to address questions of German politics, but he does so in a very different way. Mann's *Magic Mountain* and *Doctor Faustus* feature artists and intellectuals who engage in theoretical debates about the relative virtues of liberal nation states and totalitarian empires; Grass portrays lower-middle-class shopkeepers who drift in and out of the Nazi Party with little awareness of the larger issues at stake. Oskar's German father joins the party because it makes him feel important and he likes the uniform, but he later regrets his decision and chokes to death on his Nazi insignia. Jan Bronski, who may be Oskar's biological father, participates against his will in the defence of the Polish post office against the Nazis, but he has already lost touch with reality when he is summarily executed. A neighbourhood drunk sobers up when he joins the Waffen-SS, but beats animals to death in moments of unchecked rage. A repressed homosexual embraces the Nazi cult of physical fitness but is ultimately driven to suicide. The parade of opportunistic or accidental Nazis continues in subsequent volumes of Grass's 'Danzig Trilogy'.[57] Joachim Mahlke tries to compensate for his awkward appearance and social ostracism by becoming a war hero in *Cat and Mouse* (*Katz und Maus*, 1961), but he deserts the army when he realises that his efforts have been in vain; Walter Matern briefly joins the SA in *Dog Years* (*Hundejahre*, 1963), only to back out and bitterly rue his decision in later years. Grass's fiction is thus anti-theoretical and anti-heroic, but also anti-demonic; that is, he neither glorifies Nazi resistance fighters nor demonises collaborators, but rather portrays culpable individuals caught in the cogs of larger forces that they only partially understand.

By setting *The Tin Drum* in his native city of Danzig, Grass offers an explicit description of some of the most dramatic events of the Second World War and an implicit challenge to the ideology that provoked it. One of the consequences of Germany's defeat in the First World War was establishment of the Polish Corridor that cut through the formerly German territory of East Prussia and isolated Danzig (today's Gdańsk) as an independent city state between Poland and Germany. The Second World War began when Hitler decided to bring Danzig 'back home' to Germany, '*Heim ins Reich*', by launching the Blitzkrieg against Poland. Grass provides a vivid account in *The Tin Drum* of the conflict that broke out between German troops and Polish partisans on the streets of Danzig on the morning of September 1, 1939, and an equally gripping description of the depredations inflicted on the city's inhabitants by Russian troops in 1945 on their way to victory in Berlin. Between the depiction of these pivotal events in European history, Grass evokes an image of the 'lost city' of his youth that belies the ideological excuses used by the Nazis to justify their aggression.[58] According to this view, the ethnic Germans of Danzig were to be brought back into the body of the nation, just as the earlier annexations of Austria and the Sudentenland sought to redraw the boundaries of the German state in a way that included the members of a racially 'pure' nation. These efforts went hand in hand with a genocidal campaign to cleanse the German Volk of its alien others, both foreign (the Slavic peoples of Poland and Central Europe) and domestic (political dissidents, homosexuals, Jews, and others). According to this fiction, the city of Danzig was inhabited by Germans who yearned as one to return to the fold of the fatherland. *The Tin Drum* exposes this falsehood, as it depicts the population of Danzig as a heterogeneous mixture of individuals marked by religious diversity and conflicted political loyalties. Oskar's legal father does side with the Germans, but his possible biological father inclines towards the Poles, while his beloved grandmother sees herself as a Kashubian, an ethnic minority that pre-dates both modern Poland and Germany. One of Oskar's teachers adopts an orphaned member of the Roma or Sinti minority; his mother buys tin drums from a Jewish shopkeeper. One father figure is Protestant, the other is Catholic.

In later years Grass became an outspoken advocate of post-war Germany's need to think of itself as a diverse land of immigrants (*Einwanderungsland*) rather than as an ethnically unified people. Although the Nazis were the worst offenders in defining national identity in terms of ethnicity and race, they were part of a much older and remarkably persistent tradition. The Roman Tacitus began the trend when he claimed that the Germanic tribes were the original inhabitants of the region and that they had not been infiltrated by foreign peoples since.[59] When early modern German scholars rediscovered Tacitus' work, they proudly embraced his assertion of their untrammelled origins and used it in the struggle to resist the encroachment of foreign powers.[60] Even after the Nazis had provoked a world war and committed genocide in the name of racial purity, vestiges of ethnic nationalism continued to inform German law. Thus, in the wake of Reunification in 1990, those deemed ethnic Germans from other parts of Europe found it easier to gain German citizenship than the children and grandchildren of Turkish *Gastarbeiter* who had been born and raised in Berlin. Those laws have gradually changed in the early twenty-first century, as new immigrants and refugees from Eastern Europe and the Middle East have dramatically altered German demographics. Germany has indeed become a land of immigrants.

Emine Sevgi Özdamar's critically acclaimed *Life Is a Carawanserai* (*Das Leben ist eine Karawanserei*, 1992), the semi-autobiographical novel of a girl who grows up in Turkey and emigrates to Germany, could be hailed as the prototypical Bildungsroman of a new era marked by border crossings and cultural mixtures rather than loyalty to the German Heimat and the German Volk. From the perspective of the works discussed in this chapter, however, it marks only the most recent episode in the history of a genre that has been used since its inception in the late eighteenth century to reflect on the exigencies of national identity in a land marked by shifting boundaries and moving peoples. Wilhelm Meister seeks cultural unity for the Germans but confronts local wars and class conflict. The novel ends with the scattering of its characters around Europe and across the Atlantic; its sequel, *Wilhelm Meister's Journeyman Years* (*Wilhelm Meisters Wanderjahre*, 1829), follows the peripatetic protagonist as he wanders through Italy. Border crossings also play a central role in the Bildungsromane of Gustav Freytag and Gottfried Keller, although the former is anxious to draw the lines that the other seeks to blur. Thomas Mann and Günter Grass warn about the dangers of ethnic nationalism run amok in works that discuss or depict alternatives to the homogeneous nation state. The understanding of the Bildungsroman as an expression of Germany's non-political nature was a myth invented by nationalist literary critics. The novels themselves challenge that myth and the notions of nationalist essentialism that inform them. From the nineteenth-century 'nation of provincials'[61] to the twenty-first century 'nation of immigrants', the German Bildungsroman has served as a venue to depict individual development in a region with a long, and often deeply troubled, political history.

# CHAPTER 2

# The French Bildungsroman

## Alison Finch

The title of this chapter raises an immediate problem. The word Bildungsroman appears in the *Oxford English Dictionary*, its first usage dated to the early twentieth century, but not in the French equivalent, the *Grand Robert*. The database FRANTEXT, which covers nearly five thousand literary, historical and philosophical works from the tenth to the twenty-first centuries, cites only nine usages, and these start only in 1961.[1] It could be objected that French, after all, has its own term: 'roman de formation', novel of development or education. Again, however, this puts in only nine appearances in FRANTEXT, and again these are post-1960 – occurring in some of the same authors who use 'Bildungsroman', at that.[2] As we might expect, French literary critics are freer in their use of both 'Bildungsroman' and 'roman de formation', for example in studies of 1969, 1995 and 2007.[3] But the failure of either term to achieve a significant presence in the wider culture hints at a reluctance to embrace the concept itself (and perhaps also conflicting feelings about 'Germanness').

Certainly, works staging the development of a hero or heroine, his or her learning, appear in French literature from its beginnings, and, as in other national literatures, co-exist with equally long-standing picaresque narratives whose protagonists go from adventure to adventure without noticeable change of character or ethical outlook. But I shall suggest in this chapter that when authors do present such changes, it is almost always with more caveats and ironies than elsewhere.[4] This presentation has in turn had an impact on narratives outside France. French literature was, along with English, the most influential in Europe, and still is. Goethe in particular was shaped by French culture; with *Wilhelm Meister's Apprenticeship* (*Wilhelm Meisters Lehrjahre*, 1795–6) he may have initiated the Bildungsroman, but, as we shall see, that novel itself to a degree drew on French antecedents.

Goethe initiated the Bildungsroman ... but in fact, how historically specific is it? Critics are still discussing the question. In his astute, if provocative, study *The Way of the World*, Franco Moretti confines it to a very short period, roughly 1795 to 1814: he claims the 'classical' Bildungsroman is 'already over' by Jane Austen's *Mansfield Park* (1814).[5] Others, however, consider applying the term to Icelandic sagas, and yet others use it freely in analyses of Margaret Atwood or postcolonial literature.[6] As for the French novel of formation, while this had its heyday in the nineteenth century it would be surprising if it had sprung from nowhere. In the rest of this chapter, I shall outline a chronology of the 'French Bildungsroman', divided into pre-*Wilhelm Meister* and post-*Wilhelm Meister*.[7] I shall also indicate the contribution of drama and verse: it does not make sense to consider the novel in isolation from other literary forms. Until relatively recently, fiction-readers were almost all theatre-goers and lovers of poetry; novelists thinking about their plots may have in mind plays as well as previous fiction. And latterly film need not be excluded (the term Bildungsfilm has been suggested).[8]

## Before *Wilhelm Meister's Apprenticeship*

Spreading across Europe, French (or Anglo-Norman) courtly and Arthurian romance – often narrating knights' quests – provided a medieval model which doubtless eventually contributed to later 'formation' fiction. This model does not dwell on character-development as such, being more frequently concerned with confirmation of communal norms, but it does focus on a solitary hero seeking his goal.[9] However, the late eleventh-century *Song of Roland* (*La Chanson de Roland*) offers an early example of 'learning'. The Emperor Charlemagne loses his nephew Roland in a bloody battle with the Saracens; he has rejected Roland's warning that their offer of peace is deceitful, and does not know that he has been betrayed by Roland's own stepfather Ganelon, who has conspired with the Saracens. Charlemagne eventually takes vengeance on the Saracens and has Ganelon executed. The work stages not only physical but inner conflicts, for example when Roland puts pride above his duty to save his men, at first refusing to blow his horn to seek help from the retreating French army. Charlemagne is said to be weary, not to know what to do; when, at the very end, the angel Gabriel summons him to further warfare against the pagans, he weeps, tears his beard and says: 'God! how hard is this life that I lead!'[10] The *Roland* enjoyed trans-European popularity in the Middle Ages, being translated and adapted into Latin, Norse, Middle High German, Dutch, Welsh and Middle English. This foundational epic could hardly be called pacifist, yet it sets up a prototype of development in Charlemagne, who in the course of the work loses his appetite for war and whose tears verge on the inglorious. The learning is not clear-cut, does not raise characters to a higher plane. It is grounded in defeat, confusion, stubborn errors discarded too late. Nor do readers (or listeners) know if Charlemagne's future actions will change as a result.

A sophisticated complexity is also the hallmark of two leading French Renaissance authors, again highly influential outside France: Rabelais, who has bestowed on English the word 'Rabelaisian', and Montaigne, who had an international readership (including Shakespeare). In Rabelais's *Pantagruel* (1532) the hero, the giant Pantagruel, is young and initially artless, but leaves home to become a scholar and acquires judgement. Here are two aspects of the future Bildungsroman: youth and education, as well as a third for the French embodiment – it is to Paris that Pantagruel goes for his learning, a destination that will recur. But there is another side: the work is as gloriously playful as it is goal-directed, and Pantagruel's right-hand man, Panurge, is a trickster. Not only do they share the first three letters of their names, but all those of 'Panurge' are in 'Pantagruel', as if the ludic Panurge is inside Pantagruel, integral to him. And in Montaigne's *Essays* (*Essais*, 1580–8) ethical deliberation is interwoven with figurative writing and voiced through this; he prescribes wisdom but non-directively, often drolly, by way of metaphor and an emphasis on 'this is how it seems to me', not 'this is what you must do':

> I welcome and embrace truth in whosoever hands I find it. I cheerfully surrender to it, and offer it my vanquished arms as soon as I see it approaching in the distance.[11]

This light-touch 'teaching' is characteristic of a literature that since the Middle Ages had prized dexterity and hedonism. It recurs in the seventeenth century, the Great Century, as it is still called (le Grand Siècle). Many authors of the time pay lip service to the double ideal of 'pleasing and instructing' inherited from the ancients (plaire et instruire). But the pleasing matters more. Molière: 'I should like to know if the great rule of rules isn't to please'.[12] Even in works that apparently promote a moral, the picture is mixed: La Fontaine's *Fables* (1668–94) can end with advice that looks tacked on, his imaginative energy having gone into the little drama itself; while La Rochefoucauld's ambiguously worded, almost poetic, maxims tell his reader that 'humans are like this', not 'humans should be like that' (*Maximes*, 1678).

Let us pause also over the two great tragedians of the seventeenth century, Corneille and Racine, not least because Goethe refers to them in

*Wilhelm Meister*. Corneille's drama is a significant predecessor to the Bildungsroman. His best-known plays depict heroes struggling between incompatible demands, trying to see a way forward and in many cases finding it. They proclaim a newly achieved sense of self. Such is the Auguste of *Cinna* (1640–1): 'I am master of myself as of the universe; / I am, I want to be,' he declares, deciding to pardon rather than punish the conspirators who were plotting to assassinate him.[13] In Racine's plays (slightly later in the century), characters sometimes realise they have been mistaken, if only to apprehend a truth that accompanies their death or leads directly to it, as in the case of Phèdre's suicide. The most interesting play from our perspective is *Bérénice* (1671). The heroine Bérénice is at first filled with hatred for her lover, the emperor Titus, who is rejecting her for political reasons. She comes to a sorrowful acceptance of these reasons, moving away from anger and the threat of suicide. Here is development, Bildung, of a kind, albeit shot through with misery. But Racine more often creates trapped protagonists, locked inside a hell (usually) of their own making and from which there is no escape. French literati soon came to prefer Racine to Corneille, a preference in itself revealing.

The principal fictional model of the seventeenth century is Marie-Madeleine de Lafayette's novel *The Princesse de Clèves* (*La Princesse de Clèves*, 1678). It fulfils those key requirements of the Bildungsroman that have been discerned by a number of critics. The Princesse is young – indeed the only joke in the novel is about this: 'Madame de Clèves, who was at the age when one does not believe a woman over twenty-five can be loved'.[14] Apparently, she has no siblings.[15] And the novel highlights her personal development. Ignorant of the emotions, she allows her mother to arrange her marriage, then falls in love with another man; her husband dies, leaving her free to marry this other, but her experiences of jealousy, and guilt over her adulterous feelings, lead her to a decision that at the time surprised readers and still does: she leaves the man she loves. By now quite different from the unknowing young woman she was at the outset, she goes far away from the court and dies soon after.

Apart from youth, only-child status and learning, three further aspects of this novel that we have already noticed in earlier authors will recur in the French Bildungsroman. First, the learning is located in a centralised society (whether Paris or the court, to which the Princesse and her mother have just moved); this link between learning and elite residence can be tight. Second, the learning arises from a protracted and painful bewilderment. Even if the Princesse ultimately concludes that her highest value is peace of mind (repos), until then it has been less 'Now I know myself', more 'Now I do not know myself'. The longing to retain inner control vies with helplessness: 'she no longer recognised herself', 'she thought it a crime not to have felt passion for [her husband], as if this were something within her power' (235–6, 295); even five pages before the end, 'she no longer knew herself . . . her feelings were all full of trouble and passion' (310). Third and finally, far from inserting herself into the world she abandons it.

*The Princesse de Clèves* can claim to be not only Europe's first psychological novel but its first Bildungsroman, no less so for its stress on ambivalence and its culmination in a Pyrrhic victory. Furthermore, it has a female author and a female protagonist; and this heroine is endowed with insight not only by experience but, self-reflexively, through 'stories within stories': tales about unhappy love recounted to her by others. *The Princesse de Clèves* is truly pioneering. But, oddly, scholars of the Bildungsroman have overlooked it.

Learning famously leaps centre-stage with the French Enlightenment and its project to educate all strata of society, taking instruction out of the hands of the Church. If – as has been argued – the ethos of the Bildungsroman in part derives from religious ideas of self-improvement, such ideas were secularised and politicised in eighteenth-century France. Diderot's and d'Alembert's *Encyclopedia* (*L'Enyclopédie*, 1751–72), aiming to dissolve superstition and impart knowledge, travelled across Europe. The Enlightenment had started in England and Scotland, but it was France that popularised it. The satirical fictions of the century – Montesquieu's *Persian Letters* (*Lettres persanes*, 1721), Voltaire's tales (written and disseminated over about two decades up to 1775) – bring together the personas of the ingénu and the wide-eyed voyager to point up injustice and cruel anomalies in the organisation of societies and religions. These ingénus and voyagers are usually young and are progressively stripped of absurd suppositions. Clearly, they learn: by the end of his much-travelled youth, Candide has spurned the facile optimism of his mentor Pangloss. That being said, the structure of these heroes' stories and their deliberately thin personalities usually make them closer to the picaresque figures prevalent in eighteenth-century narrative than to those of the Bildungsroman: none enacts the delicate and surprising process that we now think of as Bildung. They are the cousins of Bildungsroman protagonists rather than those protagonists themselves. This sketchy characterisation is epitomised in a key work that plasters a lightly fictionalised veneer onto an educational treatise, Rousseau's *Émile* (*Émile, ou De l'éducation*, 1762). Émile and sister Sophie (the sidekick whose non-egalitarian treatment has been criticised) exist to prove points about 'development'.

However, all these works do pave the way for the great European Bildungsromane of the nineteenth century. And at least two eighteenth-century French novels can perhaps be given that designation.

The first is Antoine-François Prévost's *Manon Lescaut* (1731), still famous in both fictional and musical forms. This work presents what is starting to look familiar: a joyless Bildung. The insights of its narrator Des Grieux go hand in hand with his social and moral abjection. Des Grieux's shedding of naivety is always only partial, yet the dramatic ironies of the work, and the hero's gradual education in his own frailty and the all-importance of money, reinforce perspectives adopted by Prévost's predecessors and set agendas for key successors.

The second notable eighteenth-century Bildungsroman is Françoise de Graffigny's epistolary novel *Letters of a Peruvian Woman* (*Lettres d'une Péruvienne*, 1747). The eponymous heroine travels to France, there to discover books and freedom from stereotyping. Her Peruvian fiancé deserts her, and it is unclear if she will achieve happiness with another; but en route she finds out about her new nation and grows in personal insight. As has been pointed out, the Bildungsroman typically intertwines knowledge of community and of self. And since Graffigny's heroine explores and highlights inter alia the double standards governing men's and women's behaviour, this work can be described as the first plainly feminist Bildungsroman of France. It displays another characteristic foreshadowed by the Russian-doll tales of *The Princesse de Clèves* and that we shall come to associate with the French Bildungsroman: it is openly self-conscious. In prefatory pages it inserts itself in the wake of such precursors as Montaigne and Montesquieu, and throughout it makes play with different modes of communication (most notably South American *quipus*).

Before leaving the eighteenth century, we must air two difficulties already confronting, or pre-confronting, the establishment of the Bildungsroman in France. First, the learning promoted by the Enlightenment was sometimes expressed through the word 'perfectibilité', which means 'improvability' but is uncomfortably close to 'perfection' (the same in French and English) – close enough to invite qualms. Second, by common consent the century's greatest French novel is Laclos's *Dangerous Liaisons* (*Les Liaisons dangereuses*, 1782), which is in no way a Bildungsroman. It does have a teleology that takes us to an apparently moralising ending. But it is prized for its multi-valent structure, its irony, its verbal prowess, and above all its alluring invitation to side with the virtuosic villains. If there is learning, it is that of readers as they perceive that they have succumbed to the invitation. It would be hard for nineteenth-century novelists to escape a powerful ancestor like this, whatever their leanings towards Bildung.

## The French Revolution and *Wilhelm Meister's Apprenticeship*

Franco Moretti has argued compellingly that the 1789 French Revolution dictated the underlying premises of both Goethe's *Wilhelm Meister's Apprenticeship* (*Wilhelm Meisters Lehrjahre*) and Jane Austen's *Pride and Prejudice* (1813). (Austen's novels were by definition written in the immediate aftermath of the Revolution; she was thirteen when this occurred, and died twenty-eight years after it, in 1817. Her most notable other Bildungsroman is *Emma* (1816), but others follow the coming-to-maturity design, some of them drafted much earlier than their eventual date of publication: that is, closer in time to the Revolution.) Moretti posits that Goethe and Austen, in reaction to the cataclysms of France, are suggesting 'another way'. Wild aspirations can be grown out of; in particular, class tensions do not have to be resolved through violence. The bourgeoisie can adopt an accommodating, cooperative approach, and the aristocracy may comprehend that the middle class has qualities it can marry into. Whether or not we accept every detail of Moretti's analysis, undeniably the 1789 Revolution – far more shocking and ostentatiously ideological than the seventeenth-century English one – had a cultural impact abroad, sometimes stunning and immediate, sometimes delayed and indirect.

But if the Revolution and Terror played a crucial part in late eighteenth- and early nineteenth-century European consciousness, so too did pre-Revolutionary French literature, in a to-and-fro cycle whose intricacy is sometimes underestimated by commentators on the Bildungsroman. Goethe, as I have indicated, was steeped in French authors and French assumptions about 'taste'. The Mephistopheles of *Faust* (1808) has French attributes (his dress, his advocacy of free-and-easy 'French' or 'foreign' sexual customs). It was Goethe who would bring to the world's attention Diderot's masterpiece, the dialogue *Rameau's Nephew* (*Le Neveu de Rameau*): begun in about 1760, its first publication was in Goethe's German translation (1804). (Its earliest appearance in French, in 1823, was a re-translation of this.) It is scarcely possible to imagine a less Bildungsroman-like work than *Rameau's Nephew*, with its enjoyment of the incurably contradictory, wilfully wayward, mocking and self-mocking Nephew, and with its clinching final exchange – which clinches nothing:

HIM [the Nephew]: Goodbye, Mr Philosopher, don't you agree that I'm the same as ever? ME: Alas! Yes, unfortunately. HIM: I hope I'll be this unfortunate for the next forty years. He laughs longest who laughs last.[16]

As for *Wilhelm Meister* itself, it took cues from elsewhere – some, plausibly, from previous French fiction and drama. (Goethe refers, as we have seen, to both Racine and Corneille.) Growing into 'taste' forms part of Wilhelm's apprenticeship, and in the Germany of the time taste was invariably acknowledged to derive from French criteria. A key female character has the French name Mignon. The digressive aspects of *Wilhelm Meister*'s structure – at times surprisingly casual for the work that is supposed to be Europe's first Bildungsroman – may have been inspired by such earlier French fiction as Rabelais's *Pantagruel* and Scarron's rambling *Comic Novel* (*Le Roman comique*, 1651–7), which like *Wilhelm Meister* depicts the adventures of a company of travelling players and their dealings with provincial patrons. *Wilhelm Meister*'s easy movement between action (sometimes bedroom farce), discussion and deliberation was already integral to, say, Marguerite de Navarre's *Heptameron* (*L'Heptaméron*, 1558), an admixture of bawdy or satirical stories and conversation about these among their listeners – exploratory talk that remains dialogic. And although firm statements about Bildung do appear in *Wilhelm Meister*, others are open, for example: 'Wilhelm was beginning to feel that things work out differently in the world from what he had imagined,' not, say, 'Wilhelm was learning the path to a better moral existence.'[17]

Thus, while *Wilhelm Meister* is evidently goal-directed (the title urges us to ask: how will the apprenticeship be realised?), it is also lateral, even quirky.[18] It stages madness, androgyny, fetes, little life-stories and *mise en abyme* (self-reflectingness), most notably in the play-within-a-play-within-a-play discussion of *Hamlet*. The adolescent Mignon at times almost steals the spotlight from Wilhelm. Above all, *Wilhelm Meister* realises the Bildungsroman model through a range of tones: yes, occasionally preachy, but also sardonic, poignant, playful. The diversity is part of Goethe's genius but owes something to a neighbouring literature whose foremost practitioners had often avoided the conclusive: Montaigne's motto was: 'What do I know?' (Que sais-je?)

Post-Revolutionary France responded to this work that pre-Revolutionary France had helped to fashion. It did so most strikingly through the novelist and thinker Germaine de Staël, the poet Gérard de Nerval and the Mignon craze.

Goethe sent a copy of *Wilhelm Meister* to Staël in 1797. (Its first translation into French was in 1802.) In her *On Literature* (*De la littérature*, 1800) and *On Germany* (*De l'Allemagne*, 1807) Staël turned to Northern European and particularly to German culture, which she promulgated partly in opposition to Napoleon's rampant nationalism. Napoleon responded by ordering *On Germany* to be pulped and forcing Staël into exile. The French, then, came to Goethe (and to Romanticism) through Staël's writings. Goethe would be highly respected in France, as elsewhere in Europe.[19] But from the beginning his introduction to the French was bound up with the nation's own internal political conflicts. Furthermore, local literary traditions and French exceptionalism were not so easily overcome, erecting other barriers; for Staël's translation of extracts from *Faust* famously bowdlerised them to bring them into conformity with still-strong seventeenth-century standards of 'bienséance', propriety.[20]

Nerval was both more respectful and more imaginative. An admirer of German literature and especially of Goethe, he in his turn translated *Faust* (1827), and – a signal tribute – used *Wilhelm Meister* as a springboard in his fiction and verse. One of his prose works is titled *Aurélia* (1855), while an actress in another is called Aurélie: Aurélie is an important character in *Wilhelm Meister*. The work figuring the actress is *Sylvie* (1853), an exquisite novella which Proust would later describe as 'one of the masterpieces of French literature'.[21] Like *Wilhelm Meister*, *Sylvie* evokes the magical illusions of theatre and of doubles (the Doppelgänger was already, of course, familiar from popular and elite German culture); it is woven round journeying, performance, country fetes, half-sleeping states. Its distinctive comedy, wistfulness, rich dreaming and artfully crafted chronology are Nerval's own, but he nods to *Wilhelm Meister* throughout. And *Sylvie* puts its narrator through an apprenticeship of sorts: at the end he perforce cedes false notions and arrives at a truer view of Aurélie, who has by then befriended him. In his equally exquisite verse collection *Chimeras* (*Les Chimères*, 1854), Nerval does more than nod to *Wilhelm Meister*: as Terence Cave points out, one of the six key sonnets directly alludes to and plays with Mignon's song 'Kennst du das Land, wo die Zitronen blühn … ?', 'Do you know the land where the lemon-trees bloom … ?'[22] This sonnet is 'Delfica': 'Do you know it, Daphne, that old romance … ? Do you recognise the TEMPLE with its immense peristyle, and the bitter lemons that your teeth marked, and the cavern in which dwells the ancient seed of the conquered dragon? … ' (second ellipsis Nerval's).[23]

Also striking are the codas of these hermetic sonnets. All but one chart shifts that, while enigmatic, could be called 'moral' or at least personal, and drive to a finale that suggests a new state of mind – hopeful, even triumphant. (The exception is 'Delfica' itself.) Thus 'El Desdichado' moves through bereavement and uncertain identity to end with an affirmation of the narrator's Orphic gifts, his mastery of complexity: its last lines are: 'And I've twice, as victor, crossed the Acheron [a river of Hades], modulating in turn on Orpheus's lyre the sighs of the saint and the cries of the fairy.' The sonnets 'Myrtho', 'Horus', 'Antéros', 'Artémis' similarly culminate with affirmations, with confidence that something beyond clear knowledge has changed, or is changing, for the better.

Nerval's verse was relatively unknown in nineteenth-century France. But Goethe's Mignon became a celebrity. Cave's study charts her 'afterlives' in European music, literature and film – afterlives that populated France more thickly than elsewhere.[24] It is intriguing that this character, whose early death in *Wilhelm Meister* bars her forever from maturity, had a hold on the nineteenth-century French imagination far exceeding that of Wilhelm: an almost obsessive, almost perverse, hold. Perhaps, as Moretti suggests, post-1800 France could not or would not 'reproduce' the learning undergone by Wilhelm, however subtly Goethe had traced this. Was it because of the French exceptionalism already mentioned, a certain independence, even cussedness: 'We shall make of this work what we will'? But apart from this, France's own pre-Goethe novels of formation had doubtless been too imbued with ambiguity and dejection for much dabbling with Certificates of Apprenticeship.[25] And – a second major determinant – the Revolution's regression into chaos and horror meant that any 'upward' plot trajectory would likely be tempered with a large dose of irony in elite fiction and, to some extent, in popular culture. The androgynous and sometimes frenetic Mignon was a better fit than Wilhelm. From Lamartine's poem 'Milly' (1827) to Balzac's novel *Modeste Mignon* (1844), from Ambroise Thomas's highly successful opera *Mignon* (1866) to her post-1900 personas, Mignon represents the strongest direct purchase on France of *Wilhelm Meister*.

The strongest direct purchase; but there are the indirect ones too. Let us now look at the nineteenth-century French Bildungsroman.

## The Nineteenth Century up To 1850

The two early nineteenth-century fictions that most obviously enact Bildung are Benjamin Constant's *Adolphe* (1816) and Claire de Duras's

*Ourika* (1824), both novellas that follow the pattern of disillusion leading not to a putatively happy (because enlightened) future, but to despair and death. (Staël's eponymous heroines in the novels *Delphine*, 1802, and *Corinne ou l'Italie*, 1807, are disabused of certain assumptions by traumatic events – in Delphine's case the Revolution – but change insufficiently for their lives to be interpreted as a process of Bildung.) Arguably, Constant, Staël's lover, adopted and adapted aspects of *Wilhelm Meister* in *Adolphe*. Like Wilhelm, Adolphe is urged to take his place in professional society, but unlike Wilhelm he ignores this and other advice emanating from mentors; his Bildung does not comprise insertion into the 'practical', 'career' world, let alone the business or consumerist world, an insertion that some critics see as an important component of the novel of formation.[26] Certainly, the Adolphe we meet at the end of his life is not the egoistic youth of the outset. But what he has come to fathom is his capacity to inflict suffering, along with harsh facts about the see-sawing of desire – desire, which causes us to lose interest in those whom we think we possess securely, then to regain that interest when they appear unavailable. The lessons absorbed, there is nothing for it but to die. These lessons are presented in a suggestive manner reminiscent of La Rochefoucauld's maxims. They are often couched as a fluid invitation to wonder at the strange contradictoriness of humans – their paradoxical behaviour, the mismatch between language and emotion: 'Man's feelings are confused and mixed; they are made up of a multitude of varied impressions that escape observation; and language, always too crude and general, may designate them but can never define them.'[27] Adolphe echoes the Princesse de Clèves, too: 'In my head, I repeated what I had said; I could not understand my behaviour' (80).

For her part, Duras's Ourika realises that her black skin will forever debar her from full acceptance by polite society and will stop her marrying the man she loves. The 1789 Revolution, with its stress on egalitarianism, briefly offers hope, but soon becomes a factor in her misery as she sees this will make not a jot of difference; the innocently contented young woman she was becomes a tragic, self-hating figure. We recognise in both Adolphe and Ourika, then, that learning-to-abjection pathway, and in *Ourika* dashed political expectations play a part symptomatic of later fiction too. The brevity of these two works – the best French fiction of the first three decades of the century – suggests that France was ready for its Bildungsromane but not quite able to deliver them in extended form. (This is to exclude the long best-sellers of the early nineteenth century, many written by women and many culminating in the scenario: 'Then the scales fell from her eyes'; but these – frequently needing to earn their authors an income – sought to please the public, and their character development, such as it is, is usually unsophisticated.)

The first full-length nineteenth-century French novel that may be judged a Bildungsroman is Stendhal's *Red and Black* (*Le Rouge et le Noir*, 1830). The immaturity of its hero Julien is emphasised from the beginning, as is a physical puniness that equally suggests puerility. The immaturity can manifest itself as excessive guile and as a pride that Julien gradually under-stands is misplaced, but then only in fits and starts. The pride is responsible for his final catastrophic attempt to murder his erstwhile beloved Mme de Rênal. Meanwhile he has – as the Bildungsroman demands – learned about his society and positioned himself within it; following the inclination of the French Bildungsroman, this happens by devious means and in Paris. His acquisition of wisdom comes in the last few chapters, when he is in prison awaiting execution.

The critic René Girard has proposed that such deathbed wisdom, such conversions, characterise the greatest novels, whether French or other.[28] (Tolstoy's are among those he analyses, for example.) But Girard's volte-face schema possibly fits French fiction better than some other national literatures; his own 'formation' as a brilliant French intellectual coming from a specific culture may have contributed to his emphasis on unex-pected end-of-life enlightenment, as opposed to a steady sequence of maturing experiences such as Austen's Emma, for instance, undergoes. The contrast is not absolute but is one of degree: irony in both *Red and Black* and *Emma* provides constant correctives, and Emma comprehen-sively sees her mistakes only when she finally realises she loves Mr Knightley. However, the structure of *Red and Black* is more spasmodic. Indeed, Stendhal emphasises unpredictability (the 'imprévu', aesthetically dear to him).

Perpetuating the trend we have noted, *Red and Black* self-consciously draws attention to other fictions. Sometimes this is to mock them: in a chapter whose title, 'Elective affinities', recalls Goethe, the narrator remarks:

> In Paris, Julien's position vis-à-vis Mme de Rênal would soon have been simplified; but in Paris, love is the offspring of novels. The young tutor and his shy mistress would have found their position clarified in three or four novels … These would have outlined the role to play, would have shown them the model to imitate; and vanity, sooner or later, would have forced Julien – albeit without pleasure and perhaps grudgingly – to follow that model.[29]

And self-consciousness is writ large at a moment when the narrator goes so far as to explain why, in effect, this novel cannot be a Bildungsroman. During the prison sequence, he steps off the page to explain how Julien *would have* developed:

> He was still very young; but in my view he was a fine specimen (plante). Instead of advancing (marcher) like most men from the tender to the wily (rusé), age would have given him a goodness easily moved to pity, he would have been cured of his crazy mistrust ... But what is the use of these vain predictions? (Stendhal's ellipsis, 654)

The frustration is heightened by the use, in the first sentence, of two different tenses of the verb 'to be', difficult to convey in English. 'He *was* still very young' is in the imperfect – an ongoing process (était). But the immediately following 'he *was* a fine specimen' is, shockingly, in the past historic (ce fut une belle plante): the life is over, never to ripen. Furthermore, the narrator, virtually quitting his usual tongue-in-cheek tone, creates the illusion that he is speaking in the author's own voice. One might almost say that this brief elegy tells us all we need to know about the French Bildungsroman. It ruefully underlines both dashed potential and its own obvious fictionality; it posits 'normal' Bildung not as an evolution from error to good sense but as a more dubious passage from a kindly sensibility to crafty self-seeking ('like most men'). Trajectories of disappointment accompanied by growing worldliness will be staged by later French novelists too (not to mention by Stendhal again, in subsequent novels).[30]

*Red and Black* is original not only in its sustained wit and its subtle blend of comedy and poignancy, but also in its political awareness and its biting critique of the Church. What enabled Stendhal to lead here? Was it in part his ideologies?[31] While we should be wary of jumping rapidly from an author's credos to his or her works of imagination, plausibly Stendhal's republicanism and atheism informed his crafting of stories in which, at a time of political regression, 'betterment' may be more material than ethical, and which are larded with withering comments from the narrator. Moral stasis recurs in two of Stendhal's three great successors, Flaubert and Zola, also opponents of nineteenth-century regimes and also without religious faith; I shall return to them.

Meanwhile, however, the case of Balzac should warn us off making clear connections between fiction and personal world view. As a Catholic and apologist for the Ancien Régime, Balzac 'should have' been able to suggest more plausibly that all was not lost, that the post-Revolutionary return to religion and monarchy – however diluted – was welcome. But the literary tradition into which he was born overrode any sanguine historical assessment. Indeed, we may say that the 'French tendency' turned Balzac's ideology into the instrument for a still more ironised Bildungsroman than Stendhal's. His interpretation – that religion and royalty were but pale shadows of their former selves – gave his imagination licence to explore and exuberantly represent the shoddiness of a dysfunctional contemporary society.

This representation is both 'Realist' and 'magical realist'. As a Realist, Balzac has been lauded (by Marx among others) for his grasp of the financial and political workings of nineteenth-century capitalist France. (And like Stendhal, but unlike some other Bildungsroman authors, he depicts characters who worry where the next meal is coming from.) As a magical realist, he is celebrated for his powerful figurative writing (not least by Proust).[32] Excoriating social analyses and a genius for metaphor do not in themselves rule Balzac out as a writer of coming-to-wisdom Bildungsromane; they are after all part of Dickens's brilliance. But in this case they work towards a sense that Balzac's artistic concerns lie elsewhere than in ethical development.

The best-known young heroes of Balzac's cycle *The Human Comedy* (*La Comédie humaine*) are Eugène de Rastignac (*Old Goriot, Père Goriot*, 1834, and other novels), and Lucien de Rubempré (*Lost Illusions, Illusions perdues*, 1837–43, and *Splendour and Misery of Courtesans, Splendeurs et misères des courtisanes*, 1838–47). Eugène and Lucien come to Paris from the provinces (again). They achieve worldly acumen rather than maturity, and Lucien (again) descends into abjection: his career as a second-rate poet abandoned, he falls in with Vautrin (or Jacques Collin), the Satan of *The Human Comedy*. As for Rastignac, on the verge of conquering high society he gazes avidly down at Paris from the hilltop cemetery Père Lachaise, where he has just attended old Goriot's funeral, and addresses the city thus: 'It's between the two of us now!' ('À nous deux maintenant!')[33] The narrator describes the words as 'pompous' (ces mots grandioses). It is hard to imagine Austen, Dickens or George Eliot characterising heroines or heroes on the threshold of a new life as 'pompous'. Those authors are, as it were, more wholeheartedly behind their protagonists. We may not agree with Moretti's verdict on the English Bildungsroman: that it has something of the fairy tale about it (185–6, 213). But plainly differences exist between it and the French Bildungsroman of the same century. Balzac's heroes are of a piece with the majority Stendhal had described: they move from the 'tender' to the 'wily'.

Three other interests of Balzac's dilute any easy impression of Bildung. First, he stages in loving detail the workings of the *idée fixe* through such characters as the miser Grandet or the lecher Hulot (in *Eugénie Grandet*, 1833, and *Cousin Bette, La Cousine Bette*, 1847). Plots pivot on the sheer immutability of the obsession, which functions beyond all reason and (as in the case of Hulot) apparently never dies. (Even after dishonouring and financially ruining his family, Hulot is to be found caressing young girls and finally makes off with the kitchen-maid.) These compulsions can be tragic, comic, even marvellous in their monstrosity. What they are not is fertile breeding ground for 'progress'. Second, Balzac likes his devils, putting them centre stage and endowing them with wit and verve: Vautrin, conceivably the main character of the *Human Comedy*, shares the author's linguistic virtuosity. Third, even more than with obsession and devilry, Balzac is preoccupied with contradictoriness. He parades paradoxes of situation and especially of character, which like La Rochefoucauld and Constant he emphasises – increasingly so towards the end of his life, when he was at the height of his powers. The 1842 preface (the 'Avant-propos') that draws together the novels of *The Human Comedy* talks of complication, changeability, hiddenness. And *Cousin Bette*, for example, frequently indicates that passion and altruism itself are less interesting than the variability of their (delightfully?) odd manifestations: 'The causes operating the mechanisms (ressorts) of the soul seem to be completely foreign to the results'; 'This Scene carries, by the way, its own ethics (moralités), which are of more than one kind'; 'Beneficence has so many modes of existence in Paris that this strange expression ['a bad good deed'] corresponds to one of its variations'; 'Noble feelings pushed to an extreme produce results similar to those of the greatest vices' (respectively, 427, 290, 76, 86).[34]

*The Human Comedy* deploys incomparably ferocious and entertaining perceptions of the id – the greedy, self-defeating, chopping-and-changing unconscious; it has bestowed on us some of the greatest European novels, and certain of them display the shell of the 'personal progress' narrative. But these are Bildungsromane of a singular kind, if they are Bildungsromane.

## The Nineteenth Century after 1850

Does Flaubert, in the wake of Balzac, administer the *coup de grâce*? It would appear so. The murder is, naturally, premeditated. *Madame Bovary* (1857) teasingly references the two outstanding previous models, *Wilhelm Meister* and *Emma*. The very first free indirect narration of Emma Bovary's yearnings reminds us of 'Do you know the land where the lemon-trees bloom . . . ?' Emma, imagining the honeymoon she would have wished for, makes part of the fantasy, as it were, lemon-shaped:

> you would probably have to set off for those places with marvellous names where wedding-nights beget a more delicious lethargy! . . . As the sun is going down, on the shore of the bay you breathe the scent of lemon-trees.[35]

But Emma is no Wilhelm, lacking his social and intellectual opportunities. Then there is her forename. At one point, Flaubert even reprises a sentence or two from Austen's *Emma*. (Austen, we should remember, was using free indirect style some forty years earlier than Flaubert.) Emma Woodhouse has learned that Mr Elton is in love not with Harriet Smith but with herself: 'How could she have been so deceived! . . . Perhaps it was not fair to expect him to feel how very much he was her inferior in talent, and all the elegancies of mind.'[36] Now here is Flaubert, à propos of the botched operation Emma had urged her husband Charles to perform on the club foot of the hapless Hippolyte: 'So how could she (she who was so intelligent!) have misjudged yet again? . . . It was for him [Charles], for that creature, for that man who understood nothing, felt nothing!' (189–90). This Emma, however, is a bovine Bovary, not a well-constructed Woodhouse.

Possibly, Flaubert's Emma has a Girardian deathbed conversion. She tells the despised Charles: 'Yes . . . it's true . . . you are good!' (Flaubert's ellipses, 324). But the Flaubert who thought that 'concluding' was merely stupid was never likely to deliver a finale that could satisfy other than aesthetically.[37]

And the supreme blow is *Sentimental Education*, announcing in its title the ambition to parody all previous 'emotional educations': *L'Éducation sentimentale* (1869). This title is tricky to translate, 'sentimental' in French meaning 'emotional' without mawkish overtones; it therefore quasi-neutrally – yet brazenly – says: 'Here is a Bildungsroman' – *the* Bildungsroman, in fact (*La* not *Une* éducation). The hero Frédéric arrives in Paris as a callow young man without siblings. By the end he is still that callow, if rather less young, man. He concludes with his friend Deslauriers that an abortive visit to a brothel, which took place before the action of the novel even starts, was the best experience they'd had. Embarrassment, failure, inaction, the blurred borderline where naivety shades into silliness: this is an anti-'emotional education'. In French hands, the Bildungsroman is disappearing down its own ending.[38]

Nor can we leave Flaubert without revisiting the origin of his most famous short story, 'A Simple Heart' in *Three Tales* ('Un cœur simple', *Trois Contes*, 1876). Flaubert claimed he wrote it in response to a complaint from his friend and fellow author George Sand. (Many novels by Sand herself trace Bildung: not invariably but often, her heroes and heroines improve themselves morally, socially, financially or all three. She was internationally popular, and George Eliot, though much the better writer, saw her as a model of sorts, adopting her 'George'.) After *Sentimental Education*, Sand reproached Flaubert for doubt and cynicism, exhorting him to draw directly on 'the highest morality inside oneself'.[39] So Flaubert created the Félicité of 'A Simple Heart'. Félicité is generous, loving, selfless, and, precisely, simple. She superstitiously endows her parrot with the qualities of the Holy Ghost (who, after all, appeared as a bird to the apostles), projecting those same qualities onto it once it dies and is stuffed, and even (especially?) on her own deathbed. Félicité's goodness is inseparable from her limitations; nor does she change – the story indeed depends on her constancy in all respects. For historians of the French Bildungsroman, 'A Simple Heart' is as telling as Flaubert's two great full-length novels. Whatever his disingenuous tributes to Sand, it is a crushing riposte to her optimism. And another late work, the unfinished *Bouvard and Pécuchet* (*Bouvard et Pécuchet*, posth., 1881), caricatures the image of 'learning' to the point of demolition. (Education can receive short shrift in Flaubert's fiction.)

As for post-Flaubert fiction, Huysmans's *Against Nature* (*À rebours*, 1884) folds back on itself like *Sentimental Education*, its hero concluding that travel to London is pointless, since his imaginings about that city are preferable to the actual experience. The destination is revealing, in its own way representing a rejection of 'Northern' culture that has already subtly asserted itself in Flaubert.[40] Finally, if Zola's novels depict the coming of age of certain protagonists, it is in diluted form: their learning is not the main focus of the fiction, which prefers to detail inexorable and spectacular links between social conditions and degradation or disaster. Usually those characters of Zola's who are sagacious have been so from an early stage (for example, the Pauline of *La Joie de vivre*, 1884, or Mme Caroline in *Money*, *L'Argent*, 1891). And where hope for the future exists, this is generally expressed as a wide-ranging metaphor, as at the end of *Germinal* (1884), which looks to the later 'sprouting' of an army that will avenge the defeated miners.

Subsequent literary criticism may have helped consign less equivocal nineteenth-century French formation novels to the background. Didactic, sermonising novels did abound, but are not deemed noteworthy literary phenomena of the second half of the nineteenth century; George Sand was relegated, frequently in misogynistic terms. Instead, critics have typically esteemed elite male writers' promotion of suggestion over statement, including Gautier's celebrated dictum 'That which is useful is ugly' – in other words, aesthetic beauty must *never* be contaminated by any hint of 'applicability'. Entering into this promulgation of non-Bildung are Baudelaire's irony (not for him Nerval's affirmative codas) and his transformation of 'journeying' into urban *flânerie*. Verlaine cultivates insipidity (fadeur) as a virtue. If Mallarmé's sparsely punctuated verse conveys 'the sense of an ending', it is with the utmost ambiguity, and when he uses such constructions as 'What a . . . '/'Which . . . ' it may be unclear whether we should supply a conclusive exclamation mark or an inconclusive question mark.[41] Rimbaud's verse and prose poetry is sometimes politically utopian, but his best-known poem, 'The Drunken Boat' ('Le bateau ivre', 1871), depicts a soaring-up of the imagination, a wild, exciting journey, then three verses from the end a decidedly downbeat return to reality, introduced by 'But, true, I've wept too much!' (Mais vrai, j'ai trop pleuré!). The narrator is no longer the heroic adventurer through new worlds but a child sailing his frail toy boat in a puddle.[42] Thus canon-formation, largely dictated by the French academic establishment, has had a role and still does, despite efforts by feminist and cultural critics to rehabilitate works that (although they do not phrase it this way) might strongly depict Bildung.

### After 1900

Even with the benefit of retrospective attempts to rethink the canon, the French Bildungsroman might seem, by the end of the nineteenth century, to be not merely in eclipse but extinct. But then something remarkable happens. With *In Search of Lost Time* (*À la recherche du temps perdu*, 1913–27), Proust brings it back to life. His narrator, like other Bildungsroman heroes, is an only child in whose life Paris has an important presence. He moves from childhood to adulthood unsure of his writer's vocation and undergoing painful disillusionments in his experiences of high society, friendship and love. He finally realises that these experiences can be the subject of his book and that he can become the artist he has longed to be. The last two hundred pages of the seven-volume novel make such declarations as 'a new light dawned in me. And I understood that all these materials for a work of literature were my past life' (IV 478).

The last four decades or so have seen a tendency to shy away from the reading of *À la recherche* as a triumphant odyssey, a quest achieved.[43] This reading has been perceived as ingenuously ignoring all the gleeful detours along which the narrator proceeds, and as underestimating Proust's playfulness in favour of his supposedly solemn conclusions – in a word, it has been perceived as simplistic. To be sure, many early Proust critics emphasised the work's goal-directedness in order to short-circuit, dismiss or outright ignore its most troubling sides. Yet the repudiation of the journey's-end construction has on occasions been too absolute. In fact, the view of *À la recherche* as a 'learning' novel, a novel of initiation or even apprenticeship, has never really gone away. It moulded the discussions of such distinguished and far-from-ingenuous thinkers as Gilles Deleuze in his *Proust and Signs* (*Proust et les signes*, 1964, 1970) and later Roland Barthes in (inter alia) *Preparation of the Novel* (*La Préparation du roman*, 1978–80). And Philippe Chardin's essay of 2007 puts the Bildungsroman interpretation firmly back on the map.[44] With *À la recherche* we can have, then, the Bildungsroman, the Künstlerroman: the novel of the artist's growth to maturity. For after all, by any view Proust's narrator is different from Balzac's failed poet Lucien. Whether or not he goes on to write the work we have just been reading, the undertaking to do so is there.[45] But most readers, unencumbered by the finer points of Proust criticism, surely assume that the previous three thousand pages have indeed been written by the narrator.

And *À la recherche* represents a maturing of other kinds. It would be strange to suspect sleight of hand when the narrator finally adopts stances of humility, openness and tolerance. These come almost as closing responses to the displays of pride, mendacity and prejudice (homophobic, racist and snobbish) that have been on show throughout, to both cruel and amusing effect. Among the narrator's last statements is, for example, this one about his readers, fifteen pages from the end:

> For in my opinion they would be not my readers but the readers of themselves, my book being a kind of enlarging lens ... my book, thanks to which I would give them the means to read inside themselves. So that I would not ask them to praise or denigrate me, but only to tell me if it is indeed thus, if the words they read in themselves are indeed those I have written (IV 610).

What has sometimes been forgotten is that a Bildungsroman can be teleological *and* digressive (like music, which drives forward, reaches a resolution, but on the way is made of variations, unexpected departures, often dissonances). The Bildungsroman's tale can be both bare and eccentric, can raise ethical questions and also be ambiguous, as in *Wilhelm Meister*. To take just one aspect: the famous Bildungsromane *Pride and Prejudice*, *Emma*, *Great Expectations* are all luxuriantly comic.

Mr Bennet's remark to Mary that her singing has delighted listeners long enough, Miss Bates's repetitive non-sequiturs, Joe's rueful comments about Pip's sister Mrs Joe, in a sense participate in the broader learning depicted in those novels, yet they take on a splendid life of their own. Similarly with *À la recherche*: its ludic scenarios, its ironies, its polymorphism and its sensationally rich verbal texture do not preclude a structure of which Proust himself was proud and that led him to talk to friends and fellow authors of truths that would be revealed only at the close. 'I'm forced to paint errors without feeling I have to say I hold them for errors. Too bad for me if the reader thinks I hold them for the truth,' he wrote in a letter of 1914.[46]

What inspired Proust not only to 'suck' nourishment from nineteenth-century predecessors 'into his own great plant', as John Cocking has put it, but also to respectabilise the French Bildungsroman, set it on a new path?[47] Proust's aesthetic tastes were exceptionally eclectic and international. He admired English novelists, in particular George Eliot and Dickens. (Pip's eventual insight into his own and others' snobbery doubtless contributed to the shooting-down of the aristocracy performed by Proust's narrator.)

And Proust admired Goethe. He cites him a few times in *À la recherche* itself. In the third volume, *The Guermantes Way*, he describes the milieu of actors as 'made beautiful to a degree by Goethe's depiction in *Wilhelm Meister*' and refers to a mountain 'honoured' by Goethe's walks (II 475, 553); in sketches for that volume he cites the 'double play-acting' of *Wilhelm Meister* (II 1153). In *Time Regained*, his character M. de Charlus criticises wartime Germanophobia for its absurd claims that great German writers like Nietzsche and Goethe lack 'psychology' (IV 358). Also significant are two short essays (three pages each), one published in 1904, nine years before *À la recherche*, the other of uncertain date (found among Proust's papers).[48] The 1904 essay is a review of two books in German: one on Ruskin and the other a translation into German of Ruskin. Here Proust, on the pretext that Ruskin alludes to Goethe, delivers a double-edged compliment, referring to the 'limits' of Goethe's work, and slyly remarking that *Wilhelm Meister* is not 'all nature', as Carlyle and Emerson had suggested, but rather 'at most, all humanity. "Human, too human", we are tempted to repeat in front of this admirable book.' However, this is the last even slightly carping comment on Goethe that Proust pens, and in the same review he goes on to say that *Wilhelm Meister* and *Elective Affinities* show 'the highest intelligence that ever existed'.

The unpublished and undated essay, '[On Goethe]' ([Sur Goethe]), is the most important evidence we have of Proust's attitude to Goethe.

To judge by style and content, it is later than the review: it is written more densely, and its preoccupations are close to those of the Proust preparing to compose (perhaps already composing) *À la recherche*. It goes into far more detail about *Wilhelm Meister*, citing, necessarily briefly, the following: its debating; its 'maxims'; the interruptions in its narrative; its depiction of acting and ceremony; and the fact that Goethe's novels are 'much occupied' by the arts – including 'the art of the pedagogue'. Proust brings out the multi-layered and (in a sense) unknowable structure of *Wilhelm Meister*: Goethe 'holds, with some mysterious aim, the string that governs them [the puppets, that is the characters]'; there is a tale within a tale; some of the characters appear arbitrarily or (again) 'very mysteriously'. Proust does not allude to Mignon herself, but near the end of the essay he mentions the 'useless deployment of factitious activity in women', naming the Philine of *Wilhelm Meister* and the Luciana of *Elective Affinities*. And Proust refers not only to 'the art of the pedagogue' but also, throughout these compact pages, to the 'truths' sought by Wilhelm, who 'does not fear didacticism' (ne craignant pas le didactisme); he even cites 'the spirit of truth' evoked in the work (l'esprit de vérité). *Wilhelm Meister* presents, furthermore, 'various spectacles that can fortify the goodwill (les bonnes dispositions) of men', and it shows that which, on the contrary, may militate against 'our true development' (notre développement véritable).

Seemingly without embarrassment or equivocation, then, Proust draws attention to the Bildung in Goethe's novel and indicates its compatibility with an enigmatic mode of story-telling. Much (even most) of his commentary characterises his own novel: the 'young man with a liking for talking about truths', the appearing and disappearing characters, the role of the arts, mirror effects (the tale within the tale). It is likely that in *Wilhelm Meister* he saw one model for *À la recherche*, appreciating its flexible form, its blend of comedy and high seriousness, and its variable image of personal development.

Arguably, French novelists were ready, in this period, to move away from the ironised and treacherous trajectories narrated in so much pre-1900 fiction. Commentators have remarked on the apparent confidence in creativity to be seen in early twentieth-century art. The concept of *joie de vivre* had been welcomed from the mid-1880s on, the phrase itself launched by Zola's *La Joie de vivre* and taking a grip over the following few decades. Before World War I, it is true, the twentieth-century picture is still mixed. In Gide's *The Immoralist* (*L'Immoraliste*) of 1902, the narrator Michel goes from illness to jubilant health, with consequences that are greeted with unease by his friends and which these days make readers still more uncomfortable, Michel's health depending on sexual tourism with minors; however, the Bildung is unmistakable. *The Immoralist* was followed a decade later by Alain-Fournier's coming-of-age novel *The Great Meaulnes* (*Le Grand Meaulnes*), which recounts the familiar progress towards clear-sighted desolation. But in the same year that *Meaulnes* was published, 1913, the first volume of *À la recherche* came out; and it is impossible to look at post-World War I French fiction without taking Proust and his revival of the Bildungsroman into account. All contemporary and following authors read him and (sometimes despite themselves) were marked by him. One arresting case is that of Sartre.

Sartre attacks fiction that presents a clear-cut story or 'adventure' on the grounds that it encourages us to see our own lives as a story. This we must not do, for nothing is ordained: we are free, moment by moment, to choose, and should not allow our actions or even our thoughts to conform to some habitual or sacrosanct mould. These attacks are prominent in Sartre's own first novel *Nausea* (1939), which names and shames Balzac, among others. Sartre would go on to lambast the fiction of the Catholic writer François Mauriac for its unabashed teleology; criticisms, albeit of a different kind, are also levelled at such distinguished predecessors as Flaubert and Proust. And *Nausea* has sometimes been taken as a parody of *À la recherche*. Its narrator, Antoine Roquentin (a young man without visible siblings), is mired in his biography of the late eighteenth-century/early nineteenth-century marquis Adhémar de Rollebon. Roquentin is beset by perceptions of his physical surroundings that induce nightmarish doubts and self-loathing; these lead him to give up the biography and finally, taking his cue from a jazz piece sung by a black woman, to decide to write a different book, his own novel. But is this parody or tribute? Like Proust's narrator, Roquentin sheds his fascination with the aristocracy, and like him finds inspiration in music to create a work of art. *Nausea* bears a suspicious resemblance to a Künstlerroman. And it is difficult to characterise Roquentin's movement towards a free self as anything other than Bildung. Indeed, the existentialist project *is* one of Bildung, of formation or progress broadly understood: it is an adaptation to the present and future, not a clinging to the past.

This is not to deny that many post-World War II French writers and film-makers reject the very notion of dynamic narrative as aesthetically impoverished, even inane. Beckett implicitly, and such New Novelists as Alain Robbe-Grillet and Nathalie Sarraute explicitly, scorn teleology and create internally patterned works that incline to the groundhog day. They also scorn what they see as the over-delineated protagonists of earlier fiction. Yet the characters of both Sarraute and another New Novelist, Michel Butor, do often, by the end, grasp something vital that was initially hidden from them. The protagonist of Butor's *La Modification* (1957) boards a train from Paris to Rome, determined to leave his wife and live with his Rome-based mistress. In the course of the journey he reconsiders, and once at his destination turns back for Paris with a new sense of personal identity. Similarly, Agnès Varda's film *Cléo from 5 to 7* (*Cléo de 5 à 7*, 1962) shows Cléo, a young singer (living in Paris, without siblings that we know of), coming to terms with a possible cancer diagnosis. In less than two hours she moves from fear, superstition, the companionship of frivolous and exploitative men, to relative calm and the start of a newly reciprocal relationship. Varda enlists 'travel' – here, *flânerie* – as part of Cléo's change: she takes in the Paris around her, and eventually finds her way to a peaceful park – an arranged, ordered nature that, at a few removes, echoes parts of *Wilhelm Meister*. Even in the mid-twentieth century, Bildung may still be celebrated in French narrative.

And later? As in other national literatures, many twentieth- and twenty-first-century feminist and postcolonial French novelists and quasi-autobiographers abandon (or never adopt) the relatively static anti-drama and non-narrative prevalent in the 1950s and 1960s. They depict – almost showcase – an arrival at understanding by young protagonists or narrators (frequently one and the same). Such are works by, for example, Marguerite Duras, Annie Ernaux, the Moroccans Driss Chraïbi and Tahar Ben Jelloun, the Senegalese Sembène Ousmane and the Canadian Antonine Maillet. (Postcolonial authors have a renowned predecessor in the Martinican Aimé Césaire, whose *Notebook of a Return to my Native Land, Cahier d'un retour au pays natal*, 1939, crescendos from the slave origins of the narrator to the exultant and climactic proclamation of his own poetic voice.)

## Conclusion

The Enlightenment notwithstanding, Proust notwithstanding, and the plasticity of the model notwithstanding, France did not adopt the Bildungsroman as warmly as some other cultures. Much in the nation's literary history militated and still militates against it. In the century that should have seen it reach an acme, the nineteenth, doubts about learning were overdetermined by key precursors – Lafayette, Prévost, Laclos – and by the course of the 1789 Revolution. Three other factors may have been especially powerful during the nineteenth century. The first was the prestige of Racine, still strong despite attempts to unseat him. Second, the tradition of the *moraliste* was already working against fictional promotion of personal development, and in the nineteenth century adherence to this tradition transmuted into the prizing of suggestion over statement already mentioned. (The *moraliste* describes the vagaries of human behaviour wryly or compassionately, without passing judgement. The disliked *moralisateur*, on the other hand, lays down the approved direction. Montaigne and La Rochefoucauld are *moralistes*.) Third, from the mid-eighteenth century onwards Voltaire's *Candide* made optimism seem ridiculous: one might go a long way to avoid resembling Pangloss.

But, fragmented and quizzical though the Bildungsroman has often been in France, it is still there, still criss-crossing national boundaries. And what was true of Laclos's *Dangerous Liaisons* is true of other great French novels – even of *Sentimental Education*. The learning takes place in the reader's head. In a dialectical process, the most dismal fictional lives move to another plane – are *aufgehoben* – as readers understand their own (thwarted) needs: their desire to identify with heroes and heroines, sighing or rejoicing along with them, and their wish to savour a morally wholesome trajectory and a clear-cut chronology. Faced with even the most savage anti-Bildungsroman, readers may still feel a paradoxical exhilaration, a Bildung, as the lid is lifted on assumptions they would have preferred not to acknowledge.

# CHAPTER 3

# The Bildungsroman and Nineteenth-Century British Fiction

## Richard Salmon

Critical attempts to establish the origins of the Bildungsroman as a significant genre in the history of English-language fiction have in recent years become contentious, for reasons that are now well documented. The term itself did not appear in literary discourse in Britain until over a century after its first usage in Germany by Karl von Morgenstern in 1803. Though retrospectively viewed as a characteristic form of the nineteenth-century novel, it was not discussed by name in a British context before the beginning of the twentieth century, entering the *Encyclopaedia Britannica* in 1910.[1] Even when taking into account recognisable English synonyms or proximate terms of nineteenth-century provenance, such as the 'novel of apprenticeship' or 'self-culture', the pursuit of an originary source for the fictional narratives associated with these terms can be deemed problematic. As Susan Fraiman and others have argued, the widespread assumption that Johann Wolfgang von Goethe's *Wilhelm Meisters Lehrjahre* (1795–6) represents an urtext of the genre from which 'an English family of texts [is] seen to descend' can have the effect of distorting or erasing alternative genealogies of eighteenth- and nineteenth-century fiction in English, particularly in relation to issues of gender.[2] Eschewing the Goethean model of the Bildungsroman, Fraiman traces an alternative tradition of English 'novels of development' produced by women writers back to Frances Burney in the 1770s. Lorna Ellis, in contrast, accepts the critical utility of the German term in describing the work of British female writers but goes even further back into the mid-eighteenth century to find its earliest exponent (Eliza Haywood).[3] For the main chapter on the English Bildungsroman in his well-known study of the European genre, *The Way of the World* (1987), Franco Moretti chose to include Henry Fielding's *Tom Jones* (1749) and William Godwin's *Caleb Williams* (1794) from the eighteenth century alongside Walter Scott's *Waverley* (1814), and the more familiar examples of Charles Dickens and Charlotte Brontë. More strikingly, Moretti credits an early nineteenth-century English writer as a co-founder of the genre: the Bildungsroman, he declares, 'originates with Goethe and Jane Austen'.[4] Unlike her contemporary Scott, Austen is not known to have read *Wilhelm Meister* (which was not translated into English until after her death), so Moretti's statement proposes a parallel cross-cultural generic formation, rather than a direct lineage of cultural transmission. Other theorists of the Bildungsroman, however, have differentiated eighteenth- and early nineteenth-century English novelists from the genre, situating them within a broader taxonomy of novelistic forms. Mikhail Bakhtin, most notably, cites *Tom Jones* as an example of 'biographical' fiction in which the hero remains a fundamentally static figure, unaffected by the 'assimilation of historical time' characteristic of the Bildungsroman.[5]

Scott's *Waverley*, commonly known as the text which instigated the nineteenth-century enthusiasm for the 'historical novel', as well as taking the form of a biographical narrative of individual development, would seem to fit the criteria for the Bildungsroman outlined by Bakhtin and Georg Lukács better, but it is less clear where the novels of Austen sit within this broader taxonomic field.[6] With the exception of *Mansfield Park* (1814), as Thomas Jeffers has noted, none of Austen's novels present an extended narrative of self-formation.[7] *Pride and Prejudice* (1813) and *Emma* (1815), the two novels most commonly cited as Bildungsromane, contain narratives of transformative self-reflection within a much narrower framework, focusing on a relatively discrete sequence of biographical time. Yet Fanny Price, the heroine of *Mansfield Park*, is, for some readers, notoriously deficient in the narrative agency with which Austen's other female protagonists have been credited. Recently, Laura Green has distinguished 'novels of courtship' in the Austen-Burney tradition from 'novels of formation' in the more modern sense, though she too is sceptical of the term 'Bildungsroman' in the context of 'English and Anglophone literary tradition'.[8]

Despite these associated difficulties and disagreements, there remains a strong case for foregrounding the pivotal significance of Goethe's *Wilhelm Meister* in any account of the nineteenth-century Bildungsroman in Britain. 'Novels of development' written in English in a variety of forms predate or independently coalesce with the late eighteenth-century German Bildungsroman – some of which have indeed been cited as influences on Goethe himself – but if we wish to understand the term 'Bildungsroman' as a more nuanced, differentiated category within the broader narrative field of nineteenth-century fiction Goethe's text still presents a key point of access. Almost all the major nineteenth-century British novelists, from Scott in the first two decades to Thomas Hardy in the 1890s, were familiar with *Wilhelm Meister*, and some with other important examples of the German Enlightenment and Romantic theorisation of *Bildung*. Some popular writers of fiction such as Scott, Edward Bulwer-Lytton, and George Eliot had an extensive knowledge of, and scholarly interest in, German literature, while others, such as Dickens and Charlotte Brontë, had access to translated editions. While it is not the primary aim of this chapter to trace the influence of the German Bildungsroman on the development of nineteenth-century British fiction, such an undertaking need not be confined to seemingly marginal or obscure novels of the period. The list of Victorian novels which directly invoke or appropriate *Wilhelm Meister*, or which through varying layers of mediation reconfigure specific formal and thematic elements of the Goethean Bildungsroman, includes some of the most recognisable titles, as well as a multitude of less familiar ones (plus some which were widely known during the period, but whose profile has subsequently diminished). The following discussion encompasses the wide range of nineteenth-century British fiction that can be read in relation to the generic model of the Bildungsroman, recognising, of course, that like all acts of generic classification the model to which individual texts are aligned is, to some extent, an abstraction composed of a range of elements which are rarely reproduced in their entirety in any concrete instance. At the same time, and in contrast to some recent critical accounts of the genre, I would emphasise the relative cohesion of a body of Victorian fiction that works through the cultural legacies of the German Bildungsroman, acquiring by the end of the century its own internal momentum and intertextual frame of reference.

## Anglicising the Bildungsroman

Goethe's *Wilhelm Meisters Lehrjahre* was first translated into English, under the title *Wilhelm Meister's Apprenticeship*, by Thomas Carlyle in 1824. Carlyle was not the first British writer to be absorbed by the novel which is widely seen as the 'prototypical' German Bildungsroman; Walter Scott, who also published English translations of Goethe and other German writers, is thought to have been influenced by his reading of *Wilhelm Meister* when he began drafting the early chapters of *Waverley* in 1805.[9] The titles of these chapters read as a schematic outline of a biographical narrative of self-formation similar to that unfolded in Goethe's text: 'Waverley-Honour – A Retrospect', 'Education', 'Castle-Building', 'Choice of a Profession'. In its completed form, published a decade later, there is a marked disjunction between the manner of these early chapters and the bulk of the narrative which follows Edward Waverley's journey to the Highlands of Scotland. While, as indicated above, a plausible case can be made for reading *Waverley* as the first major nineteenth-century Bildungsroman in English, its more established status as a work of historical fiction follows from this uneven structural development. In consequence, Carlyle's role as the primary mediator of *Wilhelm Meister* and the German Bildungsroman within Victorian literary culture has become an established truth of modern criticism.[10] Though Carlyle found certain aspects of Goethe's novel troubling, and was uncomplimentary towards the title character (describing Wilhelm as a 'milksop, whom, with all his gifts, it takes an effort to avoid despising'), he interpreted its underlying significance as an autobiographical expression of Goethe's spiritual development, and a more mature philosophical statement than his early work *The Sorrows of Young Werther* (1774).[11] Carlyle, in other words, projected the narrative form of a Bildungsroman onto Goethe's life and career as a whole, culminating in the verdict which he expressed in an obituary article of 1832 that Goethe was: 'A completed man ... each side of many-sided life receives its due from him'.[12] Carlyle conceived of his relationship to Goethe as that of 'a Disciple to his Master, nay of a Son to his spiritual Father', and was accordingly self-conscious about his role as a cultural mediator: in 1827, following the success of his translation, he wrote to inform Goethe that 'your name and doctrines will ere long be English as well as German'.[13] The process of 'translating' Goethe into English, however, went far beyond a technical act of transliteration. Carlyle helped to fashion a particular interpretation of Goethe's cultural significance for early and mid-Victorian readers, in the process 'Calvinizing and Anglicizing' the form of the Bildungsroman.[14]

Carlyle's only completed work of fiction, *Sartor Resartus* (1833–4), can itself be described as an exercise in cultural translation, a remediation of *Wilhelm Meister's Apprenticeship* beyond its formal status as a novel in translation. The two texts could hardly be more different in their formal and tonal qualities, and yet, to a large extent, *Sartor Resartus* exists for the purpose of disseminating and recontextualising the philosophical kernel which Carlyle extracted from *Wilhelm Meister*. In addition to the book's central figure, the German philosopher of clothes Diogenes von Teufelsdröch, and its use of a hybridised Anglo-Germanic language, *Sartor Resartus* directly cites its parent text on numerous occasions. Sandwiched between the English Editor's bemused speculations on the meaning of Teufelsdröch's philosophy, Book 2 of *Sartor Resartus* contains an autobiographical narrative of self-formation which G. B. Tennyson described as a 'handbook of the Victorian Bildungsroman'.[15] Beginning from the 'Happy season of Childhood' followed by 'the fervid season of youth', Teufelsdröch's autobiography figures a process of 'terrestrial Apprenticeship' which negotiates the central conflicts and crises previously resolved (in Carlyle's view) by Goethe's text.[16] This narrative climaxes in an experience of spiritual conversion by which the philosopher comes to apprehend the wisdom associated with Goethean maxims:

> America is here or nowhere . . . Yes here, in this poor, miserable, hampered, despicable Actual, wherein thou even now standest, here or nowhere is thy ideal . . . Whatsoever thy hand findeth to do, do it with thy whole might. Work while it is called To-day, for the night cometh wherein no man can work. (148–9)

The citation of Lothario's advice to Wilhelm in Goethe's novel ('Here or nowhere is America') is the cornerstone of Teufelsdröch's 'hour of Spiritual Enfranchisement', an epiphany on the value of channelling the imperative of work through the constraints of present circumstance, rather than unfocused aspiration (148). As critics have often noted, Carlyle's 'Calvinizing' spin on the Goethean dictum emphasises the core virtue of labour or 'action', a form of praxis which not only shapes the self but saves it from the despair of scepticism and doubt.[17] Carlyle is sometimes criticised for an apparent reluctance or inability to appreciate the 'aesthetic' dimension of Goethe's conception of *Bildung*, but it should be recognised that work is not conceived in this context as an external imposition on the self, but rather as an intrinsic aspect of its formation. As Teufelsdröch writes: 'A certain inarticulate Self-consciousness dwells dimly in us; which only our Works can render articulate and decisively discernible' (126). The resolution of Teufelsdröch's conversion narrative strikes a balance between self-affirmation and the 'Annihilation of Self' through labour (142): affirmative to the extent that the philosopher has been able to discover his true 'Calling' as a writer, yet not as dogmatically self-certain as might superficially appear to be the case (151). Teufelsdröch's mysterious disappearance and dispersal at the end of the text approximates to the state of pilgrimage or exile which Wilhelm enters at the end of *Wilhelm Meister's Apprenticeship*, neither text providing the narrative closure which is sometimes associated with the Bildungsroman.

One of the earliest theorists of the genre, Wilhelm Dilthey, observed in an essay on *Sartor Resartus* first published in 1891: 'Carlyle's translation of *Wilhelm Meister*, his *Essays*, but especially this novel, were effective in transplanting the German Bildungsroman into English soil. It would be interesting to see what effect this *Bildungsroman* had on the English novel in general.'[18] The most immediate 'effect' of Carlyle's work of cultural translation can be seen in the plethora of 'novels of "apprenticeship"' written in transparent emulation of *Wilhelm Meister* (and, to a lesser extent, *Sartor Resartus*) during the 1830s and 1840s.[19] This body of fiction was first collectively identified by Susanne Howe in a pioneering critical study of the nineteenth-century English Bildungsroman, *Wilhelm Meister and His English Kinsmen* (1930), and includes novels by Benjamin Disraeli, Edward Bulwer-Lytton, G. H. Lewes, Geraldine Jewsbury, John Sterling and F. D. Maurice. Despite criticism by Fraiman for fostering an unhelpful veneration of *Wilhelm Meister* as an 'originary' text, Howe's study remains a valuable exercise in tracing the direct cultural influence of the Goethean Bildungsroman on early and mid-Victorian culture. Though, inexplicably, Howe chose to omit several of the major British exponents of the genre, including Dickens, Thackeray, Eliot and Charlotte Brontë, her consequent focus on writers who were already perceived as 'minor' in the early twentieth century and are now largely unread has its benefits. A common motif of the 'apprentice novels' identified by Howe is 'the sane and corrective power of action', a 'moral lesson' which Carlyle had encouraged readers of *Wilhelm Meister* to embrace, rather than dwelling on the aesthetic dimension of 'harmonious self-development'.[20] At the same time, Howe notes that the dandified, male upper-class protagonists of novels by Disraeli and Bulwer-Lytton exhibit an 'apprenticeship *de luxe*', such that it would be misleading to portray these early Victorian 'imitators' (203) of Goethe simply as purveying moralistic or pragmatic reductions of *Bildung*. Disraeli's *Contarini Fleming* (1832), for example, takes as its subject 'the development and formation of the poetic character', and ostentatiously depicts the hero's aesthetic education through travel to exotic locations. As his name suggests, the title character of the novel is self-divided by his mixed Latin and Teutonic lineage, a cultural schism which is manifested in the narrative as a series of bewildering oscillations between the pursuit of worldly power and esoteric learning. The advice of Contarini's mentor De Winter is to pursue action ('Act, act, act; act without ceasing, and you will no longer talk of the vanity of life'), yet to the end of the novel it remains ambiguous whether 'action' should be understood as a commitment to external social obligations or as a cover for the solipsistic cultivation of aesthetic experience.[21]

Bulwer-Lytton's *Ernest Maltravers* (1837) and its sequel *Alice; or, The Mysteries* (1838) similarly attempt to reconcile the personal development of the artist with social responsibility. Offering a more cohesive and schematic narrative than Disraeli's, *Ernest Maltravers* is perhaps the closest that any nineteenth-century novel in English came to a simulation of *Wilhelm Meister*. In his 1840 Preface to the novel, Bulwer-Lytton explicitly compared the 'moral education or apprenticeship' of his title character with that of Goethe's text, indicating his intention to shift the focus of the narrative of apprenticeship from 'theoretical art' to 'practical life'.[22] Within the novel itself the narrator outlines the shape of his hero's story as one of 'fierce emotions and passionate struggles, through which the Wilhelm Meister of real life must work out his apprenticeship, and attain the Master Rank' (66). Again, the 'real' and 'practical' are privileged terms within the dialectic of self-formation and social order, and the overarching trajectory of the two novels moves from the realm of the 'Ideal' towards a recognition of 'the virtue of Action – the obligations of Genius – and the philosophy that teaches us to confide in the destinies, and labour in the service, of mankind'.[23] Nevertheless, the apprenticeship served by Maltravers stages a genuine contest between alternative vocational identities – should he become a 'man of books' or a 'man of deeds'? – and as in *Contarini Fleming* the hero oscillates from one extreme to the other (117). The resolution of this debate lies in Bulwer-Lytton's conception of the modern professional author as a figure who steers a median course between commercialised popularity, on the one extreme, and solipsistic detachment from the public sphere on the other. As I have argued elsewhere, the 1830s and 1840s saw the publication of many similar narratives of literary apprenticeship, in which the generic template of the Bildungsroman was used to enable and examine the construction of new professional identities, Dickens's *David Copperfield* (1849–50) being now the most celebrated example of this sub-genre.[24] Professional development, in this narrativised form, is differentiated equally from the self-absorbed interiority of the 'Romantic' artist and a debased accommodation with the market.

Though nowadays little-known, *Ernest Maltravers* was a remarkably influential text in the mid-nineteenth century, whose presence can be traced directly through a series of subsequent novels in a similar form by the likes of Lewes, Thackeray and Charles Kingsley. In Jewsbury's *The Half Sisters* (1848), one of the two female protagonists, Alice Helmsby, is shown reading a copy of Bulwer-Lytton's novel, 'then recently published', and identifying with the situation of a character whose aristocratic self-cultivation does not result in fulfilment.[25] Ironically, the very fact that

Alice has sufficient leisure and cultural knowledge to read *Ernest Maltravers* is a symptom of her 'ennui' (82) and lack of a productive vocation of the kind embodied by her half-sister, the Italian actress Bianca. *The Half Sisters* is one of the first Victorian Bildungsromane to adopt parallel protagonists and its interest lies partly in its anticipation of more familiar novels by George Eliot. A close family friend of the Carlyles, Jewsbury is the only female writer included in Howe's survey of *Wilhelm Meister's* 'English Kinsmen'. Yet, significantly, Goethe is not the primary model for *The Half Sisters*, this role belonging instead to another seminal work of European Romanticism, Madame de Staël's *Corinne, or Italy* (1807). Like the renowned singer Corinne, Bianca is a powerful figure of female genius whose artistic talent and vocation are established from the outset of the novel and remain more or less unwavering until near the end. Jewsbury's narrative traces the process of professional development which allows her heroine to achieve artistic and public success, yet with none of the uncertainty and vacillation which characterises apprentice novels predominantly influenced by *Wilhelm Meister*. As in *Sartor Resartus*, a commitment to work is deemed prerequisite for self-realisation, and its enforced absence has tragic consequences for women's lives, as in the case of Bianca's half-sister. Through the obvious counterpoint of her dual protagonists, Jewsbury argues strenuously for the necessity of female vocational opportunities, legitimising the figure of Bianca against the prevailing masculinist 'horror of professional women'. The professional woman participates in a fulfilling though austere life of 'struggle' (214) which, in Carlylean fashion, is exalted over the 'search after happiness' (225) – that is, until the very end of the novel when Bianca undergoes a *volte face*, abandoning the stage for marriage in a manner which partially prefigures the resolution of Elizabeth Barrett Browning's Bildungsroman in verse, *Aurora Leigh* (1856).

## Novels of Self-Culture

The popularisation of the Bildungsroman as a novelistic form during the mid-Victorian period was closely related to the emergence of a wider discourse of 'self-culture' and 'self-help'. The two latter terms may appear to connote different, even opposing cultural values: 'self-culture' as an approximate translation of the German idea of *Bildung* as aesthetic education; 'self-help' as a practical instrument of social mobility popularly associated with lower- and middle-class Victorian culture. Yet in fact these terms were used synonymously in many influential writings of the period, and disentangling one from the other is more difficult than is sometimes assumed. Carlyle's Teufelsdröch, for example, wishes to 'acquire for himself the highest of all possessions, that of Self-help', by which he means a capacity for intellectual development through informal self-education with little discernible effect on his worldly status (88). The most famous of the mid-Victorian exponents of 'self-help', Samuel Smiles, used the term interchangeably with 'self-culture' in his 1859 conduct book, based on a series of lectures on education delivered to working-class men in Leeds during the 1840s. For Smiles, 'The spirit of self-help is the root of all genuine growth in the individual', and like Carlyle he educed poverty as the material basis from which growth is most likely to be achieved, precisely on account of the difficulties faced.[26] Self-help is a doctrine which espouses the capacity of individual will to resist and overcome adverse circumstance; at the same time, as the format of Smiles's collective (or group) biography indicates, this doctrine assumes the ordinariness of free will – the capacity for overcoming difficulty is not reserved for exceptional individuals. Smiles's key argument, though, was the mutual reinforcement of physical and mental labour in the work of self-culture. A 'life of manual employment' was not 'incompatible with high mental culture', he believed, and by the same token culture achieved without the discipline of labour was ineffectual. This suggests an inextricable relationship between the material and spiritual dimensions of self-help but it also refutes the suspicion that cultural aspiration is merely a cover for social mobility. Smiles clearly states that '[o]ne way in which self-culture may be degraded is by regarding it too exclusively as a means of "getting on"' (273).

Dickens is the novelist in whose work this popular contemporary discourse of self-culture is most clearly felt. The two novels by Dickens commonly associated with the Bildungsroman genre – *David Copperfield* and *Great Expectations* (1860–1) – both explore ideas prevalent within the writings of Smiles and less familiar names such as G. L. Craik and Edwin Paxton Hood. Critics have noted the broadly affirmative use of the language of self-help running throughout the first of these two novels, sometimes with unease. According to Jerome Buckley, the 'happy ending' of *David Copperfield* suggests a seamless 'integration of personality to which the hero in the novel of youth typically aspires', though it is rarely accomplished.[27] Through much of his autobiographical narrative David attributes 'the source of my success' to a 'patient and continuous energy which then began to be matured in me, and which I know to be the strong part of my character'.[28] He draws strength from the traumatic experiences

of childhood recounted in his narrative, concluding that 'the endurance of
my childish days had done its part to make me what I was' (750). Working
in a bottle warehouse in London with 'common men and boys' (157) – an
episode based on Dickens's childhood experience of the blacking factory
revealed in the unpublished autobiographical fragment which preceded his
composition of the novel – becomes a 'painful discipline' from which he
can build a stronger self (481). The latter half of *David Copperfield* recounts
David's successful apprenticeship as a professional writer in which his
determination '[n]ever to put one hand to anything, on which I could
throw my whole self; and never to affect depreciation of my work, whatever
it was' both sublimates and redeems the memories of alienated factory
labour which he would prefer to forget (560). Robin Gilmour is one of
several critics to find the Smilesian ethos of 'prudence and emotional self-
discipline' (which applies both to David's personal and professional life)
unsatisfactory as the 'official subject' of the novel. He points out the
contradictory appeal of David's exorbitant childhood memories and the
'liberating imprudence' of his friend Micawber, both of which work
against a narrow interpretation of the economy of self-help. But if
Dickens is 'far from single-minded in the presentation of David's successful progress', *David Copperfield* nonetheless contains a narrative of self-
realisation through professional vocation in a strikingly modern sense.[29]
Dickens shows David literally labouring on the construction of a self
through writing, and while the course of his formative narrative acknowledges that his work is not free from alienation, the professional identity
which he creates is met with almost instantaneous recognition and reward
in the guise of his 'rising fame and fortune' (778). Buckley identifies an
element of 'wish-fulfilment' in the autobiographical context of the novel,
though another way of reading it would be to infer that David is a rather
more exceptional figure than the bland democratic everyman suggested by
Moretti.[30]

Whereas in *David Copperfield* Dickens maintains the equivalence
between 'self-culture' and 'self-help' which Smiles sought to emphasise –
David achieves material success and social mobility only through the self-
realisation of authorship and literary fame – in *Great Expectations* this is no
longer the case. Pip's determination to 'get on in life' and to be thought
'uncommon' is the expression of his shame at being derided as a 'common
labouring-boy' by Estella, but it results not in a dialectical sublation of
labour as the source of cultural and economic value (at least not until near
the end of the novel), but rather in his complicity with the view that to
become a 'gentleman' is to be 'above work'.[31] Once removed from the

necessity to work Pip makes little progress in self-cultivation, despite acquiring the educational polish of his newfound middle-class status. The material conditions which are conventionally presumed to enable self-culture (an increase of leisure and economic resources) in fact militate against it; though limited in scope, the self-educational achievements of Biddy and Joe Gargery are given greater textual prominence than any knowledge that Pip gains as a direct result of his social elevation. Pip, of course, is not a figure of 'self-help' in either of the senses exemplified by David Copperfield: he 'know[s] I have done nothing to raise myself in life, and that Fortune alone has raised me' (463). When G. B. Tennyson describes *Great Expectations* as a distinctive expression of the 'Victorian concept of *Bildung*', therefore, he does not mean that the hero of the novel directly embodies Smilesian values, rather that '[w]hat Pip undergoes is a self-education that is of necessity painful, but also ultimately spiritually fortifying'.[32] In this case, the pedagogical function of the genre is accomplished more through a stripping away of the subjective illusions which the protagonist has nurtured during the course of his development from childhood to early adulthood, than through a process of self-affirmation, as in *David Copperfield*. The difference between these two narratives, however, is relative rather than absolute: just as David's immature perception of the world is also, to some degree, disenchanted in the course of his development, so Pip's mature consciousness must also begin a process of self-reconstruction. The staged progress of Pip's 'Expectations' across the three volumes of the original book publication explicitly frames this narrative of self-education for the benefit of the reader.

*Great Expectations* draws from Carlyle in its modelling of Pip's self-formation as a process of apprenticeship through which the autobiographical subject learns, eventually, to accept the discipline of labour. Whereas in *Wilhelm Meister* and *Sartor Resartus*, however, 'apprenticeship' is a figurative expression for a broader period of learning bounded only by the temporal confines of youth, in Dickens's novel, as in other Victorian realist fiction, the hero's apprenticeship is also a concrete social experience located within a fully articulated system of class and the division of labour. Dickens exposes the painful disjunction between apprenticeship as it is experienced in its traditional context as a form of indentured labour and the new possibilities of cultural aspiration and social mobility which it encompasses within the Bildungsroman. In *Wilhelm Meister*, as Moretti puts it, '"apprenticeship" is no longer the slow and predictable progress towards one's father's work, but rather an uncertain exploration of social space, which the nineteenth century – through travel and adventure, wandering and getting lost . . . – will underline countless times'.[33] In *Great Expectations*, Dickens presents Pip's dissatisfaction at the circumscribed prospect of his future as an apprentice blacksmith to his surrogate father, Joe. Pip is 'bound apprentice' in a scene which alludes to the threat of penal incarceration overshadowing his childhood: 'Here, in a corner, my indentures were duly signed and attested, and I was "bound," Mr. Pumblechook holding me all the while as if we had looked in on our way to the scaffold, to have these little preliminaries disposed of' (105). He soon becomes restless with the 'regular routine of apprenticeship-life' and longs to 'be a gentleman' (117). Although from the retrospective maturity of his autobiographical narrative Pip accuses himself of not valuing his apprenticeship with 'plain contented Joe' sufficiently, the 'restlessly aspiring discontented me' which leads him away from the forge is equally close to the authorial voice of the novel (108). Pip's restless movement and 'inability to settle to anything' (313) aligns him with that aspect of the 'modernity' of youth which Moretti sees symbolically represented by the form of the Bildungsroman.[34] It is important to note that Pip is unable to return to the forge at the end of the novel, even though he has come to value the unchanging social idyll which it evokes.

Self-culture and social mobility can thus be conceived as the dual imperatives of the mid-Victorian Bildungsroman – ideally aligned in mutual support, but where this relationship breaks down generating friction productive for social critique. Despite the intrinsic difficulties which both of these imperatives posed for contemporary narratives of female development, as numerous feminist critics have shown, they are equally evident in the novels of Charlotte Brontë. *Jane Eyre* (1847) has long held an anomalous position within modern critical accounts of the 'female Bildungsroman': its very prominence as an iconic text of proto-feminist self-expression – which renders it almost obligatory to include in such accounts – makes it unrepresentative of nineteenth-century novels of female development more broadly, and thereby puts it at risk of becoming strangely invisible. Ellis sums up the established view of *Jane Eyre* when she describes it as 'the quintessential female *Bildungsroman*',[35] and yet for others, including Fraiman and the editors of *The Voyage In* (1983), the Bildungsroman is not the 'quintessential' narrative form of female development.[36] Most critics are agreed on the narrative features which make *Jane Eyre* seem an exceptional novel of female development for the mid-nineteenth century, and by extension make it comparable to the contemporary male Bildungsroman. Jane's 'independence as a wanderer who must make her own way in the world' allows her to achieve a type of

'*Bildung* defined as social mobility' which, to some degree, resembles that of David Copperfield.[37] The fluid spatial movement and temporal retrospection of the protagonist, her drive to fulfil autonomous creative, professional, and spiritual needs, and her eventual reintegration within an established social hierarchy through marriage to Rochester, all have resonance in Dickens's novel. Like Dickens too, Brontë's overarching narrative template for the biographical novel was a secularised adaptation of John Bunyan's *Pilgrim's Progress* (1678), an 'insistence on life as a pilgrimage' in which the hero/ine undergoes the trials of worldly experience on their route to salvation;[38] likewise, in the contemporary novels of Thackeray the gentleman hero must find his 'way through the world'.[39] Brontë's treatment of this archetypal narrative design retains more of its original spiritual fervour than is evident in the novels of Dickens or Thackeray, and Barry Qualls has suggested a direct link to the 'Calvinized *Bildungsroman*' model established in *Sartor Resartus*, as well as to earlier Protestant spiritual autobiographies. In Brontë's fiction, as in Carlyle's, the achievement of self-formation hinges on a commitment to its apparent opposite: 'self-annihilation and renunciation, the exaltation of work as alone giving the human being purpose and identity'.[40] In *Jane Eyre*, this religious impulse to chasten the individual's desire for self-fulfilment is tempered by an equally strong Romantic impulse of self-assertion, resulting in what Kelsey Bennett has described as a 'healthy reconciliation of propensity with principle'.[41] In plot terms, Jane's two acts of resistance to the men who seek to shape her identity through marriage appear to cancel each other out: her decision to leave Rochester at Thornfield leads her in the direction of renunciation (sacrificing the propensity of her desire for moral principle), but her subsequent decision not to follow St John Rivers to India is based on a reversal of priorities (self-sacrifice in an extreme and self-conscious form is abandoned at the prompting of a natural impulse). Though the ending of *Jane Eyre* is endlessly disputed in its details, it seems clear that some kind of balance between opposing energies has been established, however precarious its foundation.

As Qualls and others have suggested, Brontë's final novel *Villette* (1853) presents a more austere and unsettling version of the heroine's internal conflict between self-realisation and the renunciation of self.[42] In some ways, Lucy Snowe's autonomy and latent aspiration to determine her own life exceed that of Jane Eyre, leading her into social environments more challenging than Thornfield. Her solitary journey to London (the 'Babylon' of Victorian imagination) en route to Villette (a city whose language and religion are entirely alien to her, but where she manages to secure a foothold as an English tutor in Madame Beck's Pensionnat) offers, for the 1850s, an extraordinary depiction of female agency outside the domestic sphere. Lucy modestly declares: 'I know not that I was of a self-reliant or active nature; but self-reliance and exertion were forced upon me by circumstances, as they are upon thousands besides,' apparently anxious to disavow any suggestion of personal ambition with professions of indecision and lack of will.[43] Of her teaching career, she remarks: 'I felt I was getting on; not lying the stagnant prey of mould and rust, but polishing my faculties and whetting them to a keen edge with constant use,' while also 'perceiving well that, as far as my own mind was concerned, God had limited its powers and its action – thankful, I trust, for the gift bestowed, but unambitious of higher endowments, not restlessly eager after higher culture' (145, 313). These carefully balanced self-assessments of her capacity for independent thought and action express both an affinity for and suspicion of the practice of self-culture. Inasmuch as this practice was conceived as a form of labour or discipline performed on the self, it represents a legitimate aspiration for the subject shaped by Protestant belief, yet it always runs the risk of detaching the self from higher obligations to God and the service of other human lives. Lucy exhorts herself to 'be content to labour for independence until you have proved, by winning that prize, your right to look higher':

> But afterwards, is there nothing more for me in life – no true home – nothing to be dearer to me than myself, and by its paramount preciousness, to draw from me better things than I care to culture for myself only? Nothing, at whose feet I can willingly lay down the whole burden of human egotism, and gloriously take up the noble charge of labouring and living for others? (450)

The suspicion of 'egotism', then, clouds Lucy's desire 'to culture' the self, the unfamiliar predicate form of the word emphasising the sense of internalised organic growth which it also held for Matthew Arnold. Like Smiles and Carlyle, Lucy considers self-culture in relation to a broad range of mental faculties, rather than in narrowly aesthetic terms, and this includes the 'cultivation' of happiness which – like Teufelsdröch – she considers a dubious goal: 'Happiness is not a potato, to be planted in mould and tilled with manure. Happiness is a glory shining far down upon us out of Heaven' (330). At the same time, there is no point in her narrative at which Lucy definitively relinquishes the desire to lead a self-fulfilled independent life. The ending of *Villette*, which confirms Lucy's professional identity as a teacher while suggesting its dependency on the romantic attachment of her male benefactor, M. Paul, and a future contingent on his fortunes, maintains its profoundly ambivalent treatment of the discourse of self-help. While there is clearly a significant gendered dimension to Brontë's ambivalence, given the prevailing cultural, economic, and legal impediments to female self-development, it should be noted that the suspicion towards self-culture grounded in religious belief was shared by some male writers of the period. Charles Kingsley, for example, wrote a series of novels concerned with 'self-development' during the late 1840s and 1850s, most notably *Alton Locke* (1850), a Bildungsroman which charts the failed literary and political apprenticeship of a working-class poet and Chartist who seeks to 'educate myself and rise in life'.[44] Kingsley similarly sympathises with and delimits the aspiration for self-improvement, especially on the part of the working classes, and he specifically critiques Goethe's 'aesthetic' ideal of cultivating the self as a form of intellectual solipsism harmful to social solidarity and religious obligation.

## Historical Time and the Laws of Development

Franco Moretti divides the long nineteenth century of the European Bildungsroman into two halves: the first half, 1789–1848, is a period of 'balance between the constraints of modern socialization, and its benefits', but in the second half, from mid-century, 'the atmosphere darkens, and a gloomy downward trajectory begins'.[45] Notwithstanding the larger cultural field of observation, and the fact that Moretti's generally dismissive view of the English Bildungsroman makes it appear unrepresentative of the genre's trajectory as a whole, this remains a useful rough distinction within the more limited cultural and historical framework of this chapter. It is often argued, in fact, that the latter half of the nineteenth century witnessed a shift away from the 'socially integrative', broadly optimistic narratives of self-formation produced during the Regency and early to mid-Victorian periods (the novels of Austen and Scott, Dickens, Thackeray and Brontë) and towards a more pessimistic 'plot of disillusionment and alienation' (the novels of Meredith, Gissing and Hardy).[46] Where critics have tended to disagree is on whether this shift marks a mutation within the boundaries of the genre, or whether it leads beyond the genre to the production of something else: an 'Anti' or 'failed' Bildungsroman. Moretti, for example, offers a very unequal treatment of the two halves of his historical period since the latter half is considered to witness the fundamental demise of the genre.[47] Within this broad schema, of course, much of the fine detail gets lost. Just as there are examples of 'failed' development in the English tradition from relatively early in the century (Kingsley's *Alton Locke* ends in the death of its eponymous hero, Thackeray's *Pendennis* (1848–50) is as much a 'novel of disillusionment' in the Lukácsian sense as the work of Balzac and Flaubert),[48] so not every Bildungsroman of the late nineteenth century adopts a tragic form or abandons the attempt to reconcile the maturation of the hero with social integration.

During the 1860s and 1870s, in particular, neither of the alternative models of the Bildungsroman which critics have tended to construct seems predominant. The work of George Eliot and George Meredith, for instance, encompasses novels which can be positioned on either – and in some cases both – side(s) of Moretti's historical divide. Eliot's *The Mill on the Floss* (1860) might be viewed as one of the earliest examples of the later nineteenth-century Bildungsroman, and it has been widely discussed as a novel which stretches the boundaries of the 'classical' genre in various respects. As a reworking of the Goethean paradigm – with which Eliot was as familiar as Carlyle and Bulwer-Lytton – the development of Maggie Tulliver has been likened by Marianne Hirsch to the inset female narrative of the 'Beautiful Soul' rather than to the main story of Wilhelm Meister. In contrast to Wilhelm's picaresque travels through social space, the process of Maggie's formation is introspective, 'located in the inner self', and spatially immobile or circular, 'culminating in death'.[49] Fraiman similarly characterises *The Mill on the Floss* as a 'failed appropriation of the *Bildungsroman* that is finally a critique of this genre and its values', specifically in revealing the masculinist assumptions underpinning the conventional pattern of the hero's development from apprenticeship to 'mastery' through encounters with the social world beyond the domestic sphere. Like other critics, Fraiman observes the poignant juxtaposition of Maggie's experience with that of her brother Tom, who undergoes a parallel, but markedly different, and in terms of practical outcome more successful, education, closer in some respects to the Smilesian image of industrious self-help (though, in fact, neither character manages to unify bodily and mental culture in the way that Smiles recommended). The tragic ending of the novel, in which both siblings are drowned, represents, for Fraiman, 'a moment when their narratives collide for the last time, and now Tom's upward-bound *Bildungsroman* is fatally assimilated to Maggie's downward spiral'.[50] In Eliot's representation of their reconciliation through death, Maggie and Tom are symbolically returned to childhood, reinforcing the sense of their arrested development, which can also be viewed as a type of evolutionary failure. More so than in earlier

Victorian fiction, Eliot ascribes the frustration and disenchantment of her protagonist's aspirations to external forces beyond the control of individual will: the collective weight of provincial society's narrow views on the forms of education appropriate for women and the determining influence of biologically inherited characteristics through successive generations. Maggie's project of self-culture fails in large measure because, for Eliot (unlike in *Jane Eyre*), the individual self can no longer be viewed as separate from the organic milieu which it wishes either to master or escape.

Meredith's early novel, *The Ordeal of Richard Feverel* (1859), offers a similarly complex appropriation of, and resistance to, the established conventions of the mid-Victorian Bildungsroman. Though not culminating in death, the hero's development from childhood, fostered by his father's pseudo-scientific educational theories, ends in a 'permanently arrested' state of incompletion, as Buckley notes.[51] In the final chapter of the novel, Lady Blandish concludes of the damaging effect of Sir Austin's 'System' on his son's emotional well-being: 'Richard will never be what he promised.'[52] According to Tennyson, Meredith 'represents a second generation of the English *Bildungsroman*' in which 'the optimism and drive of the earlier Victorians has been supplanted by a scepticism that borders at times on the cynical, and the Romantic and early Victorian organicism has been transmuted into an impersonal, almost mechanical life-force evolutionism'.[53] The language of organic growth is prevalent throughout *The Ordeal of Richard Feverel*, but in a form which makes it difficult to say whether it is merely the debased currency of Sir Austin's book of educational aphorisms, *The Pilgrim's Scrip*, or an authentic model for understanding psychological and sexual development within adolescence. One of the problems with Sir Austin's 'System' is that it attempts to regulate organic development through external cultivation and monitoring, rather than allowing for the contingencies of self-culture. As such, his organicism is itself mechanistic, conceiving of Richard as 'an organism opening to the set mechanic diurnal round' which needs to be 'fit for what machinal duties he may have to perform' (139). Meredith opposes the unavoidable influence of 'Nature' on Richard's maturation to his father's scientific modelling of the organic to often ambiguous effect.

In her later novels, George Eliot produced narratives of self-formation which largely avoid or moderate the 'downward trajectory' towards catastrophic endings and cultural pessimism. Eliot's commitment to the ideal of 'vocation', discussed by several critics, provides a normative orientation to *Middlemarch* (1871) and *Daniel Deronda* (1876) within the established framework of the post-Goethean Bildungsroman. Eliot continued to use the novel of apprenticeship to chart the professional development and integration of young men within middle-class society, as in the novels of Dickens and Thackeray, but to this she adds a recognition of what Dorothea Barrett terms the 'negative space of female vocation', as well as proposing a more exalted conception of what professional vocation might achieve.[54] Alan Mintz argues that, for Eliot, 'professional work might be in itself a significant means of self-realization and of contributing to the progress of humankind'.[55] Both motivations of the vocational plot can be found in *Daniel Deronda*, as can the unequal access to this narrative for men and women. The two central figures of the novel, Daniel Deronda and Gwendolen Harleth, occupy parallel narratives, as in *The Mill on the Floss*, whose divergence and ultimate incompatibility reveal gender divisions within contemporary discourses of self-formation, professional apprenticeship, and even historical development. Gwendolen recognises these discrepancies from an early point in the novel: 'We women can't go in search of adventures ... We must stay where we grow, or where the gardeners like to transplant us.'[56] Though not as culturally or geographically restricted as Maggie Tulliver, Gwendolen has limited opportunities for self-culture and independent social mobility. Rejecting the path taken by Jane Eyre, the modest self-reliant role of governess and the hope/fantasy of attaining self-fulfilment through marriage, she desires to achieve personal distinction and power over others, yet lacks the artistic talent and discipline to succeed as a professional singer/actress in the manner of Jewsbury's Bianca. Eliot presents Gwendolen's frustrated ambition as akin to that of 'male contemporaries ... when they felt a profession too narrow for their powers', or in darker moods as a 'general disenchantment with the world – nay, with herself, since it appeared that she was not made for easy pre-eminence' (321, 333–4). By contrast, the difficulty of Daniel's search for a vocation arises from having *too much* freedom of choice, and the consequent risk of not committing to any particular course of action, a problem discussed in *Sartor Resartus*. Daniel's characteristic deferral of vocational choice is in part conditioned by his privileged social upbringing – unlike David Copperfield, he is not forced by economic necessity into the work which comes to define him – but it is also an instinct which reflects his understanding of the nature of vocation. Commenting on Daniel's dissatisfaction with the experience of formal education at Cambridge University, Eliot envisages his 'inward bent towards comprehension and thoroughness diverging more and more from the track marked out by the standards of examination': 'He longed now to have the sort of apprenticeship of life which would not shape him too definitely, and rob him of that choice that might come from a free growth' (220). Daniel recognises that a premature adoption of a career may undermine the basis on which a vocation subsists, namely that it be a freely chosen commitment to self-realisation through work. He prefers to take the indefinite course of the Bildungsroman hero whose 'apprenticeship of life' is left deliberately vague (the Carlylean-sounding phrase is borrowed directly from the title of an unfinished novel by Eliot's partner, Lewes, himself a biographer of Goethe).[57] Like Teufelsdröch, Daniel's cultivation of passivity leads him in time to face the opposite dilemma:

> His early-widened sensibility and reflectiveness had developed into a many-sided sympathy, which threatened to hinder any persistent course of action . . . A too reflective and diffusive sympathy was in danger of paralyzing in him that indignation against wrong and that selectness of fellowship which are the conditions of moral force . . . what he most longed for was either some external event, or some inward light, that would urge him into a definite line of action, and compress his wandering energy. (412–13)

In *Daniel Deronda*, then, Eliot explicitly returns to the dialectic of 'reflection' and 'action' which earlier Victorians, such as Disraeli and Bulwer-Lytton, had derived from Goethe, and which modern scholars have identified as a key component of the 'classical' Bildungsroman.[58]

Further points of comparison between *Daniel Deronda* and *Wilhelm Meister* can be adduced, including Daniel's eventual choice of vocation through his discovery of belonging to a larger social body which has, seemingly, guided his development through the narrative with the effect of a teleological design. Daniel's Jewish heritage and incipient Zionism provide him with a collective identity and sense of purpose in which 'vocation' is viewed simultaneously as a means of inner self-realisation and a 'renunciation of the demands of self' (866). The latter formulation is Daniel's advice to Gwendolen at the moment of their final parting, but also the ethical kernel of his own search for 'some ideal task, in which I might feel myself the heart and brain of a multitude – some social captainship, which would come to me as a duty, and not be striven for as a personal prize' (819). It is another adaptation of Lothario's motto 'Here or nowhere is America', since Daniel's realisation is that 'duty' lies in a self-renouncing commitment to others, but primarily to those others with whom he feels most immediate kinship, a practice which he presumably wishes Gwendolen to adopt within her own separate sphere of action. The implication of this message may be troubling in its cultural politics, but as in *Middlemarch* Eliot's wider philosophical ambition is to

demonstrate the interconnection of individual lives and the broader processes of historical and organic development: in Bakhtin's terms, the
confluence of biographical and historical time. The narrator observes in
relation to Daniel and Gwendolen: 'I like to mark the time, and connect
the course of individual lives with the historic stream, for all classes of
thinkers' (121–2). Where Daniel notably differs from the likes of
Gwendolen and Dorothea Brooke is in the immediacy of the connection
between individual and historical narratives of development which the
discovery of his Jewish identity permits. The conversation involving
Daniel and his Jewish mentor Mordecai in The Philosophers' Club in
Book 6 explicitly broaches the 'laws of development' in respect of social
progress and the formation of national consciousness, as well as the scope
for individual agency within these broader trajectories. Mordecai's organic
theory of national development emphasises both the significance of hereditary characteristics for Daniel's self-formation and its progressive orientation towards the future: 'The life of a people grows' (585). By aligning his
own apprenticeship so directly with that of 'his people', Daniel comes close
to fulfilling the Hegelian role of 'world-historical individual', a quasi-
Messianic figure far removed from the quotidian world of the
Bildungsroman hero as often described.[59]

Published in the same year as *Daniel Deronda*, Meredith's *Beauchamp's
Career* (1876) makes for an interesting comparison in its handling of
political vocation and contemporary scientific discourses of historical
development. Like Daniel, Neville Beauchamp develops a compelling
sense of mission beyond the fulfilment of personal ability or desire; starting
from a Quixotic love of country, his ethos of self-sacrifice expands to
encompass sympathy with 'humanity' and 'the poor', committing him to
the cause of radical political reform.[60] His aim is to 'work to the end of his
time', subordinating individual/biographical life to a vision of collective
societal advancement, sometimes at the cost of insensitivity to personal ties
(216). Neville's mentor, the Radical politician Dr Shrapnel, plays a similar
role to Mordecai in his adherence to a grand narrative of social progress, in
this case comprising a quasi-Marxian account of the historical development of class struggle and the defeat of 'egoism' in the forthcoming
accession of the 'workman's era' (284). A more combative, conventionally
'heroic' but less reflective figure than Daniel, Neville embodies similar but
perhaps more acute questions for the Bildungsroman form in a period
when the pursuit of self-culture confronts seemingly uncontrollable historical forces. While Daniel's future cultivation of his Jewish 'destiny' is
envisaged by Eliot as entailing a state of voluntary exile from English

society, the terms of this rupture remain relatively benign on both sides of the cultural divide. In contrast, Neville's Radical political allegiance results in a more antagonistic posture towards the established social order. His shift from patriotic military hero to social ostracism remains unbridged at the end of the novel: for his Tory admirer Cecilia, Neville is 'solitary in the adverse rank to the world; – to his countrymen especially' (474). The ending of *Beauchamp's Career* disallows any comforting resolution of this ideological conflict on either side of the question. In the final chapter, Neville's marriage to Dr Shrapnel's daughter Jenny is considered a possible threat to the continuation of his political 'career'; the indolence of their honeymoon cruise along the Iberian coast implies the 'delusion of happiness', according to Shrapnel, and a wavering commitment to the labour of vocation (542). Both Neville and Shrapnel view women in misogynistic terms as obstacles to social progress, coding them in evolutionary discourse as agents of a 'primal' force 'perpetually pulling us backward on the march' (537). But then Neville's life is abruptly ended in 'mid career' (535) when he drowns attempting to rescue two lower-class boys from a river, saving one 'insignificant bit of mudbank life' in the process (547). As Margaret Harris notes, the imagery of this scene places Neville's 'career' in the wider context of evolutionary time, suggesting both the possibility of the random extinction of life (as in the ending of *The Mill on the Floss*) and the ongoing replacement of one life by another.[61] Neville's action is characteristically heroic and self-sacrificial, yet it results in the curtailment of both his political aspirations and romantic self-fulfilment. Whether the ending of the novel celebrates the achievement or reveals the futility of Neville's moral progress – the success or failure of his 'career' – is open to question.

## Aesthetic Education and the Late-Victorian Bildungsroman

Although the Bildungsroman of the late-Victorian period has been characterised as disrupting or inverting the traditional 'integrative' form of the genre, some of the leading intellectual influences on British culture during this period were committed to disseminating the idea of *Bildung* in something approaching its original German form. John Stuart Mill approvingly quoted Humboldt's ideas on self-cultivation and personal development in outlining his philosophy of liberal individualism in *On Liberty* (1859). Matthew Arnold in *Culture and Anarchy* (1868) defined the ideal of 'culture' in organicist terms: 'Not a having and a resting, but a growing and a becoming, is the character of perfection as culture conceives it.'[62] The Goethean attachment to 'Hellenism' with which Arnold associated culture, as opposed to Hebraic (Judaeo-Christian) morality, was shared by Walter Pater whose 'Conclusion' to *The Renaissance* (1873) justified the practice of self-cultivation in relation to the 'love of art for its own sake', paving the way for late-Victorian aestheticism.[63] While the successful attainment of self-culture may have grown more difficult to envisage in fiction of the final two decades of the century, this is not because it was replaced by a fundamentally different aspiration for individual development. In Pater especially, however, the ideal of self-cultivation is often distinguished from 'work' in its pragmatic, socially recognised forms. The eponymous hero of Pater's historical Bildungsroman, *Marius the Epicurean* (1885), displays traits of passivity and contemplative detachment reminiscent of *Sartor Resartus*, but what is missing is their rhetorical framing in relation to the instrumental labour of self-formation. Whereas the reflective self-absorption of Teufelsdröch and other earlier protagonists is intended to serve as a preparation for future action and social engagement, even when these outcomes are projected beyond the text itself, the trajectory of Marius's narrative is one of sustained internalisation and solipsistic withdrawal from worldly concerns. From boyhood Marius is 'more given to contemplation than to action', Pater emphasising his 'natural Epicureanism, already prompting him to conceive of himself as but the passive spectator of the world around him'.[64] Marius's self-conscious pursuit of an '"aesthetic" education, as it might now be termed' (117), insists on the primacy of the visual sense in responding to the phenomenal world:

> Revelation, vision, the discovery of a vision, the *seeing* of a perfect humanity, in a perfect world – through all his alternations of mind, by some dominant instinct, determined by the original necessities of his own nature and character, he had always set that above the *having*, or even the *doing*, of anything. For, such vision, if received with due attitude on his part, was, in reality, the *being* something. (293)

Here, the equivalence between 'seeing' and 'being' affects a twofold negation of the aims of self-culture, as conceived by earlier Victorian writers. Not only is Pater concerned to differentiate self-culture from material accumulation or social mobility (*having*), but also, it appears, from any form of praxis which would translate 'vision' into 'action' within the social world (*doing*).

This is not to suggest that Pater's aestheticism is altogether removed from the sphere of work or that it lacks an 'ethical' dimension. Written in response to precisely such criticism of his 'Conclusion' to *The Renaissance, Marius the Epicurean* reformulates self-culture as neither irresponsible hedonism nor an outward-looking engagement with the world, but rather what amounts to an immanent labour of the self. Marius's encounter with the classical philosophies of Epicureanism and Cyrenaicism teaches him to accept the temporal constraints of his subjective, visual experience of the world, an intensified apprehension of the present moment from which 'regret and desire' are excluded (113). Pater does not shrink from drawing anachronistic comparison with the situation of Wilhelm Meister ('*America is here and now – here, or nowhere*' (113)) and even acknowledges Carlyle's interpretation of Goethe's text. The narrowing scope of Marius's sensory/ aesthetic experience is the condition which enables him to discover a sense of purpose within time: 'his scheme is not that of a trifler, but rather of one who gives a meaning of his own, yet a very real one, to those old words – *Let us work while it is day!*' (187). Pater seeks to represent the life of the true aesthete as 'a life of industry, of industrious study, only possible through healthy rule, keeping clear the eye alike of body and soul' (122), thus obliquely continuing the tradition of Victorian self-improvement which he appears to dismiss.

Just as there are echoes of the esoteric *Sartor Resartus* in the more mainstream mid-Victorian fiction of Dickens and Brontë, so *Marius the Epicurean* presents in rarefied philosophical language a narrative template for the interests and anxieties of more recognised late-Victorian novelists, including Henry James and Thomas Hardy. The choice of 'aesthetic education' as a specific form of personal development, though by no means new to the English Bildungsroman as I have shown, became more prevalent during the 1880s and 1890s.[65] In James's *The Princess Casamassima* (1887), for example, the hero Hyacinth Robinson, an orphan of mixed working-class and aristocratic parentage but raised in the lower echelons of class society, is apprenticed as a book-binder where he is able to cultivate a Morrisean artistic sensibility: 'the delicate, charming character of the work he did ... was a kind of education of the taste, trained him in the finest discriminations, in the perception of beauty and the hatred of ugliness'.[66] Unlike some of the apprentice heroes of earlier novels, Hyacinth rejects the prospect of 'rising in the world' through the exercise of his talent, instead defining the value of his artistic work in its own terms (266). Ostensibly at least, the Smilesian equivalence between self-culture and self-help is split apart. In its place, James stages an internal conflict between Hyacinth's capacity for refined aesthetic experience and creative work, on the one hand, and his class consciousness which motivates the desire to redress social injustice on the other. In Paterian terms, *The Princess Casamassima* is a novel of apprenticeship which explores the fissures between the incompatible demands of *being, having*, and *doing*. Less content than Marius with an elevated state of aesthetic consciousness, Hyacinth is equally unable to commit to action on behalf of the revolutionary cause which he intermittently espouses, and all the while he appears to define 'culture' as the possession of symbolic capital and the commodified objects which he conspicuously lacks. Hyacinth's frustrated call for action amongst the discontented labourers and Radical agitators gathered at the Sun and Moon public house, 'in God's name, why don't we do something?' (295), suggests a form of paralysis and indecision similar to Marius's reluctance to commit to one single version of philosophical or religious truth in Pater's text. Both novels, significantly, end with the protagonist's death, figured as an act of self-sacrifice which effectively forestalls the capacity to choose a determinate course of action or belief, ironically idealising the state of uncertainty before decision.

According to George Levine, Hardy's *Jude the Obscure* (1895) might be seen as the last Victorian Bildungsroman, 'a kind of reversal of and elegy for the form and its essentially optimistic implications'.[67] Certainly, Hardy absorbs and reconfigures narrative and thematic elements from many of the texts discussed in this chapter, looking back at the distinctive nineteenth-century genre of the apprentice novel as much as he looks forward to early Modernist fiction.[68] Jude Fawley follows in the tradition of the working-class autodidact whose feats of self-education whilst employed in manual labour were recounted in the numerous exhortatory collective biographies of Smiles and his contemporaries, and more critically depicted in the novels of Dickens and Kingsley. Jude's pursuit of intellectual self-improvement draws most obviously on Arnold's conception of 'culture' embodied in his eulogy of Oxford (fictionalised as Christminster in the novel) as the 'Beautiful city' whose 'ineffable charm keeps ever calling us to the true goal of all of us, to the ideal, to perfection'.[69] Like Hyacinth Robinson, Jude seeks to maintain the purity of his aesthetic education by insisting on its separateness from vulgar social aspiration: the narrator styles him as 'a species of Dick Whittington, whose spirit was touched to finer issues than a mere material gain' (113). Yet Hardy reveals the difficulty of disentangling the mixed motivations of self-culture, just as it proved difficult to maintain a harmonious equilibrium between them. After the collapse of his ambition to study at the University, Jude berates himself for having constructed a falsely disinterested cultural ideal:

> The old fancy which had led on to the culminating vision of the bishopric had not been an ethical or theological enthusiasm at all, but a mundane ambition masquerading in a surplice. He feared that his whole scheme had degenerated to, even though it might not have originated in, a social unrest which had no foundation in the nobler instincts; which was purely an artificial product of civilization. There were thousands of young men on the same self-seeking track at the present moment. (162)

Having acted with an apparent inner conviction of his calling to a scholarly vocation, Jude now discovers that he is merely an exemplary figure of working-class self-improvement, one of 'thousands' bent on social mobility. As in *Great Expectations*, but in a more complex and overdetermined form, Hardy's protagonist is divided between his emotional attachment to the values of cultural tradition and an impulsive, dissatisfied individualism symptomatic of modernity. Jude's inability to remain content in his trade as an artisan stonemason figures one type of 'apprenticeship' in the prescriptive terms of an inherited class identity, yet, ironically, the path of self-culture which he perceives as a progressive emancipation of the individual (an 'apprenticeship of life' in the more informal sense) leads further into a claustrophobic, socially stratified past. It remains a moot question whether Jude's artisan craftsmanship would not have offered him greater opportunity for creative fulfilment than a life of classical scholarship; both practices recycle a material knowledge of the past, and Jude is at first willing to acknowledge that the mason's yard represents a 'centre of effort as worthy as that dignified by the name of scholarly study within the noblest of the colleges' (120). Once more, perhaps, the underlying problem is an inability to reconcile the work of the hand with that of the mind, bridging the division of social labour in a way which influential contemporaries such as John Ruskin and William Morris urged was necessary. Sue Bridehead quotes Mill's *On Liberty* in justification of her decision to elope with Jude: s/he 'who lets the world, or his own portion of it, choose his plan of life for him, has no need of any other faculty than the ape-like one of imitation' (255–6). The liberty of self-development, though, is from another perspective the 'modern vice of unrest' (120), as both Jude and Sue come to profess as the novel unfolds. In Sue's case, this process of disillusionment leads to the now familiar solution of renunciation ('Our life has been a vain attempt at self-delight. But self-abnegation is the higher road' (373)), whereas for Jude it results in a similar impasse to the ending of *The Princess*

*Casamassima*, in which neither side of the dispute can be chosen. Hardy's characterisation of *Jude the Obscure* as a 'tragedy of unfulfilled aims' in his 1895 'Preface' to the novel can be applied to both figures (38).

By the final two decades of the nineteenth century, however, new opportunities of professional employment for women helped to establish the social conditions for a new form of 'female Bildungsroman', distinctively different from the novels of Brontë and Eliot. Associated with, but not restricted to, the 'New Woman' figure of the 1890s, this new fiction of female self-development was also centrally concerned with the relationship between work, culture and aesthetic education. Examples such as Charlotte Riddell's *A Struggle for Fame* (1883) and Ella Hepworth Dixon's *The Story of a Modern Woman* (1894) represent women whose narratives of formation do not culminate in either domestic fulfilment or self-abnegation, but rather in a determination to 'struggle and labour, to see whether she was really fit for any work, and if so, for what'.[70] In some respects, these novels may be seen as a belated counterpart of the narratives of professional development featuring male protagonists which flourished from the 1840s, often in the form of a specifically literary apprenticeship. The emphasis on work as a kind of liberating constraint in shaping the cohesion of a mature self recalls the rhetoric of Dickens and Carlyle, which now appears more openly available to women writers. The heroine of Hepworth Dixon's novel, Mary Erle, for example, is positioned as an exemplary figure of the 'modern woman' through her desire to 'do something, to live', which makes her, according to her suitor Vincent Hemming, an embodiment of the 'modern craze for work'.[71] Work is not presented in the novel as a source of immediate pleasure or creative fulfilment, but rather as a personal compulsion which finds its rationale in economic necessity: 'One works ... because one must', she tells Vincent (181). Mary's initial aspiration to train as a professional artist proves disillusioning in its revelation of the commodification of art, and her subsequent drift into writing popular fiction and journalism echoes the satirical thrust of George Gissing's contemporary *New Grub Street* (1891). Nevertheless, literary work is not merely experienced as alienated labour by Mary (as it is in Gissing's text) since it contributes indirectly to the formulation of her identity. Unable to remain satisfied within the domestic sphere, work is the necessary medium of her self-development, no matter how negative or empty its content.

The intentional exemplarity of *The Story of a Modern Woman* calls to mind Moretti's characterisation of the Bildungsroman as 'the symbolic form of modernity', and by the 1890s it is clear that the generic architecture of this form was well established.[72] The narrator's retrospective account of Mary's childhood reading singles out Brontë's *Villette*, Dickens's *David Copperfield* and, perhaps predictably, Goethe's *Wilhelm Meister* as formative texts. A 'revelation in the possibilities of life' (53), such books provide Mary with knowledge of suffering, sexuality, and presumably work. In addition, the novel contains unmistakeable allusions to Thackeray's *Pendennis* and Barrett Browning's *Aurora Leigh* (Mary is seemingly named after the character Marian Erle). Hepworth Dixon thus self-consciously positions her representative heroine within an intertextual lineage which crosses boundaries of language and gender. The narrative carefully differentiates Mary's late nineteenth-century historical experience from that of her predecessors – she is not a mid-Victorian figure of suffering fortitude nor a 'fallen woman' – yet at the same time her 'story' of apprenticeship and (failed) vocation is an extension of theirs. While it remains important to exercise care and a due degree of rigour in applying the term 'Bildungsroman' beyond its immediate cultural and historical contexts, the extent to which British writers recognised and engaged with this genre through a distinctive body of narrative texts produced over the course of the nineteenth century has yet to be fully understood.

# CHAPTER 4

# The Bildungsroman in Imperial Russia and the Soviet Union

## Lina Steiner

The origins of the Bildungsroman are often traced to the emergence of the new conception of freedom as self-determination in early modern Europe. This secularised view of freedom entailed a transformation of humanistic culture. While traditional humanism oriented itself towards eternal ideals of truth, beauty and goodness, the new humanism that began to emerge in the early eighteenth century saw human beings as perpetually evolving beings continuous with the natural world.[1] For Jean-Jacques Rousseau, Johann Gottfried Herder and other advocates of this secularised view human beings were children of nature endowed with the powers of language and thought, which enabled them to improve themselves and the surrounding world. The educator's task was to engender awareness in the child of these innate gifts and encourage him to develop them. This vision underpinned the concept of Bildung that became one of the key-words of the German Enlightenment in the mid-eighteenth century, spreading across Central and Eastern Europe. From the 1780s to the 1880s, the Russian Empire remained politically and economically allied to Prussia and Germany, which explains why Russian intellectuals were among the first to absorb and respond to the newest philosophical, pedagogical and literary ideas arising from the land of 'poets and thinkers'. Pedagogical narratives modelled on Christoph Martin Wieland, Johann Wolfgang von Goethe and other German and Swiss authors began to appear in Russia in the last quarter of the eighteenth century, paving the way for the Russian Bildungsroman or, as Mikhail Bakhtin called it, the 'novel of emergence' (*roman stanovleniia*).

It is noteworthy that the first theoretical discussion of the Bildungsroman – a genre that Moretti has identified with a conservative liberal response to the French Revolution – was provided by a German-born scholar teaching at the Russian Imperial University of Dorpat (now Tartu, Estonia).[2] From Karl Morgenstern, who first introduced the term

Bildungsroman in 1819, to Bakhtin, whose unfinished work *The Novel of Education and Its Significance for the History of Realism* (ca. 1938) is well known to any scholar of the Bildungsroman, Russian critics have been actively engaged in theorising the relationship between the novelistic genre and the idea of self-formation.[3] Therefore, before launching into literary history, I would like to take stock of the rich intellectual debates concerning literature's pedagogical mission in Russia from the first quarter of the nineteenth century (the period that witnessed the awakening of national self-consciousness in Russia) to the second half of the 1930s (which were marked by heated polemics concerning the identity of the novelistic genre in the Soviet era).

## The Idea of *Bildung* and the Emergence of Russian Literature, 1810s–1860s

A former pupil of the famous philologist Friedrich August Wolf, Morgenstern was hardly an original mind. 'On the Nature of the Bildungsroman' distils some of the central ideas of German literary theory since the publication of Friedrich Blackenburg's 'Essay on the Novel' (1774).[4] Blackenburg was among the first to contrast the novel, which focuses on contemporary life, to the epic as a genre that focuses on the past. Taking his cue from British critics, Blackenburg had suggested that novelists should learn from Shakespeare how to portray a human character in the state of development, because only a work that sounds the depths of the human heart can be truly instructive.[5] Morgenstern repeats these ideas and adds that the novel is different from drama because it unfolds gradually and is intended for slow reading. Echoing Friedrich and A. W. Schlegel's works on the history of literature, Morgenstern examines the novel in the diachronic perspective, finding similarities between it and medieval romances that offered vernacular retellings of sacred history. Oscillating between typological and diachronic approaches, Morgenstern defines the novelistic as the domain situated halfway between heroic epic and prose chronicles (650). He proclaims the Bildungsroman to be at once the most representative and most noble novelistic category (654). It is the most representative because it best expresses the difference of this genre from the epic: in the Bildungsroman the hero develops gradually through experience whereas in the epic heroic characters appear already full-blown. It is deemed to be the most 'noble' genre because it has a beneficial effect on the reader.

Published in a provincial periodical, Morgenstern's lecture had no immediate impact on German or Russian literary life. But its very

appearance is significant insofar as it emblematises the intellectual proximity between Germany and Russia at a time when Germany enjoyed an
ascendency in philosophy and criticism, whereas Russia was just beginning
to mobilise as a *Kultur-Nation* through the development of universities,
literary societies and journals. Many Russian *literati* were able to gain first-
hand access to works written in German. Those without the requisite
language skills absorbed these ideas as they were translated and mediated
by Russian intellectuals. Thus, the idea of *Bildung* gradually became part
and parcel of Russian cultural consciousness. This new development
reflected itself through language. The terms *obrazovannost, obrazovanie,
obrazovyvat*, which were apparently coined by analogy with *Bildung* and
*bilden*, began to enter the vocabulary of educated Russians in the 1830s and
1840s.[6]

The key role in this process belongs to the so-called *Wisdom Lovers*
(*Liubomudry*), an intellectual circle that formed in Moscow in 1823 and
included Vladimir Odoevskii, Ivan Kireevskii, Aleksei Koshelev, Dmitrii
Venevitinov and Nikolai Rozhalin. As Andrzej Walicki points out, their
turn to philosophy represented a turning-away from the political interests
that typified the Decembrist movement, which suffered a fiasco in 1825.[7]
While Decembrist secret societies developed liberal political theories aimed
at transforming the autocratic state into a constitutional state, the Wisdom
Lovers thought that Russia's path to modernity required first of all the
cultivation of independently minded individuals.

Of seminal importance for the *Liubomudry* was Herder, whose philosophy of history provided a convenient paradigm for understanding Russia's
historical trajectory. Russia's sudden emergence as a European power in the
early eighteenth century presented a considerable challenge to many historians. For the founder of modern political theory, Jean-Jacques
Rousseau, Peter the Great was a destroyer of Russia's organic traditions
and his revolution a monstrosity. Because of Peter Russians lost their sense
of identity without having become Europeans. Herder countered
Rousseau, arguing that by making his subjects aware of the Western
Enlightenment Peter had not destroyed Russia's civilisation but rather
provided it with opportunities for growth and enrichment.[8]

Taking his cue from Herder, Kireevskii argued that, by bringing Russia
face to face with Europe, Peter and Russia's subsequent westernised rulers
accelerated the development of their subjects' self-consciousness.[9] A nation
that had grown slowly and unselfconsciously in isolation from world
history was suddenly confronted with a more dynamic world. Rising to
this challenge, Russians had become interested in their history and started

seeking ways to bridge the gap between their ancient traditions and the ideals of the Enlightenment. According to Kireevskii, Russia's arrival on the world-historical scene coincided with the crisis of Western culture, which manifested itself through the revolutionary upheavals in France (100). Russia's sudden emergence out of backwardness, concluded Kireevskii, was highly auspicious. While the Middle Ages and the Renaissance were the periods when Romance and Germanic cultures dominated the world, the nineteenth century was to become the age of Russia's cultural ascendancy.

Kireevskii's theory offered an antidote to Petr Chaadaev's controversial *First Philosophical Letter* (1829), which described Russia as a country devoid of history, condemned to exist in a merely vegetative way.[10] Kireevskii and other dialectical thinkers in his wake interpreted Chaadaev's despair as a symptom of Russia's spiritual awakening. Drawing on Hegel's method of dialectical negation, Kireevskii envisioned a scenario in which the educated elite would overcome their present alienation and reconnect with their environment in a more conscious and deliberate fashion. Exactly how this new synthesis would occur is left unexplained by Kireevskii. Many other nineteenth-century thinkers and authors would pick up his thread, developing various scenarios of national *Bildung* aimed at pulling the country out of its socio-economic and cultural backwardness and reconciling the educated minority with the people. Kireevskii himself eventually shifted towards a more conservative position. In his Slavophile phase he renounced the idea of progress and sided with Alexei Khomiakov's defence of pre-Petrine Russia.

The debate between the Slavophiles and the Westernisers galvanised the Russian public sphere in the 1840s. The former were sharply critical of Peter the Great and saw the culture of Muscovy as a repository of intuitive wisdom, which had been compromised by an encounter with the individualistic and instrumentalising Western rationality. Their opponents, on the contrary, defended Peter's attempt to make Russians less self-sufficient and close-minded. The central issue that divided the two camps was the idea of 'personality' (*lichnost*), which the Slavophiles saw as a result of a false route taken by Western philosophers. Their most articulate opponent was Vissarion Belinskii who was firmly convinced that the attainment of self-consciousness was a legacy of Peter's reforms. These reforms introduced a stage of 'negativity' marked by the alienation of the cultural elite from their roots and even their native language (since the end of the eighteenth century the aristocracy had spoken mainly French). Drawing on Hegel's dialectical method, Belinskii argued that the negative stage was followed by a new synthesis, which he linked to the enthusiasm caused by the anti-Napoleonic campaign. This phase found its expression in the poetry of Pushkin who was the first Russian author capable of fusing the national element with the universal. His *Eugene Onegin* (1825) was for Belinskii a perfect example of truly 'objective' national poetry that replaced the Romantic subjectivism emblematised in Pushkin's earlier Byron-inspired works.[11]

Belinskii's death in 1848 (on the eve of his arrest for his political views), the emigration of Herzen in 1847 and the arrest and banishment to Siberia of Fyodor Dostoevsky in 1849 stripped Russian society of its most out-spoken critics. Only conservative intellectuals flourished in the repressive climate of the last decade of Nicholas I's reign. However, within a few years the tide changed. Nicholas I's death (1855) and Russia's devastating defeat in the Crimean War ushered in a new epoch of liberal reforms. Concerned with rebuilding a national community, the government no longer stifled the debate on national *obrazovanie*, but, on the contrary, encour-aged writers and other professionals to make both theoretical and practical contributions. An essay by a renowned medical professor, military surgeon and public educator N. I. Pirogov, entitled 'Questions of Life' ('*Voprosy zhizni*') (1857), captures the atmosphere of the age.[12] Pirogov argues that the primary goal of any education is to raise reflective individuals who can think independently about the meaning of life. Imparting specialised knowledge is a secondary task that should be subordinated to the larger objective of forming thoughtful individuals. To achieve this goal, schools must include modern literary works in their curricula and allocate enough time for literary discussions. That German debates on *Bildung* reverberate in Pirogov's writings is not surprising given that he spent much of his career at Dorpat (where he received his doctorate and held a chair in medicine in 1836–41).

It has become a cliché to speak of the age of the so-called Great Reforms as the age of the novel. Nevertheless, it is worthwhile mentioning this concurrence of political and literary history in the present context, because the boom of the prose novel and the expansion of the 'thick journals' reflected the Russian authors' self-assigned mission as public educators. Belinskii and other critics encouraged them to think of themselves as the consciousness of their nation. However, different novelists interpreted their pedagogical mission in different ways. While some tended towards an old-fashioned didacticism that called to mind seventeenth- and eight-eenth-century moralistic prose, others were imbued with the Romantic spirit that privileged individuality and originality. The didactic approach is exemplified by Nikolai Chernyshevskii's *What Is to Be Done?* (1863), whereas a romantically inspired liberal approach can be found in the novelistic experiments by Apollon Grigor'ev. These works – in particular, the autobiographical *My Literary and Moral Wanderings* (1862–4) – answer a pedagogical imperative by unfolding before the reader an image of creative individuality that cannot be imitated but can only inspire readers to undertake their own moral and creative wanderings.

Originality and non-conformism were part and parcel of Grigor'ev's 'organic' approach to criticism. An eclectic thinker, Grigor'ev took to heart Herder's idea that Russian culture would achieve maturity by incorporating elements of other cultures. He saw himself as spokesman of a new literary generation called to overcome the divide between the Slavophiles and Westernisers through a creative synthesis of the most interesting indigenous and foreign ideas. In 'The Development of the Idea of Nationality in Russian Literature Since Pushkin', Grigor'ev followed Belinskii in analysing the history of Russian culture as a teleological process that reached its climax with Pushkin's turn to the novel.[13] But while Belinskii identified Russia's emergence into maturity with the wholly rational, disenchanted viewpoint occupied by the narrator of *Eugene Onegin*, Grigor'ev argued that Pushkin's deepest insight into Russian reality was represented by the somewhat simple-minded narrator of the *Tales of Ivan Petrovich Belkin*. For Grigor'ev the mature Pushkin was a typical genius in Schelling's sense of the term, a miraculous nexus of nature and culture whose emergence betokened Russia's impending cultural efflorescence.

### Bakhtin on the Bildungsroman

As we have seen from the previous section, in the second half of the nineteenth century Russian prose fiction was becoming increasingly self-conscious and concerned with originality. According to Boris Eikhenbaum, the first dissertation on the novel in Russia appeared as early as 1844.[14] However, it was not until the 1890s that systematic research into the poetics and stylistics of the novel was undertaken by one of Russia's pre-eminent philologists, Alexander Veselovskii. Inspired by Rohde's work on the Greek novel, Veselovskii argued that the novelistic genre was a product of a historic rupture that occurred when classical Greek culture was absorbed into a more heterogeneous imperial culture under Alexander the Great. 'The tradition of political freedom darkened along with the ideal notion of the citizen. The individual, sensing his isolation in vast cosmopolitan spaces, retreated within himself. His interest now turned to inner life in view of the dearth of social ones. For want of legends, he began elaborating utopias. Such are the topics that suffuse the Greek novel,' wrote Veselovskii.[15]

In his works dedicated to the historical poetics of the Russian novel, Veselovskii stressed its connections to hagiography and folklore. Echoing Grigor'ev's 'organic criticism', Veselovskii conceived of the modern Russian novel as the result of a cultural synthesis of various Eastern and Western traditions.[16] He called his approach 'historical poetics', signalling his allegiance to the historicist method that was then being actively developed by several philosophers and literary scholars in Germany where Veselovskii spent some time as a student and young scholar.

The historicist turn has rekindled an interest in the novel of education. For Wilhelm Dilthey, who rediscovered the term Bildungsroman in 1870, it denoted a type of novel that portrayed personal emergence simultaneously as a psychological maturation and social integration. He argued that the Bildungsroman with its emphasis on inward reflection conveyed historical experience peculiar to the age of early industrialisation in Germany.[17] Dilthey's attempt to link the Bildungsroman to German nationalism provoked intense critical debates. Georg Lukács's *Theory of the Novel* (1916) offered an influential counterpoint to Dilthey's approach. Far from expressing a uniquely German path to modernity, the novel, argued the Hungarian philosopher, centred on themes of universal significance. As a form of great epic literature, the novel strove to grasp and represent totality, which it could only do negatively, by focusing on the 'problematic individual'.

Bakhtin first encountered *Theory of the Novel* in the 1920s, while still at work on *The Problems of Dostoevsky's Art* (1929). By this time Lukács himself was already disappointed with it. Having moved to Moscow in 1930, Lukács went on to reformulate his theory and history of the novel in ways that dovetailed with the Marxist theory of consciousness. Lukács's view of *Bildung* in the 1930s involved a twofold dialectic whereby a human being underwent integration into social reality in its diverse shapes and forms, while simultaneously transforming this reality by dint of his own labour, a conception that fitted well with the newly forged doctrine of socialist realism.

The publication of Lukács's entry for the *Soviet Literary Encyclopedia*, 'The Novel as a Bourgeois Epic', was accompanied by a major philosophical debate in Moscow in 1934–5. Inspired by these polemics, Bakhtin also concentrated on the theory of the novel.[18] Among new projects conceived at this time was a book on the novel of emergence (*roman stanovleniia*). The manuscript which Bakhtin submitted to *Sovetskii Pisatel* in 1938 was lost (presumably burnt) in the early months of the German invasion in 1941. All that has survived is an initial outline, including an extensive plan of this book. An extract from this unfinished text was translated into English and published in 1986.[19] The American translators and editors of this text recognised the importance of the Bildungsroman (they used this term instead of the more cumbersome 'novel of emergence') as one of the key categories in Bakhtin's thought. As they surmised, the published extract offered but a glimpse into Bakhtin's massive project. Some recently published archival materials shed new light on Bakhtin's preoccupation with the novelistic genre in the second half of the 1930s and early 1940s. These materials reveal that the problem of personal emergence and the Bildungsroman as the literary vehicle of such emergence were at the centre of Bakhtin's attention during this crucial phase in his career.

In March of 1941 Bakhtin delivered a lecture at the Institute of World Literature in Moscow on 'The Novel as a Literary Genre'.[20] As can be gleaned from Bakhtin's lecture notes, he used the occasion to publicise the ideas he developed in the course of a decade-long preoccupation with the theory and history of the novel.[21] In defending the autonomy of the novel from the epic tradition Bakhtin reveals his debt to Lukács. He drives this point home by referring to Goethe's and Schiller's characterisation of the epic as a form of 'absolute past'. The epic, says Bakhtin, bars the genuine self-expression of creative individuality, which always looks forward towards the as yet unknown and unrealised future, rather than to the past. Only a narrative that portrayed the encounter between the mind and the world from a completely unique, unrepeatable point of view could do justice to historical reality. This type of narrative is the Bildungsroman.

Bakhtin's plan for the Bildungsroman book, most of which was probably never written, begins with a historical typology of the novel as approached from the standpoint of character construction.[22] The second part was to provide a historical overview of the novel of education and the Bildungsroman from classical antiquity to neoclassicism. The third part was to cover French, English and German novels of education, including a subchapter on the Enlightenment theory of education. The fourth part of Bakhtin's work (a large fragment of which was to survive) focused on Goethe and the novel of emergence, with separate sections devoted to *Poetry and Truth* (1811), *Wilhelm Meister's Apprenticeship* (1795) and *Journeyman Years* (1821; 1829). The final fifth part was to focus on the novel of emergence after Goethe. After surveying the development of

German, English and French realism in the wake of Goethe, Bakhtin planned to switch his attention to Russia. Among the nineteenth-century authors he planned to discuss were Goncharov, Turgenev, Tolstoy and Dostoevsky. The Soviet authors whose names figure in Bakhtin's plan were Prishvin, Fedin, Sobolev and Fadeev. The final part was to be dedicated to the work of Maxim Gorky.

The surviving drafts of this book leave many questions unanswered. For example, a large section of the extant manuscript approaches the history of literary forms from the point of view of the 'chronotope' or spatio-temporal conception of experience. Whether Bakhtin intended to reconcile this approach with the socio-linguistically inspired theory of dialogic discourse that he developed in his study of Dostoevsky remains a matter of debate. The methodology pivoting on the chronotope, which Bakhtin applied to his interpretation of Goethe, allowed him to respond to contemporary ideological pressures and give realism primary importance. For example, in 'The *Bildungsroman* and Its Significance in the History of Realism' Bakhtin appears to side with Lukács's view of the novel as part of the epic tradition intent on capturing the totality of life, thus departing from his crypto-Schlegelian characterisation of the novel as an expression of an 'unfinalised' ironic consciousness.[23] However, as evidenced by 'The Novel as a Literary Genre', the equation of the novel and the epic did not endure. Bakhtin reverted to his original position, arguing that the most progressive form is the novel of emergence, which depicts individuals who are perpetually redefining themselves, thereby creatively transforming the world.

### Early Russian Novels of Education, 1790s–1830s

As Herder points out, eighteenth-century Russians were eager to learn from many teachers at once.[24] Hence accounting for the influence of different European Enlightenment traditions on eighteenth-century Russian literature is a singularly complex task. I will limit my discussion here to Alexander Radischev and Nikolai Karamzin, two particularly influential figures whose careers, as divergent as they were, reflected a range of common tendencies in the Russian Enlightenment. These were the first Russian prose writers who sought to fuse European and traditional Russian narrative traditions.

Both Radischev and Karamzin were privileged enough to complete their education in Europe. Radischev was part of a group of students whom Catherine II sent to the University of Leipzig in 1766 to prepare for a career in the imperial bureaucracy. Though specialising in law, Radischev was erudite in both ancient and modern political philosophy. With his *Journey from St. Petersburg to Moscow* (1790), a bitter attack on authoritarianism and serfdom in the guise of a sentimental travelogue, Radischev was to secure his place in the canon of Russian radical liberalism. In 1789 he published *The Life of Fyodor Vasilievich Ushakov*.[25] Modelled on a saint's life, this moving work describes the life of Radischev's friend who organised a student rebellion against the tyranny of their supervisor Bokum. The students were victorious and Bokum was stripped of at least some of his power. Soon after these events, however, Ushakov was struck down by an incurable illness and died while abroad. To immortalise his friend, Radischev composed *Zhitie*, a subtle psychological analysis of a young man who confronts terrible suffering and untimely death.

After publishing his *Journey* Radischev was arrested and faced trial. During his imprisonment he composed another work that combined elements of hagiography and the sentimental novel of education, *The Tale of Philaret the Merciful* (vol. I, pp. 397–410). Ostensibly, the tale describes the early life of a Greek saint celebrated for his generosity. Scholars have assumed, however, that the work is autobiographical. It was in exile that Radischev completed a philosophical-anthropological treatise entitled *On a Human Being, His Death and Immortality* (1792). Drawing on Herder, Haller and other materialistic scientists, he formulated a monistic view of a human being as a perpetually evolving organism. It is here that the term 'obrazovanie' appears for the first time to describe the process of organic Bildung.[26]

Unlike Radischev, Karamzin enjoyed an uninterrupted and successful career as a writer, court official and the first state-sponsored historiographer. He completed his education in a Moscow boarding school with a two-year European tour detailed in his *Letters of a Russian Traveler* (1791–2).[27] Critics usually cite Sterne's *Sentimental Journey* as Karamzin's primary model. However, Karamzin's autobiographical hero is very different from Sterne's sceptical Yorick. His gentle soul craves not only knowledge, but also friendship and love. Wieland's Agathon seems to be his immediate literary antecedent.

One of the key motifs throughout Radischev's works, friendship, also occupies a central place in Karamzin's work. He believed that only in dialogue with friends can one evolve as a truly virtuous and wise person. Karamzin developed this idea in an unfinished novel, *The Knight of Our Time* (1803).[28] The hero of this novel, Leon, is an adolescent of aristocratic lineage whose mother died when he was a child. The central formative influences in Leon's life include an acquaintance with a fraternal society of provincial gentlemen from whom he learns self-respect and honour, and a sentimental friendship with Countess Emilia. This heroine's name calls to mind Rousseau's *Émile, or On Education*, which, along with *Confessions*, influenced Karamzin's work. The friendship between Leon and Emilia recalls the early phase of Jean-Jacques's relationship with Mme de Warens. Karamzin's text is interrupted at the moment when Leon begins experiencing the first stirrings of erotic feelings towards the Countess and has not yet acted upon them. The idyllic chronotope is arrested but not transcended in Karamzin's novel. This step was accomplished by Alexander Pushkin who followed many of Karamzin's initiatives, including the turn to history, prose and public education.

Historiography, for both Karamzin and Pushkin, was inextricably linked to education and the development of national identity. These problems appeared particularly daunting after the failure of Alexander I's constitutional project and the fiasco of the Decembrists. Culture was the only path a reformer could take, and Pushkin took up this challenge after being summoned back from exile in 1826 by Nicholas I and accepting the Emperor's offer of reconciliation with the government.

Pushkin's experiments with the prose novel belong to the same period as his historiographical works. The majority of Pushkin's novelistic projects remained unfinished at the time of his death in 1837. The only completed novel was *The Captain's Daughter* (1836).[29] Modelled in part on Scott's Waverley novels, it gives us a clear sense of Pushkin's new self-understanding as the author of entertaining and morally edifying literature. This quasi-autobiographical narrative portrays the coming of age of a provincial nobleman, Petr Grinev, set against the background of the turbulent Pugachev Rebellion (1773–5). Before sending his son off to the army, Grinev's father instructs him to serve faithfully the sovereign to whom he swore allegiance, obey his superiors and remember the folk saying, 'safeguard your clothes when they are new, and your honor when you are young' (289).

The main plot recalls a parable about a son who goes into the world to win his fortune, and whose 'weaknesses' (seen through the eyes of the hero's servant and supervisor Savel'ich) end up being the key to his happiness. Thus, Grinev's gift of a coat to a stranger who rescues him and his servant during a blizzard seems foolishly generous to Savel'ich, but later saves Grinev's life, since the stranger turns out to be the leader of the rebels, Emel'ian Pugachev. Having recognised the young nobleman, who had been generous to him following the capture of Belorgorskaia fortress,

Pugachev offers him friendship and a position of high rank in the troop. Grinev declines the rebel's offer, remaining faithful to his oath of honour as a nobleman. Rather than having him murdered, Pugachev returns Grinev's magnanimous gesture, permitting him to return to the Empress's army and even blesses his engagement to Masha, the daughter of Captain Mironov who had died defending the fortress.

The plot centred on the motif of 'honour' is mirrored by the story of Masha Mironova, whose guiding theme is 'mercy'. After Grinev is arrested and charged with treason, Masha travels to Petersburg to throw herself in front of the Empress and beg for mercy. Catherine II encounters Masha while walking incognito in the park of Tsarskoe Selo. Moved by Masha's story, she pardons Grinev and provides Masha with a dowry so that she and Grinev can marry and retire to his estate, an idyllic place he left at the beginning of his apprenticeship narrative. In the epilogue we learn that Grinev's children and grandchildren are progressively impoverished. The novel ends with a veiled suggestion (made by the fictional 'editor' of Grinev's tale) that the times have changed and that the gentry's ethical and aesthetic ideals, which linked virtue to loyal service to the Tsar, no longer guarantee happiness. But the young Grinevs are still clinging to their ancestral nest and their inherited world view.

## From the 1840s to the 1860s: Herzen, Turgenev, Goncharov

When compared to *The Captain's Daughter*, Sergei Aksakov's *Family Chronicle* (1840s–1856) appears as a consciously archaic narrative projecting an idealised image of aristocratic family life. Pushkin's narrative self-consciously combines elements of idyll, romance, fairy tale, family chronicle, the novel of ordeal and the historical novel, leaving ample room for metaliterary play and irony. The Slavophile Aksakov, on the other hand, couches the Bagrov family chronicle in wholly idyllic terms, carefully avoiding difficult social issues. This is not to deny the artistic qualities of Aksakov's prose. Gogol and Turgenev admired Aksakov's portrayal of the psychology of a young person growing up in harmony with nature, while Mirsky compared *Childhood Years of Bagrov Grandson* (a sequel to *Family Chronicle*, 1858) to Proust's *À la recherche du temps perdu*.[30]

But the larger and more prominent group of authors who came of age in the 1840s, including Herzen, Turgenev and Dostoevsky, were socially engaged and West-oriented. The suffering of the oppressed, especially the serfs and women, was the main theme of Russian stories and novels in the 1840s and 1850s. It is telling that in these and many other works from this period, including Herzen's *Who Is to Blame?* (1846) and Dostoevsky's *Netochka Nezvanova* (1849), the active role belongs to the female character who desperately struggles for happiness, whereas male protagonists give up and capitulate before 'necessity'.

The problem of social irrelevance and psychological weakness or immaturity assailing young Russian men lies at the heart of Herzen's *Who Is to Blame?* and the unfinished *Honour Above All*, Turgenev's *Rudin* (1856) and *The Nest of the Gentlefolk* (1859), Goncharov's *Oblomov* (1859), and other works composed by the authors who entered the literary scene at the moment when the critical campaign against the egotistic 'Byronic hero' and his Russian avatars (e.g. Pushkin's Onegin, Lermontov's Pechorin) was at its height. Consequently, the main task facing Herzen's Bel'tov (*Who Is to Blame?*), Goncharov's Alexander Aduev (*The Same Old Story*), Oblomov and Stolz (*Oblomov*), Turgenev's Rudin and Lavretskii (*The Nest of the Gentlefolk*) and other literary characters from the same period is to find an activity that would engage their entire intellectual and spiritual powers and enable them to grow. However, these heroes remain confined to the role of the Romantic 'superfluous man' – either because of their superficial education or because of psychological inaptitude. As for Goncharov's 'active heroes' who choose business as the sphere in which to apply their energies, they inevitably end up looking too narrow and stripped of all poetry and spontaneity. Petr and Alexander Aduev (uncle and nephew, respectively) represent two stages in this developmental process, which ultimately drains their lives of all excitement and vigour. The author's moral judgement of this *Bildung* Aduev-style can be inferred from his description of the premature decline of Petr's young wife Liza. When at the end of his sentimental education Alexander assumes the same posture of a realist disenchanted in his dreams and resigned to a life of pragmatism as his uncle the reader feels saddened. In his next novel, *Oblomov*, Goncharov chose a different strategy. Here the more interesting and psychologically convincing character is the weak Oblomov, whereas the strong and industrious Stolz lacks depth and originality. He is but a foil for Oblomov, his more down-to-earth alter ego, whose success does not compensate for Oblomov's early fading away.

In his final novel, *The Ravine* (1869), Goncharov once again focused on the sentimental education of a young man from the provinces who comes to Petersburg to realise his dreams. The hero of this novel, Raiskii, is an artist, and his experiences broaden his world view without making him disenchanted with his choice of profession. Raiskii is more of an observer than participant in the drama which involves his cousin Vera, who falls in love with a nihilist only to become disenchanted in her love, and his and Vera's great-aunt (called 'Granny') who finds out about Vera's 'fall' and interprets it as retribution for her own love affair decades ago. This incident prompts Raiskii to start composing a novel. At the end of the narrative we find him in Europe, continuing his artistic apprenticeship, unwilling to settle down and accept a life of successful mediocrity. In the end, for Goncharov it is the Romantic motif of genius and endless striving that wins the day against the Hegelian motif of giving oneself up to history and one's community.

Turgenev's continuous quest for a heroic personality – a modern Don Quixote (a figure whom Turgenev juxtaposed to the hesitant Hamlet in an influential 1859 lecture)[31] – also brought him face to face with the impossibility of completely rejecting Romanticism. While supporting Belinskii's idea of 'critical realism', he could never bring himself to share the positivistic and utilitarian world view of the radical intelligentsia, which came to dominate the editorial board of *The Contemporary* and the Russian literary scene on the whole towards the end of the 1850s. Turgenev's most influential contribution to the debate on 'realism' vs. Romanticism is *Fathers and Children* (1862).[32] In this novel he tried to bring to life the figure of a contemporary 'nihilist' (in the sense in which this term was used by Russian radicals who understood it as the antithesis to 'Romanticism' and 'idealism'). But far from being a mere caricature, Bazarov is sensitive and in the course of the novel discovers that, contrary to his scientific convictions, he is capable of deep feelings. When Bazarov's love for an aristocratic widow, Odintsova, remains unrequited he is heartbroken. Just as he tries to escape his private suffering and immerse himself in the work of a country doctor, he contracts blood poisoning from an incorrectly performed autopsy and dies. Bazarov's development is thus tragically arrested, whereas that of his friend Arkadii Kirsanov swings back to the idyllic chronotope he had left behind when he moved to Petersburg and became a student. In the end Arkadii marries and falls into his hereditary role of a country squire. It is this clash between Bazarov's tragic Bildungsroman and Arkadii's return to his roots that lends *Fathers and Children* a special intensity and precludes us from classifying it as a conventional generations novel.

Throughout the rest of his career Turgenev continued his search for heroes who possessed enough energy and creativity to grow out of the roles to which they were predestined by contemporary Russian society. Thus, Litvinov and Potugin (from *Smoke*, 1867) tirelessly seek new opportunities for action in spite of their disappointments. But Turgenev, who lost his faith in Hegelianism in the early 1850s and found consolation in

Schopenhauer's philosophy, could never write a wholly optimistic novel. However, towards the end of his career, he composed a novella, *Punin and Baburin* (1874), which contains as one of its subplots a female Bildungsroman that recalls the plot of his earlier novel, *On the Eve* (1860). Over the course of the story, which begins in the 1830s and ends in the 1860s, the heroine Muza (Muse) develops from a naive girl seduced and abandoned by a nobleman to the wife and helpmate of the revolutionary Baburin, and finally to a revolutionary in her own right.

The only work by an author from the same generation that finds a positive resolution for the problem of 'superfluity' is Herzen's *My Past and Thoughts*. As critics have observed, Herzen's memoir is structured like a Bildungsroman.[33] It records the evolution of an autonomous subject who refuses to submit to any form of external domination, be it the tyranny of the Russian Tsar, or that of bourgeois morality, or else one's own instincts and baser sentiments like jealousy and anger.

Herzen consciously modelled *My Past and Thoughts* on Goethe's *Poetry and Truth*. This form allowed him to narrate his life story, while simultaneously including a number of historical and philosophical digressions. At the heart of Herzen's memoirs is the story of a drama, which unfolded in 1849–51 and involved Herzen, his wife Natalie, his friend and fellow revolutionary Georg Herwegh, and Herwegh's wife Emma. The *ménage à quatre* in the spirit of Saint-Simon collapsed once Herzen discovered that Natalie and Herwegh had a love affair. Although he was soon reconciled with Natalie (who died in 1852), Herzen could never forgive Herwegh for what he saw as a betrayal of their friendship. Meanwhile, Herwegh challenged Herzen to a duel, which Herzen refused to fight. Some scholars maintain that, had it not been for Herzen's desire to justify his conduct to posterity, the long-contemplated project of his memoirs might never have been fulfilled. The chapters describing Herzen's family drama may have been the first ones he wrote.[34]

Born on April 6, 1812, just two-and-a-half months prior to Napoleon's invasion of Russia, Herzen plots his life story as a constant interaction between history and private life.[35] Thus, in the first chapters we learn of a special diplomatic mission that his father was asked to carry out during the Patriotic War of 1812, which involved an interview with Napoleon. Herzen's transition from childhood to adolescence begins when he and his friend Nikolai Ogarev learn of the execution of the Decembrists in 1826. The two boys make a pledge to continue the Decembrists' work.

To prepare himself for a revolutionary career Herzen embarked on a study of German philosophy. It should be noted that by the time

Herzen started to work on his memoirs his interest in Hegel had waned. What remained was a propensity for understanding the particular and the universal together, for thinking of human character not only in psychological, but also in historical terms. This dialectical design is most obvious in Part Five, which describes both the revolution of 1848 and the family drama. It is the most dialogic part in the entire book. Here Herzen incorporates fragments from Natalie's letters and reports their conversations at great length. He relentlessly analyses their past, trying to grasp why and how they grew apart.[36] A bitter disappointment with the outcome of European revolutions combined with his family drama revealed to Herzen the insufficiency of his earlier ideals and pushed him to seek new ones.

While writing and editing his memoirs Herzen had already embarked on a new philosophical path (which was to culminate in his theory of Russian socialism). However, his newly found historical optimism failed to lend conclusive shape to his memoir. In a sense, Herzen the writer outstripped Herzen the philosopher. As a political theorist Herzen reaped harsh rebuke from a wide spectrum of opposition. His Bildungsroman, on the other hand, has been found moving and inspirational by readers from different countries, generations and philosophical camps.

## Tolstoy and Dostoevsky

Lev Tolstoy made his literary debut in 1852 when his autobiographical novella *Childhood* was published in the liberal journal *The Contemporary*. In 1854, as a young artillery officer, he was dispatched to Sevastopol where he remained throughout the siege, continuing to write and sending his *Sevastopol Sketches* to *The Contemporary*. The *Sketches* were immediately published and met with great acclaim. Following the fall of Sevastopol in 1855, Tolstoy went to Petersburg, where he found himself surrounded by admiring critics and audiences. Divided on most issues, the editorial board of *The Contemporary* displayed unanimity in embracing the young Tolstoy. Chernyshevsky, who was the journal's leading critic, published a flattering review of the *Sevastopol Sketches*, in which he first coined the expression that was to become a lynchpin of Tolstoy criticism: 'the dialectics of the soul'.[37] He recognised in Tolstoy one of the most penetrating nineteenth-century literary psychologists, a true heir of Rousseau, Sterne and Goethe. This warm welcome encouraged Tolstoy to continue work on an autobiographical cycle, *Four Epochs of Development*, though ultimately only three of the four projected parts were published.

*Childhood* describes the life of Nikolen'ka Irten'ev at his family's estate up to the point when this idyll is disrupted by the death of Nikolen'ka's mother. The children and their father relocate to Moscow where the plot of *Adolescence* (1854) unfolds. Here, Tolstoy shows his hero's transition from the patriarchal world of the country to the 'civilised' world of Moscow society, focusing on Nikolen'ka's *faux pas*, hidden first disappointments in people and the world, and the development of his excessive self-love. In *Youth* (1857) the hero enters the university, where he encounters students of non-noble origin. It is here that Tolstoy's autobiographical hero first discovers his democratic sentiments and begins to raise the question that would preoccupy the author for the rest of his career: how to bridge the gulf between people of differing social and cultural backgrounds and, ultimately, transform human society into a brotherhood.[38]

From the late 1850s on, the question of personal development is intertwined in Tolstoy's mind with the problem of national *obrazovanie*, which he sees as a twofold issue involving both mass education and the re-education of the upper classes such as would make them better prepared for citizenship in a modern nation. During his second European trip in 1860–1 Tolstoy (who had been teaching children on his estate Iasnaia Poliana since the late 1840s) undertook a detailed study of European educational systems. None of these foreign systems seemed applicable to Russia whose precocious leap into industrialised modernity called for a unique approach to education. Realizing the magnitude of this problem, Tolstoy began to immerse himself in the study of Russian history, focusing especially on the Napoleonic wars and the Decembrist movement. The first version of a historical novel that would eventually become *War and Peace* – entitled *1805* – was serialised in *The Russian Messenger*, in 1865–7. The novel was first published in its entirety in 1869.

*War and Peace* is a veritable blending of the epic and of the modern genres of family novel and Bildungsroman.[39] This is because the heroic past as presented in this work is not the 'absolute' past of ancient epics, but is organically connected to the present. The main male characters of *War and Peace* – Andrei Bolkonskii, Pierre Bezukhov and Nikolai Rostov – represent three approaches to self-development Tolstoy considered typical of the Russia of his father's generation. But the re-emergence of similar character types in Tolstoy's later works – most notably in *Anna Karenina* – suggests that the heroes of *War and Peace* were not wholly anachronistic and could be found in contemporary Russia. Thus, Konstantin Levin shares many characteristics with Pierre Bezukhov and Nikolai Rostov, and Andrei Bolkonskii's aristocratic type is echoed in the images of

Alexei Vronskii and Prince Serpukhovskoi. Similarly, the carefully wrought portrait of a peasant soldier, Platon Karataev, heralds Tolstoy's subsequent attempts to feel his way into the world view of Russian peasantry and learn how to write the kind of literature peasants would find comprehensible.

Among the central characters of *War and Peace*, only Pierre can be described as a hero of the Bildungsroman whose inner evolution transcends the chronotope of the traditional novel of education. According to Bakhtin, this chronotope links psychological maturation to a biological process more or less consistent in most traditional societies.[40] Thus, a traditional novel of education is essentially the offspring or comprises some features of the family (or generations) novel with which it shares an essentially cyclical view of time. Most of the life stories depicted in *War and Peace* fall under this rubric. The same holds not only for the women, Natasha and Princess Marya, whose spiritual and religious longings are supposed to be fully satisfied by their roles as mothers and educators of their children, but also for Nikolai Rostov and even for Andrei Bolkonskii. Nikolai's maturation transforms him from an enthusiastic and sensitive youth into a *pater familias* and shrewd estate owner. Andrei, his intellectual interests and ambition notwithstanding, follows the path of honour his father instructs him to take. His obedience to his father (which precludes him from following the promptings of his heart and quickly marry Natasha) keeps him confined to a role of a freethinking but proud aristocrat, a faithful soldier who finally dies from a wound he receives at Borodino.

Only Pierre, an illegitimate son of Count Bezukhov and an unnamed mother (who could be a peasant or a foreigner of middle-class origin, like Herzen's mother) is a new type of hero, whose significance in the novel is that of an observer of world historical and personal dramas as these unfold before him. Pierre, to be sure, is no mere bystander, for he does become involved in many adventures. He gets married, joins the Free Masons, conceives a plot to assassinate Napoleon, acts nobly and decisively during the French occupation of Moscow when, among other deeds, he helps save a girl from a fire, before finally being arrested and incarcerated in a POW camp where he encounters a peasant sage, Platon Karataev. However, such experiences are presented as a form of schooling that prepares Pierre for true life, which begins only in the epilogue. It is at this point that the fourth epoch of Pierre's development begins to unfold. Although Pierre is wealthy and happily married to Natasha with whom he has several children, he is unsatisfied by life in an idyll and craves political activity. He is possessed by

the desire to improve the world, an idea that he probably imbibed when
reading of the Enlightenment authors, whose works he devoured during
his Masonic phase. The epilogue shows Pierre's transformation into
a Decembrist revolutionary.

The search for a sphere of activity that would satisfy one's spiritual
longings and social conscience but which also accommodates a happy
family life is the central problem confronting Konstantin Levin, another
quasi-autobiographical character who shares narrative space as a co-
protagonist with Anna in *Anna Karenina* (1877). Ilya Kliger has recently
interpreted this two-plot narrative as a combination of an archaic plot
dominated by a tragic sense of predestination (Anna's story) and a modern
secularised quest narrative (Levin's story).[41] I similarly interpret the plot
centred on Levin as a somewhat idiosyncratic Bildungsroman where the
hero's perpetual search for meaning in life is offset by his happy marriage to
Kitty. Family happiness grants a sense of closure to Levin's narrative,
suggesting that the answers to the questions of life that Levin is seeking
are already somehow available to him through his emotional symbiosis
with Kitty. Like most of Tolstoy's women, Kitty has an intuitive grasp of
the truths that her husband seeks in the books and through work and
conversations with the peasants. The message with which Tolstoy ends his
novel is that only a harmonious love union can yield a sense of wholeness
otherwise unobtainable by purely intellectual means. However, this conclusion did not outlive the 1870s. As evidenced by *Confession* (1879) and his
later writings, Tolstoy came to view love between family members as an
extension of self-love. For the later Tolstoy, a truly good life is one that
seeks to contribute to a worldwide brotherhood. As I will argue below,
a similar message may be discerned in Dostoevsky's lifelong preoccupation
with the problem of moral self-perfection and national formation.

Notable overlaps between Tolstoy's and Dostoevsky's humanistic
visions have not escaped scholarly attention. As Donna Orwin has
observed, Dostoevsky first noticed Tolstoy as the pseudonymous author
of *Adolescence*, which he read while in exile in Siberia, in 1855.[42] Starting
with *Humiliated and Insulted* (1861), Dostoevsky made several references in
print to Tolstoy's trilogy. Tolstoy's pedagogical activities also received
positive reviews in the journals *Time* and *Epoch* published by Fyodor and
Mikhail Dostoevsky. It was not only literary rivalry, but also a sense of
a shared responsibility for Russia's future during the stormy Reforms Age
that drew Tolstoy and Dostoevsky to similar topics.

Thus, as attested by Konstantin Mochulsky, in 1863–4 Dostoevsky
commenced work on a Bildungsroman along the lines of *Wilhelm*

*Meister's Apprenticeship* though focused on a quintessentially Russian hero.[43] This suggestion flies in the face of Bakhtin's attempt to draw a distinction between Dostoevsky's polyphonic novel and the Goethean tradition. In *Problems of Dostoevsky's Poetics* Bakhtin suggested that Dostoevsky 'saw and conceived his world in terms of space, not time', and therefore the Bildungsroman form was alien to him.[44] At the same time, Bakhtin's plan for the Bildungsroman study does list Dostoevsky among Russian authors who contributed to this genre. This apparent inconsistency not only reveals the incompleteness of Bakhtin's theory, but also alerts us to some contradictory tendencies within Dostoevsky's oeuvre.

Unable to complete his Küntslerroman *Netochka Nezvanova*, Dostoevsky returned to the themes of childhood and education through-out his post-Siberian career. At the same time, Bakhtin was right to emphasise Dostoevsky's aversion to the kind of novel of education that portrays psychological maturation as a gradual reconciliation with the status quo. With minds resembling intellectually dense, polemically aggressive 'thick journals', many of Dostoevsky's heroes perpetually 'tarry with the negative', often in ways that preclude psychological growth. A case in point is the hero of *The Notes from the Underground* (1864). Dostoevsky undoubtedly sympathised with this naysayer. But, contra Lev Shestov, we should not identify the Underground Man's world view with Dostoevsky's.[45] Shestov distinguished between the early humanistic Dostoevsky and the Dostoevsky who emerged after the Siberian ordeal. Bakhtin to some degree shares this view. Meanwhile, late Dostoevsky's creative projects and non-fictional work, including his speech at the Pushkin Festival, testify to his ongoing – or newly rediscovered – attach-ment to such Enlightenment ideals as moral self-perfection and reconcilia-tion among different nations and cultures.

As evidenced by Dostoevsky's notebooks, throughout the 1870s he had been planning a large-scale epic entitled *The Life of a Great Sinner*. Although this work remained unwritten, Dostoevsky's last four novels – *The Idiot* (1869), *The Devils* (1872), *The Adolescent* (1875) and *The Brothers Karamazov* (1880) – all bear the impress of this project focused on a Russian hero who ultimately attains spiritual regeneration. Among these works, *The Adolescent* stands out as the most intensely plotted and intellectually dense work. This novel may be regarded as a preliminary sketch to a more ambitious project that would bring together and reconcile the epic, the Bildungsroman and the Russian hagiographic traditions.

*The Adolescent* describes Russia's regeneration during the Reforms age as a twofold dialectic: first, the reconciliation between the Russian intellectuals of the 'Petersburg period' (represented by the gentleman named Versilov who was widely believed to have been modelled on Herzen) and the *raznochintsy* ('people of various ranks' represented by Versilov's illegitimate son Arkadii Dolgorukii); and second, the reconciliation between the intellectuals and the people (represented by Arkadii's mother Sophia and her husband, a saintly elder Makar Dolgorukii). The son of a gentleman and a peasant, Arkadii represents Dostoevsky's riposte to Tolstoy's Pierre Bezukhov. Despite his respect for Tolstoy's novel, Dostoevsky believed that *War and Peace* failed to transcend the horizon of the gentry and therefore could not be regarded as a national narrative. Dostoevsky's plan was to show the education of his hero as a somewhat chaotic or 'accidental' process that allows him to confront various social strata and partake of Russia's social and moral 'disintegration'. Raised in a residential school for children of the aristocracy, he later becomes involved with gamblers, schemers and terrorists. Arkadii's successful overcoming of these ordeals symbolised Russia's re-emergence from the current crisis.[46]

The main obstacle preventing Arkadii from becoming a happy and integral personality is his resentment towards Versilov. As a lonely child despised by his aristocratic classmates, Arkadii developed an *idée fixe* of becoming '"as rich as Rothschild"'. He desired wealth not in order to enjoy life, but in order to feel himself superior to others, and above all, to Versilov. To liberate himself from this spiritual 'underground', Arkadii first had to understand and forgive Versilov and develop a genuine respect and appreciation for his humble mother. One of the novel's central episodes depicts an encounter between the seventeen-year-old Arkadii and Versilov, who, having just returned from his travels in Europe, seeks reconciliation with his homeland and the illegitimate family he had abandoned there. In the course of this dialogue Versilov opens his heart and asks his son's forgiveness. But Versilov's confession alone cannot transform his alienated and embittered 'bastard' into a loving son. The main catalyst of Arkadii's regeneration is Makar Dolgorukii. To emphasise the innate moral beauty and magnanimity of this peasant, Dostoevsky gives him the name of an illustrious princely family. Returning from one of his many pilgrimages, Makar meets his end at Sophia's home. But before his death he imparts his ideal of *blagoobrazie* to Arkadii. The term *blagoobrazie*, which combines *blago* ('the good') with *obraz* ('the image'), implies ethical and aesthetic perfection. It echoes the Greek term *kalokagathia*. That Dostoevsky would attempt to find a Russian equivalent for *kalokagathia* comes as no surprise, considering his profound indebtedness to Schiller's idea of aesthetic education. Much like a Schiller play, his novel dramatises the spiritual dialectics of his conflict-ridden heroes. *Blagoobrazie* is also synonymous with the perfection of Christ, whereas its opposite, *bezobrazie* (literally, 'imagelessness'; or 'ugliness'), stands for atheism or nihilism. Versilov's drama reaches its climax when he violently dashes the *obraz* ('icon') to the ground. After this outburst he collapses and Arkadii assumes full responsibility for the family, including Versilov, Sophia, Arkadii's sister Liza and her illegitimate child.

## The End of Empire and the Revolution

The sense of harmony which prevails at the conclusion to *The Adolescent* brings to mind the idea of 'universal sympathy' developed in Dostoevsky's Pushkin speech.[47] 'If everyone followed Christ's example and learnt to understand and forgive everyone else, would not Paradise immediately come to be established on Earth?', asks Dostoevsky in one of his notebooks.[48] Dostoevsky's work on a diptych, in which his vision of universal reconciliation would find its ultimate expression (of which only the first part, *The Brothers Karamazov*, was completed), was cut short by his death on February 9, 1881.[49] The assassination of Alexander II on March 13, 1881 ushered in an era of strife and terror, which was to surpass even the darkest of Dostoevsky's visions. The need for both reform and redemption was never felt more acutely than during the reign of Alexander III, which witnessed the emergence of organised political movements and parties and the rise of decadence in literature and the arts, the increasing popularity of mysticism, theosophy and the occult. Tolstoy's activities as a religious reformer during this period testify to his continual attachment to the ideal of self-perfection, which he formulated in terms approaching contemporary neo-idealism and Solov'ev's theory of God-manhood. Breaking his vow to cease writing novels on the characters populating high-society milieus, Tolstoy took up Dostoevsky's challenge to break free from the long tradition of 'negativity' and portray a positive hero in *Resurrection* (1899).

Tolstoy's final novel focuses on the spiritual regeneration of Prince Dmitry Nekhliudov who realises that he has lived a life of error. His fall began when committing his first crime: he seduced and abandoned an orphan girl, Katiusha Maslova, who turned to prostitution thereafter. Some years later, serving as a jury member on a murder trial, he recognises Katiusha as the prostitute falsely accused of murdering a client. He resolves to atone for his crime by marrying Katiusha and following her to Siberia. However, Katiusha refuses to accept Nekhliudov's sacrifice. She rejects his proposal and eventually marries a political prisoner, Simonson. 'We need nothing,' she says to Nekhliudov, using a plural pronoun to emphasise both her peasant origins and her sense of being part of a new community – that of the spiritually unbroken sufferers.[50]

Rejected by Katiusha, Nekhliudov nevertheless breaks his engagement to a wealthy aristocrat and travels to Siberia where he begins a new life among revolutionaries, ordinary prisoners and religious sectarians. Nekhliudov's pride gradually softens as he develops a genuine attachment to the community of prisoners. As Tolstoy wrote in 1906, 'a spiritual being knows no passion or desire and is therefore conscious of its unity with everything'.[51] Tolstoy calls this spiritual form of being 'love' and interprets it as synonymous with immortality.

Although Russia was not exempt from the exigencies surrounding the novel and the general crisis of *fin de siècle* European culture, its robust tradition of realism carried over to the twentieth century. But instead of utopia, the heirs of the nineteenth-century realists confronted an increasingly polarised reality marked by intolerance and bitter strife. The Bolshevik Revolution of 1917 forced members of the intelligentsia to make their political and ideological choices in ways that entailed existential consequences. The times did not favour those who engaged in protracted self-analysis, but rather those who knew how to adapt to rapid changes. The works which most closely adhere to the nineteenth-century coming-of-age narrative, such as Ivan Bunin's *Life of Arsen'ev* (1933; 39), Maxim Gorky's *Life of Klim Samgin* (1927–36), Mikhail Bulgakov's *The White Guard* (1924) and Pasternak's *Doctor Zhivago* (1957), were all conceived in the early post-revolutionary years. All four narratives are to some extent autobiographical and illustrate different paths that Russian intellectuals were able to follow after 1917.

Written in France, where Bunin had been living since 1920, *The Life of Arsen'ev* is an elegiac tribute to the tradition of Goncharov and Turgenev, the story of an impoverished young gentleman determined to become an artist amidst the economic and political turmoil of the 1900s. Like a typical Romantic Künstlerroman, Arsen'ev's story remains unfinished and his character 'unfinalised' (in Bakhtin's sense of the term).[52]

Unlike Bunin, who came from a family of age-old gentry, Gorky was born to half-literate artisans. His autobiographical trilogy *Childhood* (1913–14), *In the World* (1916) and *My Universities* (1923) describes his difficult childhood in his grandparents' home (he was orphaned at eleven) and as a vagabond and underage worker throughout the Volga region. The protagonist in *The Life of Klim Samgin* (1925–36), unlike the author, comes from an educated family. As a university student he comes into contact with revolutionaries and becomes interested in their ideas. Although over the course of the novel Klim is often portrayed as a sympathetic character, Gorky claimed that his novel was conceived as a *roman-à-thèse* intended to unmask the intellectual and spiritual impotence of the liberal intelligentsia. This long and meandering narrative, which depicts the hero wavering between liberal bourgeoisie and revolutionary democrats, between Russia and Europe, and never reaching a decisive end, reveals Gorky's own tortuous *Bildung*. Passing through various stages, including God-building and Marxism, the author returned to the Soviet Union where he became a leader of the Writers' Union and a doyen of socialist realism.

Once socialist realism became established as the official ideology of Soviet culture, Gorky's 1907 novel *Mother* was proclaimed one of the pioneering works in this style. As Katerina Clark has observed, the novel, which pivots on two working-class people turned revolutionary heroes, Pavel Vlasov and his mother, Nilovna, exhibits features reminiscent of the Bildungsroman, where the mother is the person being 'formed'.[53] While Pavel is modelled on recognisable revolutionary martyr figures such as Rakhmetov from Chernyshevsky's *What Is to Be Done?* and Andrei Kozhukov from Stepniak-Kravchinskii's eponymous novel, Nilovna is Gorky's invention. Over the course of the story this downtrodden woman develops a self- and class-consciousness and after her son's arrest replaces him as an organiser of a revolutionary group. But Nilovna's final incarnation has already been determined when she begins her formation. She does not evolve freely, but rather assumes the likeness her son had assumed before her (Clark, 57).

## The Bildungsroman in the Soviet Period

Although Bakhtin had planned to include a chapter on Gorky in his Bildungsroman study, both *Mother* and the novels he wrote upon his return to the Soviet Union in compliance with the party's ideological agenda project very dogmatic, positive heroes. Thus, they fall short of the Bakhtinian idea of a Bildungsroman hero as an emerging individual confronting an ever-evolving historical reality. It is conceivable that in the menacing atmosphere of the late 1930s Bakhtin contemplated a compromise that would reconcile his theory with Lukács's conception of the epic as narrative told from the standpoint of a realised Marxist utopia. But the disappearance of the completed part of the Bildungsroman manuscript frees us from the need to apologise on Bakhtin's behalf. In his published work the scholar is faithful to a conception of art as vehicle of self-understanding that cannot assume the role of a handmaiden to a preformed ideology.

In my discussion I do not include those Soviet novels which follow formulaic plots and narrate the education of heroic workers, doctors, aviators, etc. in the manner far more common to hagiography than to the Bildungsroman. Instead, I would like to focus on two works that reflect scepticism vis-à-vis Soviet ideology: *Master and Margarita* (1940) by Mikhail Bulgakov and *Doctor Zhivago* by Boris Pasternak. Having little hope of being allowed to publish these works in their native country, Bulgakov and Pasternak addressed themselves to posterity.[54] Both novels display rich 'intertextuality' and can be seen as examples of 'genre hybridity'. However, in both texts one can discern a dominant genre, to which other genre and stylistic elements are subordinated. This dominant genre is the Romantic Künstlerroman, a variety of the Bildungsroman, which depicts the emergence of a free-spirited artist.

Bulgakov's novel satirises the spiritual emptiness of Soviet society of the New Economic Policy period and yearns for faith, heroism and Romantic love. One of the main plotlines focuses on the composition, destruction and miraculous retrieval of a novel about Pontius Pilate. The author of this novel is a historian whose real name is never revealed. His beloved Margarita calls him 'the Master' (alluding to Goethe's famous Bildungsroman). The Master's novel describes Pilate's remorse upon the execution of Jesus (Ieshua Ga-Notsri) and his eventual conversion. Harassed by Soviet critics, the Master loses confidence in his work and retreats to a psychiatric asylum. The devil himself must intervene to rescue the Master's work, which focuses on an age-long debate between good and evil. Woland's appearance in Moscow not only adds a dimension of phantasmagoria to a realistic social satire, but transposes a work of fiction into a philosophical theodicy.

Woland and his retinue wreak havoc in the Soviet capital, seeking to awaken the Muscovites from their 'dogmatic slumber' and shatter their materialistic world view. Confronted with Woland's supernatural powers, a young proletarian poet Ivan Ponyrev (whose pseudonym 'Bezdomny' means 'Homeless') proves naive enough to believe his eyes rather than the precepts of his atheistic ideology. He reacts by behaving like a madman and ends up being confined to a psychiatric establishment – the same one where the Master has found refuge from reality. Thus, a writer of an older generation, shaped by pre-revolutionary classical education, gets a chance to impart his wisdom to a working-class poet.

At the end of the novel the Master and his faithful beloved are granted their wish to be freed from a world that has been so cruel to them. Woland's servant Azazello gives them a special poison and then takes their souls to a place of eternal rest that resembles Dante's Limbo. At the same time, the Master's hero Pilate, who has spent almost two thousand years in the Limbo, is forgiven and allowed to ascend to heaven where Ieshua awaits him. Like the ending of Goethe's *Faust*, this ending resolves the debate on the meaning of good and evil in favour of a Christian theodicy. Meanwhile, Ponyrev, whom the departing Master named his 'disciple', gives up poetry and becomes a scholar of history and philosophy. This transformation suggests that Ivan, who has grown more self-reflective and resistant to ideology, will be able to continue the Master's research into the lives of a mysterious Jewish 'philosopher' who claimed to know the Truth and his Roman executioner tormented by doubts. It is noteworthy that Pilate's remorse and conversion are described as part of the Master's dream, which gets realised before his eyes on Woland's orders. But assuming that the Master's bequest to his disciple is to engage in further inquiry rather than retell the story the Master had composed, we cannot be sure that the story he writes will have the same ending.

Published in Italy in 1957, *Doctor Zhivago* has been revered as testimony to the resilience of the human spirit in the age of totalitarianism.[55] For Pasternak, who completed his doctorate in philosophy under Hermann Cohen before deciding to embark on a literary career, freedom as self-determination remained the guiding idea throughout his life. A great deal has been written about Pasternak's indebtedness to Tolstoy, Dostoevsky and other giants of Russian literature, as well as to Shakespeare and Goethe, both of whom Pasternak translated into Russian. Linking *Doctor Zhivago* to the Bildungsroman tradition, however, may still appear controversial to those accustomed to seeing the Bildungsroman as a coming-of-age narrative. The story of Yurii Zhivago covers his entire life and even transcends it. Spanning Russian history from the revolution of 1905 to the end of Stalinism (the novel's epilogue ends in 1953) and encompassing stories of multiple families and individuals from all social strata, outwardly Pasternak's novel resembles an epic. Upon closer scrutiny, however, Zhivago's story does not fit into the pattern of an epic hero's life. The protagonist, whose last name is etymologically related to the word 'life' (*zhizn*), dies prematurely from a heart attack. His character, however, is never 'finalised', because his rich inwardness outstrips the confines of a biographical novel or epic. Zhivago is survived by his poems (which form the final part of the novel), as well as by several friends who continue to reflect on the meaning of Zhivago's poetry and life long after he is dead. Preserved in the memories and souls of others, Zhivago's life takes on the aspect of immortality in the sense Pasternak assigns to this idea. In *Doctor Zhivago* one of the main spokesmen for Pasternak-the-philosopher is Vedeniapin, whose position, stated in part two, is openly characterised as a newly reinterpreted Christianity which links the idea of history to humanity's struggle to overcome death. According to Vedeniapin (whose name echoes the old-fashioned term *vedenie*, 'knowledge'), human beings are building a new universe in which death will no longer command the same power it had over the natural world before the emergence of human consciousness and creativity.

Zhivago participates in this unfolding of truth by becoming a natural scientist and artist who refuses to make concessions to the increasingly dictatorial Bolshevik ideology. Throughout the novel Zhivago's views on history and life are juxtaposed to the ideas expounded by the emissaries of the revolution, including Lara's husband Antipov-Strel'nikov, the partisan leader Liverii Mikulitsyn and several others. These representatives of the 'vanguard' throw themselves into the crucible because they believe in the inevitable victory of the proletariat and the coming utopia. Zhivago finds their mechanistic understanding of history both false and destructive. But instead of actively opposing them or seeking to escape to Europe (like the rest of his family), he is forever in search of a tranquil life bordering on quietism. How can we understand Zhivago's willingness to endure a life of privation and insecurity? Perhaps it can be linked to his commitment to art, which he understands not only through the prism of his uncle's philosophy (i.e. as the rewriting of the *Book of Revelation*), but also as linked to his scientific studies. It is not by chance that Zhivago's dissertation in medicine dealt with the physiology of the eye. A student of Goethe and Schelling, Pasternak imparted to his hero a deep appreciation for their *Naturphilosophie*. It underlies Zhivago's self-understanding as being part and parcel of a human organism whose sufferings he must express poetically. The connection between Christianity and the Romantic conception of art – more specifically, Schelling's conception of tragedy – comes across most forcefully in the first poem from the cycle attributed to Zhivago, 'Hamlet'. It projects the lyric poet into the persona of an actor who plays the role of Hamlet. Facing the audience whilst contemplating the difficult role he is about to play, the hero of the poem pleads with his 'Father' to spare him this bitter cup. Hamlet, whom Romantic critics had read as a quintessentially reflective hero capable of philosophical insight but incapable of action, is here reinterpreted as a Christian hero preparing for suffering in order to show humans the road to freedom.

Intellectually dense and epic in its scope, *Doctor Zhivago* bridged different ages of Russian and Soviet culture through an aesthetic whole that projected a sense of meaningfulness and totality onto a world of bitter conflicts, ruptures and losses. In a way, Pasternak's Künstlerroman offered a closure to an epoch of Russian intellectual and cultural history that was inspired by such Enlightenment ideals as moral self-perfection, autonomy and creativity. This is not to say that these ideals completely disappeared from the Soviet literature of the post-World War II period. But the traumas of the war and of Stalinist terror, combined with an increasing awareness of the vulnerability of our species brought on by the nuclear arms race, began to undermine humanistic faith that underlay the Bildungsroman tradition. Vassily Grossman's epic novel *Life and Fate*, which was finished in 1959, but remained unpublished until 1980, is the most powerful indictment of the civilisation which produced both Fascism and Stalinism, two monstrous distortions of the Enlightenment-inspired quest for perfectibility. Grossman indicts both Christian and more recent secular humanism for substituting genuine humanness with an abstract ideal of the good. Nevertheless, *Life and Fate* shows that even in the midst of war humanity survives through individual and sporadic acts of kindness. This kindness is something elementary and ingrained in our nature. It requires no special education. Thus, in a sense, Grossman's novel can be read as a critique of the ideology of Bildung as education through culture.

Stalin's death and the de-Stalinisation campaign announced by Khruschev provided a new impetus for the development of Soviet literature in the second half of the 1950s and 1960s. Upon Khruschev's policy of revivifying the cultural institutions that had lain dormant under Stalin, the Soviet Writers' Union held its second congress (which should have been held in 1937 had the Union abided by its charter) in 1954. The author of *The Thaw* (1956), the novel whose title gave the name to the post-Stalinist cultural renaissance, Ilya Ehrenburg delivered a fiery speech denouncing dogmatic socialist realism, which he compared to children's literature.[56] Genuine realists, argued Ehrenburg, should not eschew a critical confrontation with the surrounding reality. At the same time, Ehrenburg reconfirmed his allegiance to the Communist party, whose policy was supposed to lead to the triumph of humanism. Only communism would enable the development of genuine humanness and individuality, as opposed to self-ish individualism cultivated in the capitalist countries of the West. The task of the Soviet writers in the wake of Stalinism was to recover their creative vitality and freedom of thought and to devote their energies to the construction of a communist future.

In the wake of the second congress, the Writers' Union expanded its repertoire of monthly journals. In 1955 *Youth*, and in 1956 *The Young Guard* were opened with the specific aim of offering new outlets for young authors who were expected to bring a breath of fresh air into Soviet literature. This initiative led to the resurgence of interest in the coming-of-age narratives and family novels focusing on the conflicts between different generations. The generation of the fathers who had survived Stalinism was to stand trial by their sons and daughters who were eager to emancipate themselves from the Stalinist legacy of universal suspicion and Terror. At the same time, when reading novels from this period we should bear in mind that the seeming liberalisation and revitalisation of the public sphere was only one aspect of a sweeping ideological campaign launched by the Party in 1954. Surveillance and punishment were the other side of the coin. The Party and the Komsomol (its junior branch) paid extensive attention to the way the young people spent their free time, subjecting those who behaved in an 'uncultured' or socially subversive way to severe censure. Playing and listening to jazz (and later rock music), wearing stylish clothes that followed Western fashions, using slang, and other nonconformist behaviours were deemed morally suspect and could even lead to one's expulsion from university. Only those authors who were able to negotiate a compromise between free creativity and the cultural norms approved by the Party could build successful careers. It is under these circumstances that Andrei Siniavskii, Naum Korzhavin, Joseph Brodsky, Vladimir Voinovich, Georgii Vladimov, Vassilii Aksyonov and Andrei Bitov entered professional literature. Two of these authors, Aksionov and Bitov, first established their reputations by publishing narratives that approached such classic Bildungsroman themes as self-understanding and the quest for a meaningful and fulfilling life from the point of view of a transforming environment where a tendency towards liberalisation went hand in hand with suspicion and craving for approval by the authorities.

The problem of defining the purpose of one's life is at the centre of Aksyonov's 1961 novel *A Ticket to the Stars*. Published in *Youth*, this novel immediately became a sensation not only because it portrayed sympathetically a disaffected seventeen-year-old hero, but also because of its conventional form and language. The narrator's perspective in this novel oscillates between two brothers: a twenty-eight-year-old Viktor, who is finishing his dissertation in a strategically important branch of life sciences, and his seventeen-year-old brother Dimka, a rebel against the status quo who uses slang, wears Western-style clothes and, upon graduating from high school, elopes with a group of friends to Estonia instead of studying for the university entrance examinations. The parents of Viktor and Dimka belong to the Soviet intelligentsia and are completely loyal to the state. They believe that a successful academic career is the only way to get on in life – or, as they put it, 'to become a person' (*stat' chelovekom*). Their elder son follows this track and makes an important scientific discovery, but his career suffers a setback after he publicly presents the results of his research, which contradict the findings of a world-famous scientist who works at the same institute. The defence of Viktor's dissertation gets postponed for an unspecified period of time. Frustrated by this obstacle in his career, the hero gets married and brings his young wife to his parents' shabby apartment, intending to start a new family there. Meanwhile, Dimka is working as a fisherman in Estonia, the most Western republic within the USSR. The older brother visits him there, trying to convince him not to give up his chances to get a higher education. This is the last time the brothers see each other, because the plane on which Viktor leaves Tallinn crashes. Dimka attends Viktor's funeral, at which his former dissertation supervisor and other scientists give moving speeches. Maligned during his life, Viktor is posthumously canonised as a martyr for science and a true Communist. Will the rebellious younger brother stay at home and repeat his brother's path, or will he find his own way to become a full-fledged personality? In the closing scene of the novel we find Dimka on the windowsill where Victor had used to lie in his free time gazing at the stars. As both Viktor and Dimka have observed, a star-spangled piece of the sky visible from this vantage resembles a train ticket. The novel ends with the hero wondering, 'But to what destination will this ticket take me?'[57]

If in *A Ticket to the Stars* the intelligentsia's values are regarded with gentle irony, in Bitov's *Pushkin House* both the classical Russian humanism and Soviet intelligentsia that claimed to be its legatee are subjected to a thoroughgoing re-evaluation. It is noteworthy that this novel, completed in 1971, was rejected by Soviet publishers as an excessively 'subjective' work.[58] The charges levelled against Bitov by the publishing officials harked back to Hegel's critique of Romanticism. Focused mainly on the inner life of a young philologist of princely origin, Lyova Odoevtsev, who happens to be a descendant of one of the Decembrists, the novel pays homage to the Romantic age both thematically and formally. Thus, Lyova grows up surrounded by the myths of the Decembrists, Pushkin and other noble figures from the past. As a teenager, he discovers that back in the 1930s his father had betrayed his own father in order to obtain his university chair. An encounter with his grandfather, who survived the Gulag, propels Lyova's identity crisis. The narrative begins to oscillate between different points of view, constantly multiplying perspectives and inviting new interpretations of each fact or event. The author frequently interrupts his narrative in a manner reminiscent of 'Romantic irony'. Thus, he emphasises the unreliability of the protagonist's interpretation of reality.

The central intrigue revolves around an erotic rivalry between Lyova and Mitishat'ev, both of whom are interested in the same woman. An anti-Semite with an 'underground man' complex, Mitishat'ev is jealous of Lyova's illustrious name and talent. He teases Lyova and insults everyone he respects (including a Jewish senior colleague and the woman Lyova loves) until the hero can no longer contain his anger.[59] First they fight with their fists like ordinary hooligans. But for Lyova, raised as he is on classical literature, a fight can only have an ideological significance when it is stylised as a Romantic duel. To defend his humanistic values, he challenges Mitishat'ev to a duel, which they proceed to fight with museum pistols. Mitishat'ev fires and Odoevtsev falls down. At this point the author enters the story, offering two conclusions. In one of them Lyova, like Pushkin, is killed by an ignoble opponent. In the other version he survives, cleans up the mess in the museum and next day returns to work and gives a tour of Leningrad to an American writer. The author offers three different epilogues. This *mise en abyme* reveals the difficulty of finding a proper way to extricate the hero from the outmoded and somewhat narcissistic role of a 'beautiful soul'. Trained as a philologist, Lyova Odoevtsev seems a captive of a past whose ideals and values, albeit still respectable, can no longer endow one's life with a genuine purpose. But how can someone raised in an ivory tower assert himself outside of the protected space of a literary museum? The appendix entitled 'Achilles and the Tortoise (The Relationship between Hero and Author)' reveals Bitov's indebtedness to Bakhtin (who also served as a prototype for Odoevtsev's grandfather). If we interpret *Pushkin House* in the terms of Bakhtin's early work on narrative theory, we realise that this text is in fact autobiographical. The author possesses no 'surplus of vision' and therefore cannot 'finalise' the hero, a Romantic truth-seeker whose nostalgia for the heroic past conceals an aversion to the present and an anxiety about the future.

The author's dissatisfaction with his own age and uneasiness about the future are quite understandable, bearing in mind that *Pushkin House* was completed during the so-called stagnation period, when the country's economic backwardness and cultural isolation could no longer be excused or masked by optimistic slogans. This was also the time when censorship, which was somewhat relaxed under Khruschev, became as strict as it had been before the Thaw. Those authors who dared to reveal their frustration with the reigning ideology were either silenced or ignored. Some of them, including Aksyonov, Vladimov and Solzhenitsyn, emigrated (either willingly or by force). Others stayed behind and continued to write with only a glimmer of hope of ever seeing their works published. Still others sought ways to compromise with the regime by avoiding topics of political significance and concentrating on daily lives of ordinary people. The 1970s and 1980s witnessed a resurgence of interest in science fiction, fantasy, the short story and lyric poetry. This period also witnessed the heyday of the 'village prose'. Vassilii Shukshin, Valentin Rasputin and other authors whose provincial and rural origins made them outsiders vis-à-vis the urban intelligentsia gave a new impetus to prose fiction by rekindling an interest in the countryside. Sentimental or Romantic at their core, these authors represented the village community as a precious wellspring of organic creativity threatened by urbanisation. The village prose signalled a definite impasse in modernity with its confidence in historical change and progress and therefore presented an antithesis to the Bildungsroman.

The decline of the Bildungsroman in the last two decades of Soviet history was symptomatic of a larger crisis in a society that was about to implode. Throughout its two-hundred-year history this genre, which had emerged alongside Romantic historicism, remained concerned with the inner lives of individuals who saw themselves not as mere playthings of history, but rather as its agents. With the loss of faith in traditional Marxism this Romantic humanism was also beginning to lose its credibility. The advent of postmodernism constituted a response to this crisis. However, as evidenced by Bitov's *Pushkin House*, the scepticism and irony characteristic of postmodernity are not necessarily nihilistic, but can engender creative exuberance. And out of this sheer playfulness new forms of vision and humane awareness can emerge. Thus, when the hero of this novel collapses in a fight with a hooligan we witness the demise of an old-fashioned Romantic humanist, but the playful author resurrects Lyova and endows his consciousness with a host of contradictory feelings. Different voices resound in his mind and he seems ready to rush in several directions at once. Overwhelmed, he feels that he is turning both into the statue of Peter the Great (the so-called Bronze Horseman) and into Pushkin's unfortunate hero, Evgenii.[60] The monolithic classical hero dissolves in front of our eyes, as the linear narrative of maturation is interrupted and transformed into a polyphonic multiverse populated by hosts of different 'heroes' and 'authors', each with their own vision of reality.

In the wake of Bitov's work other Russian postmodernists took turns at deconstructing the Bildungsroman and its more dogmatic Marxism-inspired offshoot, the socialist realist novel. Thus, Victor Pelevin's debut novel *Omon Ra* (1992) masterfully parodies Ostrovskii's *How the Steel Was Forged* and other didactic novels of emergence.[61] In the course of the narrative Pelevin's hero, the young pilot Omon Krivomazov, gets disabused of his illusions about the superiority of his country and its space programme which he wishes to join. As his mind becomes more and more independent from the dogmas he has been fed since childhood, his consciousness is opened to another reality, one that he first discovers through meditation when looking at the starry skies. Pelevin's postmodern hero taps into Nirvana. This discovery saves him from despair or madness, providing an escape from the historical reality in which he feels trapped. Freed from the constraints of time and space, the hero's consciousness ascends to a higher realm. The title of the novel, which alludes to the Egyptian sun god Ra, suggests that the hero reaches the ultimate stages of illumination. Thus Omon Ra completes the quest for enlightenment upon which Russian authors and their heroes embarked at the end of the eighteenth century.

# CHAPTER 5

# The American Bildungsroman

## Sarah Graham

An adolescent on the journey to maturity is a perfect metaphor for the United States: young, adventurous and optimistic.[1] This accounts for the enormous popularity of the Bildungsroman, with its central motif of personal transformation, amongst American writers and readers.[2] Cherished examples of the genre, such as Horatio Alger's *Ragged Dick* (1868) and Louisa May Alcott's *Little Women* (1868/69), affirm the nation's founding promises through the achievements of their protagonists. The emphasis on 'life, liberty and the pursuit of happiness' established by the Declaration of Independence (1776) and the image of the USA as the 'land of the free and the home of the brave', enshrined in its national anthem, 'The Star-Spangled Banner' (1814), are embodied in protagonists who overcome obstacles to achieve triumphant self-realisation.[3] Their victories affirm the validity of the 'American Dream', which holds that all citizens can improve their circumstances, however deprived their origin, and a sense of connection to the nation is reinforced by the Pledge of Allegiance (1892).[4] Frequently reiterated by politicians – in 2009, President Barack Obama asserted, 'We remain a young nation ... Our capacity remains undiminished' – entrenched beliefs such as these inform many classic American Bildungsromane.[5]

Yet America's image as youthful has also been understood in negative terms. Writing during the post-war boom in teenage culture, literary critic Frederic Carpenter commented on America's 'adolescent civilisation, with both its mixed-up confusion and its splendid potentiality'.[6] It is fitting, given this ambivalence, that American novelists have used the Bildungsroman more than any other genre to expose the nation's shortcomings. Despite the assurances embedded in America's doctrines, the protagonists of many well-known Bildungsromane express dissatisfaction with it. A turbulent history of civil and international wars, slavery, migration, economic decline, and inequalities of class, race and gender contest the dependability of its ideologies. The young heroes and heroines of

American Bildungsromane repeatedly find that the past, whether individual, familial or national, weighs heavily upon them, and they see little in the adult world to encourage them in optimism about the future. Their disquiet about growing up and the disillusionment that often results from their journey to maturity signifies wider anxieties about the nation's prospects and principles.

The majority of studies of the American Bildungsroman focus on specific identity groups, reflecting the country's diversity.[7] This chapter approaches the subject differently, seeing the genre as divided into two strands: in the first strand, the novels affirm the conventional American ethos, which is exemplified in the work of Horatio Alger; in the other strand, the novels question those same values and beliefs. This chapter focuses on this second strand, discussing texts published since the mid-nineteenth century and evident across subsequent decades to the present, revealing a literary heritage of the Bildungsroman being employed to critique American society. It begins by comparing the US Bildungsroman to the European tradition and considers why the genre figures so largely in American culture. It then discusses Bildungsromane about white working-class male youth, the social group most likely to see itself as the potential beneficiaries of America's promises of prosperity and happiness in exchange for labour and commitment to the nation. Alger's idealistic *Ragged Dick* is contrasted with later Bildungsromane, which repeatedly call American beliefs into question. Mark Twain's *Adventures of Huckleberry Finn* (1884) interrogates the morality of slavery, while Stephen Crane's *The Red Badge of Courage* (1895) queries the ethics of war. Jack London's *Martin Eden* (1909) raises doubts about class mobility, and John Steinbeck's *The Red Pony* (1937) exposes the impact of rural poverty. The analysis then turns to more recent depictions of disadvantaged adolescent boys, such as Larry McMurtry's *The Last Picture Show* (1966), Cormac McCarthy's *All the Pretty Horses* (1992) and Philipp Meyer's *American Rust* (2009), which all depict the realities of living in modern America for the poor. McMurtry's and McCarthy's texts are both set just after the end of the Second World War: the dismal lives of the protagonists undermine the positive image of that era and of the periods in which they were published. Meyer's novel, set in the early twenty-first century, focuses on the social crisis of industrial decline at a time when political attention was directed towards external threats. In these Bildungsromane, economic gain is neither available to all nor lasting, and the characters' sense of dispossession mirrors that of many Americans who cannot realise their dreams.

The next section focuses on Bildungsromane about girls, who grow up aware of the nation's promises but come to feel excluded by their gender. This part of the chapter looks at representations of white working-class girls, such as *Bastard out of Carolina* (1992) by Dorothy Allison, and depictions of middle- and upper-class girls, who might be expected to enjoy a greater level of opportunity. These include *What Maisie Knew* (1897) by Henry James, Edith Wharton's *Summer* (1916), Harper Lee's *To Kill a Mockingbird* (1960) and Sylvia Plath's *The Bell Jar* (1963), all of which express a specifically female sense of disenchantment with American society. Bildungsromane about Americans whose sense of social marginality is even stronger than that of white girls are considered in the last section, which examines texts that focus on African Americans, Native Americans, Jewish Americans and LGBTQ+ Americans. These representations of ethnic, racial, cultural and sexual difference not only reflect the hostility such groups endure, but also convey the protagonists' response to a dominant order that excludes and represses them. In closing, the chapter examines the best-known American Bildungsroman of the twentieth century, J. D. Salinger's *The Catcher in the Rye* (1951), to show that even white, affluent male youth, the group most likely to support the nation that has endowed it with privilege, is driven to critique American society. In sum, key novels depicting the movement from youth to maturity frequently express pessimism, disillusionment, anger and resistance to the American story of progress and success that conventional Bildungsromane endorse.

### The American Bildungsroman and the European Tradition

After US independence, American culture strove to free itself of European influence. This heritage, evident in early literature by writers like Washington Irving and Edgar Allan Poe, was supplanted from the mid-nineteenth century onward by a focus on the emerging nation, as seen in the work of such authors as Nathaniel Hawthorne and Herman Melville. The American Bildungsroman emerges in this same period because, as Kenneth Millard observes, young protagonists are paradigmatic of the nation: 'the figurative language of adolescence [is used] to describe the New World's emergent autonomy as a colony ... independent of Old World habits'.[8] Even in the mid-twentieth century, critic Barton C. Friedberg connected the popularity of fiction about youth – which he termed 'the cult of adolescence' – to America's determination to be free of European influence, driven by its 'extreme individualism' and a 'spirit [that] has not been worn out and debased in a gigantic struggle against an old and overbearing cultural tradition'.[9] Given this desire for origin-ality, it is not surprising that the American version of the form differs in distinct ways from its European forebear, for example in its willingness to criticise society. This inclination is much less evident in the European Bildungsroman, from the text many critics see as foundational, *Wilhelm Meisters Lehrjahre* (1795–6) by Johann Wolfgang von Goethe, onward.[10] In his classic study of the European Bildungsroman, *The Way of the World* (1987), Franco Moretti argues that depictions of developing youth in the nineteenth century help their readers assimilate modernity.[11] In the American Bildungsroman, by contrast, the experiences of young protago-nists tend to heighten, rather than dispel, what Brigid Lowe terms 'the anxieties of a modern age', thereby calling the aspirations of the new nation into question.[12]

The American Bildungsroman further departs from the European tradi-tion in its teleological drive. A classic novel of development charts the progress of its young protagonist through trials of various kinds and concludes with an epiphany that brings insight. For Moretti, '[a] *Bildung* is truly such only if, at a certain point, it can be seen as *concluded*: only if youth passes into maturity, and comes there to a stop there [sic.]'.[13] Mikhail Bakhtin, in his influential essay on the Bildungsroman, also identifies evolution towards a definable point as vital to the genre: it traces the 'path of man's emergence from youthful idealism and fantasies to mature sobriety and practicality'.[14] A Bildungsroman, says Bakhtin, '[depicts] the world and life as *experience*, as a *school*, through which every person must pass', highlighting the centrality of education, as sug-gested by its German name ('bildung', education or formation; 'roman', novel).[15] This emphasis on conclusion and resolution is much less evident in the American version of the genre, indicating a preference for prolonged emerging over categorical endings: a process of *becoming*, rather than defined *being*. Although the European Bildungsroman does depict 'conflict between the ideal of *self-determination* and the equally imperious demands of *socialization*' (15), this typically ends in the protagonist's acquiescence to social norms, which signals entry into adulthood and an end to develop-ment. However, in many American Bildungsromane the protagonist's resistance to the established order is conveyed by a refusal to undertake the rituals that signify the end of youth, such as marriage or employment.

The attitude towards conformity expressed in many key American Bildungsromane reflects a tension between the nation's twin ideals of individualism and citizenship. In a conventional Bildungsroman, the protagonist's compliance with social standards is rewarded with material and social success. Moretti argues that in the European Bildungsroman, death – literal or metaphorical, such as exclusion from a community – is the only alternative to conformity, typically symbolised by marriage (22–3). In texts of this kind, therefore, the main characters are either married or dead at the narrative's close, a capitulation to the prevailing orthodoxy that limits the genre's capacity for social critique.[16] By contrast, in the American Bildungsroman, individualism is presented as a laudable quality not incompatible with national ideals: 'Trust thyself', Ralph Waldo Emerson counsels in his canonical essay, 'Self-Reliance' (1841), 'every heart vibrates to that iron string'.[17] The American version of the genre communicates the nation's image of itself as committed from its founding days to individualism and readiness to 'speak truth to power'.[18] Thus, protagonists frequently question and reject social norms and often choose marginality over convention, autonomy over accommodation.

The protagonist's capacity for social resistance and dissent in the American Bildungsroman evokes a deviation from the classical model that Moretti can locate in very few European texts, namely Alexander Pushkin's *Eugene Onegin* (1825–32) and Stendhal's *The Red and the Black* (1830). In these narratives, the heroes' lives are 'a sequence of battles, a sort of personal campaign' in which 'youth does not find its meaning in creating countless "connections" with the existing order, but in breaking them' (75). Rather than accepting the hegemonic order like most protagonists in the European tradition, these characters are alienated and resist socialisation. Moretti attributes the advent of this 'entirely new narrative form' (75) to the widespread conflict in Europe in the years of the French Revolutionary War and the Napoleonic era (1792–1815), suggesting that war can foster disillusionment.[19] Comparably, the United States is 'the child of world wars': conflict between Britain and France on American soil encouraged its founding, and it endured lengthy military campaigns around the turn of the nineteenth century, including the American Revolutionary War (1775–83), the Northwest Indian War (1785–93), and the War of 1812 (1812–15).[20] Indeed, there was rarely a day of peace from the establishment of the republic until the end of the Civil War (1861–5), which cost more lives than the combined American fatalities of both World Wars.[21] So, while Moretti believes that a few European Bildungsromane are influenced by war, which accounts for the heroes' sense of estrangement from society, in the American variety the impact of prolonged conflict manifests itself more widely. This is evident not only in characters whose conflicted state of mind mirrors the nation's involvement in civil and international warfare, but also in the antipathy many protagonists' feel for a society they perceive as callous and wasteful of young lives.

The American Bildungsroman shares with the European tradition a tendency towards nostalgia that affects the development of its protagonists. Lowe sees in 'Romantically inflected *Bildungsromane*' of mid-nineteenth century Europe adult characters who '[seek] to re-enter an Edenic childhood'.[22] This regressive impulse, fired by a sense of loss, is equally evident in American texts: rather than maturing, many young protagonists would rather return to their earlier life, often to reconnect with someone or something significant they lost as they matured. As Joan Didion observes, there is a recurring emphasis on threats to innocence in American culture: 'How many times can America lose its innocence? In my lifetime, we've heard that we've lost our innocence half a dozen times at least'.[23] Thus, protagonists in American Bildungsromane echo wider concerns about individuals, communities and the nation being imperilled by political trauma and social change: the assassination of leaders such as John F. Kennedy and Martin Luther King, the terrorist attacks of 9/11, greater sexual permissiveness, and increased gender and racial equality. The perception that childhood has a purity that is endangered by the process of growing up is evident in many Bildungsromane, in which the protagonists' fear of growing up and the depiction of adults as flawed and unreliable reinforces a connection between maturity and corruption.

## White Working-Class Boys

As in the European tradition of the genre, portrayals of young white men dominate the American Bildungsroman. However, in contrast to European Bildungsromane, in which the 'middle-class man' is the 'structural *sine qua non* of the genre', American novels of formation often depict working-class protagonists (Moretti ix). Moretti attributes this feature of the classic Bildungsroman to the static nature of class in Europe: the condition of the extremely poor or wealthy changes little, or very slowly, and it is only '"in the middle" [that] anything can happen – each individual can "make it" or "be broken" on his own' (248, note 5). The wider range of class positions in the American Bildungsroman not only implies a higher level of class mobility than in Europe, but seemingly also affirms the power of the American Dream and the assertion in the Declaration of Independence that 'all men are created equal' in the USA. While middle-class boys, who have already secured the benefits of living in the 'land of opportunity', might embrace society or at least feel safe in criticising it, working-class boys have far more reason to invest themselves in an ideology that offers liberty, happiness and prosperity. Nevertheless, male protagonists of all classes implicitly or explicitly censure American society, querying the validity of the pledges it makes to its citizens. With one exception, the novels discussed here show young white men as misguided in their commitment to the nation's ideals, let down by its hollow promises, or repelled by its values.

The fiction of nineteenth-century novelist Horatio Alger represents the American Bildungsroman in its most orthodox form. Its unswerving optimism and affirmation of the nation's promise mean that it 'remain[s] a shorthand for America itself and the opportunities it offered to all'.[24] Alger's poor, uneducated heroes are humble, cheerful adolescents, committed to correcting any 'faults and defects' in themselves that might have contributed to their impoverished situation, and never cynical, rebellious or resistant to the adult world.[25] The popularity of Alger's fiction has embedded its ideologies in American culture: his novels had sold between seventeen and twenty million copies by the late 1920s.[26] His legacy is not only evident in the work of The Horatio Alger Association of Distinguished Americans, Inc., which aims to challenge the belief that 'the American Dream [is] no longer attainable' by providing scholarships for young people, but also in everyday discourse, such as the speech delivered to the House of Representatives in 1998 by politician Tom Lantos, who referred to Holocaust survivors as people whose 'stories involve a degree of courage and determination unmatched in the most ... inspiring of Horatio Alger's stories'.[27] Inevitably, then, Alger's version of the genre is profoundly influential on the American Bildungsroman.

Alger's most famous novel, *Ragged Dick*, set in mid-nineteenth-century New York, charts the improbable rise of a fourteen-year-old homeless boy from boot-black to a career in a bank within a year. Carol Nackenoff contends that Alger's fiction was 'inaccurate as a description of the world even when written'.[28] To account for Dick's unrealistically rapid ascent, the text makes much of his positive qualities, underscoring that individual effort is essential to success: 'our hero was very much in earnest in his desire to improve ... he was willing to work ... Dick was naturally a smart boy ... determined to make the most of himself' (86). The novel parallels Dick's progress with that of Manhattan's Central Park (under construction when the novel was published), to stress that he is a symbol of modern America and the opportunities it offers. A sign of the city's immense wealth, Central Park was also intended to express altruism and 'refute the European view that Americans lacked a sense of civic duty and appreciation for cultural refinement'.[29] When Dick visits the park early in the novel, it is 'still very rough and unfinished' (42), much like him. However, at the novel's conclusion he observes, 'They're getting on fast at the Central Park. It looks much better than it did a year ago' (107). Like Dick, the Park undergoes a transformation in a year; both are emblems of the advancement of American society.

By presenting Dick's achievement as quickly and easily attainable, Alger seeks to convey that the American Dream is not a fantasy. However, although his 'manly and self-reliant' (6) qualities are presented as the key to his victory, Dick has a string of benefactors who ensure that he prospers. They advise him to see his future as his own responsibility – 'A good many distinguished men have once been poor boys. There's hope for you, Dick, if you'll try' (27) – but they also assist him in ways that make a material difference to his advancement. Dick's 'bildung' – his education – is not characterised by psychological development, epiphany and subsequent reflection, but by the acquisition of connections and agency. Alger's novels were disparaged for minimising the realities of poverty and the considerable help his protagonists receive, and for equating success with material gain.[30] *Ragged Dick* could be dismissed as simply an unrealistic, didactic text. However, as Rychard Fink observes in his 1962 introduction to the novel, 'Anyone who wants to know his country should get acquainted with Horatio Alger,' confirming its close relationship with American ideology.[31]

*Ragged Dick*'s uncritical stance on American attitudes stands in marked contrast to a revered Bildungsroman published just sixteen years later, Mark Twain's *Adventures of Huckleberry Finn*. Whereas Alger's novel offers limited access to the protagonist's consciousness, Twain creates an intimate relationship with the reader through direct address: Huck's opening remark is, 'You don't know about me, without you have read a book by the name of "The Adventures of Tom Sawyer", but that ain't no matter.'[32] Twain's use of the vernacular became a defining feature of many later Bildungsromane, most notably Salinger's *The Catcher in the Rye*, and the two are often compared. Further, by stating that it will be possible to 'know about' Huck without having read about Tom Sawyer, Huck promises access to his thoughts as well as his actions. Such insight encourages the reader to identify with Huck, and to understand how his experiences contribute to his development.

Set in 1830s Missouri, a slave-owning state until the end of the Civil War in 1865, the novel depicts a world in which slavery is widely accepted. Huck's adventure on the Mississippi River with Jim, a fugitive slave, is a literal and psychological journey that changes his perception of slavery. Marc Redfield contends that 'To undergo Bildung is to identify with humanity: a humanity that is itself an ongoing process of self-realization or becoming.'[33] Huck's process of identification with Jim leads to him realising 'how good [Jim] always was' (223). This affects Huck's views so radically that he decides to help the enslaved man escape bondage, although he knows this is illegal and judged immoral. Showing he understands that freeing Jim will be considered sinful, when Huck tears up the note he has written that would reveal Jim's location, he resigns himself to damnation: 'All right, then, I'll *go* to hell' (223). However, Huck is ambivalent about his community's ethics from the outset, and ultimately decides to leave it and 'light out for the Territory' because 'aunt Sally she's going to adopt me and sivilise me and I can't stand it' (296). This preference for the unregulated 'Territory' shows that Huck comes to equate 'civilisation' with principles he cannot accept, and chooses to live outside its jurisdiction instead.

Stephen Crane's *The Red Badge of Courage* also intimates the dangers of unthinking commitment to dominant American values. The persuasive quality of the maxim that the US is the 'home of the brave' is evident in adolescent protagonist Henry Fleming's eagerness to risk his life. He has 'dreamed of battles all his life' and, believing there is 'much glory' in the ongoing Civil War (1861–5), enlists on the Union side.[34] Henry longs for a war wound, known colloquially as a 'red badge of courage', assuming it will make him a hero. However, by consistently referring to him to as 'the youth', the narrative indicates that his aspirations are naive. Once Henry is with his regiment his excitement turns to anxiety that he will not be able to resist fleeing the battlefield in fear (88). The 'ecstasy of self-satisfaction' (117) he experiences having survived his first battle dissolves when he runs away with 'the zeal of an insane sprinter' (120) as a second skirmish begins. To mask his inadmissible cowardice, Henry tells his comrades that he was caught up in 'Ter'ble fightin' and had 'an awful time' in which he 'got shot. In th' head' (154). Though he reiterates several times that he was shot, his 'red badge' actually comes from being accidentally hit on the head with a rifle by a soldier of his own side. In contrast to an orthodox Bildungsroman, in which the hero gains self-awareness through experience, Henry's opportunistic deception shows that he has gained no insight into the myths of war. Through him, Crane undermines cherished ideas about American character by portraying those caught up in conflict as victims of myths about bravery and self-sacrifice.

Many depictions of working-class youth in American Bildungsromane
show the protagonists facing sadness and disappointment, despite the
promise of the Dream. Jack London's *Martin Eden* conveys that the
fulfilment of ambition may be as devastating as failure. The eponymous
hero is a twenty-year-old sailor living in San Francisco at the turn of the
twentieth century. Perceived as an 'uncouth young fellow', he is in reality 'a
mass of quivering sensibilities', an autodidact who loves literature and
longs for formal education.[35] His name suggests that he is innocent, like
the Biblical Adam before the Fall, and evokes the mid-nineteenth-century
vision of the ideal American that R. W. B. Lewis summarised as a 'figure of
heroic innocence and vast potentialities, poised at the start of a new history'
in his landmark literary study, *The American Adam* (1955).[36] Eden fights his
way to renown as a writer, apparently affirming that the US is a place of
opportunity in which effort is rewarded, but he is unfulfilled and isolated
by success. Having previously viewed upper-class life as paradise, he now
sees 'intellectual futility' (476) in the bourgeoisie. Confirming the significance of his name, he realises that his true Eden was his previous life as
a ship's stoker, and he is now 'in quest of the Paradise he had lost' (477–8).
The narrative thus takes him full circle, underlining how little he gained
from his efforts. Eden's epiphany that he belongs neither to the working
nor upper class leads him to drown himself, his despair an indictment of
the false hopes engendered by America's ethos that class mobility is
possible and desirable.

Further proof that Alger's triumphal stories are more the exception than
the norm in American coming-of-age fiction is found in John Steinbeck's
*The Red Pony* (1937), a four-part novella set on a ranch in the Salinas Valley,
California, around the turn of the twentieth century. In each part, young
Jody Tiflin faces loss of some kind and each experience shapes his development over three years. In the first part, 'The Gift', his authoritarian
father, Carl, buys him a 'red pony', a colt to train. The vitality of the young
animal reflects Jody's exuberance, and the pony's sudden death symbolises
the passing of Jody's innocence. In the second part, 'The Great
Mountains', an elderly Spanish American man, Gitano, visits the ranch.
When Gitano steals Carl's oldest horse and rides away into barren mountains, Jody understands that he is going there to die. His death is emblematic of the demise of paternal authority, as Jody withdraws from his
unsympathetic father. In the third part, 'The Promise', Carl vows to give
Jody the colt from his best mare if the boy will tend to her while she is
pregnant. Disaster ensues, however: the birth is difficult, and the mare is
killed to save the colt, signifying the loss of the mother, as Jody must

inevitably loosen that bond, too. In the final part, 'The Leader of the People', Jody's grandfather visits. The empathy that Jody shows for his grandfather conveys that he is no longer a child enthralled by the old man's tales of past glories, but a maturing adolescent who understands that his grandfather misses the excitement of the life he once had. R. Baird Shuman argues that this final section 'shows Jody's change from a self-centred boy into a feeling young man who has finally attained the status of a human being', but the melancholy that suffuses the novel counters the optimism Shuman infers and implies that Jody's adulthood will be testing.[37] As a historical novel, *The Red Pony* not only hints at the trials the new century will bring Jody and all America, in war and economic turmoil, but also to the Depression of the 1930s, when it was written, which brutally deprived countless working people of security.

In later Bildungsromane, decline rather than progress continues to be the fate of the white working class. Even in post-war America, famed for an economic boom, the privations of rural life crush aspiration, as shown in Larry McMurtry's *The Last Picture Show*, set in the early 1950s in the small West Texas town of Thalia. Ironically named after the Greek Muse of comedy, this is a grim environment in which to grow up. Its sterility and hopelessness blight its citizens, including the central character, an unambitious high school senior named Sonny, who plays sports inexpertly, works menial jobs and pursues women. The rest of the town's youth have no appetite for improvement either, and their sense of inertia is mirrored in the novel's circular structure: the narrative begins in November 1951, when an ominous 'cold norther' wind is 'swirling long ribbons of dust down Main Street' and ends a year later, on an almost identical day, a 'cold, sandstormy morning in late November'.[38] Although Todd Womble argues that the stultifying atmosphere of the town fosters dreams of freedom – 'the characters feel trapped, suffocated, and their sole desire is to somehow escape the limits of the place in which they live'– most are passive and defeated.[39] When the town's cinema closes, its final show is *The Kid from Texas* (1950), about teenage outlaw Billy the Kid, who died aged twenty-two. Echoing this, the concluding chapter details the premature death of another 'kid from Texas', a young man with learning difficulties named Billy, who keeps Thalia's pool hall swept clean. He endlessly sweeps the dusty streets and roads, too, a futile labour emblematic of lives without purpose. At the narrative's close he is killed by a truck while wearing patches over both eyes, unaware of the danger this blindness poses. The death of this innocent conveys the desolation and atrophy felt by all the town's youth, and suggests that innocence has also died in post-war

America, despite its much-vaunted prosperity and optimism. There is neither nostalgia for the past in this novel, nor hope for the future of the younger generations.

Cormac McCarthy's *All the Pretty Horses* is also set in post-war Texas, but focuses on a protagonist desperate to realise his ambitions. In 1948, sixteen-year-old John Grady Cole aspires to emulate an American icon, the cowboy. However, a new era of increasingly mechanised labour is a threat to that aspiration. Growing up with his grandfather on a ranch shields John Grady from social change, but when the old man dies his mother sells the ranch because, as the family's lawyer tells him, 'not everybody thinks that life on a cattle ranch is the second best thing to dyin and goin to heaven'.[40] In fact, there is nothing John Grady wants more, but his skill with horses masks his lack of life experience, leading to disaster. He leaves Texas on horseback to find work as a cowboy in Mexico, turning away from the country that has dispossessed him of traditional labour. Rather than realising his dream, though, his problems escalate in Mexico: he pursues a forbidden relationship with the daughter of a Mexican ranch-owner and lands in prison, where he kills a man. He returns to Texas to find that his father has died. Without home or family, John Grady faces the future alone in a country that has nothing to offer the man he wants to become. The closing image – of him riding 'into the darkening land, the world to come' (306) – is one of foreboding and uncertainty, his prospects bleaker at the novel's close than at the start. While *All the Pretty Horses* contains many tropes of the Bildungsroman (a young man's trials on the path to maturity), John Grady's failure and his continued journey subvert the genre's conventions and query the nation's pledge of opportunity for all.

America's promises continue to elude the young in the twenty-first century. The title of Philipp Meyer's *American Rust* not only evokes 'American Dream', but also 'Rust Belt', a term for a group of US states, including Pennsylvania, where the novel is set, which have suffered high unemployment and population drain following deindustrialisation. Best friends Isaac English and Billy Poe grew up together in the town of Buell; once prosperous, it has been forced into terminal decline by the closure of its steel mill, countering the nation's celebrated trajectory towards progress and prosperity. Now twenty years old, neither young man has managed to leave Buell, although Isaac has the intellect for university, and Billy had a college sports scholarship lined up, implying that they too are rusting. Isaac breaks free of the town's hold when he steals his father's '*rainy-day fund*' and sets off for Berkeley University, California, to fulfil his dream of studying astrophysics, his chosen subject communicating that he has set his sights far from home.[41] Billy accompanies Isaac for the first few miles, and the two are caught up in an event that changes their lives: three homeless men attack Billy, and Isaac, in a desperate effort to defend his friend, accidentally murders one of them. Billy, imprisoned for the murder, sacrifices himself so that Isaac can pursue his education, believing that he has no prospects in a country where the only employment opportunities are those created by economic collapse, 'taking apart old mills and factories' (289). Surely, thinks Billy, '[y]our country is supposed to do better than that for you' (289), seeing such work as evidence of both the nation's failure and its desire to erase the past until there is 'no record . . . to show that anything had ever been built in America' (289). Like John Grady in *All the Pretty Horses*, Billy represents a social class whose expectations have been shattered: it is no longer possible to 'go with the current and expect it to turn out fine' (290). In the 2008 election, Barack Obama's Democrats held Pennsylvania, and famously promised, 'Yes we can to justice and equality. Yes we can to opportunity and prosperity. Yes we can heal this nation. Yes we can repair this world. Yes we can.'[42] However, *American Rust* suggests that if the nation's promises were not fulfilled for white working-class adolescents in the twentieth century, the twenty-first has offered them little more.

## White Girls

Since the Bildungsroman is traditionally a male-dominated form, it is not surprising that fewer texts focus on girls. Those that do show that growing up is a gendered experience. This affirms the central tenet of the groundbreaking study of the female Bildungsroman, *The Voyage In: Fictions of Female Development* (1983), edited by Elizabeth Abel, Marianne Hirsch and Elizabeth Langland: 'the sex of the protagonist modifies every aspect of a particular *Bildungsroman*: its narrative structure, its implied psychology, its representation of social pressures'.[43] Class position is one of the 'social pressures' that makes an impact on girlhood. Repeatedly in Bildungsromane, girls who grow up struggling with 'family dysfunction, hunger, discrimination, and the day-to-day indignities of life in poverty' face sexual exploitation, too.[44] In Betty Smith's *A Tree Grows in Brooklyn* (1943), Francie Nolan grows up in an impoverished family at the turn of the century and is exposed to sexual predation. Francie is assaulted in the hallway of her building by a 'pervert' who has his 'lower garments opened'.[45] Although she matures into a bright and self-possessed adolescent, she literally bears the scar of her experience because her father burns her leg with carbolic acid to 'fix' (253) the place where the attacker touched her. Other underprivileged white girls suffer even more, evidenced by the sexual abuse depicted in later texts such as Carolyn Chute's *The Beans of Egypt, Maine* (1985), Dorothy Allison's *Bastard out of Carolina* (1992), Gail Anderson-Dargatz's *The Cure for Death by Lightning* (1995) and Karen Russell's *Swamplandia!* (2011). Female adolescence, Barbara White observes, 'portends a future of continued secondary status'.[46] This is borne out by Bildungsromane about girls, who bear the brunt of economic deprivation, are most vulnerable to sexual violence, fight to obtain a measure of the autonomy granted boys, and are routinely denied the 'liberty and happiness' ostensibly promised to all Americans.

The right to 'life' guaranteed by the Declaration of Independence recognises the importance of autonomy and a sense of identity for well-being. Thus, the extent to which both Southern society of the 1950s and her own family fail Ruth Anne Boatwright, the narrator of Allison's *Bastard out of Carolina*, is encapsulated in the way she is denied a name and thereby dispossessed of an identity. Without her father's details on her birth certificate, she is deemed 'a bastard by the state of South Carolina', despite her mother's repeated attempts to revise the record.[47] Kenneth Millard points out that the low status connoted by this term is underscored by its use in the novel's title, contrasting with Bildungsromane named for their protagonists such as David Copperfield, Jane Eyre and Huckleberry Finn.[48] In contrast to these classic texts, which all have positive outcomes, the absence of Ruth Anne's name implies that she will not enjoy a similar destiny. Underscoring this gloomy intimation, Ruth Anne's relatives call her 'Bone', a nickname derived from her small size (at birth she is 'no bigger than a knucklebone' [2]), which suggests fragility and death as well as whiteness. While this seems to acknowledge the child's defencelessness, her family fails to protect her from the persistent cruelty of her stepfather, 'Daddy Glen'. Thus, Bone's life is shaped by an enduring sense of illegitimacy and powerlessness. James R. Giles describes her as 'horribly abused though ultimately triumphant', but although it is possible to infer self-acceptance from Bone's assertion, on the novel's last page, 'I was who I was going to be ... a Boatwright woman' (309), she is not necessarily triumphant.[49] The cumulative effect of extreme poverty and severe abuse, culminating in her rape by Glen, is that her adult life will be irretrievably damaged by her childhood. Thus, her comment may signify her resignation that at twelve years old she is fated to be, like her mother and aunts, a woman who endures perpetual hardship. The novel's final image of 'the night clos[ing] in around' Bone and her aunt (309) conveys their entrapment in poverty and brutality: as Millard observes, in this novel, 'social class is a defining cultural discourse and institution, one from which there is little possibility of escape'.[50] Stripped of her innocence before she has even entered her teens, Bone is prematurely aged by Glen's viciousness: 'I was so old my insides had turned to dust and stone' (306). She blames herself for being his victim and attributes her mother's loyalty to him to her failures as a daughter. In this Bildungsroman, American society is implicitly held to account for neglecting a social group often dismissed as 'trash' (3) – a stereotype of 'poor whites as "incestuous and sexually promiscuous, violent, alcoholic, lazy, and stupid"' – and held responsible for its disadvantaged situation.[51] The novel counters this by communicating forcefully that Bone's thwarted development and depleted expectations are as much the fault of the nation as the family.

Middle-class girls in American Bildungsromane are not exempted from distress as they mature despite the privileges they enjoy. This rebuts the perception that social advantage shields the young and raises doubts about the real value of prosperity in America. One of the best-loved examples of the genre from the nineteenth century begins with a complaint about hardship from a middle-class protagonist: '"Christmas won't be Christmas without any presents", grumbled Jo'.[52] Jo March, the central figure in Louisa May Alcott's *Little Women* (1868/69), grows up in genteel poverty with her three sisters. Beth, one of the sisters, dies, but the others marry and have children of their own, watched over by their selfless mother, Marmee. Alcott's is a didactic Christian text intent on showing that there is no 'greater happiness' (495) for girls than marriage and child-rearing, so it is not surprising that it has a positive ending, despite the difficulties the sisters face on their journey to adulthood. However, as with Horatio Alger's novels about working-class boys, the optimism of *Little Women* is a notable exception in depictions of middle-class girls.

Growing up in London in the late nineteenth century, Maisie Farange, the central figure in Henry James's *What Maisie Knew*, is exposed from the age of six to cruel treatment by her parents that blights her childhood and shapes her maturation. Like Bone in *Bastard out of Carolina*, Maisie blames herself for her parents' behaviour, believing that 'everything was bad because she had been employed to make it so', including their acrimonious divorce.[53] Being female and a small child at the start of the novel, Maisie is an unusual protagonist for a nineteenth-century Bildungsroman, but the novel conforms to the genre's conventions in that she develops psychological maturity, undertakes a journey that changes her (a short trip from England to France is 'a crossing of more spaces than the Channel' (159) as it signifies the end of Maisie's relationship with her mother), and reaches an epiphany in her adolescence. From the outset, Maisie sees 'much more than she at first understood' (18) about her parents, then as her self-awareness develops, comes to realise that she 'had known all along a great deal' (159), and finally accepts that she is 'distinctly on the road to know Everything' (216), the capital letter hinting that some of her knowledge is unsavoury. Maisie loses her innocence, but acquires the capacity for moral judgement. When she chooses to live with her working-class governess rather than her upper-class step-parents, she rejects the tawdry behaviour of 'her own people' (271) and becomes, as critic Alfred Habegger observes, 'free, fine, noble, and upright'.[54] The novel intimates that if Maisie's reward for loss of innocence is moral perspicacity, then the miseries of her 'bildung' may have been worthwhile.

Charity Royall, the seventeen-year-old heroine of Edith Wharton's *Summer* (1917), like the protagonist of *What Maisie Knew*, suffers from the cruelty of people more privileged than she, but Wharton's novel is also a frank depiction of the risks of sexuality for girls, a topic James does not address. As such, *Summer* is a Bildungsroman that exposes gender inequality and the contrasting roles and responsibilities assigned to young women and men, especially in sexual relationships. Charity makes a life-changing decision when she becomes pregnant in her teens and decides to keep her baby, even though she is unmarried, showing that across the novel she develops from a disaffected, shallow girl to an ethical young adult. Charity's name reflects her status as a girl rescued from poverty by a benefactor, but his name, Royall, is much less appropriate, since he is a middle-class, heavy-drinking, womanising lawyer who derides Charity's birth family as 'half human'.[55] This reversal in the stereotypical behaviour of the poor and the privileged queries the power invested in the middle and upper classes as moral arbiters who are not called to account for their behaviour, while the working class are judged negatively. Emphasising this, the father of Charity's baby is a professional man, Lucius Harney, an architect, to whom Charity gives 'all she had' (128) – her virginity – only to be abandoned for a wealthier girl when she becomes pregnant. Royall's offer of marriage seems close to incest, and when Charity accepts him she appears to be relinquishing her autonomy and aspirations, even her ethics. Karen Weingarten argues that Charity is trapped by the social and legal regulations that govern a woman's body, especially when she is pregnant, so her 'decision to marry Mr. Royall can barely be considered as such'.[56] Despite her limited options, though, Charity acts according to her own sense of morals. Her progress from compliance to self-determination in the face of male dominance marks the novel as a proto-feminist Bildungsroman.

Harper Lee's *To Kill a Mockingbird*, like *Adventures of Huckleberry Finn*, exposes the injustice of racism by presenting it through a child's eyes, but it also implicitly critiques the white male professional for failing to avert injustice, and American society for adhering to nineteenth-century attitudes to race long after the end of the Civil War. Set in Alabama in the 1930s, the novel charts three years in the life of the narrator, Jean Louise, nicknamed Scout, her older brother Jem, and their gender-nonconforming neighbour, Dill. Despite his rhetorical brilliance, lawyer Atticus Finch, Scout and Jem's father, cannot persuade a white jury to recognise the innocence of a black man, Tom Robinson, accused of rape by a white woman, Mayella Ewell. The children's faith in the adult world is shaken by this display of unequivocal racial prejudice, intensified by the fatal shooting of Tom Robinson before his appeal against the conviction reaches court. These incidents confirm the children's sense that their father, although lauded by the town's black citizens for his commitment to justice, is 'feeble' because he did not save Tom.[57] When Scout and Jem are viciously attacked by Mayella's father, their reclusive neighbour, Arthur 'Boo' Radley, saves them by killing their assailant. Being rescued by this social outsider rather than their father complicates Atticus's status as protector within the family, just as his failure to save Tom Robinson caused the children to doubt his power in the community. When Scout observes that she and Jem live in an 'old neighbourhood' (100), the underlying implication is that both its racism and its belief in white superiority are relics of the past that her father has not been able to change. So, although the novel is set in the 1930s, it comments on the necessity of the Civil Rights movement that was gathering strength when it was published in 1960, using a child's growing awareness of injustice to question American resistance to social change and the complacency bred by white privilege.

Despite the alterations that the Second World War brought to gender roles, Sylvia Plath's *The Bell Jar* (1963) suggests that growing up in post-war America engenders as many anxieties as opportunities. Its protagonist, nineteen-year-old Esther Greenwood, becomes seriously ill as she tries to fulfil the American Dream – for her, a glamorous career in Manhattan – but finds it impossible to reconcile the varied pressures upon her as a young woman. As Rachael McLennan argues, 'Esther desires to conform, fears she may not conform, and actively resists conforming to the prescriptions of . . . society.'[58] Attempting to negotiate these mutually exclusive desires is Esther's downfall. Ostensibly, multiple options are available to her as a young woman, represented by the text's central metaphor of a fig tree on which every fruit represents 'a wonderful future'.[59] However, whichever one she chooses entails 'losing all the rest' (81), leading her to feel that making any choice is impossible. Early in the narrative, Esther observes that although she is 'supposed to be having the time of [her] life' (2), she feels instead, 'very still and very empty' (3), unable to negotiate the pressures upon her. Her sense of entrapment, as if under a bell jar – a metaphor for the masculine world of science that seeks to diagnose and treat her unhappiness, embodied by her boyfriend, Buddy, a medical student – drives Esther to multiple suicide attempts. Her realisation that the future is complex and alarming positions *The Bell Jar* as a critique of post-war America that challenges its positive image of affluence and possibility. Specifically, though, Esther's misery derives from her instinct that it is not possible for a woman to be happy and successful in the public world and the domestic sphere simultaneously. Her feelings are affirmed by sociological studies of the era, especially Betty Friedan's *The Feminine Mystique*, published in the same year as Plath's novel, which revealed the dissatisfaction felt by many middle-class women about the limitations of their lives.

## Bildungsromane of Difference and Diversity

African American writers have employed the Bildungsroman to describe the effects of growing up in a country where racial prejudice is rife, part of the nation's history, and often upheld by law. Langston Hughes's *Not without Laughter* (1930) conveys the poverty his young hero faces, but he depicts the pleasures of family bonds as well as the disadvantages of living in a segregated black community. In stark contrast, Richard Wright's *Native Son* (1940) communicates that black Americans, after centuries of brutal oppression, may respond with rage and violence to their situation. Wright's protagonist, Biggar Thomas, grows up in miserable circumstances, forced to work instead of getting an education; unable to see any better prospect, he turns to robbery and then to rape and murder. He is emphatically a 'native son', a product of America, and the novel suggests that the impact of society's racism on his life must be acknowledged. Likewise, Ralph Ellison's *Invisible Man* (1952) blends the picaresque and Bildungsroman to condemn the US for neglect of its black citizens. As Claudine Raynaud observes, the African American Bildungsroman can be read as 'a negation … of the American dream'.[60] Toni

Morrison's *The Bluest Eye* (1970) focuses on how girls suffer from the effects of entrenched racism: sexually abused Pecola Breedlove is the victim of both her brutalised father and of a racist society that teaches African Americans to value whiteness. Claudia MacTeer, the narrator, expresses resistance through her hatred of Shirley Temple and white dolls, but there is no escape for Pecola except into mental breakdown; the devastating effects of white norms, epitomised by the extracts from the Dick and Jane reader that frames each section of the narrative, are fully evident in the tragic story of Pecola's demise. The history of race relations in the US weighs heavily on the protagonists of Ntozake Shange's *Betsey Brown* (1985), set in St Louis, Missouri in 1959, and Thulani Davis's *1959* (1992), set in Turner, Virginia. Both employ the Bildungsroman to explore the impact of *Brown* v. *Board of Education of Topeka* (1954), the case heard in the Supreme Court that desegregated US public schools, paralleling their heroines' battle to come of age with the nation's turmoil over the rights of black Americans.

Not all African American Bildungsromane end in despair. Although Geta LeSeur argues that '[c]hildhood as presented in the African American Bildungsroman is depressing, like America's Black history', in James Baldwin's *Go Tell It on the Mountain* (1953) and Paule Marshall's *Brown Girl, Brownstones* (1959), both set in 1930s New York, there is ultimately some sense of optimism for the protagonists, despite the hardships they face growing up.[61] As the novel closes, Baldwin's John Grimes '[finds] himself smiling', cleansed of the anxieties about his sexuality that plague him at the beginning of the narrative, and ready to challenge the power of his cruel stepfather.[62] Marshall's Selina Boyce also must come to terms with the impact of her parents on her life – her strong, stern mother and loving, feckless father – and is ready to emulate them both, by returning to the Caribbean as her father longed to do, and becoming (as her mother was at eighteen years old) her 'own woman'.[63] Even Celie in Alice Walker's *The Color Purple* (1982) and Precious in Sapphire's *Push* (1996) eventually find a little happiness and hope after years of brutal abuse.

Native American Bildungsromane often engage with the legacy of violent colonisation that dispossessed people of their land and forced them onto reservations to live with attenuated resources, agency and prospects. Native culture is profoundly threatened by geographical relocation and the dispersal of communities because its founding stories are deeply related to place and passed through generations by retelling. Many Native American Bildungsromane convey the challenges posed by these issues in their depiction of young protagonists navigating their position in

Native and non-Native society. In some texts, this entails accepting the problems and opportunities created by a dual identity. In others, it means choosing to embrace Native society exclusively, sometimes after a sojourn outside it. *The Surrounded* (1936) by D'Arcy McNickle (Flathead) explores the effects of colonisation through the experiences of Archilde Leon. His mother believes that 'An Indian boy ... belong[s] with his people', but Archilde is disenchanted by Salish reservation life, asking his sister, 'what you think a fellow can do here – steal horses ... ? Drink and run around?'[64] However, his views change as he spends more time with his family and community until, as Enrique Lima explains, 'Archilde's formation as an individual coincides with his realization that he is part of the Salish whole', suggesting that integration into Native American culture is a more positive outcome for the protagonist than immersion in non-Native America or attempting to construct a binary sense of self.[65]

The difficulties entailed in balancing tribal identity with the demands of white-dominated society recur in Native American Bildungsromane across the twentieth century. N. Scott Momaday (Kiowa) addresses such issues in his formally experimental novel *House Made of Dawn* (1967), which emerged in the era of the 'Red Power' movement for Native rights, and traces the attempt of Abel, a Second World War veteran, to locate his place as an individual and member of a tribe. As in Momaday's text, the central character in *Ceremony* (1977) by Leslie Marmon Silko (Laguna Pueblo) is a war veteran, Tayo, whose reintegration into his community is jeopardised by trauma. Returned home from combat, he cannot stop vomiting and will starve to death if he is not cured. Jude Todd reads Tayo's affliction as indicating his need to 'purge and purify his stomach from the lies fed to him since childhood' by community, school and army so that he can heal and progress.[66] These canonical novels and more recent coming-of-age narratives by lauded Native writers like Louise Erdrich (Ojibwe), such as *The Round House* (2012) and *LaRose* (2016), and Sherman Alexie (Spokane/ Coeur d'Alene), especially his short-story sequence *The Lone Ranger and Tonto Fistfight in Heaven* (1993), all depict Native experience from the inside, placing at the centre of the narrative those previously marginalised and silenced. These writers use the Bildungsroman not only to depict but also to decry the unequal position of Native peoples in the USA.

The relationship between the individual and the nation is foregrounded in many Bildungsromane about members of marginalised groups. For example, becoming an American citizen is often complicated for migrants and their descendants by a residual attachment to a place and culture outside the USA. Early Jewish American examples of the genre often parallel migrants' 'coming to America' narratives with coming of age, as they share elements such as identity formation and adjusting to change. Abraham Cahan's *The Rise of David Levinsky* (1917), which has been described as 'a Jewish American Horatio Alger story', demonstrates this shared ground.[67] Section titles in the novel such as 'Home and School', 'I Lose My Mother', and 'I Discover America' certainly suggest that Levinsky's life in New York is a familiar story of trial and triumph in the New World. However, the final section, titled 'Episodes of a Lonely Life', makes clear that despite his accomplishments, David is 'not happy'.[68] He concludes, 'There are moments when I regret my whole career, when my very success seems to be a mistake' (529); no hero of Alger's would countenance such doubts. Achieving the American Dream has brought David no gratification because it has alienated him from his roots in the migrant community.

In Anzia Yezierska's *Bread Givers* (1925), the protagonist also has a complex relationship with her origins. The novel represents 'a neglected aspect of Yiddish culture, . . . the woman's experience of immigration', in which Yezierska's heroine, Sara Smolinsky, defies her father and fights to support and educate herself in the demanding environment of New York, refusing to be another subservient 'bread giver' like her mother and sisters.[69] Anticipating Virginia Woolf's essay, 'A Room of One's Own' (1929), Sara is desperate for the luxury of 'be[ing] alone in a room' with a 'door I could shut' (158); once attained, she studies for a teaching career. In many ways a tale of migrant – and female – victory, Sara still regrets that she cannot be reconciled with her tyrannous father, whose misogynistic beliefs – '[a] woman without a man is less than nothing' (294) – have shaped her life. As Carol B. Schoen remarks, the novel identifies the 'tensions between the ancient Jewish mores that assumed male domination and the American ideal of individual freedom'.[70] Although Yezierska's novel is both a classic tale of the American Dream attained and a Bildungsroman that is in many ways conventional, it conveys the double trial of becoming American and becoming a woman. It also eschews simplistic resolution: Sara recognises at the narrative's close that her father, and the culture he represents, is a 'weight . . . still upon me' (297). As Martin Japtok observes, Sara bears comparison to Selina in *Brown Girl, Brownstones*, as both young women have the '[strong] individualist leanings' typical of heroines of the Bildungsroman, and both struggle to reconcile this with their ethnic and racial heritage.[71]

*The Adventures of Augie March* (1953) by Jewish American Saul Bellow announces itself as a Bildungsroman by echoing the title of Twain's

*Adventures of Huckleberry Finn* and thereby simultaneously evoking and revising the nation's literary heritage.[72] Bellow's hero has a voice that recalls Walt Whitman's self-confidence as well as Huck's demotic: Augie's narrative begins, 'I am an American, Chicago born – Chicago, that somber city – and go at things as I have taught myself, free-style, and will make the record in my own way: first to knock, first admitted'.[73] Augie echoes David Copperfield in his self-conscious reference to making 'the record' of his life, but rejects Dickens's chronological structure in favour of describing whatever comes to his mind first. Indeed, challenges to the conventions of the Bildungsroman are central to this novel: Nicholas Nardini observes that Bellow sends Augie 'on an episodic ramble through a long series of apprenticeships that leave him increasingly disillusioned with the very notion of education and no closer to an identity than before'.[74] Bellow's rejection of classic Bildungsroman tropes is an assertion of difference and, like the other Jewish American writers discussed here, he communicates his protagonist's ambivalent relationship with both his heritage and his present situation by manipulating the genre.

Like Jewish Americans, migrants from around the world who settle in the US often find that their country of origin and its traditions exert a strong pull. Maxine Hong Kingston's feminist Bildungsroman, *The Woman Warrior: Memoirs of a Girlhood Among Ghosts* (1976), expresses the hybridity of its Chinese American narrator through a hybrid narrative form that incorporates legend, autobiography and family chronicle. As she grows up in California in the 1950s and 1960s, the narrator is puzzled and alienated by the gender norms of her parents' country of origin, China, which simultaneously encourages and punishes female assertiveness. Kingston's mother tells her that she will become 'a wife and slave', but also tells her the 'song of the warrior woman, Fa Mu Lan', a Chinese heroine.[75] This mixed message is repeated in post-war America through the contrasting messages of femininity and feminism. Christy Rishoi observes that, as Kingston matures, she learns to 'name the inconsistencies and eventually construct a different way of being for herself', accepting uncertainty and a heterogeneous identity that resists the monoculture conceptualised in the American 'melting pot'.[76] Kingston's ambivalence about Chinese culture discourages her identification with it – she states firmly, 'I am not a Chinese woman, never having traveled east of Hawaii' – but in other migrant Bildungsromane a sense of attachment to a place outside the US is acknowledged by (re)visiting it, often to connect with extended family.[77] This features in Julia Alvarez's *How the García Girls Lost Their Accents* (1991) and Junot Díaz's *The Brief Wondrous Life of Oscar Wao*

(2007), both of which focus on the children of migrant families from the Dominican Republic. Yolanda García and Oscar Wao negotiate, not always successfully, their sense of being connected to two countries and yet not fully belonging in either one as they journey between the two locations. On a smaller scale, the family home in the new world can be simultaneously a source of attachment and constraint. Esperanza Cordera, the central figure in Sandra Cisneros's *The House on Mango Street* (1991), is a Latina girl who comes to see the titular house as the place 'I belong but do not belong to': a symbol of the family and culture she loves, but also what she must leave behind to succeed.[78]

Like 'coming to America' narratives, 'coming out' stories (about the revelation of non-normative sexuality or gender identity) typically incorporate the motifs of coming of age. Since social convention is heteronormative, Bildungsromane about LGBTQ+ characters often relate their search for acceptance of alternative gender roles and sexuality in a hostile environment. These narratives communicate that promises of equality and happiness are rarely kept for those who challenge convention, and social integration means denying fundamental aspects of the self. In some novels, protagonists retreat from the nonconformity they sense in themselves. In Carson McCullers's *The Member of the Wedding* (1946), the wartime setting reflects the conflict over gender identity experienced by a boyish girl, Frankie, as she develops. Her acquiescence to a date with a soldier is driven by a desire to be more feminine; when the encounter threatens to become sexually intimate, she escapes by fighting back. Subsequently, unsettled by her own show of strength, she retreats to a more heteronormative gender identity and more feminine name, Frances. Truman Capote's *Other Voices, Other Rooms* (1948) was described by one of his associates as 'the fairy *Huckleberry Finn*', identifying it as a queer revision of the classic American Bildungsroman.[79] Capote depicts the development of adolescent Joel and his fascination with his cousin, Randolph, who wears 'a seersucker kimono with butterfly sleeves' and 'a lady's ring'.[80] Joel's identification with Randolph leads him to recognise that he, too, is gay and has a feminine gender identity. Capote's novel associates same-sex desire with opposite-sex gender performance, as Gary Richards observes: 'the gay men and boys of *Other Voices, Other Rooms* are passive, foppish, and effeminate' and often attracted to hyper-masculine men.[81] Capote's characters reject the norms of gender and sexuality, refusing to be cowed by the intolerant attitudes that vilify gay men.

By depicting experiences legally or tacitly prohibited, literature can counter bigotry as well as conveying its impact on sympathetic characters.

Although the protagonists of *Carol* (1952) face prejudice, Patricia
Highsmith's portrayal of the relationship between a young woman,
Therese, and the older, married Carol is especially notable for showing
the two happily united at the novel's close, contesting the typical representation of same-sex relationships as dysfunctional, miserable and ephemeral. Edmund White's *A Boy's Own Story* (1982) challenged literary
convention not only in its content but also as a conscious response to the
lack of gay Bildungsromane. Its adolescent hero struggles with a sexuality
he knows is taboo, and although White contends that the protagonist's
'confusion could be interpreted as a general teenage malaise about love and
sex', the novel specifically counters anti-gay prejudice by offering access to
the boy's complex emotions, a strategy employed by many later novels of
gay adolescence.[82] Larry Duplechan's *Blackbird* (1986), published at the
height of the homophobia that arose in the US in the era of AIDS,
confirms that the Bildungsroman remains a valid form for exploring
sexuality and repudiating oppression. As 'the first contemporary black
coming out story', his depiction of gay African American adolescent
Jonnie Ray highlights the role played by intersectionality in identity
formation.[83] Despite greater acceptance of LGBTQ+ life in some quarters
and increased visibility in the cultural mainstream, Bildungsromane that
represent non-normative identities continue to resonate not only because
they acknowledge that sexuality forms a major part of adolescence, but also
because they often question the extent to which ideologies of equality and
freedom embrace all Americans.

The recurring use of first-person point of view in Bildungsromane transforms perceptions of the Other by creating an intimate relationship with the
reader that makes unexamined prejudice much harder to sustain. Jeffrey
Eugenides's *Middlesex* (2002) intensifies this effect by presenting several
different lives from the perspective of a single first-person narrator. Cal
Stephanides is identified as female at birth and raised as a girl, but begins
to masculinise at puberty and lives as a man from his late teens onward; he
tells the story of his heritage and sense of isolation retrospectively, from
middle age. Cal intercuts his account of growing up intersex with the story
of his Greek grandparents' migration to America, despite the impossibility
of describing first-hand events that occurred before his birth. This strategy
conveys with great sympathy the most private emotions of a variety of
gender and sexual nonconforming citizens to whom Cal is related, so
when they are denied the opportunity to be happy and self-determining in
twentieth-century America, the injustice is clear. Much like the immigrants
of earlier Bildungsromane, American-born-and-raised Cal cannot locate

a place in his home country where his intersex identity is liveable, and his adulthood is a continuous search for belonging. Eventually, he moves to Berlin, reversing the journey from the Old to the New World undertaken by his grandparents. In leaving the US, Cal implicitly criticises American society for failing to accommodate gender and sexual difference.

## Conclusion

The evident capacity of the Bildungsroman to represent diverse experiences contributes to its popularity in American literature, as does its strategy of presenting the nation from the perspective of youth. While depictions of disadvantaged and marginalised characters give the Bildungsroman its critical power, many novels portray discontentment amongst the most socially privileged youth. Affluent white boys express deep dissatisfaction with the nation, despite the comfort and opportunities they enjoy as its pre-eminent citizens. The most famous example of this is Salinger's *The Catcher in the Rye*. Its narrator, Holden Caulfield, begins his account of his misadventures in New York with a reference to one of the most famous Bildungsromane in literary history: 'If you really want to hear about it, the first thing you'll probably want to know is where I was born, and what my lousy childhood was like, ... and all that David Copperfield kind of crap, but I don't feel like going into it'.[84] The reference to Copperfield indicates that Salinger's novel is a Bildungsroman, too, but one that will revise the genre by withholding personal revelations. In a further rejection of the classic model, Holden resists assimilation into a society he holds in contempt and expresses no interest in conforming to norms of sexuality, aspiration, or material acquisition. To Holden, the elite world he is born into is facile, unfulfilling and 'phony': he envisages adulthood as a time to 'make a lot of dough and play golf and play bridge and buy cars and drink Martinis' (155), none of which seem meaningful to him. The superficiality in post-war America is the antithesis of Holden's deceased younger brother, Allie, a loving innocent who valued poetry, and the conventional masculinity that demands emotional repression makes it impossible for Holden to mourn Allie's death openly. Holden's misadventures build to a crisis when he realises that escape from the adult world is impossible. Although he appears to have resigned himself to the inevitability of entering adulthood when he watches his sister Phoebe ride a carousel, in the short closing chapter he asserts, 'I don't *know* what I think about [all this stuff]' (192) and refuses to commit himself to conformity in the future. Rather than concluding with integration and acceptance, Holden's journey is set to continue, his alienation from society akin to that of all marginalised and dispossessed young Americans. Together, their stories suggest that America's promise of life, liberty and happiness has yet to be fulfilled.

# CHAPTER 6

# The Modernist Bildungsroman

*Gregory Castle*

What modern art has to do
in the service of culture
is so to rearrange the details
of modern life, so to reflect it,
colour that it may satisfy the
spirit.
And what does the spirit need
in the face of modern life?
The sense of freedom.

Walter Pater

Colour there is in this sphere world,
colour of the red anemone,
as seen under clear water . . .

H. D.

## Bildung and Portraiture

The modernist Bildungsroman is a genre in crisis, or so the dominant critical narrative tells us. Since Franco Moretti's influential *The Way of the World* (1987), many scholars (myself included) have been drawn to a reading of literary history that charts the destiny of a genre under the pressure of modernist experimentation and innovation.[1] The specific nature of this destiny has been a point of conflict, however. Tobias Boes, for example, sees a powerful transformative impulse in the Bildung concept throughout its literary history and points to its wide-ranging influence in philosophy, theology, natural science and history and finds a cosmopolitan openness in the Bildungsroman from the start.[2] In exemplars like James Joyce's *A Portrait of the Artist as a Young Man* (1916) and Alfred Döblin's *Berlin Alexanderplatz* (1929), Boes finds an 'individuating rhythm' that emerges in contrapuntal relation to dominant narratives of formation. Jed Esty tells a somewhat different story in his study of the novel of development in an age of empire by showing how the disjunctive and alienating temporality of 'colonial migration and displacement' leads to 'a breakdown in the allegorical function of the coming-of-age-plot'.[3]

The stunted or stalled development of young people at the periphery of Empire, Esty argues, cannot be explained by the classical concept of Bildung; nor can it be narrated in the classical Bildungsroman.[4] For both critics, the crisis of the form has to do with social environments that are inimical to the successful or ideal achievement of Bildung, though Boes is more open to the idea of understanding Bildung as the process by which individuals overcome such environments through creative formal accommodations.

My position is that the crisis originates *within* the Bildung concept and is the necessary condition of its narration, if the latter is to accord with the sense of self that emerges out of the modernist protagonist's experience. The Bildung concept in its classical mode refers to self-formation, the dialectical process by which one's sensibilities and faculties, in 'spontaneous cooperation' with others, are brought together in a harmonious and unified expression of self.[5] Wilhelm von Humboldt, in the 1790s, emphasised this aspect of cooperation because he believed that Bildung required a commitment from the State to nurture and protect it, a commitment that made inner life a truly dialectical engagement with the social world.[6] However, the history of the Bildungsroman reveals a fundamental contradiction between the ideal promised by Bildung in the classical narrative form and the condition of relative *unfreedom* that makes achieved Bildung impossible for the protagonist. Even the Bildungsheld of Johann von Goethe's *Wilhelm Meister's Apprenticeship* (1795–6) is constrained by the terms laid down *in advance* by authoritative mentors.[7] For the modernist protagonist who evades or refuses the consolations of achieved Bildung, this contradiction is aggravated by the conditions of late-modernity, which included economic inequality, racial and gender discrimination, political instability, rapid social transformation (movements up and down class hierarchies and across disparate geographies), techno-bureaucracy, the 'culture industry' and the myriad depredations of Empire. In negative dialectical fashion, the broken promise of the classical form created, for modernist Bildungshelden who resist such conditions, new narrative possibilities for representing self-formation and the temporality of inner life that organises and sustains it.[8]

Bildung arises as a crisis in modernism precisely because the dialectical harmony of the protagonist and her world, promised by the classical Bildungsroman, never comes about; there is no achieved Bildung, no self-consciousness of inner life in harmony with all other aspects of life. I want to suggest that this negative dynamic is conveyed most compellingly through the 'portrait of the artist' motif – the emergence in literary language of what Max Saunders calls 'im/personality', a critical form of *self-impressionism*: 'What modernist impersonality is impersonal about is arguably nothing less than personality.'[9] This motif, with its strong emphasis on *self*-portraiture, characterises a dominant strand of modernist fiction, in which portraits of the artist are effectively accounts of the dynamism and expressive capacity of inner life. The genealogy of this practice, as I illustrate it here from English-language exemplars, includes Walter Pater's *Imaginary Portraits* (1888), which Saunders regards as an important early work in modernist *auto/biography*, one that shadows forth a self-portrait within the portrait of the artist.[10] I argue that the portrait of the artist motif is central to Oscar Wilde's *Picture of Dorian Gray* (1890) and James Joyce's *A Portrait of the Artist*, early modernist Bildungsromane featuring protagonists who want *to be* artists and whose inner lives are modelled on that of their creators. This genealogy also includes E. M. Forster's *A Room with a View* (1908), which retains formal features of the classical Bildungsroman and offers a form of portraiture that works with the protagonist *and* her milieu to produce what I call a 'portrait of aesthetic life'. Virginia Woolf's *The Voyage Out* (1915) and Dorothy Richardson's *Pilgrimage* (beginning in 1915) introduce new modes of representing this life, chiefly in free indirect styles that blur the line between the artist and the subject of the portrait. H. D.'s fiction of the 1920s, particularly *HERmione* and *Asphodel*, reorients modernist portraiture by connecting Bildung, in startling new ways, to aesthetic environments and by intensifying the autobiographical component that subtends any formative fiction and the portrait of the artist motif it employs. I end by looking at Elizabeth Bowen's *The Last September* (1929), which sustains the portrait of the artist motif but also registers a less welcoming attitude towards inner life and the aesthetic milieu it requires. The postcolonial dimension of exile and diaspora that Joyce's *Portrait* introduces as an elegant aesthetic solution to an ethical dilemma, Bowen redefines as the aesthetic homeland of a deracinated Bildungsheld. In late modernist and postcolonial contexts, the portrait of the artist motif survives, but often at the expense of the protagonist's inner life, which may no longer correspond to or accommodate the created or *expressed* world of the work.[11]

As I will show in what follows, modernists tended to be of two minds about the self, the formative process, and the legibility of gender in both: on the one hand, a strong trend runs through modernism of the male artist-hero whose formation, in a negative dialectical fashion, is both a critique of classical Bildung and a rehabilitation of its central aesthetic values (a process Theodor Adorno calls *instauration*). On the other hand, an equally strong trend features female protagonists whose desire for the aesthetic life is grounded not in a heroic posture towards art but in a revolutionary way of understanding and acting on (and in) the sensible world. At a certain limit, a 'portrait of aesthetic life' emerges that reframes the question of self-formation in terms of the general environment of the protagonist's aspirations rather than of the ideal of achieved Bildung. In both cases, we see two separate developments – the changing fortunes of the Bildung concept and the narrative means of expressing aspiration for it – that intersect with provocative and productive results in the modernist Bildungsroman. Aspiration, liberated from a failed ideal, offers in compensation the pleasures and rewards of its perpetual unfolding; and the protagonist, by resisting the dialectical closure of achieved Bildung, forges new values in the only spaces open to her, inner life and the aesthetic milieu it generates. The portrait of the artist motif captures this transformation of inner culture – the garden of *Bildung* – into the consolations (or desolations) of aesthetic life.

## Freedom and Inner Life

Modernist Bildungshelden move towards horizons they have made for themselves; they resist, by and large, the allure of socialised subjectivity and of any attempt to assimilate the moment of aspiration to the destiny outlined with cruel economy by Hegel:

> [T]he subject sows his wild oats, builds himself with his wishes and opinions into harmony with subsisting relationships and their rationality, enters the concatenation of the world and acquires for himself an appropriate attitude to it. However much he may have quarrelled with the world, or been pushed about in it, in most cases at last he gets his girl and some sort of position, marries her and becomes as good a Philistine as others.[12]

Bildung is at once a model of the seemingly fruitless dialectical process described here and the ideal of achieved Bildung towards which the process is *supposed* to move, a contradiction that the 'good Philistine' misrecognises through endless compromise. By contrast, the modernist Bildungsroman recognises this internal contradiction not as a problem meant to be solved but as the negative dialectical condition of its possibility. The Bildungsheld's refusal to sanction the ideal – the result of discovering it to be a sham – becomes the starting point for imagining new modes of self-formation and social belonging that do not depend on achievement and that reward aspiration as a goal in itself.

This is the inverse of what we see in the urtext of the tradition, Goethe's *Wilhelm Meister's Apprenticeship*, in which achievement ultimately supplants aspiration and the protagonist, Wilhelm, conforms to Hegel's outline, albeit in the lofty terms of the certificate of achievement granted by his mentors in *Die Turmgesellschaft* ('society of the tower'). Wilhelm's achievement is naive and uncanny; his return home – *status quo antebellum* – is made under the cover of an idealised escape from it. What changes in modernism is the Bildungsheld's refusal to accept a similar destiny in the form of a merely symbolic, that is to say *unattainable*, ideal. Her refusal of the terms offered by tradition constitutes a negative dialectical moment, an affirmation of non-identity, of individual aspiration *as such*, and a rejection of achieved Bildung, which amounts mainly to a rejection of the manipulation by others. This refusal is not so much a failure to achieve as it is a *falling-away* from the teleology of achievement; it is a productive *failing* on the part of a hero whose aspirations are spent more often on resistance to ideals than on their realisation. If the classical Bildungsroman conceals this failing (or misrecognises it as failure) it does so in order to sustain the illusion of a self-sufficient, self-identical person. The modernist Bildungsroman, by dramatising what is concealed, draws our attention to the rupture of the ideal that has haunted the Bildung concept from the start.[13]

The practice of failing advances the fortunes of the protagonist by enabling a counter-narrative of self-appraisal and self-fashioning in which aspiration and the moment of its passing constitute an outlaw realm of aesthetic life. The word *aesthetics* (Greek αἰσθητός, 'sensible, perceptible') designates sensation, that which is available to the senses; art is that mode of thought and creative action that focuses on what we perceive in experience, what we feel emotionally and what we use, in terms of media, to convey these perceptions and feelings. In using the phrase *aesthetic life*, I take my cue from Wilde, whose lecture on the 'The English Renaissance of Art' (first delivered in America in 1881) calls for a 'passionate cult of pure beauty, with its flawless devotion to form, its exclusive and sensitive nature'.[14] In one of his most popular lectures, 'House Decoration', he champions the 'noble design' that he feels is 'a necessity of human life'.[15] Wilde advocates for nothing less than an aesthetics of everyday life: 'all the arts are fine arts and all the arts decorative arts' he claims and, by so claiming, valorises the beauty of what is often seen as practical, ephemeral or insignificant: the milieu of the everyday, the banal, the merely decorative.[16]

Wilde follows a path already explored by Friedrich Schiller, one of the architects of Bildung, who writes in *Letters on the Aesthetic Education of Man* (1795) that 'to replace morals by Morality, happy events by Happiness, the facts of knowledge by Knowledge itself – that is the business of physical and moral education. To make Beauty out of a multiplicity of beautiful objects is the task of aesthetic education'. The fundamental importance of the latter, and the artistic liberty afforded by the multiplicity of objects, is announced at the end of letter II: 'if man is ever to solve [the] problem of politics in practice he will have to approach it through the problem of the aesthetic, because it is only through Beauty that man makes his way to Freedom'.[17] Just such a project of aesthetic education is at the heart of classical Bildung: it fosters inner life and provides the mechanism by which the subject *under these conditions of freedom* engages in the social world by way of harmonious dialectical compromise. The modernist Bildungsroman sustains this pedagogical project (if not the harmonious compromise) in depictions of classroom instruction, formal and informal mentorship, and the rarified ad hoc proceedings of like-minded 'free spirits' (to use Nietzsche's phrase) who talk of art, literature, and the very fact of their aesthetic education.[18] To be sure, aspiration for Bildung and an aesthetic education can lead one to pursue an artistic calling – think of Stephen Dedalus in *Portrait* or Hermione in H. D.'s *HERmione*. But it can also prepare one for an aesthetic life in which a sensitivity to and aspiration for the beautiful commands one's sense of self and one's relation to the rest of the world. When I speak of the portrait of the artist motif in modernism, then, I am referring to a representation that weaves the protagonist into the milieu in which she moves, much as one's inner life occupies the space opened up by the 'spontaneous cooperation' with others that Humboldt finds necessary for Bildung.

The underlying requirement for modernist portraiture is the Schillerian idea of freedom through beauty. In the conclusion to *The Renaissance* (1874), Walter Pater writes, 'What modern art has to do in the service of culture is so to rearrange the details of modern life, so to reflect it, that it may satisfy the spirit. And what does the spirit need in the face of modern life? The sense of freedom.'[19] Out of this sense of freedom comes an inner life understood as a wilful rearrangement of ourselves:

> To such a tremulous wisp constantly re-forming itself on the stream, to a single sharp impression, with a sense in it, a relic more or less fleeting, of such moments gone by, what is real in our life fines itself down. It is with

this movement, with the passage and dissolution of impressions, images, sensations, that analysis leaves off – that continual vanishing away, that strange, perpetual, weaving and unweaving of ourselves.[20]

One way to accommodate this weaving and unweaving – formation and *de*formation – is to recognise its vital role in the framing of a portrait, the narrative attempt to form an impression of the momentary passage of the self. This is why the portrait of the artist motif in modernism must be seen outside a static notion of portraiture.

Pater's idea of portraiture is kinetic; it maps shifts in mood, attitude and reflection that are 'more or less fleeting', moments that are always 'vanishing away' even as they weave back into place. 'Passage and dissolution' constitute the portrait's warp and woof, the mechanism of a resemblance that defies analysis yet also unerringly captures the milieu of inner life in which this weaving and unweaving take place.[21] In his *Imaginary Portraits* (1887), Pater creates artistic personalities like Antony Watteau, who is possessed by an 'incurable restlessness one supposed but the humour natural to a promising youth who had still everything to do.' This *having still everything to do* corresponds to the futural condition of aspiration, in which what matters for Antony is not 'realised enjoyment' in the sense of an achieved goal, but rather 'the thought of the independence' that such enjoyment 'has purchased him, so that he can escape from one lodging-place to another, just as it may please him'.[22] Such 'incontinence' is natural to Denys L'Auxerrois, who exemplifies the artist who must fall away from every ideal, for he occupies a 'prosaic world' in which he 'remains the aspiring, never quite contended being he is' (*IP* 47).

Pater's imaginary artists possess a talent for resemblance, for creating 'a solid and veritable likeness of [life] and of its ways' in artworks that possess an 'unreal imaginary light' (*IP* 27, 32). We find it in L'Auxerrois's 'new, free, generous, manner in art', which resembles without imitating 'the richness, the flexibility of the visible aspects of life' (*IP* 56, 62). This same 'imaginary light' also illumines the darker spaces of portraiture, as in Pater's account of Sebastian von Storck, who senses the 'one lively spirit circulating through all things – a tiny particle of the one soul, in the sunbeam, or the leaf – and understands it as an 'abstract being', a 'pallid Arctic sun, disclosing itself over the dead level of a glacial, a barren and absolutely lonely sea' (*IP* 108). Like Duke Carl of Rosenmond, in the final portrait, Sebastian experiences daily life as a series of 'transient affections', which threaten 'the freedom, the truth, the beatific calm, of [his] absolute selfishness'. The space of his inner life inspires both a 'fantastic sense of wellbeing' and 'a sort of fanatical devotion'. Indeed, in a fine irony that is Gothicised in Wilde's *Dorian Gray*, the artist becomes so absolutely selfish that 'he die[s] to self'. Inner life, which corresponds to this mode of artistic selfishness, thus becomes an escape from the 'lodging-place' of identity, an utterly free space that is 'but the passing thought of God' (*IP* 109).

This resemblance between the artist's inner life and the thought of God animates 'Duke Carl of Rosenmond', a Gothic allegory of classical *Bildung*, set in the late eighteenth century, in which the protagonist confronts 'the essentially aged and decrepit graces' of his model, 'the French ideal, in matters of art and literature'. In negative dialectical fashion, the Duke's 'essentially youthful temper … invigorated what he borrowed' and made his 'aspiration towards the classical ideal' (*IP* 124) a vital alternative to an exhausted model. He floats in a timeless realm of sensation, possessed, like Antony Watteau, by a 'strange restlessness' that he believes may be the 'imperfect reminiscence' of an 'earlier life' (*IP* 133). He believes that 'past ages' are enlivened by a 'historic soul' and exist 'for the entertainment, the expansion, of the present' (*IP* 145). Though the Duke disappears from the stage of his own life in the mysterious advent of a 'victorious army', his spirit appears to rise again in the figure of Goethe, who is 'the fulfillment of the *Resurgam* [L. "I shall rise again"] on Carl's empty coffin – the aspiring soul of Carl himself, in freedom and effective, at last' (*IP* 153).

Pater captures this essentially Schillerian sense of freedom and efficacy in a series of portraits that, by virtue of being imaginary, are the products of his own subjectivity, his inner life, projected through the filter of his narrators, who are themselves part of the aesthetic milieu in which the imaginary artists exist. But rather than imitate their creator by mirroring in his prose the autobiographical reality he experiences, his portraits offer a resemblance to him that passes like a shadow in the world of the work. Pater is thereby legible in his creations, precisely in the way that Basil Hallward, in Wilde's *Dorian Gray*, suggests: as evidence that the artist shares a lifeworld with the artwork, which bears, as it were, a family resemblance to his own inner life. If portraiture *misrecognises* the self in such resemblances, it does so in order to foreclose a more destructive, idealising misprision: the dialectical closure of achieved *Bildung*.

## Deformation and Autobiography

The modernist portrait of the artist motif represents the experience of protagonists whose aesthetic appreciation of everyday life effectively revamps the Bildungsroman by opening up new possibilities (both thematic and formal) for Bildung. These protagonists take on the responsibility of refashioning life along new aesthetic contours. Wilde is famous for having said that '[t]o become a work of art is the object of living',[23] and he gave this epigram a Gothic treatment in *Dorian Gray* by literalising the motif of the portrait and transforming the concept of self-development into its opposite, a dissolution without passage. Dorian Gray and his friends live a heightened aesthetic life, in which aspiration becomes tantamount to artistic production. The ideal of an aesthetic life – in which, as Goethe says, you 'give yourself up to your impressions' – is one that Wilde developed from Pater, James McNeill Whistler and John Ruskin – the full sweep of English aestheticism, which he extolled in 'The English Renaissance of Art'.[24] This ideal sanctions Dorian's education in art *and* his Faustian wish for youth, a wish that comes to haunt him and leads to his *in*aesthetic death. Lord Henry's relation to Dorian appears, on one level, to be a mentorship in queer aesthetics, in which the beauty of the male body and the idea of the self-as-art are celebrated. But on another level, he manipulates the younger man in order to intensify his own vicarious pleasures and produces at best a simulacrum of his own ego-ideal. Basil Hallward differs only in the intensity of his desire for the younger man and in the moralistic ground he tries to establish for his mentorship (first came love, then came religion), for he too plays (with) Dorian, just less adroitly and with less discretion.

When Dorian finally reflects on the idea of selfhood, he does so while reviewing his portrait gallery, which provides proof of a family resemblance, though for Dorian, it does not substantiate blood ties. It does nothing more than affirm the power he possesses to 'multiply . . . personalities'. He rejects the 'shallow psychology' of polite society that would regard him as a singular person and assents instead to the idea of a 'complex multiform creature'.[25] Yet he also falls prey to 'that pride of individualism that is half the fascination of sin' (*DG* 109). Lord Henry senses this contradiction and seeks to assimilate it into the grander contradiction between art and life when he tells Dorian, '"Life has been your art. You have set yourself to music. Your days are your sonnets"' (*DG* 165). His efforts fail, however, for the 'imaginary portrait' of his protégé's aesthetic life is no better than the actual portrait of Dorian's life stowed away in the attic: each enables a radical misrecognition of his formative experience and of the contradiction that enables art. Dorian is trapped in a painted world of resemblance; and his inner life, now of a piece with the painted world, is no longer the engine of his Bildung. He hopes that the changes he sees in the portrait are the expression of a 'subtle affinity between the chemical atoms' (*DG* 81). That he lashes out against Basil makes sense if we understand his rage as being vented against the very idea of a portrait that captures his essence when he is fully aware that his essence is change, the 'strange, perpetual, weaving and unweaving of ourselves', that for Pater constitutes the moving totality of the self. Unlike Stephen Dedalus a generation later, Dorian cannot move the process of his own formation into alignment with the portrait of the artist trope that animates his desire, for that trope is an *imposition* on the part of mentors whose perversion lies in their willingness to impose.

While in some ways *The Picture of Dorian Gray* offers a lesson in the excesses of aestheticism, and can be read as an indictment against Dorian's fateful desire to become his own portrait, it is simultaneously a critique of accepted ideas about the self, subjectivity and the relation of the other in the formative process. Wilde portrays the self as internally split and contradictory and formation as a process driven by arbitrary impositions of power and influence. Ultimately, Dorian sacrifices his life to regain the power of his own formation through an acceptance of his own *deformation*, a sacrifice that serves primarily to memorialise the self he has lost. If he tries to seize himself back at the cost of the life he once hoped to preserve in amber, it is because he has come to realise the nature of aspiration, which requires the very field of time and change that he thoughtlessly wished away. This is what he seeks to achieve by destroying the portrait *and* the artist, for in doing so he brings back into himself the temporality of his own formative being.

As a portrait of the artist, *Dorian Gray* is overdetermined: all parties to the portrait find themselves in it, thereby dramatising the inherent multiplicity of subjects in literary portraiture, a point Wilde makes explicitly when he confesses that *Dorian Gray* 'contains much of me in it. Basil Hallward is what I think I am; Lord Henry what the world thinks me; Dorian what I would like to be – in other ages perhaps'.[26] Wilde's modernist portraiture does not seek to establish an exact correspondence between representation and its subject, between his own age and some other, but rather to create a resemblance to the subject portrayed, a world of the work that takes in maker, milieu and medium. The figure in the portrait exists semi-autonomously in a shadow relation to the creator's concrete social reality it only (and necessarily) resembles; in a similar fashion, the creator exists in the work. The phenomenologist Mikel Dufrenne explains this mutual inhabitation by noting that the art work is 'doubly tied to subjectivity': first 'to the subjectivity of the spectator [or reader], from whom it requires the perception necessary for its manifestation'; and second, 'to the subjectivity of the creator, from whom it has required the activity necessary for its creation, and who expresses himself through it, even – and especially – if he has not expressly desired it!'[27] It follows that the artwork – in this case, the modernist portrait of the artist – serves a primarily hermeneutic function: it anchors the inner life of the protagonist to the autobiographical real – specifically, the world of the author and of her aesthetic life and vision – and, by virtue of this anchoring function, conveys something of the immediacy and intimacy of the creator's lived experience. In this way, portraiture moves closer to inner life and, ultimately, *self*-portraiture.

This aspect of portraiture, the pre-eminence of inner life, is developed in Joyce's *Portrait* in a free-indirect style of 'narrated monologue' that is crucial to representing both the artist and his formative milieu.[28] A young Catholic Irishman, Stephen Dedalus, must struggle against the inevitable failings of achieved Bildung and at the same time try to understand the allure of his own aspirations, his 'wayward instincts':

> All through his boyhood he had mused upon that which he had so often thought to be his destiny and when the moment had come for him to obey the call he had turned aside, obeying a wayward instinct. Now time lay between: the oils of ordination would never anoint his body. He had refused. Why?[29]

By refusing the call to serve the Church in favour of his own desire, Stephen not only moves past boyhood; he moves past the temporality of formation that makes boyhood *formative of* achieved manhood of a certain kind, valorised by the 'oils of ordination'. And he does so by claiming time for himself, creating what Tobias Boes calls an 'individuating rhythm', a disjunctive mode of self-formation in which the subject 'appears as a monadic entity cutting a solitary path through historical time and into the promise of modernity'.[30] Stephen realises, as a very young man, that '[n]ow time lay between' him and the world of his father, a time full of promise, the temporality of his own aspirations that *necessarily* fail to conform to the goals of a socialised subjectivity, specifically the Bildung concept urged upon him by his father who calls for him to associate with – that is, *to be like* – 'fellows of the right kidney' (*P* 80).

If Joyce's *Portrait* stands out in early modernism as the paradigmatic expression of the portrait of the artist motif, it does so because it brings together the grandeur of achievement and the quicksilver pleasures of aspiration, and it thematises the conflict between them in a free-indirect style that blends with and becomes part of the portrait's texture. Stephen borrows from the external world to give familiar shape and dimension to the 'inner world of [his] individual emotions', and this inner world is, in turn, mirrored in his thoughts, couched 'perfectly in a lucid supple periodic prose'. His immediate environment seeps into the inner world he contemplates; a phrase he speaks to himself – 'A day of dappled seaborne clouds' – becomes allied with the day itself and 'the scene harmonised in a chord'. He invites the world of experience – 'slowdrifting clouds, dappled and seaborne' – into the inner life he fashions beyond the reach of that world: 'He heard a confused music within him as of memories and names; then the music seemed to recede, to recede, to recede,' then 'Again! Again! Again! A voice from beyond the world was calling.' He finds himself ('Again!') confronted with a world beyond *this* one, where the 'slender masts' on the Liffey 'flecked the sky and, more distant still, the dim fabric of the city lay prone in haze'. The world of the work, 'prone in haze' like the city, and the inner world of the artist come together '[l]ike a scene on some vague arras', visible 'across the timeless air' (*P* 146–7).

At this pivotal point, Stephen feels, though he does not yet recognise, that what matters is not achieved Bildung ('the dignity of the office he had refused') but the sheer force of 'his own soul going forth to experience, unfolding itself sin by sin' (*P* 90). The theological cast to his thought is overcome in part by an aesthetic standpoint that calls for 'a new personal experience' (*P* 145). We do not find out what this experience might be in *Portrait*, but *Ulysses* suggests that it has to do with the young artist abandoning his hierophantic posture and turning a corrective gaze on his own aesthetics of epiphany, which, in *Portrait*, excludes the author from the world of the work. From a godlike perspective the artist may strive to remain 'within or behind or beyond or above his handiwork' (*P* 189); but like the 'voice from beyond', this perspective belongs to his own inner world, which fails *necessarily* to isolate him from his creation. He emerges as a high priest whose desire to realise the truth in art leads to self-exile in an attempt to find congenial grounds (in a word, Paris) for the aesthetic life he desires. In part because of the strong autobiographical component – it is well known that *Portrait* follows closely the outlines of the author's own boyhood and youth[31] – Joyce offers us a vision of such a life in strategic balance with the external world it incorporates through mimetic borrowing. As a portrait of the artist, *Portrait* captures the dynamism of its protagonist's inner life, his ambition 'to rearrange the details of modern life', as Pater suggests, and thus bend the world to the demands of his 'wayward instincts'.

## Free-Indirect Intimacy

The aesthetic life in *Portrait* is the culmination of a process whereby the artist ultimately disappears from the artwork, 'invisible refined out of existence'; properly speaking, it is life *in* the aesthetic object, 'purified and reprojected from the human imagination' (*P* 189). Stephen has not yet created for himself a condition of ordinary living that entails a commitment to beauty in the enjoyment of life and the moment's aspiration that it affords. As in Wilde's *Dorian Gray* and Pater's imaginary portraits, the male artist figure predominates and the aesthetic life appears rarefied and exclusive, to the point of being cut off from the realm of ordinary sensible experience. Forster's *A Room with a View* offers us a very different example of how the early modernist Bildungsroman portrays artistic life, and does so by focusing less on the desire to be an artist than on the desire to live the aesthetic life. Lucy Honeychurch works against existing norms for (male) development and registers, in her responses to her milieu, not only the persistence of aspiration but the emergence of new relations to those norms from the standpoint of inner life. To accomplish this, realism is made to do subtle and effective work. *A Room with a View* includes meticulous description; a sensitivity to aesthetic milieu; a self-conscious, dramatised narrator, who is at times self-deprecating but also commanding, even omniscient; and at least three levels of ironic distance: the narrator's with respect to the action and characters, the characters' with respect to each other, and the reader's with respect to the narrator. If the autobiographical real gains a purchase on the text, it does so by virtue of identifications Forster makes with his narrator and characters, much as we see in Wilde, though perhaps less explicitly, and by virtue of the reader's intimate relation with the dramatised narrator.[32] Finally, as a late example of the New Woman movement, *Room with a View* drives a critique of the masculine privilege of ambition and the Bildung-script in which women play a fore-ordained role as *helpmeet* to the male hero of development.[33] Lucy challenges the protocols of the conventional Bildungsroman by taking command of her own aesthetic education, despite a paucity of opportunities to further it, and by remaining open to unconventional mentors. It is this challenge, and the ambivalence it generates around the idea of marriage and personal happiness, that is conveyed in Forster's portrait of aesthetic life.

Literary portraiture, as we have seen, is the impression of a personality sustained in a dynamic resemblance, the aesthetic operation that links the work (the portrait) both to the maker and to the person (or a likely *type* of person) who occupies the position of sitter or subject. Forster's portrait of Lucy owes much to Pater and the general curriculum of English aestheticism, steeped in Greek, Roman and Italian art and culture. A crucial part of such a curriculum is the extended tour of Italy depicted in *A Room with a View*, during which Lucy's aesthetic sensibilities come alive, as when she visits the church in Santa Croce and finds 'frescoes by Giotto, in the presence of whose tactile values she was capable of feeling what was proper'.[34] She is eager to know the details and provenance of the aesthetic life into which she desires entry and to recognise *for herself* what 'had been most praised by Mr. Ruskin' (*R* 33).

Once she returns to England and Windy Corners, Lucy becomes absorbed in her own desires and ambitions. An 'unknown emotion' arises from a sudden sense of herself coming 'into view' – indeed, of seeing the 'whole of life in a new perspective' (*R* 42, 47) – which leads her to aspire deeply and urgently: 'she wanted something big, and she believed that it would have come to her on the wind-swept platform of an electric tram' (*R* 65). Lucy knows instinctively that aspiration works by way of the 'wind-swept' arrival of something surprising rather than by clear-sighted knowledge of a goal. She shares with Pater's restless artists a capacity for 'rebellious thoughts' and a sense of herself as somehow unfinished or inauthentic, existing in a state of unfreedom that her fiancé Cecil threatens to sustain in marriage. The reader is confronted with a protagonist whose affect communicates that she has not yet begun to live (in this she resembles Pater's Duke Carl of Rosenmond with his Byronic sense of belatedness). Her first encounter alone with George Emerson, a young man travelling with his father, disturbs and fascinates her in equal measure precisely because it seems to mark the starting point of her life. He derails her conventional sense of timing and propriety by suddenly kissing her while they are alone in 'a little open terrace, which was covered with violets from end to end', beating 'against her dress in blue waves' (*R* 115–16). If George's first kiss seems to halt her in her tracks – 'I thought I was developing' – the second starts her up again because it is the external manifestation of her own aspirations, the intense, sensual *promise* of life that the first kiss put into motion: for she '*had* developed' (*R* 122, 276; my emphasis).

Like Dorian Gray, Lucy's true talent is for living – chapter nine is titled 'Lucy As a Work of Art' (*R* 164ff) – and like him she struggles tremulously to identify as an artist, as when she thinks of herself as 'a kind of poetess sort of person' (*R* 182). Her halting, tense relation to music mirrors her struggle to come to terms with her aspirations. Like Miriam Henderson in Richardson's *Pilgrimage*, she wants to immerse herself in the worlds created by music and to feel 'the sadness of the incomplete – the sadness that is often Life, but should be Art' (*R* 208). She recognises that the goal of art is ultimately that of life – to exist in a form of incompleteness that testifies not to an inferior unfinished state but rather to the dynamism of a formative process. She is brought to this point of reflection by an unlikely mentor, George's father – '"rather a peculiar man"' (*R* 215) – who helps Lucy realise the nature of her own formative desire, which, until then, had seemed to her like a vague muddle. The narrator tells us that 'she never gazed inwards . . . If at times strange images rose from the depths, she put them down to nerves' (*R* 242). But not gazing inward does not mean that she has no inner life. When the narrator tells us that she 'disliked confidences, for they might lead to self-knowledge' (*R* 332), we are struck with how satisfyingly *wrong* the narrator is, for Lucy first gets a taste of self-knowledge amid the 'blue waves' of violets, when she opened herself, and her inner life, to another.

Self-*mis*recognition, volitional and canny, leads Lucy to a genuine understanding of her inner life, which enables her to remain open to Mr Emerson's shocking proposal: '"You must marry, or your life will be wasted".' He is not advocating the idea that Lucy should subordinate her own formative desires to George's; indeed, quite the opposite appears to be the case when he tells Lucy, '"He is already part of you"' (*R* 351). His appeal – '"Marry him; it is one of the moments for which the world was made"' – is not that of the patriarch who wishes his son to complete his Bildung-process in a satisfying way; his concern is rather that '"love is answered by love"'. Lucy's anger subsides as Mr Emerson leads her to a vision about herself, for at this moment, 'as he spoke the darkness was withdrawn, veil after veil, and she saw to the bottom of her soul' (*R* 352). Her resistance is overmatched by their shared recollection of '"the mountains over Florence and the view"' and by his admonition that she must '"go cold into a battle that needs warmth, out into the muddle that you have made yourself".'

In the final chapter, George and Lucy return to the Pensione Bertolini, where they first met. Lucy feels isolated because her family reacted badly to the match, so George 'carried her to the window, so that she, too, saw all the view' (*R* 360). From this perspective, all of the world is open to them, just as George's father had promised. They find all the trouble they have gone through worthwhile, for being together 'was the great joy that they expected, and countless little joys of which they had never dreamt' (*R* 360). In the aesthetic milieu that first brought them together – the room with a view in the Pensione Bertolini – they rediscover the rhythm of their own aspirations ('countless little joys'), neither subordinated to the other, both accountable only to a benign fate, symbolised by the young Italian cabman, whose song can be heard outside their window and may have 'set this happiness in motion twelve months ago' (*R* 358): 'Youth enwrapped them; the song of Phaethon announced passion requited, love attained . . . The song died away; they heard the river, bearing down the snows of winter into the Mediterranean' (*R* 363–4).

Forster's novel is rare among modernist Bildungsromane in that a female protagonist manages to marry happily *and* to enrich her inner life. However, the question of marriage is far more complex and the gains for the Bildungsheld more rewarding in works by Woolf, Richardson and, later, H. D. Volume one of Richardson's *Pilgrimage* and Woolf's *The Voyage Out* were published in 1915 and both articulate a desire for an aesthetic life free of the constraints imposed by marriage.[35] Woolf's protagonist, Rachel Vinrace, pursues this desire while languishing with her fellow expatriates in the fictitious South American port of Santa Marina. Given the freedom and novelty this arrangement affords her, she has a decided advantage over a woman like Lucy Honeychurch, whose life in Windy Corners was conventional and restrictive, though her sojourn in Europe begins to open up the kind of possibilities discerned by Woolf's protagonist. Rachel's aspirations submit Bildung to a dilatory temporality, a time of dreamy longueurs and deep study, 'idle moments' when she has to struggle to regain 'some consciousness of her own existence', for life was like 'a light passing over the surface and vanishing, as in time she would vanish'. In the rarified milieu of her inner life, she is aware of the external world as 'things that existed . . . . so immense and so desolate', while a clocked ticked 'in the midst of the universal silence'.[36] Her interactions with her contemporaries, the intellectual discussions dominated by men, the endless speculation about marriage – all of this drives her into the solitude of her inner life, where she is free to surround herself with music and literature and to reflect on her own existence. During the long illness that closes the narrative, Rachel ceases to strive for the singular self she most desired and seems to share her being, for a moment, with that of her fiancé Terence Hewitt, who at the time of her sickness feels 'peace invading every corner of his soul'. Her death comes as 'nothing', he says; 'it was to cease to breathe'. But her death also created something new, 'the union which had been impossible while they lived' – for now, 'he seemed to be Rachel as well as himself' (*VO* 412). Woolf does not give us illness as redemption, and the inner life as a safe harbour from social convention; I think she stages illness to create a zone of indistinction in which something like a mutual aspiration moves towards an impossible future: a world in which Bildung can be shared. For in the moment of her passing, she and Terence 'possessed what could never be taken from them' (*VO* 412). And while she seeks out death as a way to safeguard her wish 'to be alone' (*VO* 405), after dying she inspires peace and happiness among others, a form of 'spontaneous cooperation' by proxy. The aesthetic life she sought for herself turns out to be her bequest to Terence and to their friend, the artist St John Hirst, who comes to feel, with her passing, a 'profound happiness'. It is telling that when he heads to bed, at the novel's end, the voices of the community 'sound gratefully in [his] ear' (*VO* 436–7).

Richardson's *Pilgrimage I* presents us with a similar protagonist, one whose aspiration for Bildung is just as ardent if less refined than Rachel's. Richardson's narrative, unvaryingly tied to Miriam's wayward conscious-ness, pauses for long periods to record her study and reflections, and in the first three volumes these reflections are often explicitly directed towards the realisation of an aesthetic life. But if Rachel succeeds in creating an environment amenable to intellectual self-improvement – a room with a piano and 'a mess of books on the floor', where she can read or do 'absolutely nothing' (*VO* 31) – if the isolation of her father's ship and leisure time in Santa Marina provide her with the freedom to study and learn, Miriam has to struggle in a strait-laced school environment, with limited resources, cramped quarters and little free time. Yet like Rachel, she explicitly aspires towards Bildung, claiming to live in her own 'German atmosphere'.[37] And like her, she displaces the goal of marriage by affirm-ing, again explicitly, the value of her own aspirations.

In Richardson, as in Joyce and Woolf, free-indirect style enables the merger of creator and creation, of consciousness and language in a way that aligns the protagonist's inner life with the world of the work. This alignment becomes the 'subject' of portraiture. Gill Hanscombe suggests that Richardson sought to 'write about the subject she [knew] best, which, she maintained, was her own life'.[38] And in this, she follows Dufrenne, who says that 'it is precisely the sole virtue of the aesthetic object not to explain but to reveal its creator'.[39] In her foreword to *Pilgrimage*, written in 1938, Richardson speaks of Balzac and 'the power of a sympathetic imagination, uniting him with each character in turn, [which] gives to every portrait the quality of a faithful self-portrait'.[40] Self-portraiture on this model elicits not the self-revelation of an autobiographical plot, which we may say is the case with Joyce, or the identifications we see in Wilde and Forster, but rather a mood of general empathy, so that *every* character resembles the author. Richardson, like Woolf and H. D., stakes a claim to this general empathy, which allows her discreetly to touch down on the autobiographical real in ways that are veiled and obscured by fictionalising tropes and alternative modes (choric, plural, shared) of Bildung.[41]

Because Miriam's aspirations for Bildung are revealed primarily in moments of self-reflection, Richardson required a technique that would capture both the quicksilver urgency of her protagonist's experience and the continuity of her reflections. In a manner that looks forward to the later Woolf and H. D., Richardson transforms the portrait of the artist motif by representing the atmosphere of Miriam's aspirations in a style of free-indirect intimacy that keeps an ever-changing and conflicted flow of thoughts within the limits of an inner world dominated by the desire for an aesthetic life. Richardson was thus able to represent the 'individuating rhythms' of Miriam's thought, the moments of heightened aesthetic awareness that illustrate both the inner life of her desires and the social accommodations that make it possible.[42] Woolf tried to understand this style and decided that Richardson had 'invented, or, if she has not invented, developed and applied to her own uses, a sentence which we might call the psychological sentence of the feminine gender'.[43] I believe this better describes Woolf than it does Richardson, whose style produces sentences that only she could write or Miriam think. They are certainly not essentially feminine, for Miriam seems to *despise* women, whom she finds to be 'so terrible' (*H* 436). Her sentences flagrantly reveal the very quality that Woolf disparaged when she referred to Richardson (and Joyce) as having succumbed to the 'damned egotistical self'.[44] But the intense interiority of Richardson's Bildungsroman, or for that matter Woolf's, is not due to a solipsistic inward turn but to quite the opposite, an *outward* orientation towards the self paradoxically grounded in inner life: 'She stirred; her hands seemed warm on her cool chest and the warmth of her body sent up a faint pleasant sense of personality. "It's me," [Miriam] said, and smiled' (*PR* 150). Yet at the same time, her body is *not* her. Gazing in the mirror she thinks, 'I *am* German looking today [...] But I haven't got a German expression [...] Never mind. I look jolly [...] It's something. It isn't me. It's something I am, somehow [....] Oo – crumbs! This is no place for *me*' (*PR* 150–1). Miriam contemplates herself in a way that draws out the German other that engages her inner life and that highlights the duplicity of portraiture, the way it reveals indiscreetly the image of the creator, for Miriam's awareness of her embodied self ironically calls our attention to the impossibility of representing the autobiographical real. Her difficulty representing herself is of the same order as Richardson's; the 'faint pleasant sense of personality' informs both Miriam's self-representation and Richardson's 'sympathetic imagi-nation'. The (mis)alignment of the two results in literary self-portraiture.

Like Joyce, Richardson rehabilitates classical Bildung, but does so in a way that underscores the Bildungsheld's understanding of the specifically *German* ideal of 'being a "person of leisure and cultivation"' (*PR* 28). *Pointed Roofs* recounts Miriam's first teaching post in Hanover, where she began creating her 'German atmosphere'. Later, in *Honeycomb*, we learn that '[n]o English person would quite understand – the need that the Germans understood so well – the need to admit the beauty of things . . . the need of the strange expression of music, making the beautiful things more beautiful' (*H* 374). Miriam focuses on the key art forms of German philosophical aesthetics (poetry and music) and follows Schiller, who believed that 'mak[ing] Beauty out of a multiplicity of beautiful objects is the task of aesthetic education'. For Miriam, it follows that art must strive, despite the inevitability of failure, to give a total picture (*Gesamtbild*) of life – 'Music and poetry told everything [. . .] they put you in the mood that made [. . .] things go on shining until the end' (*H* 374). Like Lucy Honeychurch, she seeks the 'featureless freedom' that music affords: 'She would play something she knew perfectly [. . .] and let herself go, and listen. That was music . . . not playing things, but listening to Beethoven,' who 'had always been real' (*PR* 56). In the world of music, human time is 'dissolved, past and future and present and she was nothing but an ear, intent on the meditative harmony which stole out into the garden' (*PR* 205). Such momentary suspensions of time define and orient her; they provide an 'ever-recurring joyous sense of emergence', of being 'alive and changeable, able to become quite new' (*PR* 90, *H* 302–3).

Miriam's aesthetic desire soon confronts education as an obstacle. The headmistress of the school, known only as Fräulein, has a rigid, neo-Humboldtian notion of teaching, according to which the teacher must be '"human sunshine, encouraging all effort and all lovely things in the personality of the pupil"' (*PR* 160). Indeed, the teacher must '"enter into the personality of each pupil"', a prospect that could not be less amenable to Miriam, whose sense of self-cultivation is fearlessly changeable and self-centred and resistant to the dialectical charms of a pedagogy that absorbs the teacher in the student. In fact, the two volumes following *Pointed Roofs* document, in a manner consistent with other modernist Bildungsromane, the downfall of Miriam's faith in education, once she begins to teach in England. By the time she lands with the Corries in Newlands (in *Honeycomb*), Miriam has grown worryingly cynical about the children she teaches: 'They would grow up and be exactly like their parents,' never knowing '[s]cience, strange things about India and Ireland, the aesthetic movement. Ruskin; making things beautiful' (*H* 383).

We could speak, as Jed Esty does in his study of postcolonial Bildungsromane, of a failed or stalled or suffocated Bildung, and regard Miriam's development as a series of symptoms of her failure to realise her ambitions. But I believe that these opening volumes represent not a *failure* to achieve but a chronicle of a productive *failing*, a disorientation of character, that leads the protagonist to a greater sense of her own aspirations. Miriam seems *to outgrow* the desire to achieve a vocation, which she misrecognises as a failure to become a particular 'kind of person': 'They wanted a governess [. . .] It was a mistake; another mistake' (*H* 352). Ultimately, she just wants to exist, as a kind of artistic being, in a world free of people. She finds this other world in books which come to occupy her in ways that are increasingly distant from her pedagogical responsibilities: they are '[m]ore real than actual people. They came nearer [. . .] In a book the author was there in every word' (*H* 384). Like other modernist Bildungshelden, Miriam is surrounded by people and talk, by the process and rewards of education; but unlike them, she has no intellectual confidant of the sort who could serve as a whetstone, as Mr Emerson serves for Lucy, or Cranly for Stephen. She dreams of the kind of aesthetic life – Richardson saw it as 'aesthetically revelling' in life[45] – that would allow her to 'sing all day in the garden' and play to her husband on the piano; 'they would share the great secret, dying of happiness. Die of happiness' (*H* 396). And she ruthlessly lays claim to this secret, which is nothing less than the beauty of life: 'Bright mornings, beautiful bright rooms, a wilderness of beauty all round her all the time – at any cost. Any life that had not these things she would refuse [. . .] It was her right' (*H* 403).

The desire for the aesthetic life supplies its own goal, its own terms of achievement, which are not those celebrated in the marriage plot; the husband mentioned above is little more than an *objet d'art*. All that is needful is to sustain the moment of beauty infinitely. Miriam's turn to painting at the end of *Honeycomb* signals a new creative capacity to her aspirations. Her 'German atmosphere' of cultivation and personal freedom, 'that strange inner life' that was 'independent of everybody' (*H* 431), will come to protect her in subsequent volumes. A Bildung-plot built on such an atmosphere – 'the offering of the moment' (*H* 383) – could conceivably extend into eternity, which accounts for the 'long form' that Richardson uses to narrate the waxing and waning of Miriam's aspirations, the gravitational fluctuations of her 'strange inner life', which encompasses everything: "'I'm something new'" she rejoices, "'a kind of different world'" (*B* 260). It is precisely this world-making capacity, coupled with an unrelentingly intimate free-indirect style, that animates the portrait of the artist motif in *Pilgrimage I*; for at bottom, what is at stake in modernist portraiture is the creation of a world grounded in (and on) the inner life of the protagonist.[46] If Forster portrays the aesthetic life as a reward hard won by a young woman who has learned along the way to value her own aspirations for it, then Richardson's and Woolf's protagonists eschew a promised reward and instead make an accommodation with existing conditions – what I've been calling the aesthetic life – such that aspiration alone constitutes the reward they desire. In Richardson's case, a trace of the autobiographical real serves to strengthen this accommodation by virtue of the similarity between the creator's consciousness and the inner life of her creation. In this respect, Richardson develops an essential aspect of Wilde's *Dorian Gray*: the presence of the creator *within* the portrait she creates.

## Bildung and the Aesthetic Life

The portrait of the artist motif serves a similar world-making function in H. D.'s work, particularly the *HERmione-Asphodel* sequence that I am identifying here as H. D.'s auto/biographical Bildungsroman.[47] A dense matrix of auto/biographical relations and misprisions is expressed in an allusive and creative free-indirect style that works by resemblance and analogy rather than imitative mimesis to convey non-linear, fragmented and citational strands of thought. As in Richardson's *Pilgrimage*, we see in *HERmione-Asphodel* how literary portraiture allows the autobiographical real to become a vital part of a textual economy in which the expressed world of the work becomes nearly co-extensive with the contours of inner life – itself a confluence of author and character – with the result that the represented world appears utterly subordinated to it, much as Dorian's 'real' life was subordinated to a portrait of him. With H. D., we see just how far the artistic construction of inner life constitutes *in its own right* an expressed world, free of the constraints that would limit representation to an imitation of the real. The resulting resemblance between the inner world of the author as creator and the expressed world of the work is paradigmatic of the aesthetic object, if we follow Dufrenne, and this resemblance is nowhere more self-evident than in H. D.'s portrait of aesthetic life. The expressed world of H. D.'s novel is a confluence of inner lives – that of the creator and her avatars, that of the reader as well – that generates a play of resemblances that extends beyond the formal empathy that allows Richardson to regard the author as united 'with each character in turn'. For it is also a confluence of genres, of the Bildungsroman and the *roman-à-clef*, that makes possible an ambiguous appeal to the autobiographical real, an appeal not to the reality behind fictions that H. D. creates but to the difference between reality and fiction that the *roman-à-clef* masks through its factual facade.

As Sean Latham has pointed out, the *roman-à-clef* is a duplicitous form because it borrows an 'aesthetics of detail' from the realist novel precisely to prevent any kind of full or candid disclosure of 'genuine facts about real people'.[48] This aestheticisation of 'genuine facts' and 'real people' brings in its train alternatives to the biographical temporalities that typically organise formative fictions. These alternatives made it possible for H. D., as it did for Woolf, to convey the sense of Bildung as an experiment in the aesthetic life, one that refuses the demands of an ideal or the dictates of a model and, as we have seen, one that refuses the necessity to stick to facts even when one is assuming the 'factual' status of the autobiographical real. Aspiration for its own sake arises as the ongoing reward of the aesthetic life, marked in singular moments of the kind that sum up in a *flash* (as opposed to a *fact*) a whole process of formation, that illuminate a point of rupture or rapture in the pursuit of self-harmony – the 'exquisite moment' that, in *Mrs Dalloway*, compresses time into 'a diamond, something infinitely precious'.[49]

*HERmione* focuses on a life of moments. The protagonist, Hermione (H. D.), is stranded at her parents' home in rural Pennsylvania after failing at 'a somewhat exaggeratedly-planned "education"' at Bryn Mawr. She is a precocious artist-in-the-making who finds that she must reject the authority of her father and brother, whose 'theorem of mathematical biological intention'[50] alienates the ethereal and artistic Hermione, who resists the middle-class standard described by Hegel: 'harmony with subsisting relationships and their rationality'. She also resists the provocative new explanations of life coming out of psychoanalysis, indeed any explanation 'that posts signs over emotional bog and intellectual lagoon . . . "failure complex," "compensation complex," and that conniving phrase "arrested development"' (*HER* 3–4). These new standard metrics do not apply to her:

> Her development forced along slippery lines of exact definition, marked supernorm, marked subnorm on some sort of chart or soul-barometer. She could not distinguish the supernorm, dragging her up from the subnorm, letting her down. She could not see the way out of marsh and bog. She said, 'I am Hermione Gart precisely.' (*HER* 3)

The standards of success and failure ('supernorm'/'subnorm') give way to the self-legitimising act of naming, in which intellectual and artistic aspirations are nourished in the space of inner life where formative temporalities do not rise or fall according to an ideal of achieved – that is, successful – Bildung.

By naming herself 'precisely', Hermione seeks to free herself from 'forced' development and the manipulation of others: 'Hermione Gart hugged HER to Hermione Gart. I am HER. The thing was necessary. It was necessary to hug this thing to herself' (*HER* 33). Hermione's name is thus separate from HER (and from 'H. D.' and Hilda Doolittle), yet her selfhood is *a thing open to other equivalent things*: 'Names are in people, people are in names' – 'Trees are in people. People are in trees' – 'Things are in people, people are in things' (*HER* 5, 134). She emphasises this fluidity by displacing her own 'proper' name: 'I am out of *The Winter's Tale*,' she says (*HER* 32), though later she says 'that's not me'.[51] A sense of radical deracination leaves her 'clutch[ing] toward something that had no name yet' (*HER* 8) – something floral and aquatic, sensual but evanescent. '"Some plants,"' she tells her fiancé George Lowndes (Ezra Pound), '"some small water creatures give a sort of jellyfish sort of birth by breaking apart, by separating themselves from themselves."' He stops her with kisses. '"Oh God, hamadryad, forget all that rot"' (*HER* 118). Of course he tells her to forget it, so that he may be the one who separates Her from herself with his habit of giving her affectionate names out of Greek mythology.

Hermione spends a lot of time with George, whose aesthetic values and sense of the way poetic language works gives her the opportunity to form her own ideas about art; but she feels that there is 'something harlequin about him' (*HER* 33). He seems to parody the very high culture he advocates, which is not hard to believe, given the elegantly ironic classical poetry that Pound was writing at the time (around 1908).[52] At the same time, he oppresses her: 'George like a sponge had smudged her smooth face with kisses, had somehow, now she recalled it, smudged out something' (*HER* 118). While she feels intellectually dominated by him, he is at the same time a liberating influence. Sometimes, with him, she can feel how one moment can hang fire, 'shaping an eternity, shaping the whole of Her' (*HER* 188–9). Fayne Rabb (Frances Josepha Gregg), a friend from college, has a similar effect on her, though she is more playful, sensual and loving than George. Fayne tells her, '"You're as little as a bird that has no wings, no beak, no feathers. You are the sort of thing a caterpillar would be before it were born"' (*HER* 144). These animal metaphors are more astute than George's mythic cognomens, and Hermione luxuriates in Fayne's attentions. Their mutual regard creates an appealing private world. Fayne's visits help to create a space that accommodates languorous aesthetic musings and recitations from Swinburne, an erotically charged milieu that enables a form of shared Bildung: 'Save yourself and offer them a sort of water creature. Keep marble for yourself and keep marble for marble. Keep a marble self for a marble self, Her for Her, Her for Fayne exactly' (*HER* 177). This merger of selves is staged as marmoreal self-portrait, an aesthetic milieu memorialised 'exactly' in a shared moment: 'keep marble for marble'.

Hermione's perceptual values descend from the Paterian school of English aestheticism, with its emphasis on 'the inward world of thought and feeling', where we find 'a drift of momentary acts of sight and passion and thought'.[53] She learns 'to accept value in one gem, one strip or stripe of colour, accept red as you get it, in coral or blue as you get it, perfect star sapphires in eye-sockets' (*HER* 53). Her Bildung-quest is a series of such acceptances: 'The boom of the bee in her ear, his presence like an eclipse across the sun brought a visual image of the sort of thing she sought for' (*HER* 13). She experiences a pure but inchoate desire for a 'sort of thing', an aspiration that is not oriented towards achieved Bildung, but towards the shifting horizon of her own being, which is not always *her own* being. This sense of disorientation informs the culminating scene of Hermione's illness. For H. D., as for Woolf, illness is a not metaphor but a paradoxical and seemingly self-harming tactic of misrecognition; while ill, Hermione is able both to grasp the true nature of her family's errancy *and* to execute a deliberate misunderstanding of her own ambition in order to leap ahead of herself and posit a plausible future. When she is in the grip of fever and isolated from her family, she forms a bond with her nurse, Amy Dennon, to whom she speaks, in a long dramatic monologue, about the luminous importance of the moment: '"I want to sit here sensing this moment that is dawn and morning. A moment and an infinitesimal fraction of a moment and dawn slides into morning like starlight into water. There is a quivering, a slight infinitesimal shivering. The thing that was is not"' (*HER* 212). In a moment's passage, Hermione has access to her own suspended being, a form of waiting that is fatally evanescent: 'The thing she realized in that moment, that fraction of waiting, lost' (*HER* 213). But 'coming through the moment there were memories, red hyacinths in snow, red cyclamen seen through avid blighting lava' (*HER* 214–15). This idea of the moment, in which the past and the future converge, makes possible a new kind of freedom: for in the state of perpetual belatedness – a state of being *out of time*, like starlight falling long after it was emitted – the subject is no longer bound to the teleological logic of achieved Bildung.

H. D.'s self-portrait of the artist seeks to capture this *untimely* sense of Bildung by depicting an inner life that both preserves the self ('Keep a marble self for a marble self') and overcomes it in an act of self-disavowal: 'I want to take nursing,' she muses, aspiring to Amy's self-lessness. 'Valiantly I will keep Her under. I will incarcerate Her. Her won't anymore be' (*HER* 215–16). Hermione's self-image, by turns marmoreal and fluid, resists settling into anything other than an uncanny resemblance to herself. But like Miriam, she knows instinctively that she cannot betray the very self she has created in resistance to 'subnorm' and 'supernorm'. The goal of her contradictory aspirations is definitely not to resolve the contradiction in favour of a vocation in which she becomes the nurse she desires, *for the moment*, to be. She resists this role by making aspiration itself – Pater's 'drift of momentary acts' – her vocation: 'A moment will stand in a starched apron and the moment will save Her's being' (*HER* 216).

The *disposition of the moment* is the key to Her's aesthetic life, and in *Asphodel* she has to learn how to recognise and sustain that life in a new European milieu during an unprecedented time of war. She struggles to align a new sensorium (so much blood, strained nerves, unexpected cowardice and bravery – wholly new affective responses to pain, suffering, death) with a Paterian sense of self as constantly shifting and changing: '"I am burning away that's all,"' she tells Fayne. 'The clear gem-like flame' (*A* 52). She isolates herself from all precedent:

> My grandfather read Shakespeare – that's why, Hermione. But that's not me. That's not me. They can laugh if they want cry if they want, become rhapsodic over Her Gart, Hermione Gart or Hermione. But I'm something different. It's nothing to do with them. I'm something else. Different.' (*A* 53)

Hermione echoes Miriam's '"I'm something new" . . . a "different world"' in a declaration of aspiration embodied as a perpetually emergent *new thing*. Such an understanding of selfhood involves a sense of time that can accommodate a negative orientation – 'I saw myself grow up against my self' – and that enables a powerful and generative misrecognition: 'I am priestess, infallible, inviolate. I am chosen. No Penelope. Cassandra? Madness rings me' (*A* 151).

If the movement towards recognition of the moment's aspiration structures *HERmione*, aesthetics and the aesthetic life structure *Asphodel*. Early in the latter, the criteria for an aesthetic milieu are set out: 'Religion of love-of-beauty wasn't this thing. But still they wanted something, looked for something . . . The image of truth, of beauty is in this marble bowl forever . . . a Grecian urn. Where is he, Keats of that somewhat washed out ode? Let me get to him' (*A* 20). The repudiation of aestheticism does not quite stick, nor does slighting Keats's great ode diminish the importance of the key terms in it for the protagonist, who arranges her inner life in a way that showcases the beauty of the moment as a form of truth. Just as Miriam finds comfort during adversity in 'the offering of the moment', so we find that Hermione is consoled by the momentary pleasures of a still-rich aesthetic life. George plays a less vital role, now that he is in his European element and less dependent on her for emotional and intellectual support. She moves in a circle that includes her new husband Jerrod Darrington (Imagist poet Richard Aldington), Cyril Vane (Scottish critic and composer Cecil Gray, father of H. D.'s daughter) and Beryl (poet and novelist Bryher, H. D.'s partner); yet her own artistic accomplishments are obscured amid a welter of social engagements, war-time work, personal trauma, and the birth of Phoebe Fayne Darrington (Frances Perdita Aldington). She becomes close to the pianist Walter Dowel (Walter Morse Rummel), 'Debussy's favourite pupil' in Paris (*A* 27), and her early reflections on him and music revive the more intellectually carefree mood of *HERmione*. There is also a sense that Dowel, like George, is of the same Nietzschean *sort* as Hermione: 'There is a sort of aristocracy of the spirit . . . Things don't just happen. Art is sweating and going blind with agony' (*A* 28). She is not interested merely in beautiful objects (Miriam's simple claim), but in a life of spirit that is affectively powerful and that inevitably bleeds into whatever art one chooses to create. The artistic milieu in which Hermione moves evokes the real world of the author, whose inner life becomes one with the expressed world of the work. Auto/biography enters into art because art must be open to the agony of the creative spirit.

The wartime context of *Asphodel* puts a new kind of pressure on artistic aspiration. In isolation, with Darrington distracted or away in France, Hermione retreats to her art and her inner life. War has cast a 'wrong enchantment' over everything; art is 'all smudged out' and a new aesthetic is forced upon her, one that imposes the 'dastardly beauty of destruction' (*A* 118) to make up for the beauty that has been destroyed. Hermione's response is to envision 'for a moment . . . a layer of ourselves, in another sphere of consciousness', where present objects share their existence with a distant past and become 'imbued with . . . an epic quality' (*A* 152). She describes the world-making power of art

('Layers of life are going on all the time,' *A* 152), which, at this pivotal moment in her development, corresponds with an inner life that must compensate for the privations of war:

> Everything is to each but it is only in developing one's own genius, one's own mean personality (which is one's innate daemon) that we can reach the realization of some sphere which is for all time, eternal, flowing as water, colourless, transparent which falling imbues the very common chair you sit in the very ordinary book you lift and open with some quality that is one with the Revelation of Saint John the Divine or the orders of Sappho. *Colour there is in this sphere world, colour of the red anemone, colour as seen under clear water.* (*A* 152; my emphasis)

This remarkable passage conveys well the sense of time falling into eternity that characterises Hermione's inner life, one in which 'everything is to each' and the 'common chair' and 'ordinary book' share a time-space with Sappho and Saint John. In the highlighted sentence, the ambiguity of deictic reference ('colour *there*' vs. 'in *this* sphere') contributes to a general sense of otherworldliness, for like the expressed world of the work, inner life constitutes its own 'sphere world', though it is beholden to the world of representation for 'colour'.

This layering of possible worlds within art and inner life, I suggest, is a function of the (re)adjustment of perspective that Hermione sees as the artist's task: 'Things seen in perspective become things to be grappled with. Art. *Isn't art just re-adjusting nature to some intellectual focus?*' (*A* 175; my emphasis). Her aesthetics grants the inherent artistic value of the everyday and the ordinary – 'Mysteries were written in the air and you asked answers of the mysteries and were granted them' (*A* 155) – but it also requires that the artist focus, select, construct. 'The things are there all the time, but art ... make[s] a focus, a sense of proportion ... focussing on one small aspect of life' (*A* 175).[54] This notion of art as adjustment of focus and perspective is in keeping with a mode of portraiture that takes misrecognitions ('odd distorted images') and frames them (by 'grappling' with them) so that their 'right perspective' can be appreciated, but only by virtue of creative errancy:

> Lips were coral lips, smooth, lips were Eros lips, the mouth was too perfect though the nose plunged forward dangerous, too large, ploughing as it were a way before it, but the nose in this light was put on, rightly placed, giving too much character to the characterless child face ... The nose gave too much character and the eyes spoiled all the effect of peace, and of nonentity ... Something was wrong. (*A* 185)

Contradiction (at once 'characterless' and 'too much character') and a violent kineticism (plunging, ploughing) govern a portrait (of Beryl) that deliberately misrecognises its subject and thereby allegorises the internal logic of the portrait of the artist motif. The narrator refuses to align the subject of the portrait with the painted image – the subject's nose, which is 'rightly placed', provokes an excess of character, which spoils the 'effect of peace' – and this aesthetic disorientation reflects her own inner world, where she finds herself no longer moving 'on a straight line' but advancing 'in a spiral', until she 'grew more vague, no, more distinct, but distinctness in vagueness that was more tantalizing' (*A* 193). Inner life, made vital through free-indirect style, transforms narrative *mise en scène* into portraiture.

The patent contradiction in Hermione's depiction of Beryl captures the tantalising uncertainty, both temporal and spatial, of modernist portraiture: 'more vague, no, more distinct'. Though we know the protagonist in *HERmione* and *Asphodel* corresponds to H. D., the latter's free-indirect style substitutes resemblance for faithful likeness with the effect that Hermione takes on a life of her own, precisely by plunging forward into Beryl. Hermione is two-faced, duplicitous, like the *roman-à-clef* genre H. D. uses to conceal herself in plain sight. The portrait of the artist motif returns to its beginnings, for in H. D., as in Wilde, we find '[t]wo Greek faces, one on top of the other, both Greek, neither Greek, each spoiled by each' (*A* 186).

## The Intransitive Subject

After the mid-1920s, use of the portrait of the artist motif falls off, as fiction turns either to radical experimentation and innovation (which entails a firm repudiation of the Bildungsroman and other conventional forms for narrating the self) or to a resurgent realism less interested in Bildung-plots than in narratives with greater social, geographical and historical scope. However, we have a fine late-modernist exemplar in Elizabeth Bowen's *The Last September* (1929), which, like H. D.'s *Asphodel*, depicts a young woman's desire for an aesthetic life amid times of war. But unlike H. D. – and for that matter Richardson and Woolf – Bowen employs an ironic, understated realism, akin to what we see in Forster. The protagonist, Lois Farquar, is about the same age as Miriam Henderson, but is cast adrift in Danielstown, her aunt and uncle's Big House in County Cork during the Irish War of Independence (1919–21). The Naylors are Irish Protestants, members of the Ascendancy land-owning class, and they have little sense of the reality of their besieged situation. Lois senses that her own chances for a normative development are not good; at best, '[s]he thought of herself as forcing a pass'.[55] This is due in part to the suspension of normal life in wartime, but it is also due to Lois's sense of not quite belonging anywhere. As Mrs Vermont, one of the British Army wives, says of her, she '"is so – I mean, well, you know – vague, isn't she?"' (*LS* 46). This vague judgement fails to capture the sharpness with which Lois 'forc[es] a pass' through obstacles to gain some control over her own destiny. Bowen's narrator, like Forster's, portrays a young woman who has to grapple with her own inner life; but whereas Lucy 'never gazed inwards' Lois seems to have nowhere else to gaze, a self-reflective stance misrecognised as vagueness.

Jed Esty sees in *The Last September* a 'dilated, inverted bildungsroman plot' that is reduplicated in the 'permanently adolescent status' of the Anglo-Irish Ascendancy.[56] But what might seem like a developmental inversion may in fact be the temporal condition of inner life (recursive, repetitive, suspended, proleptic) when it becomes (as it was for Hermione) a retreat from the world of representation into one determined by her own 'individuating rhythm'. Lois's detachment from her youth – which 'seemed to her . . . rather theatrical', a vision of her that 'grown-up people expected' (*LS* 40) – is a sign not so much of stunted development (or the diminished symbolic value of youth) as of resistance to a cultural script that would have her marry young and stifle her artistic aspirations. When she overhears herself being discussed by others, she panics because '[s]he didn't want to know what she was, she couldn't bear to: knowledge of this would stop, seal, finish one' (*LS* 83). She is torn between marrying a young British subaltern, Gerald Lesworth, and trying to pursue her still-unformed ('vague') artistic aspirations. A family friend, Marda Norton, encourages her in a way that draws out every enthusiasm a young woman harbours when she is in isolation from meaningful social relations. Alongside a dreary, predictable marriage plot – marked by the leitmotif 'I must marry Gerald' – something queer and unsettling unfolds: '[s]ophistication opened further horizons' (*LS* 141, 114).

Lois is drawn to Marda in ways she only partly understands. '"[S]he's a girl – at least a kind of girl,"' she tells Gerald. '"She's awfully attractive"' (*LS* 127). Later, when Marda asks to see her artwork, her attraction to the older woman becomes more complicated as she finds herself being mentored. Her aspirations are thrown into doubt by Marda's less than encouraging response to her drawings. '"I think you're cleverer than you can draw, you know,"' she tells her. '"Why can't you write, or something?"' (*LS* 141–2). Marda understands what Lois can only intuit: that her aspirations, signified chaotically but powerfully by her 'cleverness', are what drive her, a quality of quicksilver intelligence that could never be satisfied with Gerald, who is dull-witted, emotionally clotted, and oblivious to the promise that Marda recognises. Though she is herself engaged, because she is '"sick of all this trial and error"', Marda warns Lois off the idea of marriage: '"If you never need anyone as much you will be fortunate"' (LS 146). Yet this *need* is precisely what she *needs*. When Marda goads her by saying, '"you like to be the pleasant young person"', Lois replies that she likes '"to be in a pattern"', '"to be related; to have to be what I am. Just to *be* is so intransitive, so lonely"' (LS 142).

Bildung is, for Lois, less about the harmony of inner culture than about social connectedness. She hungers for the kind of community that all the other Bildungshelden discussed in this chapter paradoxically find in the negative dialectics of inner life. Her desire for transitivity is an explicit rejection of the social class that made her failure at achieving anything like classical Bildung a foregone conclusion. The disjunctive tempo of development that Esty sees as a symptom of colonial dispossession emerges, on this view, as the faltering process by which a young woman comes to acknowledge her own aspirations and the dialectical necessity of overcoming her natal community in pursuit of new forms of social belonging. Lois's aspirations are thrown into confusion and doubt when Marda leaves, and Gerald's violent death cuts her adrift. She has '[n]owhere particular' to go after Danielstown is torched by the IRA, but she is not rootless. We can only assume she is heading off to art school – '"I should go to the Slade,"' she says, agreeing with her aunt (LS 254) – and this assumption aligns Lois with Stephen Dedalus, who similarly vanishes into a suggestive but untold future. Perhaps, like Hermione, she will sustain a healing misrecognition by studying art, when she should, as Marda counselled, 'write, or something'. By going 'nowhere particular', she rejects social expectations and the achievement signified by marriage, but she also opens up an avenue to the aesthetic life, in which aspiration is its own reward.

Bowen gives us not so much a portrait of the artist or of the aesthetic life as a preliminary study of both for which there is no follow-up work. The glimpses we receive of Lois's inner life suggest that she is herself a preliminary study. When she tries to focus on the space of her own being and the pace of her aspirations, she is frightened (in a way that other modernist Bildungshelden are not) by the *loneliness* of her intransitive position. Her desire *to relate*, like that of Hermione and Miriam, is grounded in the desire for an aesthetic life, for beauty and artistic aspiration: she too is '"something new . . . a kind of different world"' (B 260).

What differs, and this makes a big difference, is the colonial mentality that infuses Lois with a sense of grandeur and a sense of loss, both stemming from the original sin of Protestant Ascendancy rule. Even though she understands the power of the moment, the moment does not (yet) compensate for the threat to aspiration after every social support has been stripped away. In a manner that adumbrates the postcolonial Bildungsroman, Bowen portrays the diasporic subject as an intransitive subject, one whose self-formation is tied ineluctably to the need to *be in a pattern* and *to relate* rather than to be sequestered in inner life, in a safe but otherworldly garden of Bildung, posing for a portrait.

# CHAPTER 7

# Bildungsromane for Children and Young Adults

## Fiona McCulloch

The Bildungsroman, translated from German as the novel of education or the novel of formation, is ideally positioned as a pedagogical model of childhood development within children's and young adult (YA) fiction. Literature for children often concerns itself with a journey or quest which the young hero or heroine must undertake in order to advance themselves and, often simultaneously, their society. The journey, of course, is a symbolic manifestation of the child's Bildung process of maturation, encouraging them to shift beyond their comfort zone and step into the unfamiliar or hitherto unknown. This culminates in challenging rites of passage, where they overcome some difficulty or barrier or struggle that sets a course through which they navigate along a trajectory that is the ideal route for a Bildungsroman narrative. In turn, the intended reader of children's and YA fiction is induced towards emulating this process of self-development with a view to socialising or readying them for their place as future citizens. As they come to understand themselves more thoroughly, so too do they more fully comprehend their relationship with the external world. Thus, as well as depicting the education or development of the young, the Bildungsroman can also be used in a didactic way, to shape the development of its readers. Education policies direct the formation of the individual within the so-called hidden curriculum, culminating in the moulding of a compliant and productive citizen who has internalised society's hegemonic values. As an educational tool, the Bildungsroman presents the growth and development of a character that embodies the criteria of personal and social success, and manages to successfully inhabit both a personal narrative and be forged by a social script. Success, in traditional Bildung terms, is managed by social class stratification, so that 'the self-discovery and self-definition of the protagonist tend to be more emphatically social, conjured up in large part by new prospects of social mobility, a world of possibility at once exhilarating and fearful'.[1]

That desire for, yet terror of, the unknown is an ideal format for children's literature and the protagonist's progress.

Since the Bildungsroman 'demonstrates middle-class confidence in the individual who can learn from experience and, through initiative and effort, occupy a respectable place in society', it is a powerful ideological component of children's and YA fiction that socialises the next generation of citizens within and beyond its textual frame.[2] As Ellen McWilliams warns in her assessment of Toril Moi's feminist critique of liberal humanism, 'the idea of the Bildungsroman as educative (and thus as exerting an influence over the reader) can be dangerous, given its potential to reinforce the kind of tyrannous relationship between author and reader that Moi describes'.[3] How much more dangerous and exploitative is that tyrannous relationship, as has often been critically attested when it is built upon the adult/child power imbalance of children's literature?[4] According to Deborah Cogan Thacker and Jean Webb, 'While all literature is based on a power relationship, and all is dependent on a shared understanding of language, children's literature is based on a relationship that is less equal than that between adult reader and adult author.'[5] Thus, in many ways, the Bildungsroman for children and adolescents must come with a trigger warning that tyrannical authority over the intended reader's self-development is very much at stake. Yet, just as McWilliams advocates that the emergence of feminism, post-structuralism and postmodernism ushered in a more playful *jouissance* regarding the genre, children's literature is also prone to these socio-political and theoretical shifts, enabling it to probe and reassess rather than simply mimic hegemonic structures. One will always encounter the power imbalance within children's and YA fiction, but there is ample room for manoeuvre in terms of irony, intonation and play regarding its dialogical engagement with discursive hegemony. As such, children's and YA literature interrogates childhood as a contested and dynamic rather than settled space.

This chapter will explore the ways in which the genre has been used in novels to set an example for young readers. It will selectively discuss exemplary texts that accentuate and illuminate facets of self-development and socialisation, as well as offering an account of whether there might be instances when the societally conservative elements of the Bildungsroman are interrogated or perhaps even subverted. In other words, it will offer an exegesis of a variety of literary texts that contain elements familiarly located within the Bildungsroman genre. Traditionally regarded as a Western, middle-class male format, frequently berated for its 'often unapologetic investment in masculine, bourgeois ideologies' (McWilliams 9), such implications for working-class or female protagonists will be of particular interest, as well as those who may be marginalised through sexuality or ethnicity, for instance. Jeanette Winterson's *Oranges Are Not the Only Fruit* (1985) is an excellent case in point, since it portrays the development from childhood to adulthood of a northern, working-class lesbian and, as such, undercuts many of the hegemonic expectations of the Bildungsroman. Further, James Joyce's *A Portrait of the Artist as a Young Man* (1916) offers the perspective of a Catholic Irishman growing up during the country's colonial rule by Britain. While these are not examples of YA fiction, they nevertheless offer useful instances of the Bildungsroman's heteroglossia.

Interestingly, Giovanna Summerfield and Lisa Downward (2010) argue that the Bildungsroman contains a spiritual element that can be traced to its historical links with Freemasonry. They challenge Victor Watson's claim that 'Children's books did not go in for spiritualism'[6] while pointing out that Watson simultaneously 'refers more bluntly several times to terms like "sin/virtue"'.[7] Additionally, they reject the male-dominant hierarchical model of the genre in favour of a complex 'spectrum', concluding that 'from its inception the Bildungsroman has destabilized traditional notions of gender' (Summerfield and Downward 5, 6). Likewise, McWilliams argues that the female Bildungsroman is interrogating and reshaping the genre's traditions so that it is 'not simply defined by resemblance to the classic template, but is rather sustained in the mapping of an odyssey of selfhood in which the internal machinations of the self are foregrounded; in this way the female Bildungsroman reinvigorates the genre' (McWilliams 12). It is not an obsolete, static genre, then, but a format that can be revisited time and again, and injected with political and theoretical impetus from feminism, postmodernism and so on. Such rejuvenated re-formation of the genre is undoubtedly also the case with the children's literature category, since childhood itself is prone to socio-historical shifts and geopolitical discourses that shape concepts of identity. Thus, our journey through classic to contemporary children's and YA texts will itself be one of dynamic heterogeneity rather than fixity. This is particularly vital for a literature aimed at future citizens, since it must be able to circumvent the masculine hegemony of Bildungsromane traditions in order to chart new spatial territories of regenerative possibility for fledgling identities that allow room for manoeuvre regarding counter discourses.

To briefly recall Summerfield and Downward's observations regarding spirituality as a facet of the Bildungsroman, including children's fiction, an interesting example can be found in Frances Hodgson Burnett's *The Secret*

*Garden* (1911), which puts much emphasis upon the restorative and regenerative power of nature's healing, referred to in the text as Magic, and
Burnett was a Christian Scientist. Watson also alludes to the significance of
magic in Burnett's and other children's texts, but he does not couple this
with her interests in Christian Science or spiritualism. Or there is the
Reverend Charles Kingsley's *The Water-Babies* (1863), with its interest in
the spiritual rebirth of the orphan Tom. The Victorian period, to be sure, is
a time of reflective self-development in literature: Maureen Moran notes
that the Bildungsroman met Victorians' 'voracious appetite for accounts of
the individual's moral, intellectual and spiritual formation'.[8] This ultimately reflects the Victorian spirit of self-reliance and success disseminated
through such works as Samuel Smiles's *Self-Help* (1859). But, in children's
literature, this spiritual development persists, with the likes of C. S. Lewis's
*Narnia Chronicles* (1950–6) often regarded as Christian allegory. Then
there is the more contemporary *His Dark Materials* (1995–2000) trilogy
in which Philip Pullman challenges Christianity as an inhibitive social
discourse to spirituality within humans and the wider cosmos. But even
within these earlier apparently conservative Bildung narratives, there is
ample room for deconstructive readings that can offer moments of resistance against any dominant hegemonic values that may be overtly
imposed. So, for instance, one might read Narnia's White Queen through
a feminist lens and consider how she is demonised within a phallocratic
narrative, or how Burnett's text can offer a space for feminist resistance to
dominant models of femininity. Even so, endings can be problematic.
Often they can revert to the restoration of a conservative status quo, as in
the case of Mary's overshadowing by Colin in *The Secret Garden*, which
feminist critics have reviled. Others, though, have regarded this as symptomatic of descriptive rather than prescriptive endings, where, in the case of
Burnett, she is merely reflecting the gendered inferiority bestowed upon
girls and women in keeping with the novel's socio-historical context.

As with Summerfield and Downward's view that the Bildungsroman
moves along a varied spectrum rather than remaining within a fixed position, it is worth noting that the genre itself becomes something of a self-
conscious journey of spatio-temporal development and maturation. As the
world turns so too does the genre evolve, extending its reach to maintain an
association between a protagonist and the extraneous influences that
impact upon the pivotal narrative. As with any hero/heroine, to survive
the Bildungsroman must adapt to its literary and social surroundings and
circumstances rather than becoming bogged down in the weight of conventions. In a discussion of Virginia Woolf's *To the Lighthouse* (1927),

Downward argues that the prismatic multiplicity applied to Mrs Ramsay is 'evidence of Bildung that is concerned with potentiality for becoming rather than being, which is static' (Summerfield and Downward 165). This flexible mutability of character is vital in accommodating female narratives within the Bildungsroman format, since it generates a transcendence of classic conventions that favour an otherwise male-dominated genre restricted to narrow constrictions of social enterprise and material wealth as demarcations of success. This 'perpetual state of becoming' (Summerfield and Downward 165) signals a fluidity and open-endedness that adds a refreshing mutation to the Bildungsroman and demonstrates its evolutionary if not revolutionary potential in terms of gender, sexuality, and social class, as we noted earlier with Winterson's *Oranges*. Jeanette is regarded as something of a changeling, an uncanny child that flouts the expectations imposed upon childhood by familial, religious and societal hegemonies. By queering the genre's conventions, Winterson furthers the spatio-temporal ability of the Bildungsroman to break coherent linearity and convey a social maturation of self-fashioning that acknowledges a broader church of citizens through a postmodern feminist prism that queries and problematises rather than standardises selfhood. Though not YA fiction, Winterson's text offers a useful general consideration of the Bildung genre and, notably, it is part of some school curriculums.

Insofar as the Bildungsroman mobilises itself into a fluid spatial becoming rather than fixity of being, this precisely suits the malleability of childhood and adolescence as an unfixed site of dynamic potential. Before we turn to some specific examples from children's and YA fiction, it is worth pondering that concept of becoming alongside Rosi Braidotti's thesis of philosophic nomadism as a means of disputing the fixed Western Cartesian *cogito* in favour of an endless flux that transgresses borders and offers new possibilities of selfhood and nationhood. Braidotti situates a cosmopolitical resistance amidst the plethora of deterritorialised identities that interrogate and transgress Western hegemonic norms. Through 'transformative becoming', she argues that a 'sustainable ethics for a non-unitary subject proposes an enlarged sense of interconnection between self and others, including the non-human or "earth" others'.[9] Thus, the self/other binary, including anthropocentrism, is dismantled, ushering in a transpositional posthumanism that fuses *zoe* and *bios* insofar as 'Life is half-animal, non-human (*zoe*) and half-political and discursive (*bios*)' (Braidotti 37). Western society privileges and empowers *bios* as hierarchically superior to *zoe*, but Braidotti envisages a cosmopolitan citizenship that dismantles such borders of difference and relates equally to all life, including environmental or planetary relations. Similarly, contemporary YA Bildungsromane often reconfigure the traditional relationship between protagonists and the natural world, encouraging their self-development to resist anthropocentricism.

While children's literature has persistently been linked to nature since the influence of Romantic discourses upon childhood innocence, nevertheless the child was often in a position of dominance over its environment, as in the case of boys' adventure stories, where there is a colonial impetus at play. More recently, though, children's and YA fiction is demonstrating a responsible ethics towards ecological themes and creating equilibrium between protagonist and planet. This is particularly crucial in the face of environmental concerns like climate change or oceanic pollution, and gives rise to YA texts like Saci Lloyd's *The Carbon Diaries* (2009–10), Julie Bertagna's *Exodus* (2002–11) trilogy or Beth Revis's *Across the Universe* (2011–13) trilogy. As with Bildungsroman conventions, the development of the hero/heroine is dependent upon their relationship with society and, particularly, the planet. YA fiction like Revis's trilogy also posits questions about being human, so pushing the boundaries of the Bildungsroman into uncharted posthuman territories.[10] In keeping with themes of transition in Bildung texts, contemporary YA fiction responds to a world that is itself rapidly evolving with the challenges of globalisation. As Rachel Falconer notes, 'Because young adult fiction has sought to articulate questions about rapid transitions, identity crises and epiphanies, it is proving to be a ready medium in which to capture the felt, everyday experience of a world on the cusp of fundamental change.'[11] Thus, as a particular focus point, contemporary YA fiction will provide an in-depth study of the evolving Bildungsroman to consider its place within current socio-political trends, such as globalisation, transnationalism and cosmopolitanism. In current YA fiction, the Bildungsroman is reaching beyond the frontiers of the nation state to imagine the world and is thus helping to shape future citizens. This is in keeping with ways in which contemporary Bildungsromane renegotiate and interrogate traditional generic conventions, so that 'in spite of the ideological limitations foregrounded by many critics, the Bildungsroman is destined to remain a medium of expression for new generations of emerging voices, whether in relation to gender and sexuality or to ethnicity and race' (McWilliams 21). All of these socio-political issues to be found in adult texts are of concern for children's and YA fiction, so I would add that the Bildungsroman is not only concerned with how the young person is shaped but also helps to shape a rapidly changing and prismatic world.

For Braidotti, cosmopolitan empathy is fundamental to societal development in terms of empowerment against globalisation and its grass-roots solidarity offers an imaginative yet political resistance to the strictures of the hegemonic status quo. This directly challenges selfish individualism and replaces it with a commonality of purpose: just as Summerfield and Downward argue that the Bildungsroman is a process of becoming, so too does Braidotti note that 'Cosmopolitanism needs to "become-world", i.e. embrace diversity' and respond to 'pan-human perspectives'.[12] Likewise, thinking beyond borderlands of difference, many contemporary YA texts pedagogically encourage the intended reader to identify with the other rather than simply the self so that Bildung development assumes an ethical identity to be a sign of successful maturation. Similarly, Tobias Boes recognises a national/transnational link, arguing that the Bildungsroman is a fluidly performative fiction in its interplay between local and global, where 'nationalism and cosmopolitanism become one and the same, and the *Bildungsroman* affirms a place in world literature that in reality it possessed all along'.[13] In a globalised world it is not enough for the Bildungsroman to develop the socialised individual within a specific national or regional locale; it must respond to the demands of a shrinking and interconnected globe where each protagonist's journey has a transnational coalescent impact. For instance, Gillian Cross's *Where I Belong* (2010) discusses the connectivity between Somalia and London, geopolitically linking each within a wider global relationship, while Theresa Breslin's *Divided City* (2005) considers the effect of Glaswegian sectarianism in relation to the transnational diaspora of asylum seekers, fleeing similar religious and ethnic conflicts.[14] Character maturation depends heavily upon an understanding of others beyond the immediate familiarity of one's locale.

Another vital means of reconfiguring the individual at the centre of traditional Bildungsromane is to introduce multiple key characters so that children and adolescents recognise the importance of socialisation rather than isolation in a world that requires cooperative communication. So, in Breslin's text, while Graham's story initiates the narrative, it is quickly dependent upon his newfound friendship with Joe and their involvement with the asylum seeker Kyoul along with his girlfriend Leanne. Kyoul and Leanne remain more peripheral characters, yet their contribution is nevertheless vital to shaping the maturation of Graham and Joe's Bildung progress. Another Breslin text, *Remembrance* (2002), set during the First World War but with clear parallels to contemporary conflicts, presents several main characters rather than just one, since it focuses upon the impact of war on a small Scottish community's young people who become embroiled in the conflict. Their psychogeographical journey towards socialisation occurs in the extreme circumstances of embattlement and leads to a maturation beyond their years that is fraught with trauma alongside a cosmopolitical understanding of the futility of difference on such a harrowing global scale.[15]

After a general consideration of the Bildungsroman within children's and YA fiction, it is now expedient to focus on some specific examples more closely. Charles Kingsley's *The Water-Babies* (1863) relates the fantasy adventure of the young orphan Tom and yet is firmly located in the grime of Victorian social realism. Mistreated by his master, Grimes, he exists on the peripheries of society and is not privy to the childhood bliss experienced by Ellie, the young girl residing in the mansion whose chimneys he is sweeping. When Tom inadvertently ends up in her angelic white bedroom after climbing down the wrong chimney, immediate chase is given to this filthy child of the believed dangerous classes. He is miraculously cleansed and renewed in the river, signifying a Christian intervention of death and rebirth to render him fit for polite society and to rid the Victorians of their fear of the lower classes, whom Kingsley himself referred to in a sermon as dangerous 'human soot'.[16] Tom's journey of education removes him from the influence of his drunken and debauched master and transplants him into the underwater nursery care and biblical doctrine of Mrs Doasyouwouldbedoneby and her sister, Mrs Bedonebyasyoudid. It is in here that he learns to become an idealised child rather than 'a savage' or 'little black ape', swallowing a good deal of Christian doctrine so that his soul becomes as cleansed as his newly washed exterior.[17] The old husk of Tom, however, lies by the river bed, suggesting that only his death has allowed him to be raised up the social ladder. While the novel does offer an interesting critique of urban squalor, the treatment of orphans and the fallout of the Industrial Revolution in terms of environmental pollution, nevertheless it remains firmly conservative in its religious discourse and view of the working classes as a Darwinian social pollutant and threat to the jingoistic imperial 'English bulldog' superiority (74). Rather like Isaac Watt's poem in praise of labour, so famously lampooned by Lewis Carroll's *Alice's Adventures in Wonderland*, Kingsley's *The Water-Babies* warns against the sinful vagaries of idleness and pleasure, lest one should endure the evolutionary regression experienced by the nation of the Doasyoulikes, who are returned to a primitive ape-like status. In keeping with Victorian fears of degeneracy, the class threat to the status quo is quashed with Tom's evolution into a more respectable figure fit to inhabit the ranks of British society[18].

Similarly, Frances Hodgson Burnett's *The Secret Garden* (1911) concerns itself with instilling an idealised childhood within unruly children so that they can become fit for respectable society and learn their place within it. Mary, until she is transplanted into the English country garden of her uncle's gothic mansion, is 'quite contrary'. The Bildung journey is geo-physical, transporting her from colonial India where she, like the plant she attempts to nurture, fails to grow, to the fertile replenishment of English soil in her homeland that she has never previously visited. Michael Cadden discusses this transplantation in relation to the theme of blood as lineage in the text, where 'home is linked to racial essentialism [and . . .] to issues of blood'.[19] Thus, she can only thrive in close psychogeographical proximity to her 'real' English self, instead of the yellow-skinned, ill-tempered and sickly simulacra confined to a stifling Indian atmosphere: 'her hair was yellow, and her face was yellow because she had been born in India and had always been ill in one way or another'.[20] From the outset Mary's tyrannical sickness is attributed, even by the lower-class Martha, to a geopolitically displaced other: '"I dare say it's because there's such a lot o' blacks there instead o' respectable white people"' (27). Childhood can only be respect-able, apparently, if it is nurtured within the freshness of English climes. The Garden, then, becomes a site of socialisation, akin to Friedrich Froebel's teachings on the kindergarten as a space of childhood develop-ment. Similarly, Mary adjusts to her new life in England by replenishing herself in the Secret Garden: both garden and child are rejuvenated and come alive, each benefitting from the other's contact. Her spoiled cousin, Colin Craven, is equally healed in the redemptive garden, learning that his tantrums do not render him the centre of the universe but, instead, he must find his place in society and assume the authority of his father's lineage. As part of the Bildung development, Mother Sowerby influences the children's socialisation, imparting the knowledge that '"When I was at school my jography told as th' world was shaped like a orange an' I found out . . . that th' whole orange doesn't belong to nobody"' and, as such, '"What children learns from children . . . is that there's no sense in grabbin' at th' whole orange – peel an' all. If you do, you'll likely not even get th' pips, an' them's too bitter to eat"' (195–6). The influence of the Garden, Dickon and Mother Sowerby helps to socialise Mary who, in turn, extends this influence to Colin.

But, with a male heir of Misselthwaite Manor, the garden shifts in terms of gender and class politics from being tended to by Mary and the lower-class rustic Dickon, to being owned by Archibald Craven's descendant Colin, who asserts "'I'm your master . . . you are to obey me. This is my garden'" (226). This is in keeping with a colonial mindset, the territory claimed by English masculine authority, yet Colin is described as the young Rajah. His tyrannical authority is supplanted onto Indian tyranny so that 'colonialism and the English class system are conveniently displaced into the alleged social patterns of the Oriental scene'.[21] The haunting slippage of the sign, though, may still resonate with the colonial British Raj. Being overshadowed by her cousin at the end, understandably has inflamed many feminist critics, since Mary is decentred and left on the sidelines in favour of Colin and his father. The boy is no longer emasculated in his bedridden hysterics, but strides beside Archibald, ready to take up the reins of running the family business when the time comes. The garden protects both children, alongside Dickon and his mother, Susan Sowerby, who nurture these weak fledglings until they are fit for British rule. In terms of gender, though, Mary will always be cast in second place:

> *The Secret Garden* concludes by foregrounding the conservatism which has also been implicit in its portrayal of class relations. Just as Mary is removed from the focus of attention at the end of the novel, so Dickon, the working-class child who has been central in the regenerative process, is completely forgotten in the finale's emphasis on reconciliation between father and son. The novel's main narrative experience of childhood freedom is thus framed by the removal and the return of parents. Similarly, the social hierarchy of prevailing English class and gender divisions is perpetuated by the una-shamed return to the status quo and the exclusion of Mary and Dickon from the centre of love as well as from power.'[22]

The subversive potential of the female Bildungsroman is replaced, then, by upholding hegemonic masculinist values within a conservative closure. However, Heather Murray asks, 'What are we to make of a woman-authored text which so validates the *status quo*, which erases the presence of the lower-class boy of the moors, and so disposes of its heroine? . . . Is Burnett here descriptive rather than prescriptive, telling us the way of the world rather than how it ought to be?'[23] Rather than necessarily endorsing such discursive patriarchal positioning, Murray contends that Burnett may in fact simply be reflecting the dominant ideologies of her text's socio-historical context. Particularly as a woman writer of the period, Burnett would have been under pressure to appear conventional. But there are certainly moments too of potential gothic resistance to such conservative realist modes so it may well still serve as an example of feminist disruption of the conventional Bildungsroman rather than a mirrored regurgitation.[24]

L. Frank Baum's *The Wonderful Wizard of Oz* (1900) is refreshing in its centralisation of a female protagonist who journeys to Oz in a cyclone and then must locate its Wizard in order to return home to Kansas. Dorothy Gale has been regarded as a feminist pioneer by critics like Alison Lurie who see her as a 'New Woman', more akin to a 'Victorian hero ... than a Victorian heroine', given her strength and aptitude displayed throughout her quest along the yellow-brick road to pursue and attain her dream of returning home to her beloved Aunt Em.[25] Gail Murray suggests that this may explain the popularity of these texts, since:

> Unlike all the other American children's fiction of the period – series books, boys' adventure tales, girls' domestic novels – the Oz stories appealed to both boys and girls. In Dorothy Gale, Baum created a female protagonist who embodied both feminine virtues (compassion, kindness, acceptance of those different from herself, concern for others' feelings) and masculine attributes (rationality, assertiveness, single-mindedness, courage, perseverance).[26]

As an active female adventure, this reconfigures the conventional male Bildungsroman and allows spatial development of feminist attributes that reconstitutes the conventional values of the genre.

Yet, as Deborah Cogan Thacker reminds us, 'Dorothy returns to the domestic sphere at the end of the story, and ceases to play a part in the larger world' (Thacker and Webb 90). As such, the entire journey is ultimately aimed towards the female child becoming content with her inherited lot as a woman within the confines of the home, signalling her domestic affinity with Em who, like Dorothy, used to be lively and full of spirit, until the Kansas Dust Bowl drained her of all optimism and joy. But one must not forget that in the wider series, Dorothy's dissatisfaction with domesticity is evident in her returns to Oz. In the first text, a sense of being engulfed and dwarfed by her surroundings is evident: 'When Dorothy stood in the doorway and looked around, she could see nothing but the great grey prairie on every side. Not a tree nor a house broke the broad sweep of flat country that reached to the edge of the sky in all directions.'[27] It is an arid landscape drained of vitality:

> The sun had baked the ploughed land into a grey mass, with little cracks running through it. Even the grass was not green, for the sun had burned the tops of the long blades until they were the same grey colour to be seen everywhere. Once the house had been painted, but the sun blistered the paint and rains washed it away, and now the house was as dull and grey as everything else. (5–6)

A panoramic narrative gaze focuses upon the vast void of terrain, panning closer until it scrutinises the elementally oppressive impact upon human inhabitants. Like a gravitational force the life is sucked out of everything, emphasised by the repetitive references to 'grey', a lifeless and soulless environment where inspiration evaporates. This drab exterior shifts to an equally grey interior living space, where inhabitants and landscape are indistinguishable. Though alive, they have ceased to enjoy life's pleasures; demonstrations of love and affection are thwarted, leaving only shells or shadows of humanity behind, resonant of F. Scott Fitzgerald's *The Great Gatsby* (1925), in which a poverty-struck area known as the 'Valley of Ashes' is populated by 'ash-grey men' who move soullessly around, as though already dead. Both American novels convey a sense of exhaustion at the overwhelming pressure of succeeding with integrity in the American Dream.

The optimism of the American Dream does not take root in Baum's representation of the Kansas frontier, which has dramatically affected and altered Dorothy's aunt, for 'When Aunt Em came there to live she was a young, pretty wife. The sun and wind had changed her, too. They had taken the sparkle from her eyes and left them a sober grey; they had taken the red from her cheeks and lips, and they were grey also. She was thin and gaunt, and never smiled now' (6). Em's youthful optimism is robbed by the harsh environment into which she has become assimilated, and her marriage reduced to domestic responsibility. Em's lacklustre eyes signal her soulless outlook upon a world that has blighted her, while her husband too is broken by endless toil: 'Uncle Henry never laughed. He worked hard from morning till night and did not know what joy was' (6). Trying to eke out an existence amidst this harsh landscape has left its imprint upon the very faces of these characters, almost like the cracks in the clay of the sun-baked prairie. As Yoshido Junko argues:

> Pioneer farmers toward the end of the century were experiencing many and drastic changes ... the extension of the railroads across the continent, especially between 1870 and 1880, stimulated the rapid increase in population of new settlers on the frontier ... Kansas, in particular, saw excessive cultivation of farmland. Then the drought in 1887 caused serious damages to the agricultural products in west Kansas ... During four years after 1887, half of the pioneer farmers left Kansas.[28]

The coalescence of individual and landscape in Baum's narrative, then, depicts the struggles facing citizens and nation on their journey to self-development.

Sensitive to her surroundings, as a child Dorothy does not have much cause for laughter, reared in an unforgiving environment with a seemingly heartless and reserved aunt and uncle. An orphan figure, she is deracinated from the familiarity of home and it is unsurprising that she spends the entire novel searching for home. But, in keeping with children's literature and childhood as a source of redemption for adult society, she sounds a discordant note of hope in this otherwise bleak existence. As the child heroine, she brings colour to an otherwise dreary Kansas landscape. But one remembers that Em too was once joyful, serving as a reminder of Dorothy's potential fate should she not journey to Oz. Junko writes:

> It is her aunt and uncle who are exhausted with the greyness and the hardships of pioneer life. There is no mention of Dorothy being actually overwhelmed by the greyness. On the contrary, Dorothy is portrayed as a pleasant and innocent girl whose cheerfulness is protected by Toto. She represents the happiness, innocence, and hope that Aunt Em and Uncle Henry have lost in the course of their pioneer lives. (159)

But Dorothy's unconscious psyche harbours feelings of alienation and lack which trigger the fantasy journey to offset any threat that she too will become contaminated by her surroundings. Though Dorothy does not articulate a wish to escape the grey Kansas prairie, nevertheless her desire is not uttered in language but through the Lacanian imaginary or Kristevan semiotic domain of an unconscious storm. In her search for a welcoming home, Glinda informs her that she could have "'gone back to your Aunt Em the very first day you came to this country'" (157). Dorothy must search for what was always there, but only becomes evident after her journey, since her quest to return home to Kansas is a psychogeographical journey towards locating a desire found in the reconstituted surrogate mother figure, Aunt Em. In Kansas, before Dorothy journeys to Oz, there are multiple images of deprivation and hunger, paralleled with a continual plenitude of eating (with the occasional fear of hunger) in the fantasy realm, where 'she ate a hearty breakfast' and 'breakfasted like a princess off peaches and plums from the trees beside the river' (19, 50). The pre-Oedipal association with a desire for the security of the absent mother is clearly established during the cyclone – it serves as a metaphorical protective womb for Dorothy during the external chaos of the storm where 'she felt as if she were being rocked gently, like a baby in a cradle' (7). A psychometeorological rupture, the storm is as much a part of Dorothy's unfulfilled desires as it is an atmospheric phenomenon: as

Dorothy *Gale* she rages internally with the same tempest that transports her over the rainbow.

Structurally, Dorothy's journey to the centre of Oz corresponds roughly with the centre of the novel. When she reaches that central location, her journey spirals her back towards her starting point, so the novel ends circularly where it began. But because she has embarked upon a Bildung journey, home is necessarily altered to accommodate her heart's desire – it is now somewhere she can be content because in her absence the longed-for mother figure has rediscovered her capacity to love. Em emphatically greets Dorothy as '"My darling child!"' and shows overt emotion, 'covering her face with kisses' (160). Dorothy connects with a reconfigured mother figure as Em claims her as her own, thus fixing Dorothy's desires in her domestic terrain, 'where Aunt Em finally becomes Aunt M, that is, a mother with an abundance of maternal affection'.[29] As child heroine, she has also returned some colour to the drab adult habitation, thus returning adult culture to a coexistence with the needs of childhood fantasy. Thus, Dorothy 'must make reality endurable by ensuring that it can sometimes be transcended' (Gilead 85). The hope is that Dorothy's quest for fulfilled desire will have altered things enough that she will not follow in Aunt Em's footsteps.

Unlike the conventional recognisable realist realm of the symbolic order, described by Sarah Gilead as 'an adult world oppressively ruled by the reality principle' (83), Oz exists as an imaginary or Kristevan semiotic disruption of that real world: it provides a fictional space to accommodate unconscious anxieties and desires. In privileging this space, the Bildungsroman is transported from traditional realism to the experimental site of fantasy. During her initial arrival in the fantasy realm, a witch tells Dorothy that Kansas has no witches – '"But, you see, the Land of Oz has never been civilized, for we are cut off from all the rest of the world"' (12). Unlike the repressive standards and encroachments of the civilised world, the fantasy dimension of Oz is free of such constraints and offers a spatial exploration of one's inner self. Fantasy has the capacity, like the unconscious, to convey a complex mixture of light and darkness, which teaches Dorothy that '"The country here is rich and pleasant, but you must pass through rough and dangerous places before you reach the end of your journey"' (19). Part of that journey, as in many children's texts, involves passing through a forest, which carries connotations of darkness, danger and erotic threats lurking beyond the safe parameters of home until her journey returns her to safety.

Although a circular journey, Dorothy returns to a new home that has been built in her absence, suggesting the potential for new beginnings and feelings of belonging. Her replenished relationship with Em sparks a rejuvenation within Dorothy's aunt, since developmental change has extended to the landscape: cabbages are growing and water is available. Although she falls asleep during the cyclone, so that her 'journey from Kansas to Oz is dreamlike' (Gilead 83), the novel does not confirm whether Dorothy was dreaming – the cinematic story sees her awaking from a dream, but Baum's text describes a physical return as 'she rolled over upon the grass several times' (159). As with the cabbages, signs of rooted-ness and fertility are evident with grass now visible in a hitherto arid landscape. Rather than allow an oppressive patriarchal regime, Baum's text colours the realist conventions of the Bildungsroman with childhood imagination, fantasy and an active female heroine, thus pushing the frontiers of the genre and interrogating its male privilege. Success is not measured in accordance with the monetary tenets of the American Dream or the conventional Bildungsroman but, instead, depends upon a loving and stable home that, in turn, extends its hope to generate dynamic change in people and their locale.[30]

Ursula Le Guin's *A Wizard of Earthsea* (1968) offers an insight into the education and development of the young wizard Ged, and provides the first instalment of the *Earthsea Chronicles*. Semi-orphaned, from the outset he is an outsider; his mother 'died before he was a year old'.[31] His father remains emotionally detached from Ged, whilst meting out a harsh treat-ment of 'blows and whippings' (12). Like Dorothy in *The Wizard of Oz*, Ged too finds himself caught up in a struggle for emotional stability and a home that he can feel part of. As an alienated loner, he also embarks upon a quest, much of which involves the search for and understanding of his own selfhood. Thus this Bildungsroman charts his progress, maturation and development from childhood to adolescence, pushing the frontiers of the genre given that, like Oz, it exists within a fantasy rather than realist dimension. His quest for identity – a journey towards maturity and wisdom and, eventually, adulthood – is bound up with the power of naming in Le Guin's text. Ged's other name, Sparrowhawk, evokes asso-ciations with flight. In a novel that emphasises the importance of equili-brium, Le Guin's feminist writing applies the flight metaphor to envisage a character whose maturation is intertwined with imagination and creativ-ity, often regarded as feminine traits, in order to interrogate dominant representations of masculine heroes and offer alternative role models that resist patriarchal hegemony. Similarly, Hélène Cixous is considered to invoke the 'metaphor of "flying" to suggest the ways in which women can speak/write'.[32] Millicent Lenz concurs: 'The stages in his movement towards maturity are marked by his changes in name.'[33] Given Ged's position as a wizard, the text portrays the developmental process and mastery of his art in terms of his ability to create and wield authority. In his youthful pride, he unwittingly unleashes a shadow and only by acknowledging this other to be a fundamental part of the self is he reconciled to his actions and matures as an individual. As such, he comes to the realisation that 'All my acts have their echo in it; it is my creature . . . Almost with my own tongue it speaks' (177). Unlike the rigid boundaries of selfhood explored in conventional Bildungsromane, Ged's maturation breaks such rigidity to embody otherness as a means of extending and enriching one's identity.

Ged's journey in search of the Jungian shadow takes him to a place significantly called 'Lastland. East and south of it the charts are empty' (Le Guin 189). From emptiness comes a space for creativity and rethinking one's borders between self/other. In this desolate mindscape the boundary between the recognisable and the unknown that distinguishes self from other dissolves. Lastland's uncharted territory mirrors the shadow: 'it was darkness itself that had awaited him, the unnamed thing, the being that did not belong in the world, the shadow he had loosed or made. In spirit, at the boundary wall between death and life, it had waited for him these long years' (97). To unleash something, of course, is to create it, and this is underscored with the power of language which, in turn, metafictionally reflects the text, where the 'creation of new words [is] vital to the building of new fictive worlds' (Lenz 75). To create or make echoes *makar*, a Scottish term for a poet, again signalling the link between making and art. By facing and naming his fear, Ged manifests a strength which overturns an acrimonious division from his shadow self and allows balance to be restored in a harmonious fusion of self/other, and Le Guin herself has referred to *Earthsea* as being 'about art, the creative experience, the creative process' (Lenz 47). Even the novel's title lends itself to a blurring of boundaries: Earthsea is a geographical and fictional liminal space located neither fully on land or sea, but composed of both, where solid and liquid become indistinguishable and interdependent, 'bringing together the components of land and ocean into linguistic unity, expressive of the metaphysical oneness' (Lenz 75). It is an ideal coalescence of self/other that reflects Ged's pursuit of his doppelganger. That is why 'Ged spoke the shadow's name, and in the same moment the shadow spoke without lips or tongue, saying the same word: "Ged." And the two voices were one voice. Ged reached out his hands, dropping his staff, and took hold of his shadow, of the black self that reached out to him. Light and darkness met, and joined, and were one'

(197–8). Finally, Ged recognises that his alter ego is not separate, but incorporates a facet of his true self: like the facial scars he bears because of his struggle with the shadow, trying to reconcile himself to it has caused a journey pitted with psychological scarring. He becomes the epitome of Taoist teaching and philosophy: both Yin and Yang, self and other, a harmony of light and darkness or masculine and feminine. His pedago-gical journey embodies Taoism's translation as the path or route, rendering it an ideal Bildungsroman format. Ged's shadow is unleashed because he has no knowledge of the consequences, demonstrating how destructive knowledge can be in the wrong hands. He learns that with power comes responsibility, and this crucially important philosophical and political message imparted by Le Guin remains as relevant today in any thinking about power and ideology as well as Bildung development.

As Ged's quest draws towards its conclusion, he realises that 'All power is one in source and end, I think. Years and distances, stars and candles, water and wind and wizardry, the craft in a man's hand and the wisdom in a tree's root: they all arise together' (182). Part of his maturation is the awareness that he is merely part of a wider force, a part of nature, and the individual power given to him as a wizard must be employed for the benefit, not the destruction, of that wider force. This ecological concept of connectivity rather than individual-ism pushes forward the Bildungsroman so that Ged's heroism is merely part of a wider energy and cosmological force. It is not enough, then, to act as an individual; one must consider the impact of one's actions in their reaction, so the Bildung progress cannot be at the expense of wider considerations. Further, the conventions of Western selfhood familiar to the genre are interrogated: the traditional representation of white supremacy set against the savage darkness of colonised natives is undermined and reversed here. When Ged, who is dark-skinned rather than a conventional white hero, protects his village from colonising invaders, 'the Kargad Empire ... are a savage people, white-skinned, yellow-haired, and fierce' (17). Le Guin herself notes:

> I see Ged as dark brownish-red, and all the other people in the book (except the Kargs and Serret) as brown or brown-red, to very dark or black (Vetch). In other words, in the Archipelago 'people of color' are the norm, white people are an anomaly. Vice versa on the Kargish islands ... what drives me up the wall is cover illustrators – trying to get them not to make everybody white, white, white.[34]

It is her intention to push boundaries of masculinity and race in order to challenge conventional generic traits and enable the Bildungsroman to depict other selves.

Thus, *Earthsea* is a creative space where phallogocentric language holds no authority, for in the closing pages, there is a cyclical repetition of the epigraph, 'Only in silence the word'. By moving beyond the fixed labels of language, Le Guin charts new territory in which new selves can emerge in a place where the other is not defeated by the self, but embraced:

> Ged had neither lost nor won but, naming the shadow of his death with his own name, had made himself whole: a man: who, knowing his whole true self, cannot be used or possessed by any power other than himself, and whose life therefore is lived for life's sake and never in the service of ruin, or pain, or hatred, or the dark. (199)

Through Ged, Le Guin charts a space where one can integrate instead of demonising others, and live beyond the myopic prejudices of Western discourses: he poignantly puts down his phallic staff and connects with rather than destroys that which he fears. In turn, Le Guin challenges dominant notions of self and extends the parameters of the Bildungsroman so that self-development is only achievable by recognising one's integral relationship with others. The competitive individual eking out their fortune in a ruthless society is dispensed with here in favour of community values and social justice for all as a means of reaching self-formation and development. Her Bildungsroman refuses to settle into generic conformity, but agitates by providing a socially marginalised voice, thereby dialogically inviting counter-narratives to be heard in society.

The Bildung development of contemporary heroes and heroines depends more on solidarity and community than solitary selfhood. So J. K. Rowling's *Harry Potter* (1997–2007) series charts the maturation of Harry from age 11 to adolescence, with a prologue briefly considering his adulthood. Although he is marked out by his scar as a singular hero, nevertheless his progress is dependent upon others, including Ron, Hermione, and the Order of the Phoenix. The Dursley household where Harry must initially reside is obsessed with being 'perfectly normal'[35] and crushes any imaginative impetus, which continually suppresses Harry's self-awareness while simultaneously emphasising his alterity as the norma-tive family push him to their peripheries and dehumanise him as a slug-like creature. Their suburban uniformity is at pains to police selfhood as a coherent and stable concept, whereas Harry's maturation depends upon dynamic change and otherness. As with Le Guin's northern setting, Rowling transports Harry to a fantasy Scottish realm, where its wildness allows for spatial possibilities of development beyond the confines of stifling suburbia. As with Ged's shadow self, part of Harry's identity is fused with Voldemort, allowing him to speak Parseltongue and to see inside his nemesis's mind. Rather than alone, then, "'you and Lord Voldemort have journeyed together'" because "'Lord Voldemort doubled the bond between you when he returned to a human form'"[36], signalling that one's trajectory is never isolated and contained but will blur into others' identities. Dumbledore's warning that "'we are only as strong as we are united, as weak as we are divided'"[37] serves as a reminder that the self is never an island, so that the Bildungsroman acquires a community cohesion rather than individualism. In Rowling's series, isolationism and lack of empathy impoverishes and fractures communities, generating division and violence, such as Voldemort and his Death Eaters' desire for pure-blood racial eugenics rather than a diverse, dynamic and vibrant cosmopolitanism which, according to Hermione, "'all stems from this horrible thing wizards have of thinking they're superior to other creatures'".[38] Division and discord are surmounted through a journey towards maturation, poignantly led by young people as investors in future society.[39]

The rise of the YA novel is dependent, according to Roberta Seelinger Trites, upon the emergence of postmodernism as a system which questions power structures, including the Romantic notion of the self, a concept of growth which Bildungsromane are preoccupied with. As such, 'the popularity of the traditional Bildungsroman with its emphasis on self-determination gives way to the market dominance of the Young Adult novel, which is less concerned with depicting growth reverently than it is with investigating how the individual exists within society'.[40] In other words, YA fiction self-consciously probes the Bildungsroman genre so that adolescents can consider fully their relationship with capitalist society rather than simply adhere to its conditions. Trites distinguishes between the Bildungsroman as a genre where the individual reaches the maturity of adulthood and the Entwicklungsroman, where growth occurs but not beyond childhood. The latter is associated with children's literature, while YA fiction is identified as Bildungsromane, given the maturation to young adulthood. We could, then, argue that *Oz* and *The Secret Garden*, for instance, are Entwicklungsroman, but it seems more apt not to tie oneself up in knots of endless subcategorisation (such as Erziehungsroman or Künstlerroman), but to simply note that all of the texts discussed contain elements of educational growth and self-development and, as

such, contain facets of the Bildungsroman. But I do agree with Trites that
YA fiction is more concerned with probing and problematising the concept
of selfhood in a world saturated with ubiquitous power and constructed
identities.

Philip Pullman's *His Dark Materials* (1995–2000) primarily concerns
itself with the growth and development of its heroine, Lyra Belaqua, and
her resistance to the narrative of her existence that she has been told. As is
often the case with the Bildungsroman, she embarks upon a quest that
combines social concerns with her own understanding and self-
development. Like Harry Potter, Lyra's journey is intertwined with societal
issues, ranging from freeing oneself from authoritative religious discourse
to convening with other worlds. Thus, Will, her counterpart from another
world in *The Subtle Knife* (1997) is integral to Lyra's maturation as she
learns other cultural norms and advances towards a comprehension of her
place within the cosmos. Referred to by the witches as the new Eve, her
identity is much greater than the boundaries of her selfhood, as she is part
of a larger battle for enlightenment and knowledge in a world favouring
obedience and ignorance. Even from a young age Lyra displays non-
conventional traits and wilfully disobeys those who attempt to confine
her, often displaying masculine traits, such as playing with boys, smoking
and swearing, so defying rigid conventions of condoned female behaviour
and allowing for an active heroine who impacts upon her environment.
The ability to understand other worlds beyond the narrow parameters of
one's recognisable reality is crucial in Pullman's trilogy, as the Bildung
development pushes conventions and boundaries and creates new spatial
possibilities of existence that transcend selfish individualism in favour of
multiple interconnecting diverse worlds.

Further, individualism is subsumed within a broader cosmological context, where we are but a mere speck formed from stardust out there in the
vacuum of space, and it is no accident that Lyra, in keeping with her
namesake constellation, embarks upon an interstellar journey towards
maturation, culminating in her realisation of 'being one with her body
and the earth and everything that was matter'.[41] This ecological coalescence
between human and environment forms part of an endless recycling
process where, upon death, 'all the particles that make you up will loosen
and float apart', becoming 'part of everything', since 'All the atoms that
were them [i.e. the dead], they've gone into the air and the wind and the
trees and the earth and all the living things. They'll never vanish. They're
just part of everything' (335). Pullman utilises scientific knowledge to
utterly disrupt and advance the Bildungsroman so that the bodily

thresholds of individual self-development are dismantled and, even upon death, one's contribution to the cosmos inevitably continues. In turn, the discourses that contain selfhood in a constricted, unquestioning coherence are interrogated so that Lyra's relationship with authority becomes one of resistance rather than compliance.

Similarly, Julie Bertagna's *Exodus* (2002–11) trilogy depicts a strong heroine in the form of Mara Bell who must save her people from the rising seas caused by climate change in a futuristic dystopia. While Pullman's trilogy alludes to ecological crises and focuses upon an Oxford heroine, Bertagna's trilogy centralises environmental degradation as the pivotal issue for her Scottish heroine's journey. Mara is not part of the privileged society of New Mungo, a sky city inhabited by those saved from the floods. Instead, she is an other, like the climate refugees trying to enter the city. However, with its corruption and greed, New Mungo is rejected by Mara in favour of relocating her followers to Greenland, which is translated in the text as 'the land of the people'.[42] Bertagna's trilogy offers a reconfigured female Bildungsroman, where Mara excels in her development, taking responsibility to relocate her people and create a counter-community to the corrupt privilege of the phallic structure of the patriarchal sky city. Again, the feminist narrative reconfigures generic norms, as social success at the expense of others is vilified in favour of mutual solidarity and cooperative community. In Bertagna's vision, Mara's achievements are based upon her empathetic capacity to understand and act for the greater communitarian good.

While the individual is linked vehemently to society, nevertheless this is not conventional socialisation and interpellation within the parameters of standardised norms; instead Mara subverts the hegemonic conventions of dominant society and sets up her own resistance movement for the good of those deemed abject non-citizens in the eyes of the privileged elitist sky cities. In an elitist dystopia like New Mungo citizen status is reserved for 'what it judged to be the best of human beings' (196). On the contrary, Mara's heroine status is earned precisely by flouting traditional Bildungsroman conventions of success. Instead, Bertagna charts a new narrative of self-development that forms part of a polyphonic feminist treatise that values the environment and all of its inhabitants as integral to human survival. Rather than self-development beginning and ending with individualism, Bertagna's vision regards intergenerational dialogue to be vital in terms of selflessly preserving a future for the next generation rather than ruthlessly pursuing commercial success without regard for tomorrow's citizens. By breaking the frame of competitive individualism,

Bertagna's trilogy recasts and rebalances the Bildungsroman as a narrative of collective responsibility so that environment as well as society is prized. Mara is cast as a figure who resists the phallic sky city structures created by the patriarchal character Caledon and, by doing so, she attempts to create a counter-narrative of heroic maturation within a feminist Bildungsroman.[43]

Gillian Cross's *Where I Belong* (2010) charts the development not of one protagonist, but three major figures, with another character's life related through omniscient narration. The three first-person narratives of Freya, Abdi and Khadija and the omniscient narrative outlining Mahmoud's life disrupt the conventions of Bildungsromane to tell multiple stories which, in turn, are connected to the wider world. So London and Somalia, rather than being poles apart, are shown to be integrally connected in a globalised world. The title focuses attention upon the 'I' of conventional narratives, only to multiply and fracture its coherence into a plethora of heterogeneous *becoming*. As these characters mature, they recognise that they are not isolated from external influences, but are very much part of a wider community and global structure in which 'we're all connected'.[44] Within the infrastructure of globalisation's shrinking world, geopolitical events in a seemingly remote region will resonate and have an impact upon one's immediate proximity: 'We're all linked together by emails and phones and the great spider's web of media that spans the world. That's where the story is set. The world' (1). Thus, in Cross's global vision, Somalian piracy coalesces with London's world, given the diaspora of many people fleeing this war-torn region and, in turn, is connected to the west's neoliberal enterprise of breaching Somalia's fishing grounds. The close proximity of nations is emphasised by comparing the Earth in cosmological terms:

> 'I hadn't even noticed the moon, but there it was, way above the tallest buildings . . . I stared up at it and for some reason I suddenly thought about Somalia again. The people there were three hours ahead of us, which made it the middle of the night. Was there a Somali girl looking up at the moon as well? If there was, she could probably see a thousand times more stars than I could. But it was the same moon.' (37)

Space and time condense here so that Freya, the British girl, becomes a compound world citizen who experiences cosmopolitan affinity with global others who share the same sky. This shifts the Bildungsroman from an individual's socialisation outwards to a centrifugal progress of collective global association and development.

Beth Revis's *Across the Universe* (2011–13) trilogy is a YA futuristic dystopia that pushes the Bildungsroman format beyond the very thresholds of humanity into a post-human existence. While Cross's novel contemplates our connectivity with the universe, as one character contemplates how all people view the same moon, Revis's fiction, rather like *His Dark Materials*, embarks upon an interstellar journey in order to explore and interrogate thresholds of self/other. But Revis envisages an alien world that is also posthuman. Amy, the heroine, falls in love with Elder, a cloned future leader of a spaceship which has been prevented from landing on Centauri-Earth, the original mission to reach an exoplanet given the climactic decline of Earth. Elder is apprentice to Eldest, the current cloned leader and, upon his demise, Elder becomes the next Eldest. To blur the boundaries between human/posthuman through a love story, albeit heteronormative, enables Amy to question the very tenets of what makes us human and how scientific development in the hands of corporate entities has impacted upon the world environmentally, economically and socially. Revis's trilogy interrogates the Cartesian *cogito* of liberal humanist selfhood, raising questions about racial and gender politics in its depiction of a futuristic posthuman world that looks back at the history of human conflict based upon difference. Its reconfiguration of selfhood through posthumanism brings into question the discursive hegemony of Western childhood and liberates the self as a prismatic and fluid becoming rather than a fixed point of final destination. Spatio-temporality is redundant in the vacuum of space where Amy is awakened after being cryogenically frozen for several years so that the conventional realist development of the Bildungsroman is utterly reshaped to take account of a futuristic post-planetary existence. Existentially, she recognises 'My life, my *former* life, already is history . . . What if I recognize myself, staring up at me from the pages of a history tome older than I am?'.[45] She has shed the skin of her old Earth-bound identity to incorporate her new existence within the expansion of space: 'I guess it doesn't matter that I had a life on Earth, and that I loved Earth, and that by now, my friends have all lived and gotten old and died' (20). Childhood boundaries and temporal chronology are dismantled so that she is an anachronistic coalescence of child/adult, signifying the uncharted territory of adolescent mutability that would be all too familiar to Revis's Earthling readers. Revis introduces a new frontier in the Bildungsroman, incorporating spatio-temporal disruption to an individual's self-formation, as well as introducing posthuman identities within a reconfigured ontological model.

Saci Lloyd's *Momentum* (2011) strives to counter compliance with the values of a neoliberal status quo by encouraging her adolescent readers to identify with outsiders. In her dystopian neoconservative vision, society is rigidly demarcated between Citizens and Outsiders, the latter denied any rights and constantly prone to brutalisation at the hands of the military police, known as Kossacks. Hunter, a privileged Citizen, and Uma, a disenfranchised Outsider, are willing to risk everything to transgress this boundary and create a resistant narrative through their love story. Highly critical of the technological turn in contemporary society and the distraction techniques of social media, Lloyd describes the Citizens as being somnambulated by constantly manipulated media, so that they are ensnared in virtual reality rather than awake to the political reality of the conditions in which they are living at the expense of those robbed of their rights. As well as living predominantly through social media in the form of constantly streamed entertainment, the Citizens have internalised a hatred of the Outsiders, with the reality of the situation falsified by those in power so that the non-citizens serve as sources of political scapegoating: 'The government cut society in two, setting rich against poor – and whipped the so-called Citizen into a frenzy of anger against anyone who was different from them. That's when the ID system came in.'[46] In many ways Lloyd is challenging her intended readers so that they reconsider media hostility towards vulnerable sectors of society, such as benefits claimants and asylum seekers, for instance. In a world affected by global economic downturns, Lloyd urges her reader to look beyond easy targets and to think critically as they journey towards adulthood. The Bildung development in Lloyd's text depends upon active adolescent agency rather than passive compliance in order to educate oneself about this dystopian society and its demonisation of others. Society and its institutions must be held to account rather than simply ratified, demonstrating that individuals should question the composition of selfhood and belonging within any nation state. Only by resisting an interpellated subjectivity, Lloyd argues, can a Bildungsroman fully develop its adolescent characters.[47]

Louise O'Neill's *Only Ever Yours* (2014), often compared to Margaret Atwood's *The Handmaid's Tale* (1985), charts the Bildung maturation of a female 'eve' called freida. In freida's dystopian world, teenage girls are subdivided into 'companions' (to produce male heirs for their husbands), 'concubines' (to serve as prostitutes), or 'chastities' (nun-like figures who train the next generation of eves). Thus, freida's future is rigidly and narrowly demarcated: she too is destined to serve as a male companion, become a concubine or live in nun-like chastity to train the next generation of eves. As with Revis's text, O'Neill's females have been privy to scientific posthuman development in order to produce a perfection defined by the strictures of patriarchal authority. Instead of a birthday, they have a design date. O'Neill recasts the Bildungsroman format within the parameters of dystopian YA fiction, presenting a school story where girls are taught nothing but gender-defined domestic duties to prepare them for their future roles in an extreme patriarchal environment. Freida's self-development is through an education that demands perfection in terms of body image and compliance to the authority of the Father, the leader of this tyrannical society. Devoid of any human rights, her growth is confined and restricted so that any sense of education in the familiar Bildung text is utterly inverted. Instead, she must erase any sense of self in order to fulfil the inane duty demanded of her as a female. As such, there is no space for self-development, only selfless complicity in a misogynistic regime, where even girls' and women's names are without capital letters to ensure that they remain overshadowed by male citizens. Any emotions must be held in check and suppressed since 'No one likes an angry girl'[48] and, in terms of beauty, 'there is always room for Improvement' (58). The natural Bildung progression from childhood to adulthood is constantly interfered with by scientific manipulation of the female body to create what is deemed perfection according to the judgemental male gaze. In such a male-dominated dystopia that values only youthful beauty, the Bildungsroman formula of chronological maturation is, as noted, disrupted and, ulti-mately, halted: 'Not everyone wants to be a companion. They get termi-nated at forty. Do you know what forty looks like?' (170). *Only Ever Yours* offers a feminist resistance to the conventional male-dominated Bildungsroman by depicting the ways in which patriarchal authority stifles and manipulates female identity. By offering such a claustrophobic Bildung environment, O'Neill's text conversely carves out a niche for young women's voices to be heard as an active empowerment for her intended reader that involves an educative self-development beyond the trappings of hegemonic gender narratives.

At first glance, the Bildungsroman seems a static genre, conservatively supportive of the status quo and determined to produce a text that serves as a finishing school for the ideal citizen, fully socialised into accepting their position within a hegemonic norm. However, closer consideration and inspection reveals a dynamic and restless literature, prone to spatio-temporal evolution and keen to embrace an identity of *becoming* rather than reaching a final destination. Nowhere is this more acutely evident than in the YA category of fiction, given its ability to question authority, challenge its intended reader and offer a paradigm shift to unsettle the conventions of traditional Bildungsromane in favour of deconstructing the many social narratives which the self is prone to. It is a genre, then, of voyage, of discovery and of coalescence with others that challenges, redefines and resists readings of self-completion and that, ultimately, questions social values. Often the protagonist does not epitomise the heroic white Western heteronormative ideal; instead s/he is diverse, transnational, marginalised and cosmopolitically seeking alternative ways of being that overturn the selfish individualism of the capitalist success story in favour of eco-conscious counter-narratives. In this process of becoming, one does not strive for the trappings of individualist dominance and power, but the communitarian solidarity of home and belonging. The heart is the asset of maturation while competitive accumulation robs humanity of its full potential in the reconfigured Bildungsroman. Rather like adolescence itself, it is a genre of mutability that offers the potential of *becoming* through interactive narratives that resist dominant modes of being.

CHAPTER 8

# The Female Bildungsroman in the Twentieth Century

## Maroula Joannou

The origins of the classical Bildungsroman, the apprentice or 'coming-of-age' narrative, are associated with the rigid class and gender hierarchies of the eighteenth-century German Enlightenment and dated to the publication in 1795–6 of Johann Wolfgang Goethe's *Wilhelm Meisters Lehrjahre*, first translated into English as *Wilhelm Meister's Apprenticeship* by Thomas Carlyle in 1824. However, Lorna Ellis's analysis of Eliza Haywood's *The History of Miss Betty Thoughtless* (1751) supports the argument that the female Bildungsroman existed well before Goethe or his English translators.[1] Women writers have contested the central ideas on which the classical Bildungsroman from *Wilhelm Meister* onward has been premised: that the self-realisation of the individual and the individual's socialisation into society are one and the same; that happiness is the 'subjective symptom of an objectively completed socialization'.[2] Twentieth-century women writers including Dorothy Richardson, Doris Lessing, Angela Carter, Jeannette Winterson and Sarah Waters have questioned the temporal logic of the classical Bildungsroman as they have disputed the ameliorative optimism of the form. In multiple reworkings women have rejected the conventional ending in marriage as a metaphor for the social contract, the '"pact" between the individual and the world, that reciprocal "consent" which finds in the double "I do" of the wedding ritual an unsurpassed symbolic condensation' (Moretti 22). They have eschewed its realism using a variety of non-realist genres such as the gothic and the grotesque, the utopian and the dystopian, the fantastic, the fable and the fairy tale.

It is necessary to revisit Goethe's *Lehrjahre* in order to understand its twentieth-century inflections in writing by women. The young Wilhelm embarks on a hazardous journey of self-discovery and after numerous misadventures learns the error of his ways and modifies his youthful idealism. Reconciled with his father, a prosperous merchant, and with the mores of his own society, the mature Wilhelm acquires an aristocratic fiancée, Natalie, and an occupation as a responsible landowner. Wilhelm's love for the actor Mariane is closely bound up with his theatrical ambition and his desire to embark on a career as an actor and dramatist in defiance of his father. Mistakenly believing her to be unfaithful, Wilhelm abandons Mariane who dies giving birth to his son, Felix. Wilhelm also rescues Mignon, a waif with a beautiful singing voice, who has been abducted by a wandering troupe of acrobats and becomes Wilhelm's devoted servant before succumbing to an incurable illness. Terence Cave explains the gendered asymmetries of the *Lehrjahre*:

> The women in the novel circle round him like planets in a solar system; their development is not at issue, and their fate often depends on the errors he makes as well as some of his more felicitous moves, of which rescuing Mignon must count as one. Unlike Wilhelm, Mariane and Mignon don't make it beyond adolescence; they also get no useful Bildung.[3]

Indeed the indicator of Wilhelm's maturity is amnesia; the adult Wilhelm and the reader alike forget Mignon and Mariane who must be consigned to the period of his youthful folly and immaturity. In other words, Mariane and Mignon are Wilhelm's mistakes. As Georgia Christinidis reminds us, 'If those who achieve *Bildung* in *Wilhelm Meister* are guided by fate, those who fail (and an exceptionally large number of characters fail to achieve *Bildung* and die) cannot be held responsible for their failure.'[4]

Angela Carter has provided two ingenious twentieth-century engagements with *Lehrjahre*, reinventing Goethe's marginal characters in *Heroes and Villains* (1969) and *Nights at the Circus* (1984) respectively, prolonging their fictional lives beyond adolescence, and providing them with the missing Bildung (education, formation, development of talents). If the classical Bildungsroman has the reader perceive the text through the eyes of one chosen protagonist, Carter offers a veritable galaxy of players in the circus that replaces the theatre in *Lehrjahre* as the fictional auditorium in which parts small and large can be played.

Carter knew her Goethe. The setting of her dystopic fable, *Heroes and Villains* is post-apocalyptic, a white tower of concrete and steel in which Marianne, who is given the same name as Goethe's character although it is spelled slightly differently, is ironically instructed in civilisation and the liberal arts by her father, a Professor of History, after a nuclear war has effectively annihilated the idea of progress, the cornerstone of the rational enlightenment on which the *Lehrjahre* is grounded. Insulated from the world outside, Marianne is tutored by her father to believe in the values of a society that no longer exists. Marianne leaves the ivory tower to join

Jewel, a marauding Barbarian living outside the civilised encampment, the antithesis of the noble savage in her father's researches. Rousseau's roman-ticised savage embodies the natural goodness and perfectibility of the human species whereas Jewel rapes Marianne and makes her his wife ('There's no choice in being a wife. It is entirely out of one's hands').[5] In a novel that is ludic in the extreme, the childhood game in the title *Heroes and Villains* is the one game that Marianne refuses to play, 'Because I do not know which is which any more, nor who is who, and what can I trust if not appearances?' (125). Nor will Marianne meekly submit to the feminine passive role. On Jewel's death she proclaims defiantly, 'I'll be the tiger lady and rule them with a rod of iron' (150).

In *Nights at the Circus* Mignon is a circus artiste, a victim of abuse, beaten 'as though she were a carpet' by the primitive Ape-Man, as she was in her previous incarnation in the *Lehrjahre* by the acrobats.[6] This time, Mignon is rescued by the aerialiste, Sophie Fevvers, half woman, half swan. Mignon starts a love affair with the Princess of Abyssinia, a black perform-ing artiste from the Windward Islands, whom she partners in a dancing tiger act: 'Mignon she kissed on the mouth and the two girls clung together for a little longer, only a moment longer, than propriety allowed although, such was the vigour of the ovation, nobody noticed except those to whom it came as no surprise' (192–3). Carter's outcome revises the gender politics of the *Lehrjahre*.

The coming-of-age journey in the classical Bildungsroman is based on the assumption of the male self as the universal self. The quest – whether geographical or the inner quest for spirituality or truth – is a quintessential aspect of human experience, not only in the Bildungsroman but also in literary forms such as the picaresque, the Arthurian legend, and epic high fantasy, J. R. R. Tolkien's *The Lord of the Rings* (1954), for example. If, however, one is a woman, the quest cannot be contemplated in the same way. It is not possible for a woman to venture forth into the unknown if the very act of stepping out onto a public thoroughfare exposes her to the risk of jeopardy to the person, ridicule, loss of reputation, or sexual assault. Even the flâneuse wandering about the streets of the city out of idle curiosity is liable to be mistaken for a prostitute. Virginia Woolf grasped this essential difference in the story of Shakespeare's sister in her feminist polemic *A Room of One's Own* (1929). Judith runs away to London for the same reason as William (and indeed Wilhelm) – to seek her fortune on the stage – but is met with derision, seduced, becomes pregnant, and takes her own life. Woolf also grasped the difference in *Orlando* (1928), a fantastical Bildungsroman in which she has the time-traveller, Orlando, heavily encumbered by the Victorian crinoline, lament the loss of freedom of movement which she had enjoyed in her previous incarnation as a man.

The characteristic journey of the hero in the classic apprenticeship novel is essentially that of the hero in stories of male adventure, legend and myth. In *The Hero with a Thousand Faces* (1949), Joseph Campbell suggests that the 'standard path of the mythological adventure of the hero is a magnification of the formula represented in the rites of passage: *separation – initiation – return*'. Borrowing the term 'monomyth' from Joyce's *Finnegans Wake* (1939), Campbell suggests that this path 'might be named the nuclear unit of the monomyth'.[7] But this formula does not correspond to the life journey of a female protagonist or the rites of passage to womanhood. A woman's quest for her identity may be explorative rather than goal-orientated, epistemological rather than teleological, relational rather than linear, circuitous or circular rather than direct, or shifting rather than fixed. Thus narrative which purports to represent the complexity and contemporaneity of that quest must do so in terms other than the formulaic ones of severance, induction and return to the point of origin.

In *The Voyage In: Fictions of Female Development* (1983), a path-breaking collection of essays that inverts the title of Virginia Woolf's *The Voyage Out* (1919), Elizabeth Abel, Marianne Hirsch and Elizabeth Langland emphasise the interiority of a woman's journey of self-discovery and the difference between the life experiences of women and their male counterparts. Thus the 'voyage in' (a psychological journey) undertaken by female protagonists is very different to the 'voyage out' (the physical journey) undertaken by male protagonists. Indeed the physical journey undertaken by Rachel Vinrace in *The Voyage Out* is literally responsible for her death which happens when Rachel embarks on an expedition to South America during which she encounters a young writer, Terence Hewett, and 'dies from a fever mysteriously contracted when she contracts to marry'.[8] The editors question the psychological and social forces that prevent the young woman from achieving maturity, and ask why death should provide Rachel with her 'only escape from a violent and confining social world and from the female body that frustrates her spiritual and artistic cravings' (4). They also suggest that even 'the broadest definitions of the *Bildungsroman* presuppose a range of social options available only to men' (7).

Is there, then, a sense in which this assessment of the Bildungsroman form as unsuited to female experience reinforces conventional perceptions of femininity as unsuited to engagement with the wider world? Might it indeed be argued that the essential characteristics of the genre have made it fundamentally incapable of depicting the experience of women? Why is

it that American literature can provide the reader with no female equivalent of *Huckleberry Finn*? Disillusionment, disappointment, diminution in
stature and the dashing of idealistic aspiration, if not disaster and death, are
all too common for the heroine. As Penny Brown puts it, 'the enquiring
and aspiring intellect and unfocused ambitions are seen to be diminished
and channelled into a position of powerlessness by contact with life's
experiences and patriarchal norms, and the harmonious cultivation of
the whole personality is far more likely to be fragmented or stunted by
compromise, frustration or betrayal'.[9] It was not only novelistic convention which curtailed the narrative possibilities for female characters; these
narrative constrictions were re-workings of social expectations. Is authorial
investment in 'enstopped' girlhood – Maggie drowning in George Eliot's
*The Mill on the Floss* (1860), the adumbration of Lyndall's life in Olive
Schreiner's *The Story of an African Farm* (1883), Cathy's death after child-
birth has symbolically denoted her entry into womanhood in Emily
Brontë's *Wuthering Heights* (1847) – authorial contestation of the generic
ethos of maturity? Are all three authors, who felt the need to publish under
male pseudonyms to avoid the reception of their work being adversely
affected by knowledge of their sex, refusing to ratify Victorian womanhood
and the restrictive social environment that they knew would have lain
ahead for their young heroines had they lived longer?

The Victorian novel illustrates the relationship between formal conventions and social conventions and how society's values and expectations
were represented and mediated through such means as characterisation,
explicit authorial statement and narrative. Charlotte Brontë's *Jane Eyre*
(1847) and *The Mill on the Floss* reanimated the genre by questioning the
preoccupation of the classical Bildungsroman with male perfectibility as
well as its restrictive proscription of femininity. Charlotte Brontë and
George Eliot link the life predicaments of their respective protagonists to
the situation of Victorian women and girls in general. Powerless, mother-
less and penniless, Jane Eyre is incarcerated in her aunt's house where she is
subjected to emotional, mental and physical cruelty while courageously
standing up to those who bully and mistreat her: the sanctimonious Mrs
Reed, her obnoxious cousin John Reed, and later the hypocritical Mr
Brocklehurst at Lowood School. Jane consistently demonstrates resilience
and moral strength throughout her ordeals: the 'more solitary, the more
friendless, the more unsustained I am, the more I will respect myself'.[10]
Thus Brontë's heroine satisfies the generic expectations of maturation and
the symbolic closure of the novel is secured with Jane happily married to
her former employer, Edward Rochester, albeit with the inequalities of

power reversed by her inheritance of a personal fortune and the onset of her husband's blindness that reverses their earlier master and servant relationship.

*Jane Eyre* and *The Mill on the Floss* are concerned thematically with questions of liberty and autonomy; with women's desire to become their own persons ('I desired liberty; for liberty I gasped; for liberty I uttered a prayer; it seemed scattered on the wind' [99]). When Rochester attempts to dress Jane in unwanted finery after their engagement, for example, she retorts that she will go out as a missionary to 'preach liberty to them that are enslaved – your Harem inmates amongst the rest. I'll get admitted there, and I'll stir up mutiny' (316). In *Jane Eyre* the passionate, defiant child with right on her side matures into the passionate, discriminating, defiant adult prepared to withstand tyranny on behalf of herself and others, thus setting a precedent of assertive female development in Bildungsromane that many later women writers were to follow.

Eliot too depicts Maggie's youthful rebellion as a rebellion against Victorian notions of femininity. Maggie runs away to join the gypsies, cuts off her long hair and struggles to reconcile her longing to escape her provincial upbringing with her keenly felt responsibility to her family during her father's bankruptcy. Maggie's Bildung is thwarted not only by scandal and disgrace after her attempted flight from St Oggs with the handsome Stephen Guest, but also by the repression of her own desires when she renounces the pleasures of the intellectual life in order to pursue an austere path of self-sacrifice under the influence of the medieval mystic Thomas à Kempis. Maggie's collusion in her own oppression typifies a pattern of female self-denial that is to resonate chillingly in twentieth-century apprentice novels to which I return, such as May Sinclair's *The Life and Death of Harriett Frean* (1922), Radclyffe Hall's *The Unlit Lamp* (1924) and Winifred Holtby's *The Crowded Street* (1924).

The loss of educational opportunities and the failure of adults to recognise the intelligence and academic potential of girls is a *leitmotif* in *The Mill on the Floss* and subsequent coming-of-age novels such as Doris Lessing's *Martha Quest* (1952). Martha is ill before a crucial examination at eleven and eye problems prevent her sitting the matriculation exam, so her formal education is cut short and she is never prepared for a career. Maggie's father thinks her 'Too 'cute for a woman'[11] and she is denied the tuition in geometry and the Classics afforded her brother Tom, although she is the cleverer of the two. When ten-year-old Maggie asks Tom's tutor, '"couldn't I do Euclid, and all Tom's lessons, if you were to teach me instead of him?"', they both respond with incomprehension

revealing the type of attitudes about women's ability to reason logically
that were to take many years to change:

> 'No; you couldn't,' said Tom indignantly. 'Girls can't do Euclid: can
> they, sir?'
> 'They CAN pick up a little of everything, I daresay,' said Mr Stelling.
> 'They've a great deal of superficial cleverness; but they couldn't go far into
> anything. They're quick and shallow.' (171)

If, as Gayatri Spivak suggests, Jane Eyre has acquired the status of a feminist
ideal, then this is at the expense of Bertha Mason, Rochester's abused Creole
wife, who is incarcerated in a foreign country and denied a voice with which
to speak. As Spivak puts it, 'In this fictive England, she must play out her
role, act out the transformation of her "self" into that fictive Other, set fire to
the house and kill herself, so that Jane Eyre can become the feminist
individualist heroine of British fiction.'[12] In *Wide Sargasso Sea* (1966) the
Dominican-born Jean Rhys enters into a dialogue with *Jane Eyre*, dignifying
the unnamed 'madwoman in the attic' with the name Antoinette in
a postcolonial Bildungsroman which reimagines the demented figure of
gothic convention as a woman driven to *extremis* by the traumas of slavery
and empire. Rhys writes: 'Of course Charlotte Brontë makes her own world,
of course she convinces you, and that makes the poor Creole lunatic all the
more dreadful. I remember being quite shocked, and when I re-read it rather
annoyed. "That's only one side – the English side" sort of thing.'[13] In having
Antoinette narrate her own account of her traumatic formative experiences
in the post-Emancipation Caribbean, Rhys 'writes back' against the
Victorian Bildungsroman, reinstating in *Wide Sargasso Sea* the marginalised
voice of the oppressed colonial subject that *Jane Eyre* had suppressed.

In *Unseasonable Youth* (2011) Jed Esty coins the term 'anti-developmental'
to denote those novels of arrested adolescence which demonstrate the
impossibility of the classical Bildungsroman adequately representing the
perspectives of colonised subjects given the crisis between the European
nation state and its colonies in the late stages of empire.[14] The crisis registers
the disjuncture between an imperial, Enlightenment narrative of perpetual
progress and the lived histories of modernisation. Esty revisits Rhys's
*Voyage in the Dark* (1934) to show how Anna Morgan's journey from the
West Indies to England is punctuated by the 'recursive logic of Anna's
nonprogress': abandonment by her family and lover, and insecure jobs as
a chorus girl and masseuse, culminating in the sadness and futility of
a botched abortion. Anna is unable to reconcile her West Indian and her
British heritages and fits in nowhere. A white privileged descendent of the

slave-owning plantocracy, she feels herself to be a despised colonial subject in London. As Esty puts it, Anna's 'disorientation and her failure to mature or progress are symbolically rooted in the massive anachronisms produced by late colonial life in the West Indies, so the uneven modernization of Anna's childhood echoes and anticipates the uneven development of her own psyche' (167, 168).

In *Black British Literature: Novels of Transformation* (2004), Mark Stein makes the case for the Bildungsroman as a genre 'uniquely suitable for the process of the redefining of Britishness' and, despite the 'risk of inflicting yet another Eurocentric body of thought onto post-colonial texts', for understanding a growing corpus of literature by black British authors.[15] Stein contends that 'the Black British novel of transformation … has a dual function: it is about the formation of its protagonists as well as the transformation of British society and cultural institutions' (22) because the formation of the subject takes place within the social world that the subject encounters and shapes.

Joan Riley's *The Unbelonging* (1985) is the first modern Bildungsroman published in Britain by a Jamaica-born woman. Isolated, rejected and misunderstood by classmates and teachers, eleven-year-old Hyacinth arrives in Britain to live with her father and stepmother but is taken into a children's home after his sexual abuse. Hyacinth longs for happiness and dreams of self-betterment, the staples of the poor immigrant's imagination. Her consoling fantasy, the return to Jamaica, materialises but produces further disillusionment, underscoring the unpalatable truth that there is no longer a 'home' or place of return. *The Unbelonging* was followed by other Bildungsromane by black British women authors including Andrea Levy's *Every Light in the House Burnin'* (1994), Meera Syal's *Anita and Me* (1996), Zadie Smith's *White Teeth* (2000), and Monica Ali's *Brick Lane* (2003). Their works are concerned with various states of 'unbelonging': individuation, alienation, displacement, heritage, and the effects of white racism upon girls growing up in first- or second-generation immigrant families.

Andrea Levy's first novel, *Every Light in the House Burnin'*, tells of Angela Jacob's childhood in a cramped council flat in Highbury, North London, with her mother, a primary school teacher, and her father, a chain-smoking postal worker who arrived in Britain on the SS *Empire Windrush*, the passenger liner which inaugurated mass migration from Jamaica in 1948. Angela's own story ends with her father's lung cancer and her anguish at his treatment in an understaffed NHS hospital. Inadequate resourcing and institutional indifference result in Mr Jacob's premature discharge from hospital and his attempted suicide: 'I always thought that they released you from hospital when you were fit. Perhaps once, but now they needed the beds.'[16] Faced with institutional inhumanity and incompetence – the hospital fetches a rabbi to his bedside although her father belongs to the Church of England – Angela entertains fantasies of assaulting the nurse who addresses her father as 'old man Jacobs' (152), but her dreams of extracting violent revenge only serve to underline the reality of her powerlessness. Dave Gunning writes of this novel, and of Levy's second, *Never Far from Nowhere* (1996), 'the bleakness of these texts, the persistence of a melancholic notion of loss, and the idea that any move forward is countered always by a parallel step backwards demand that the concept of the black British *Bildungsroman* is divorced from the sense of celebration that so often accompanies it'.[17]

In Meera Syal's *Anita and Me* (1996), Meena Kumar's parents are Indian Sikhs who migrated from the Punjab to a Midlands mining village after the Partition in 1947. The ambivalent friendship between Meena, who comes from a stable loving home, and Anita Rutter, whose wayward mother has abandoned her chaotic family, invites the obvious comparison between the aspirational incomers and the abject white English working class. Meena's innocence is cruelly ruptured when Anita joins Sam Lowbridge's gang in a white racist assault upon an Asian bank manager at the same time as she becomes involuntary witness to a tragic death. *To Kill a Mockingbird*, Harper Lee's 1960 Bildungsroman about children caught up in the violence and racism of the American deep south, which inspired Syal to write her own novel, is the present Meena chooses to give to Robert, her first boyfriend.[18]

At school, Meena exaggerates her Englishness and her Midlands accent to avoid being bullied. In hospital, she resolves to become the cliché of a dutiful Indian daughter: to 'grow my hair long and vaguely feminine', 'write letters to India', 'learn to knit' and 'always tell the truth' (284). A reinvention of self heals the laceration of her 'unbelonging': 'I now knew I was not a bad girl, a mixed-up girl, a girl with no name or no place. The place to which I belonged was wherever I stood and there was nothing to stop me moving forward and claiming each resting place as home. The sense of displacement I had always carried round like a curse shrivelled into insignificance' (303). This erasure of Meena's old self is a reaction to her mimicry of Englishness and demonstrates how subjectivities and ethnicities are mutable at the end of the twentieth century.

For much of its history the Bildungsroman was grounded thematically and structurally in the 'naturalness' of gender polarities. A woman was valued as an object of male desire and female quest narratives were often

deflected into romance and marriage. In contrast, 'For the male protagonist, marriage is not a goal so much as a reward for having reached his goal;
it symbolizes his gratification.'[19] In *Rebel Women: Feminism, Modernism
and the Edwardian Novel* (1994), Jane Eldridge Miller argues that the
'principal forms of nineteenth-century British fiction were, at the most
basic level of narrative dynamics, inimical to the representation of feminist
rebellion, for they inevitably moved towards or endorsed stasis; the status
quo, and social integration through marriage, and thus ran contrary to the
heroine's desire for independence, rebellion and social change'.[20] Miller
contends that Edwardian feminism changed both the public perception
and self-image of the unmarried woman, and, in so doing, allowed her
a fuller life and more significant role in society.

Twentieth-century representations of women were predicated upon
a *fin de siècle* social and cultural revolution in the position of women and
in the growth of feminist consciousness. The changing nature of the female
Bildungsroman depended on the success of Victorian and Edwardian
novelists in writing about women with sexual honesty and psychological
realism and in creating modern protagonists who refused to be constrained
by marriage and motherhood. Indeed, Esther Labovitz contends that the
female Bildungsroman becomes possible only as '*Bildung* became a reality
for women, in general, and for the fictional heroine, in particular. When
cultural and social structures appeared to support women's struggle for
independence, to go out into the world, engage in careers, in self-discovery
and fulfilment, the heroine in fiction began to reflect these changes.'[21]
Female Bildungsromane altered markedly in content and form in consequence of the massive demographic changes and social upheavals of the
First World War and the campaigns which secured the vote for women
over thirty in 1918. The genre's development was also to be radically
affected by the knowledge of psychoanalysis as Freud's writings were
translated into English after 1913. Stylistic and formal innovation was
influenced by new understandings of character, memory and time associated in literature with the 'stream of consciousness', and with modernism
as a literary and philosophical movement transforming the humanities, arts
and social sciences and rejecting many of the certainties of Enlightenment
thinking in which the Bildungsroman had originated.

May Sinclair became interested in psychoanalysis in or about 1913
through the Medico-Psychological Clinic in London: 'At the present
moment there is a reaction against all hushing up and stamping down.
The younger generation is in revolt against even such a comparatively mild
form of repression as Victorian Puritanism. And the New Psychology is

with it.'[22] In *The Life and Death of Harriett Frean* (1922) Sinclair draws heavily upon psychoanalytic paradigms, including Freud's ideas on repression and sublimation, to illuminate the harmful effects of Victorian domestic ideology upon women and girls brought up like Harriett to behave beautifully and to put responsibility to others above their own intimate needs. As Suzanne Raitt suggests, *Harriett Frean* 'reads almost like a case study of one of the effects of repression as Jung outlined it in *Psychology and the Unconscious*, which Sinclair reviewed in 1916' (251).

Sinclair had also reviewed the opening volumes of Dorothy Richardson's ambitious thirteen-part novel sequence, *Pilgrimage*, in *The Egoist* in April 1918 expressing her admiration for Richardson's development of a new literary technique, the 'stream of consciousness', to chart the inner life of the young Miriam Henderson. In *Honeycomb*, the cigarette-smoking Miriam is living with the Corrie family and wrestles with the contradictions of the freedom to leave home and earn her own living in the metropolis: '"I suppose I'm a new woman – I've said I am now, anyhow", she reflected, wondering in the background how she would reconcile the role with her work as a children's governess.'[23] Sinclair's reading of *Pilgrimage* informed the writing of her earlier Bildungsroman, *Mary Olivier: A Life* (1919). Originally published alongside *Ulysses* in *The Little Review*, this is a chilling interiorised modernist dissection of the Victorian family life in which a sensitive heroine is damaged by an emotionally distant mother.

Jean Radford points out that *The Life and Death of Harriett Frean* can be read 'as a delayed response to Maggie [Tulliver]'s question which has echoed down the corridors of women's writing: "Is it not right to resign ourselves entirely, whatever . . . may be denied us? I have found great peace in that for the last two or three years – even joy in subduing my own will."'[24] Harriett is born in 1845, the cossetted daughter of adoring, cultured parents. Her subsequent life of inactivity and self-denial contrasts markedly with Sinclair's own personal history. Sinclair joined the Munro Ambulance Corps founded by Dr Hector Munro whom she knew through the Medico-Psychological Clinic, and served briefly in Belgium in the 1914–18 war. *Harriett Frean* is the author's indictment of the Victorian society of her formative years which had consigned middle-class girls and women to the pursuit of moral beauty rather than self-fulfilment. Harriett's mother teaches her daughter to put others first and to contemplate bad manners as shameful:

> 'Well, I'm glad my little girl didn't snatch and push. It's better to go without than to take from other people. That's ugly.'

Ugly. Being naughty was just that. Doing ugly things. Being good was being beautiful like Mamma. She wanted to be like her mother.[25]

In declining a proposal from a man who loves her but is engaged to her best friend, Harriett deems self-sacrifice to be more important than her own happiness. The futile gesture of self-renunciation brings short-term moral satisfaction but comes back to haunt her in an empty house that becomes a mausoleum to patriarchal values: "'There *is* a standard." Harriett lifted her obstinate and arrogant chin. "You forget that I'm Hilton Frean's daughter'" (116). Unlike Mary Olivier whose sexual energies are sublimated into poetry, philosophy and the sciences, Harriett declines into a lonely old age, eventually dismissing her faithful servant whose fecundity becomes too much to bear. Lacking emotional closeness and any outlet for her feelings, she finds consolation only in the past. As her life atrophies Harriett realises the extent to which she had become complicit in her own subjugation, but by then it is too late.

Winifred Holtby and Radclyffe Hall are more traditional in their reliance on omniscient narrator, linear plot and detailed description of place than the formally innovative Sinclair. *The Crowded Street* and *The Unlit Lamp* dramatise intense life-sustaining female friendships and intimate how women might find personal fulfilment in public service or by joining the professions that were admitting women in greater numbers in the 1920s. Muriel Hammond in *The Crowded Street* and Joan Ogden in *The Unlit Lamp* come of age in dull provincial communities which stifle their creativity, initiative and imagination. Marshington is a village in Yorkshire, resembling Cottingham where Holtby grew up. Seabourne is a south-coast seaside town like Bournemouth where Hall was born. The guidance of a mentor of their own sex is *de rigueur* for the male hero but not the female characters in the classical Bildungsroman.

Holtby and Hall afford Muriel and Joan excellent role models in the characters of Delia Vaughan and Elizabeth Rodney respectively. *The Crowded Street* is a *roman-à-clef* with Delia Vaughan a thinly veiled Vera Brittain, Holtby's lifelong friend and confidante. Muriel wants to study mathematics after reading *The Life of Mary Somerville* but intellectual curiosity is not encouraged at the school. On the contrary, Mrs Hancock, the head teacher, advises her to learn dressmaking, recognising that 'for most of her parents, the unacknowledged aim of education was to teach their children to be a comfort to them'.[26] What matters above all else in Marshington is success in the marriage stakes. Muriel registers her own sense of difference as she watches other women, including her sister,

Connie, manipulate their sexual attractiveness in order to find themselves a marriageable man.

Delia offers Muriel work in London as her housekeeper and gives uncompromising advice which her protégée takes to heart: 'But the thing that matters is to take your life into your own hands and live it; accepting responsibility for failure or success. The really fatal thing to do is to let other people make your choices for you, and then to blame them if your schemes should fail and they despise you for the failure' (261). Inspired by Delia's feminist political activism, Muriel turns down a proposal of marriage in favour of an 'idea of service – not just vague and sentimental, but translated into quite practical things' (305).

*The Unlit Lamp* began with Hall's encounter with two women in a hotel; a 'gentle, tyrant mother and virgin daughter withering on her stem' as her unpaid amanuensis.[27] The central protagonist, Joan Ogden, aspires to a career in medicine, encouraged by Elizabeth who invites Joan to live with her in London. But Joan timidly allows herself to become a victim of convention: 'she had not the courage to say straight out that she intended leaving her mother's home for that of another woman ... It was *unusual*, and because it was unusual she had been embarrassed.'[28]

Like *Harriett Frean, The Unlit Lamp* is infused with a sense of wasted opportunity and time running out. Joan is the type of spinster to which the country has grown accustomed after the First World War: 'Millions all over England! They begin by being so young and fine, like Joan perhaps; and Mother how do they end?' (124). Despairing of Joan's equivocation, Elizabeth settles pragmatically for a marriage of convenience. Trapped in Seabourne, Joan overhears two stylishly confident young women who remind her of her younger self: 'women of the type that she had once been, that in a way she still was. Active, aggressively intelligent women, not at all self-conscious in their tailor-made clothes, not ashamed of their cropped hair' (301). Yet the differences are remarkable: these young women are happy and fulfilled, harbouring no feelings of disappointment or wasted potential. Joan recognises herself as 'the forerunner who had failed, the pioneer who had got left behind'. She is, as her young counterparts point out, 'what they used to call a "New Woman"' (300).

The dislike of suburban and provincial attitudes found countless echoes in twentieth-century coming-of-age narratives all over the English-speaking world, ranging from Doris Lessing's *Martha Quest* (1952) to Sylvia Plath's *The Bell Jar* (1963) and Margaret Drabble's *Jerusalem the Golden* (1967). The adolescent Martha's antipathy to the racism of her white settler parents is articulated in *Martha Quest* in which she dreams of a 'noble city, set four squared and colonnaded' with 'splashing fountains, and the sound of flutes'. She watches 'many-fathered children', 'dark-eyed', 'fair-skinned' and 'bronze-skinned', playing hand-in-hand.[29] The visionary city of Martha's utopian imagination presages an optimistic future of racial harmony and is at once the antidote to, and antithesis of, everything that she has known in the veldt. In *Jerusalem the Golden* Clara Maugham's stultifying childhood in Northam in Yorkshire, loosely resembling Drabble's home city of Sheffield, instils a horror of domesticity and the quest for what Clara's drab home life lacked: beauty, culture and sophistication. These qualities are personified for Clara in the glamorous figure of her new friend, the sophisticated Clelia Denham whom she meets as a student in London.

But departure to the city in search of excitement and self-knowledge is not always shown to bring the rewards of which women dream. In *The Bell Jar* Esther Greenwood's fragile sense of self appears irreparably damaged when the coveted opportunity to work as an intern on a glamorous women's magazine in New York materialises. Indeed, the resultant sense of failure and rejection when her plans go wrong is as painful as any disappointment that she had experienced in her earlier life in a Boston suburb.

In *The Unlit Lamp* the love between Elizabeth and Joan is depicted elliptically, through metaphor and allusion. But the desire of two women to live together is represented as utopian and unrealisable – the near absence of any literary tradition in which women were able to express same-sex desire clearly creating problems for the lesbian reader and the writer alike. Hall's *The Well of Loneliness* (1928) was the first Bildungsroman written from an unapologetically lesbian perspective. However, the ill-fated love affair between Stephen Gordon and Mary Llewellyn did much to perpetuate the notion of the lesbian condition as inexorably agonised and anguished that dominated literary representation for much of the twentieth century.

The postmodern lesbian Bildungsroman, a literary genre expressing the contemporaneity of lesbian experience and exploring the genesis of the lesbian subject, originated in the movement for gay and lesbian rights of the 1970s. Writers who identified as lesbian were able to establish a different trajectory of lesbian writing, sometimes critically reclaiming the achievements of Radclyffe Hall and lesbians of the past while generating a more varied and diverse set of modern lesbian identities and subjectivities. They often revisited the heteronormative assumptions of the traditional Bildungsroman in order to make explicit its homophobia and to affirm and to celebrate lesbian love.

Rita Mae Brown's lesbian classic *Rubyfruit Jungle* (1973) illustrates the staples of the genre: the protagonist's discovery of her love for another woman, the condemnation she is made to feel by her own family, and her rejection by a disapproving community (often followed by betrayal or abandonment by that very lover). The central character's psychological acceptance of her sexual orientation and its implications for her life is in marked contrast to the adjustment to societal norms made by the male protagonist in the traditional Bildungsroman. In this landmark coming-of-age novel, the exuberant Molly Bolt is born illegitimate, poor and working class. Academically gifted and ambitious, she is also tough, brazen, loud-mouthed and shameless. Despite being excoriated for having sex with a fellow student while still in high school, and later having her precious scholarship rescinded as a punishment for a same-sex relationship at university, the unrepentant Molly manages to survive a picaresque journey from the slums of Pennsylvania to New York City with her self-esteem untarnished and her buoyant sense of self intact.

The heroine of Jeanette Winterson's debut novel *Oranges Are Not the Only Fruit* (1985), who is also called Jeanette, is brought up in a working-class household in Lancashire by a strict Pentecostal evangelist mother who believes that she is one of God's elect. The fictional Jeanette's realistic coming-of-age narrative is related in chapters named after the eight books of the Old Testament. These are interspersed with elements of fairy tale and fantasy which mock the pieties of her mother's religious circle. Winnet Stonejar, a character who lives in a magical kingdom and is a sorcerer's apprentice, features in one of the fantasies and is an anagram of Jeanette Winterson. It is impossible to tell fact from fiction in a postmodern parody that knowingly equates the mundane domestic facts of a little girl's life with major Biblical events.

Winterson subverts the quest and self-discovery plot of the traditional Bildungsroman by making self-knowledge contingent on the protagonist's open acknowledgement of lesbian sexual desire as Jeanette innocently falls in love with her school friend, Melanie. In this, as in other lesbian Bildungsromane that revise the heterosexual discourse of the apprentice novel, the 'coming out' story is the all-important rite of passage. Melanie and Jeanette find themselves subjected to a grotesque ritual of exorcism by the fundamentalist religious sect to which the mother belongs, and Jeanette's refusal to express contrition confirms her inevitable departure from her mother's home and the affirmation of a positive lesbian identity.

In Sarah Waters's picaresque best-selling *Tipping the Velvet* (1998) the young Whitstable oyster girl, Nan Astley, is faced with the pain of rejection and disillusionment after her first love affair, with the beautiful cross-dressing Victorian music hall artiste, Kitty Butler, is abruptly ended by the latter's marriage of convenience to her manager. Nan is then befriended and abused by the wealthy Diana Lethaby, the owner of a high-class bordello. After a series of sexual escapades and misadventures with men and women on the streets of the metropolis, which illuminate the performative nature of the sexual role-playing to which Nan has to resort in order to survive economically, she finds happiness in a mature loving relationship with Florence Banner, who introduces her to socialist and feminist ideas and to her radical circle of friends in Victorian London. Although Waters's carefully researched neo-Victorian lesbian Bildungsroman is ostensibly concerned with the lesbian subcultures of the past, 'Women engaging in same-sex relationships in the Victorian era were', as Paulina Palmer reminds us, 'on the whole invisible'.[30] The importance of *Tipping the Velvet* lies largely in Waters's subversion of the Bildungsroman from a lesbian perspective in order to revise attitudes to same-sex love and social and transgression *in the present.* The novel is widely accredited as being the first to move lesbianism into the literary mainstream in Britain and to make this acceptable to a mass readership.

   Viewed from a feminist critical perspective, or indeed from any radical perspective with an investment in social change, the classical Bildungsroman appears socially conservative and reintegrative in its ideological project, as identified by Franco Moretti and others: the affirmation of the societal status quo.[31] In contrast, the works by women I have discussed contest the notion that personal fulfilment is to be achieved as a consequence of one's successful integration into society and that the relationship between the individual and society is essentially homologous. From *Wide Sargasso Sea* to *Martha Quest* and from *Jerusalem the Golden* to *Tipping the Velvet*, the female Bildungsroman concentrates on the *difference* between the needs of the protagonist and the expectations that society has of her *as a woman.* Thus the protagonist's troubled relationship to her family and her resistance to authority not only account for many of the tensions and contradictions in the narrative but also contest the genre's traditional investment in bourgeois ideology.

   As Rita Felski contends in *Beyond Feminist Aesthetics* (1989), the feminist Bildungsroman 'combines the exploration of subjectivity with a dimension of group solidarity which inspires activism and resistance rather than private resignation, and makes it possible to project a visionary hope of future change'.[32] Ellen Morgan too sees the novel of apprenticeship as 'admirably suited to express the emergence of women from cultural conditioning into struggle with institutional forces, their progress towards the goal of full personhood, and the effort to reconstruct their lives and society according to their own vision of meaning and right living'.[33] While the woman writer and reader alike may experience her life's journey as very different to a man's (a psychological 'voyage in' rather than a physical 'voyage out') the authors with whom I am concerned have inflected the Bildungsroman to present sophisticated models of individual, interiorised personal development, bringing marginal voices, lesbian as well as hetero-sexual, black as well as white, to the centre and have consistently accen-tuated individuality rather than normalcy.

# CHAPTER 9

# The Postcolonial Bildungsroman

## Ericka A. Hoagland

In the opening chapter of Nuruddin Farah's haunting and disturbing novel *Maps* (1986), a child is born. The room in which he enters the world is dark and cold; his only company in this empty space his dead mother. Wearing a crown of his mother's blood, the child is discovered by the woman who will become the only mother the boy will know. She will tell him stories about that fateful day, but the mystery of his first moments on Earth will cling to him. Though he insists that he was consciously '*present*' at his own birth, he cannot resist returning to that moment over and over again, an integral component of a perpetual process of self-discovery that begins with a newborn's first cry.[1]

Askar's attempts to map his identity must contend with what Derek Wright describes as the freakish outcomes of 'colonial whimsy', in which 'ethnic and geographical spaces [have been] subordinated to the free play of colonial signifiers' (96).[2] In Farah's novel, 'sexual, national, and ontological boundaries are straddled', and Askar embodies this balancing act between identities in perpetual tension (Wright 100). He is, Wright observes, 'both a real child and the epic miracle-child of his adoptive mother's oral tales who was present at his own birth and born out of his mother's death' (100). Born just a day after his father's death and possibly discovered as much as a full day after his birth, and with bloody fingerprints on his neck, raising the question of whether his birth mother tried to kill him before she died, it is no wonder that Askar tells the reader 'I know of no birth like mine' (Farah 24). His birth and the circumstances surrounding it function as the first confirmation of Askar's difference: he is not like other children. Indeed, there is no way he could be. Born in the disputed Ogaden territory and the child of Somali nationalists, he is adopted by an Ethiopian woman, Misra, with whom he builds a terrifically intimate bond, one in which both see the other as extensions of themselves. In his rejection of the world of children, the child Askar opts instead for the world of adults, and finds himself in neither. This liminality follows him throughout childhood and into early adulthood, and explains, in part, his obsession with cartography. As a child of uncertain borders, maps offer, so it would seem, a resolution to that uncertainty, until he learns of their perfidious nature. He comes to understand that he and Misra have been the victims of cartographic violence in both the colonial and postcolonial periods as the Horn of Africa has been repeatedly redrawn, and neither, ultimately, is able to escape the ideological, cultural and ethnic divisions that have been resurrected and created with each literal and figurative map that Farah shows to the reader.

Lost as he is in 'the eternity of a search for who [he] was' (Farah 26), Askar speaks to the predicament of many postcolonial Bildungsroman protagonists, who are perhaps fated never to stop searching, to never stop wondering who they are and where they belong. In situating Farah's novel as a sort of frontispiece to this discussion of the Bildungsroman in Africa, and focusing specifically on Askar's birth, I am drawing attention to one of the striking ways in which the question of identity is highlighted in postcolonial Bildungsromane such as *Maps*. A significant portion of *Maps'* scholarship has understandably been concerned with Farah's exploration of identity formation in the context of postcolonial nation-building, and the novel's treatment of gender politics. Both of these concerns factor greatly in the Bildung of *Maps'* protagonist Askar, and reflect in turn how the Bildungsroman has been appropriated and adapted by postcolonial writers to engage in socio-political and ethical critiques of the colonial legacy and its postcolonial aftermaths, such as the conflict between Somalia and Ethiopia over the Ogaden in which Askar and Misra are fatefully/fatally embroiled. Farah's playful gesture to Dickens in Part One's epigraph and the clearly Dickensian overtones of the opening chapters likewise reflect the postcolonial Bildungsroman's active and regularly subversive engagement with its literary forebear.[3] In that sense, Askar can be read as the 'magically intuitive and preternaturally memoried' response to the Dickensian child protagonist.[4] In talking about the postcolonial Bildungsroman as Maria Helena Lima, Maria Karafilis and others have done in their work, this chapter seeks to tease out the interventions and departures from the traditional Bildungsroman made by the postcolonial iterations of the genre, particularly the African Bildungsroman. By necessity such work requires contending with the Bildungsroman's Eurocentrism, to which José Santiago Fernández Vázquez offers a useful response: 'one of the reasons why postcolonial writers turn to the *bildungsroman* is the desire to incorporate the master codes of imperialism into the text, in order to sabotage them more effectively'.[5] Granted, the genre's 'problematic relationship with a colonialist ethos makes the Bildungsroman a rather odd choice for postcolonial writers (86), but Vázquez's observation underscores the embedded subversive potential of the genre, which has always been characterised by a self-reflexivity critical of the dominant order, even in Bildungsromane in which the status quo is upheld. For Maria Helena Lima, however, the choice by postcolonial writers to use the Bildungsroman represents a paradox, since she believes that the genre 'helps to reproduce the cultural imperialism that inevitably separates the Third World intellectual from the community and culture of his or her birth'.[6]

As Vázquez's and Lima's observations highlight, the postcolonial Bildungsroman is first and foremost characterised by the cultural imperialism and 'colonialist ethos' it has ostensibly inherited from the traditional Bildungsroman. Lima provides a necessary caution as we attempt to answer the question, 'Why the Bildungsroman?' For me, Pheng Cheah offers the most succinct answer to that question, and one which is sensitive to the concerns that Lima and others raise. He notes that the Bildungsroman 'is the most appropriate symbolic expression of' the search to alleviate the sense of homelessness experienced by those without a sense of community or nation as a consequence of the onslaught of colonialism.[7] He also raises another concern, pointing out that, for many, 'the predicament of decolonization is that there is [often] no preexisting community for the individual to be reconciled to' (243). On the one hand, this fact makes even more urgent the reclamation of indigenous culture and the assertion of a national identity; on the other, it highlights the possibility of a perpetuation of a deeply ambivalent self that has no recourse but to seek futile admittance into the dominant order.

What that last point serves to underscore is a meaningful, but by no means central, defining characteristic of the postcolonial Bildungsroman: the ongoing remediation of colonialism's traumatic legacy throughout the self-maturation process. Closure, at least in the way we would understand it in the European Bildungsroman, is neither forthcoming nor assured. As we will see below in an examination of the African Bildungsroman, however, it is prudent not to assume that the 'tragic representation of colonized childhood' is a default mechanism for readers and critics of these texts, regardless of how useful this particular modality is in articulating the generally political and ethical nature of Bildungsromane like the African Bildungsroman.[8] Nonetheless, the concern with colonialism is just one of several significant departures the postcolonial Bildungsroman makes from the Bildungsroman genre. The depiction of a broken, or even impossible, maturation process, and an ethical critique of the society into which the protagonist seeks entrance, which typifies the anti-Bildungsroman tradition, may also be discerned in the postcolonial Bildungsroman. The postcolonial Bildungsroman's active engagement with both of these traditions, and most notably, its dismantling of the ideological suppositions of the Bildungsroman, speaks a plain truth of genre in general: it does not exist in a vacuum, cut off from socio-historical forces and changes, and its definition, always subject to the desires of its interlocutors, is not immune to challenge or change. The emergence of a rich Bildungsroman tradition in postcolonial African literature is a powerful example of that truth.

Like the European Bildungsroman, the inherent conflict in postcolonial Bildungsromane is that between the 'ideal of *self-determination* and the equally imperious demands of *socialization*'.[9] In postcolonial Bildungsromane, however, this conflict is often intensified by the shadow of colonialism, the brutality of civil war, widespread disenfranchisement, and fractured family politics. This leads us to Simon Hays's forthright question: 'What happens [then] to the bildungsroman – its conventions, stylistic tics, techniques, parameters – when it goes postcolonial?'[10] This chapter is an attempt to answer that intriguing and by no means easy question.

## A Few Preliminaries

In the title of his piece on the African Bildungsroman, Ralph A. Austen speaks of 'struggling' with the genre, a reference to the various challenges that inevitably arise when applying a literary form already marked by debate to a body of texts that appears to have developed both within and against that same tradition. If the 'struggle' for Austen is at least in part how to reconcile his use of the term in order to introduce an unfamiliar body of literature (African literature) via a familiar literary form to his own literature students, despite the term's many pitfalls and contradictions, the struggle is also about what amounts to a political choice, not so much on the part of the author, but of the literary critic. Without belabouring the point, this choice could be seen as 'authoriz[ing] imperialism in its representations of both the empowered Western individual and the exotic colonial other'.[11] It is this very assumption that studies on the non-Western Bildungsroman seek to dismantle; that is, the use of 'Bildungsroman' as both literary category and ideological signifier as perforce doomed within postcolonial contexts to be nothing more than a pale, misguided reconstruction of a genre already (in)famously described as a 'phantom' and 'pseudo genre'.[12] That last point is important: if we hold that Marc Redfield is correct in arguing, *pace* Jeffrey Sammons, for the genre's spectral nature, as well as calling into question its inviolability as a genre, the postcolonial interventions and interrogations into the Bildungsroman are less a kind of blind and desperate wish-fulfillment than they are a political and aesthetic *statement*. The uneasy relationship between the Bildungsroman and its non-Western articulations is well-documented, most notably in studies on the Caribbean Bildungsroman (including the early studies by Geta J. LeSeur and Maria Helena Lima) as well as the African Bildungsroman. This work frequently entails exposing the ideological limitations of the genre, which are thrown into particularly sharp relief within postcolonial contexts, while also highlighting the genre's abiding usefulness as a tool for interrogating and representing the self-formation process as a culturally and historically contingent process. When thinking specifically about the African Bildungsroman tradition, it is worth recalling Mpalive-Hangson Msiska's description of 'African novelistic practice as a gradual process of indigenization', one in which what 'particular writers adopt as strategies of novelistic adaptation will always be a function of the aesthetic and ideological horizons that constitute their lived reality'.[13] Ralph A. Austen agrees: the Bildungsroman, whether European or African, 'always has to confront larger social contexts' (228), and this recognition is vital if we are to look at the genre beyond its original European contexts, and thus allow it to engage dialectically with other 'lived realit[ies]'.

As Marc Redfield sharply observes in *Phantom Formations: Aesthetic Ideology and the Bildungsroman* (1996): 'The *Bildungsroman* exemplifies the ideological construction of literature by criticism' (vii). Or put another way, the Bildungsroman is a '[genre] that generates its own theory' (44). Such a manoeuvre helped, if I may briefly oversimplify Redfield's highly nuanced argument for a moment, to account for the genre's paradoxical non-existence, a peculiarity that Redfield attaches to, on the one hand, the especially 'deferred occurrence' of the term in literary circles in the early twentieth century to refer to a nineteenth-century genre (40). On the other hand, there is also the term's tenuous relationship to the very texts it is used to describe, highlighting the additional problem that, the more rigorously one adheres to its 'extravagant aesthetic promises', the more ambiguous the genre appears (40). Literary theory was put into service to account for, and effectively perpetuated, these tensions, with the end result that the genre exists *because* of its theory. And Bildungsroman theory, Redfield points out, remains healthy only by continually calling the Bildungsroman into question, which accounts for both the still active discussions on the genre and the tacit refusal to draw clear and definitive borders for the genre.

For Jed Esty, 'Genres are almost always empty sets that shape literary history by their negation, deviation, variation, and mutation.'[14] Much of the work by Bildungsroman scholars, including Frederick Amrine, Jeffrey Sammons, Franco Moretti and Marc Redfield, attests to this observation, as does the work of scholars on the postcolonial Bildungsroman, which in many cases relies on that very point. For if nothing else, postcolonial Bildungsromane have shaped the more recent literary history of the Bildungsroman writ large precisely through what Esty usefully describes as a 'process of . . . unmaking' (18). And, returning to Redfield, because the genre appears to exist in large part due to its theory, Esty's unmaking process, 'which is always coeval with [the Bildungsroman's] making' (18), reinforces Redfield's other point that the more the genre 'is cast into question, the more it flourishes' (40). As we move into a brief consideration of the colonial and postcolonial Bildungsroman, it is worth noting that the earlier questions regarding the choice of the Bildungsroman by postcolonial writers and in what ways the genre changes in their hands can neither be asked nor answered without keeping in mind these salient observations by Esty and Redfield.

## The Colonial and the Postcolonial Bildungsroman

In his own study of the Bildungsroman, Bakhtin emphasises 'man's essential *becoming*' and applies the general description of the 'novel of human *emergence*' to texts in which the 'changes in the hero himself acquire *plot* significance'.[15] Bakhtin separates the novel of emergence into five types, each of which is defined by the type's relationship to time. Time in the first two types is cyclical in nature, and both present man's emergence as 'repeating itself in each life' (22). The novel of education, or Ezriehungsroman, is such a type, with the outcome being that the individual 'becomes more sober, experiencing some degree of resignation' at the text's close (22). The third type follows biological time, and 'emergence here is the result of the entire totality of changing life circumstances and events, activity and work' (22). The fourth type, didactic-pedagogical, moves towards the real historical time which characterises the fifth type, in which man's emergence is no longer private: he 'emerges *along with the world*' (emphasis original, 22–3). It is the fifth type that, for our purposes here, is most powerfully attached to the postcolonial Bildungsroman, specifically, Bakhtin's idea of real historical time in relation to the narrative character of this genre. Particularly for the postcolonial Bildungsroman, the interplay between real historical time and man's emergence, the insistence on placing the postcolonial subject within history rather than outside of it, as the history of colonialism had insisted, made more possible the emergence of the postcolonial subject. This is, in fact, the task at hand for many postcolonial Bildungsromane.

According to Jed Esty, the close of the nineteenth century triggered an identity crisis for the Bildungsroman. Colonialism effectively 'disrupt[ed] the bildungsroman and its humanist ideals, producing jagged effects on both the politics and poetics of subject formation'.[16] Esty connects the stunted growth of the modernist/colonial Bildungsroman protagonist with 'the uneven development of colonial modernity' (415). Citing modernism's experimental ethos, and the rise of racist logic at the expense of progressivism, Esty usefully bridges the gap between the nineteenth-century Bildungsroman celebrating social mobility and progress and the colonial Bildungsroman that reflected a more uneasy relationship with the Bildungsroman's traditional narrative, and the gap – far narrower, I argue – that exists between the colonial and postcolonial Bildungsroman. The 'colonial Bildungsroman' as I am thinking of it here in relation to the emergence of the African postcolonial Bildungsroman should be understood as a part of the genre's progression into postcolonial literary spaces and concerns. As such, Africa has both a colonial Bildungsroman tradition which relates the maturation process of the colonised individual during the colonial period, and a postcolonial Bildungsroman tradition. Seen in this way, we can observe that while these are two distinct genres, they also do not exist at entirely cross purposes. In fact, it is useful to see these two in a dialogical relationship. For example, Camara Laye's *L'Enfant Noir* (1953), while being an autobiography, has long been noted for also employing the Bildungsroman structure. In his recounting of his childhood in colonial Guinea, Laye explores the alienating effects of his colonial education, an education he understands is also crucial to his future success. The village/city trope is thinly veiled as the two choices facing him: the backward, or at the very least, static indigenous culture represented by his father and his village, Kouroussa, and Guinea's capital, Conakry, which is a stepping-stone to the ultimate goal, France, where Laye is headed at the novel's end. This trope is, of course, a device rooted in the European Bildungsroman tradition, and central to the maturation process of the protagonist. Cast within colonial and postcolonial contexts, this trope takes on added meaning. As Apollo Amoko observes, when the young man in *L'Enfant Noir* chooses France, he is making clear 'that he will not be heir to his father's traditional throne'.[17]

In the European Bildungsroman, the protagonist is not vacating his culture and assuming the practices and values of another culture; he remains always within his culture of origin, and that surety of place, so easily taken for granted in the Bildungsroman, is the site of much anxiety and despair in the colonial and postcolonial Bildungsroman.

Jed Esty's study of Olive Schreiner's *The Story of an African Farm* (1883) opens up another conceptual space for the colonial Bildungsroman worth brief consideration. Novels like Schreiner's feature colonial, rather than colonialised, protagonists, a not insignificant difference from the kind of colonial Bildungsroman with which this part of my chapter is concerned. As such, Schreiner's novel is not overly preoccupied with colonialism as an institution; its concerns lie squarely with two of its protagonists, Waldo, a frustrated artist, and Lyndall, a New Woman who chafes against the restrictions of a patriarchal society. Contrast Schreiner's novel with J. M. Coetzee's *Boyhood: Scenes from a Provincial Life* (1997), a fictionalised autobiography of Coetzee's childhood, roughly between the ages of ten and thirteen, also in South Africa, during apartheid. While apartheid should not be read as a substitute for colonialism, it is nevertheless rooted in systemic racism like colonialism, and part of *Boyhood* concerns itself with the destructive influence of racism over relationships and social structures. Coetzee recounts, for example, his family's mixed-race houseboy Eddie being whipped for a minor infraction, and he imagines some future in which Eddie will take unsparing revenge for the indignities racial privilege have forced him to endure.

In thinking about the movement from colonial to postcolonial Bildungsroman, then, we are thinking about more than just chronological progression. If anything, colonial Bildungsromane like Laye's novel anticipate the thematic concerns that are even more central in the postcolonial Bildungsroman, such as hybridity, ambivalence and trauma. But we must also attend to the inherent problem presented by the term 'postcolonial Bildungsroman' before we can begin to define it. As Esty points out, the 'deep contradictions of colonialism ... as a discourse of progress' encapsulate 'the problem of the bildungsroman in the age of empire'.[18] More specifically, 'colonial modernity disrupts the progressive yet stabilizing discourse of national culture' on which the traditional Bildungsroman depended (Esty 414). Or as Simon Hays more plainly observes, the 'inherently contradictory' nature of the label 'postcolonial bildungsroman' cannot be ignored (318). Hays suggests positioning 'postcolonial' as a modifier of the Bildungsroman, 'in the sense that the narrative conventions of the form are reproduced not to be either rejected or embraced but because in the suspension between rejection and embrace lies the possibility for ongoing struggle' (341). The postcolonial Bildungsroman is thus seen as an act of subversion and inversion, a political act of counter-colonisation, a reimagining and reinvention, a process of becoming through the act of unmaking its predecessor and unmasking the Bildungsroman's ideological flaws.

In her study of the Caribbean postcolonial Bildungsroman, Maria Helena Lima offers the concept of 'generic transculturation' to describe the cultural transformation and translation of a genre 'to serve [the] particular needs' of regions, like the Caribbean, that have experienced European colonisation (433). As previously noted, this fact makes the popularity of the Bildungsroman amongst postcolonial writers all the more puzzling for critics like Lima, especially since she contends that 'the *Bildungsroman* gives mankind [the] illusion of a distinct, self-present subjectivity' (437). Furthermore, because the self-realisation of the Western bourgeois subject has throughout the Bildungsroman's history been linked to the oppression of cultural and racial others via colonialism, the Bildungsroman appears to be a poor mechanism for exploring the formation of the postcolonial subject. Thus, it has been necessary for colonial and postcolonial Bildungsromane to engage in 'generic transculturation' if the genre is to be of any social, cultural and political use. An example of this may be seen in Lima's intriguing observation that many postcolonial Bildungsromane 'begin with a death rather than with the more conventional birth of the Bildungsroman protagonist' (441). Lima interprets these deaths as being 'inextricably tied to the underdevelopment that has been imposed on the region by colonization (and neo-colonialism)', signifying a kind of 'homelessness brought about by colonization' (441, 442). The absences brought about by both death and homelessness begin to explain why, in Lima's estimation, the postcolonial Bildungsroman, at least in the Caribbean articulation that she studies, cannot in the end offer its protagonist the closure and wholeness that the European male Bildungsroman protagonist could expect. Yet Tambu, whose own wider Bildung is made possible by her brother's death which opens Tsitsi Dangarembga's *Nervous Conditions* (1988), does not have such a fate, and thus Lima's observation, while useful, is not broadly applicable to all postcolonial Bildungsromane.

There is another observation Lima offers about the postcolonial Bildungsroman worth outlining here, namely, why this form of the genre regularly focuses on a short period in the protagonist's life. This narrative choice serves to highlight the interrupted, erratic and fractured development of the postcolonial Bildungsroman protagonist. Rather than giving access to a self in steady development, the reader is instead presented with fragments, flashes. Time, this choice seems to say, is not on the protagonist's side, and in the long view of colonial history at least, it never has been. The luxury of a gradual development is symbolically denied to both the protagonist and the reader, and underscores the 'displacement and alienation [chronicled] in post-colonial texts' as well as the urgency of the formative process for the protagonist (442). What I mean by that last statement is simply this: where the 'stakes' for the European Bildungsroman protagonist are relatively low, by comparison the stakes in the postcolonial Bildungsroman are often quite high.

## The African Bildungsroman and Its Variants

The previous point assumes an urgency in postcolonial Bildungsromane that perforce does not exist in the European, or 'classical', Bildungsroman. As Moretti notes, however, the classical Bildungsroman did, in fact, contend with its own urgent issue: it spoke to an emerging age, modernity, into which the protagonist (and by extension, the readers who accompanied the protagonist on his journey) was unceremoniously 'plunged', without, significantly, 'possessing a *culture* of modernity' by which to understand and navigate this new epoch.[19] If I may reformulate Moretti's point a bit, when we attend to the question of the Bildungsroman in its postcolonial, and more specifically, its African articulations, we do so recognising that 'culture' is a far more transient and hybrid entity than it has ever been before in Africa. Mindful, too, of not just colonialism's cultural and geopolitical impact, but the ever-growing reach of globalisation (and the increasing economic disparity which accompanies it), as well as the post-millennium rise in terrorism and wide-scale political disenfranchisement, what has 'happened' to the Bildungsroman, to return to Simon Hays for a moment, is nothing short of a wholesale dismantling of the Bildungsroman's core suppositions that occurs alongside the continued instabilities perpetuated by sharply uneven power dynamics.

What emerges is an ideologically distinct expression of the Bildungsroman that frequently coheres, if not wholly in spirit, then in basic design, to the classical Bildungsroman. In his study of genre and the postcolonial African novel, Mpalive-Hangson Msiska argues that the African novel is 'marked by a structure of fidelity and transgression in which genre practice is expressed as a dynamic contingent production and sublation of the settled dominant of a given instance, a dialogic tension between the Self and Other'.[20] The 'post-colonial sensibility' that is created out of the intersection between 'colonial culture and [the] anti-colonial opposition to that culture' informs 'the history of genre practice in Africa today', and this is certainly true of the African Bildungsroman (76). While I again caution against reducing that form to merely a reactionary mode, always already imbued with anti-colonial politics, there is little question that anti-colonial and anti-neocolonial opposition is regularly at work in the African Bildungsroman. Msiska suggests that the African novel 'emerged from the *interpellative* limitations of the colonial novel', an observation just as applicable in accounting for the modifications that the Bildungsroman has undergone in its postcolonial reworkings (79).[21] Furthermore, 'the new genre', he writes, 'depends for its identity and legitimation on that very arch-genre, with which it counter identifies and whose regulatory parameters it breaches' (89). Thus, it is possible for the postcolonial Bildungsroman to be a subspecies of the European Bildungsroman 'as well as an autonomous practice', to contribute 'to the stabilization of the Bildungsroman while also 'disturb[ing] its core iden-tity' (89).

Msiska's observations about genre practice in Africa provide a useful context for charting the emergence of the African postcolonial Bildungsroman, which I situate firmly within the deep tradition of African autobiography. Like the Bildungsroman, the autobiography – specifically the child autobiography – emphasises the self-in-process. The African autobiography of childhood has a long history, reaching back to the colonial era and into the present day, where the child auto-biography has seen growth most notably in autobiographies and memoirs of the child soldier. For Denise Escarpit, the 'proliferation' of the African autobiography of childhood in the colonial and postcolonial periods 'signals a "permanence" of childhood in African letters' (qtd in Sow 498). Like the postcolonial African novel in general, these autobiographies are regularly and 'profoundly situated in historical transformations' and 'are typically associated with emergencies ... cris[es], and trauma[s]' (Sow 498). These 'dominant patterns', which also include explorations of 'racial, gender, and/or class prejudice' suggest an African childhood distinctly and almost solely marked by struggle, disenfranchisement and unhappiness (Sow 499). This brings us back to Esty's process of making and unmaking, which he notes will have discernible patterns. African Bildungsromane such as *Maps, Purple Hibiscus* (2003) by Chimamanda Ngozi Adichie, *Nervous Conditions*, and *Sozaboy* (1985) by Ken Saro-Wiwa certainly reflect these patterns, but as Sow implicitly notes in his study of *L'Enfant Noir* and Wole Soyinka's *Ake: The Years of Childhood* (1981), these patterns outline only one possible engagement with colonialism and by extension, the quality of the childhood lived in a colonised and decolonising context. Even more revealing is Sow's observation about child autobiographies written before or in the nascent years of postcolonial studies: 'literary engagement with colonization and decolonization was less of a requisite' (500).[22] Certainly these words gesture back to the dominant patterns Sow describes above, but also embedded in these words is, I think, a recognition of the expectation of colonialist critique in African narratives of childhood, both autobiographical and fictional, by readers and critics. If Sow is correct in his observations, and those observations – however problematic – are applicable to understanding and defining the African Bildungsroman, and I argue that they are, then the genre appears to pivot on this axis point, since, at first glance, so many examples of the form offer narratives that replicate those dominant patterns. And if *that* observation is correct, then the African Bildungsroman always culminates in one of two outcomes: the protagonist triumphs over the crises sown by colonialism's influence, or the protagonist is left even more disenfranchised and disillusioned.

Let us return for a moment to Marc Redfield's argument that the European Bildungsroman as referential category and genre practice emerged as the result of a series of philological and aesthetic manoeuvres by literary critics in the mid-twentieth century that were in turn retro-actively applied to a collection of texts from the previous century, among them Johann Wolfgang von Goethe's *Wilhelm Meister's Lehrjahre* (1795), which became the genre's urtext, as well as applied to more recent pieces which were argued to continue the literary tradition established by those older texts. Of course, 'generic terms are no doubt usually supposed to lag behind the phenomena to which they refer', Redfield observes (40), though the 'lag' of which he speaks, as previously noted, was rather long. Just as, if not more, important is that giving the genre a history legitimised its use, in fact, its very existence. And while Redfield is dubious of the very genre he states 'does not properly exist' (vii) because of the Bildungsroman's sup-posed dependency on literary criticism to set and maintain its ideological and aesthetic parameters, he appears nonetheless to believe in the genre's basic existence, or at the very least, its 'indestructibility' (42). I highlight this point in order to lay out some initial statements as we move from the broader mapping above, and into somewhat more specialised avenues of inquiry regarding the African Bildungsroman. First, there is no question that the Bildungsroman, and by extension the African Bildungsroman, exists, regardless of the problematic nature of the genre's initial birthing. Second, that texts such as the African Bildungsroman are terrifically important to the overall study of the form precisely because, as Ralph A. Austen points out, in deviating from 'its "classical" European model' (215), the African Bildungsroman usefully calls into question the very tradition from which it derives. Third, recalling Vázquez's point that postcolonial writers use the Bildungsroman in order to 'sabotage' the 'master codes of imperialism', we are reminded of the often urgent political work that the Bildungsroman can do, and has done throughout its history (Vázquez 86). Finally, Franco Moretti reminds us that during the nineteenth century, the Bildungsroman 'performed three great symbolic tasks' (230). Within its pages, the volatile nature of social change was made manageable, through the inevitable passage into responsible adulthood of the searching, questioning youth. It had affirmed an 'anti-tragic modality of modern experience' (230). And it had presented its readers with an 'unheroic hero' much like themselves, whose socialisation into the middle classes required a more cooperative and malleable sense of self. In the English expression of the form, freedom is sacrificed for happiness, and 'youth is subordinated to "maturity"', while the French novelists were more apt to insist on 'youthful dynamism' (8). In keeping with Moretti's paradigm, I would like to suggest three great symbolic tasks common to postcolonial Bildungsromane such as the African Bildungsroman: first, an active syncretic literary-cultural aesthetic that acknowledges the deep and diverse epistemological and ontological traditions of pre- and postcolonial societies; second, its dialogic engagement with pre-colonial, colonial, and postcolonial history; and third, its attempts – not always successful – to offer an alternative to the master narrative of compromise and accommodation in the self-formation process. These tasks function as tools in the larger remediation process described above, and emphasise subjectivity and agency over submission and assimilation.

One of the earliest African Bildungsromane uses the first task to underscore the difficulties attending realisation of the third task. Camara Laye's *L'Enfant Noir* is arguably the urtext of the African Bildungsroman, though this positioning is somewhat problematic because the text is an autobiography. As a general rule Bildungsromane are fictional texts, and labelling autobiographies like Laye's text a 'Bildungsroman' presumably threatens an aesthetic cornerstone of the genre. However, as Apollo Amoko notes, both African autobiographies and African Bildungsromane 'participate in the same conversations regarding the fundamental nature of African societies in the wake of the encounter with colonialism' (Amoko 196). Laye's text, set during the author's childhood in French Guinea, recounts various events, including his participation in his tribe's circumcision ritual, as well as his visits to his grandmother's village, and culminates in him leaving for France to continue his studies. Critics of the text have been troubled by its supposed refusal to adhere to the 'familiar traumatic and tragic itinerary of the colonized' (Sow 503), its tendency to be 'a little too nostalgic, a little too good to be true' (Olney, qtd in Sow 501). Indeed, that itinerary is embedded in the African Bildungsroman to such an extent that it is extremely difficult, and perhaps even ill-advised, to define this articulation of the Bildungsroman without first mapping out that itinerary. And yet, as Alioune Sow's work with the African autobiography of childhood has shown, this itinerary is far from problematic. 'It is expected,' he notes, 'that representations of childhood [in the African autobiography] will be mapped onto representations of the constraints of African history' (502). While conflict has always been an integral part of the Bildungsroman in all of its articulations, Sow's insight points us in the direction of an uncomfortable reality that haunts the African Bildungsroman, and that is the prioritisation of the colonial and postcolonial experience in relation to the self-formation process, specifically as it conflicts with indigenous systems of knowledge and affiliation, by both critics and readers of those texts. The danger of such thinking is that African discourses which are not framed *vis-à-vis* the 'rhetoric of autonomy, resistance, and emancipation' outlined by Achille Mbembe in relation to the concept of 'Afro radicalism' will be labelled inauthentic, and hence delegitimised (qtd in Sow 502). Or, to return to Olney, seen as 'too good to be true', which is essentially the same thing.

Let us look for a moment at Laye's observation, early in the novel, that 'I had left my father's house too soon,' which on the one hand reflects the text's bittersweet nostalgic lilt, but because its rhetoric refrains from being inflammatory, the text, per Mbembe, is not a legitimate form of African discourse.[23] More immediately referencing his lack of understanding regarding the magic charms his father routinely used each night to protect himself from evil spirits, Laye's statement can be more broadly understood as a larger lamentation for a culture he only physically inhabits. He is a 'phantom' in his own culture, which itself recedes further and further away from him the more time he spends away from his father's workshop and in the Western classroom. In this sense, Laye is not unlike the protagonist Medza in Mongo Beti's *Mission terminée*, published just four years after Laye's novel, in 1957, and which is another early example of the African Bildungsroman. Medza has also been alienated from his own

Cameroonian roots due to his Western education, which shortly upon his return to Beti country and as he spends time in the village of Kala, he discovers is hardly useful. As David J. Mickelsen observes, the education that Medza has received is both 'curiously undirected', and has not 'as in most *Bildungsromane*, trained him to make informed choices in a world in flux'.[24] One effect of this for Medza has been that he has 'no long-term commitment to the group, no concern for the perpetuation of the tribe' (422). Laye, on the other hand, is more painfully aware of the cost, individually and communally, that accrues as more young men such as himself opt for or are encouraged to pursue Western education or leave the village for the city. 'Do we still have secrets,' he asks (109); 'it appears as if we are ceasing to be what we were, and that we are truly no longer what we were' (75). Even more pointedly, recalling a harvest custom, Laye again admits, as he does frequently throughout the novel, that 'I could have discovered [the meaning of the custom] by asking the old villagers who retained this kind of knowledge deep in their hearts and memories. But I was not old enough or curious enough to inquire, nor did I become so until I was no longer in Africa' (56).

Laye's lack of curiosity and his failure to understand the deeper loss that such a lack facilitated until, looking back, he begins to total it all – the impact on his family, his cultural alienation – sharply contrast with Medza's failure to appreciate the cost of his own cultural disinterest. This in turn can account for two outcomes for Beti's protagonist: Medza's stunted maturity, and his rejection of 'those groups which have attempted, in various degrees, to assimilate him: his family, the colonizing power, and Kala' (Mickelsen 423). Wholly detached and disenfranchised, Medza drifts. Here we can see several elements of the African Bildungsroman, beginning with Laye's recollections which are so heavily tinged, not with nostalgia, but with regret. In its emphasis on the tension between two cultures, both of which are vying for the protagonist physically, psychologically and intellectually, the African Bildungsroman frequently underscores Mickelson's observation that 'once having been shaped by Western education, the African can never go back' (427). Laye most certainly knows this, and to some extent, so does Medza. His abandonment of all his responsibilities, including leaving his new wife, at the very least suggests his ambivalence about himself and his future. This uncertainty, sometimes realised in the form of mental and physical collapse, as in the case of Nyasha's struggle with an eating disorder in *Nervous Conditions*, returns us to the challenges attending the third task of the African Bildungsroman. The outcome of Laye's, Beti's, and to some extent, Dangarembga's texts perpetuates the idea that the African Bildungsroman, as I previously noted, can only end on one of two notes, and that the latter – the protagonist disenfranchised and disillusioned as the story closes – is so powerful that the other outcome, or any other outcome for that matter, is inconsequential and impossible.

Take, for instance, Chimamanda Ngozi Adichie's 2012 African Bildungsroman, *Purple Hibiscus*. The fifteen-year-old protagonist Kambili Achike, along with her older brother Jaja and their mother, lives under the violent rule of Kambili's father, Eugene. Regularly beaten for minor and imaginary infractions, the family suffer for the sins of colonialism – in this case, Eugene's fanatical embrace of Catholicism. Eugene expects his children to perform at the top of their classes. He reminds his daughter that God 'expects perfection. I didn't have a father who sent me to the best schools. My father spent his time worshipping gods of wood and stone. I would be nothing today but for the priests and sisters at the mission.'[25] As with so many families of domestic violence, Eugene's public image gives little indication of his violent private self. A respected and prosperous businessman, he is the owner of a newspaper speaking against Sani Abacha's regime. Eugene is also known for generosity in the community, though his family lives very modestly, despite their wealth. He is frequently mentioned in sermons as a shining example of truth, a reflection of Christ's 'Triumphant Entry' into Jerusalem from the Mount of Olives (5). As the crisis of the Abacha regime builds, so too does the crisis within the Achike household, culminating in two vicious beatings: the first on Kambili, who is beaten so severely she spends several days in the hospital, and is even given last rites; and the second causes Kambili's mother Beatrice to miscarry. The humanitarian abuses of Abacha's presidency are clearly mirrored in Eugene's domestic violence; in fact, it is difficult not to see Abacha's shadow attached to Eugene. Indeed, both men appear to have suffered the same fate, if rumours regarding Abacha dying of poisoning are true. Unable to bear the abuse and oppression of her husband, and incapable of leaving him, Beatrice poisons her husband. His death, however, does not completely free his family, any more than Abacha's death has freed Nigeria of the corruption and violence which continue to haunt the country.

To return, then: at first glance, *Purple Hibiscus* adheres to the dominant patterns that mark African narratives of childhood. As the uneasy closure of the novel suggests, however, there is neither complete triumph nor total defeat for the Achike family. Jaja is in jail for his father's murder, having confessed in order to protect Beatrice; Beatrice struggles with even the simplest of tasks, such as brushing her hair; and Kambili, while still dreaming of her father's approval, is also plagued by nightmares of 'the silence of when Papa was alive', which leave her 'screaming and sweating' some three years after Eugene's death (305). Yet Kambili feels that she can 'talk about the future now', a future in which her brother is free, and the family can visit Aunty Ifeoma in America (306). Adichie has, in effect, both adhered to the dominant patterns *and* rejected the inevitable outcome of those patterns, and through Kambili argues that the Bildung process cannot, should not, be rendered down to a win–lose proposition.

It is with that caution that I now turn to discussing what I see as notable variants within the African postcolonial Bildungsroman tradition. The first situates formal education at the narrative's core: the reader accompanies the protagonist as he/she matriculates, culminating, if the protagonist is capable, in further education, often abroad at a Western university. It is this type that most mirrors the social mobility novel form of the European Bildungsroman. *Nervous Conditions*, and the characters of Tambu, Nyasha and Babamukuru, are meditations on this formula in a postcolonial context, and each represents various points in the process. Babamukuru purportedly is the successful culmination of this process of acculturation within and accommodation with colonial culture and its expectations, but he also reflects its gendered, classist and racist limits. He has banned his children from speaking Shona, thus effectively cutting them off from an important part of their own culture, and is deeply ambivalent about Tambu pursuing a university education, preferring instead that she settle into respectable married life. His daughter Nyasha is caught in the dilemma created by the 'contradictions of identity brought on by colonialism, patriarchy, and modern capitalism', a dilemma which is physically enacted through her anorexia and bulimia (Hays 338). Initially, Nyasha's disorder appears to be merely linked to her father's rigid academic and social standards, to being a 'good girl' (Dangarembga 205). As she speaks to Tambu late one night, she indicts colonialism for what it has done "'to me and to you and to him [Babamukuru]'" (204). She takes her history book between her teeth and starts tearing it apart, growling about "'Their history. Fucking liars. Their bloody lies'" (205). When her parents rush into her bedroom after hearing the commotion, Nyasha tells her father that she refuses to be trapped and to hate him, which is what "'they want'" (205). Curling up on her mother's lap, she whispers, "'I'm not one of them, but I am not one of you'" (205).

Nyasha's psychological breakdown causes Tambu, the novel's primary protagonist, to question her own future. While she is about to continue her

Western education at the novel's close, and appears to be more capable of negotiating the contradictions of her situation than her cousin, she is nonetheless worried about 'the problem that is [the] Englishness' (207). If we recall Maria Helena Lima's words regarding the 'impossible paradigm' represented by the male European model, which both Tambu and her uncle Babamukuru consciously and subconsciously use to measure themselves, and which throws Nyasha into despair and self-destructive behaviour, then Tambu's self-development, regardless of her knowing 'what could or couldn't be done' (Dangarembga 208), is destined to be 'truncated' (Lima 436). Simon Hays's reading of the novel, on the other hand, works against Lima's: he argues instead that the novel's ending highlights the 'ongoing dialectical struggle' that is crucial to understanding Dangarembga's purpose in *Nervous Conditions*, and by extension, the purpose of the postcolonial Bildungsroman. Both Lima's and Hays's points are valuable, though Hays's reading offers a more dynamic and less cynical way to approach the postcolonial Bildungsroman.

The second variant of the African postcolonial Bildungsroman can be found among texts that belong to another significant genre of the African novel: the war narrative, which frequently presents a violent coming of age for those caught in the crossfire. 'Unlike [traditional] rites of passage . . . war kill[s],' Franco Moretti observes, 'and its only mystery didn't decree the renewal of individual existence, but its insignificance' (229). According to Moretti, the First World War was the 'cosmic coup de grace' to the European Bildungsroman, which found itself increasingly out of step with a youth and a world it no longer recognised (230). Likewise, the civil wars that marked the post-decolonisation period throughout Africa were a violent response to the hopes of renewal ushered in by the independence movements that began shortly after the end of the Second World War. African war novels like Ken Saro-Wiwa's *Sozaboy* emphasise the insignificance of the individual, particularly the ignorant 'sozaboys' ('soldier boys') like Mene who significantly misunderstand the politics and reality of war and war-making. The African war Bildungsroman is apt to present a stunted Bildung process as an inevitable consequence of war; this is especially the case in the memoirs and fictionalised accounts of the child soldier experience. Such texts include Emmanuel Dongala's *Johnny Mad Dog* (2002), Uzodinma Iweala's *Beasts of No Nation* (2005), Ahmadou Kourouma's *Allah Is Not Obliged* (2000), Chris Abani's *Song for Night* (2007), Chimamanda Ngozi Adichie's *Half of a Yellow Sun* (2005), and the memoirs *A Long Way Gone: Memoirs of a Boy Soldier* (2007) by Ishmael Beah and *War Child: A Child Soldier's Story* (2009) by Emmanuel Jal.

The titular character of Dongala's novel is a striking example of an individuation process interrupted, twisted and corrupted by war: Johnny Mad Dog, at sixteen, has been transformed into an insecure sociopath, immune to the horrors he inflicts on others. His claims of being an intellectual are undone by his inability to articulate the conflict in which he is embroiled beyond an empty 'us vs. them' rhetoric, and are a sad reminder of one of many things Johnny has lost in his journey as a child soldier: a basic education. The education he does receive is terrifying in its callousness, and Johnny learns, albeit rather incompletely as he does not understand, is unable to see, that this observation also applies to him: 'Really, people are awful. They have no heart.'[26] Like *Sozaboy*, Shimmer Chinodya's *Harvest of Thorns* (1990), and other African war novels, *Johnny Mad Dog* eschews romanticising war in any way; even anti-colonial resistance movements, such as those depicted in *Harvest of Thorns*, are stripped of their seemingly noble nature. Brotherhood is perfidious, and the 'cause' is rendered down to the most flimsy of propaganda. The new names the soldiers are given or take for themselves erase their former identities, while turning on its head the image of the honourable soldier: the comically awful names that Johnny and his fellow soldiers adopt (one first refers to himself as 'Idi Amin', and then later as 'Chuck Norris') expose their childlike fascination with figures of strength and brutality, not to mention Western popular culture (another refers to himself as 'General Rambo'). Most powerfully, these texts open up the question of what is to become of these children when the war is over. As narratives that also engage in socio-political critique, the African war Bildungsroman exposes nations in crisis, individuals atrophied and traumatised, uncaring bureaucracies, and a West all too eager to exploit that instability for its own gain.

Mortality is a chief lesson in the African war Bildungsroman, just as it is in the AIDS Bildungsroman, which I offer here as a third variant of the African postcolonial Bildungsroman. Novels such as Violet Kala's *Waste Not Your Tears* (1994) and Carolyne Adalla's *Confessions of an AIDS Victim* (1996) chart a particular Bildung process that revolves around the revelation of the protagonist's HIV-positive status and how the protagonist responds to this knowledge. These protagonists assume an 'Everyman' quality to highlight the ubiquity of the virus itself; their journeys towards deeper, and significantly, correct information about a virus steeped in rumour and misinformation speaks to the heavily didactic purpose of these texts. Just as important are these texts' criticisms of patriarchal privilege, gender inequality and misogyny that make responding to the AIDS threat terrifically difficult in traditional African cultures. In Marjorie

Oludhe Macgoye's novel *Chira* (1997), for example, AIDS is 'chira', a misfortune that has befallen Kenyan Luo culture as the result of social taboos being broken. The protagonist Gabriel's 'AIDS *Bildung*' is interwoven within a critique of the 'devastating moral corruption [that has spread] from top to bottom, from the political leaders to the ordinary people'.[27] Steven F. Kruger argues that AIDS narratives 'may help shape broader cultural understanding of the complex and conflicted phenomenon of AIDS' (qtd in Armstrong 133).[28] Like the African war Bildungsroman, the African AIDS Bildungsroman serves a deep, urgent purpose, tying these narratives to a variation of the socialisation process that focuses on specific socio-political crises that threaten bodies, communities and identities.

The final variant focuses on African postcolonial Bildungsromane in which the figure of the nation looms especially large in the Bildung of the protagonist, as is the case with Farah's *Maps* or Moses Isegawa's *Abyssinian Chronicles* (1998). The family dynamics depicted in *Maps* work through the 'resurrected ethnocentrisms' of postcolonial Somalia and Ethiopia:[29] Askar is 'the human analogue of the Somali Ogaden', his foster/adoptive mother Misra loosely represents the Ethiopian occupier of the Ogaden, but more significantly, 'the irretrievable hybridization' that the Ogaden has undergone over centuries (Wright, 'Parenting', 177, 180). Derek Wright argues that Askar ultimately seeks to assert a 'chauvinistic Somali concept of the Ogaden', and thus his process of Bildung must be understood as sharply defined by ethnocentrism and tribalism. His 'becoming', to return to Bakhtin, is thus contingent on refusing Misra her multiplicity. When the text concludes with Askar's arrest for his unspecified participation in Misra's murder and mutilation, Farah is presenting to his readers the 'triumph' of tribalism, and reminding them of its dangerous role in postcolonial nation-building. Moreover, Askar's maturation is thrown into doubt, as his sectarianism and othering of Misra prevent him from recognising the alternative to tribalism that Misra and others like her represent. Instead, 'Africa's internal imperialisms have taken over from where the alien, external ones left off' (Wright, 'Parenting', 184).

So, it appears that the imperative of nation-building supplants, or at the very least complicates or delays, the needs of the self in the African nationalistic Bildungsroman. In Isegawa's *Abyssinian Chronicles*, another sophisticated treatment of identity and nation formation as Bildungsroman, the seven 'chronicles' into which the narrative is divided chart both the history of Uganda over sixty years (between roughly 1930 and 1990) and the development of the protagonist Mugezi and his family.

Isegawa even more literally links the formation of the self with the nation by tying specific moments in Mugezi's development to key events in Ugandan history, such as the chronological proximity of Mugezi's early schooling with the 1966 emergency (Armstrong 130). However, in his reading of Isegawa's novel, Andrew Armstrong argues that Mugezi's personal history should not be read as a 'refraction[s]' of his nation's (130). This point usefully reminds us that the tendency to transpose the nation over the self in nationalistic Bildungsromane is not an inevitability, or the only lens through which the protagonist's self-formation process may be accessed. If this were the case, then the Bildung of protagonists like Mugezi or Askar are little more than reactionary or reflexive responses to social and political processes and contingencies, rather than dynamic and subjective choices. By 'integrating the social process with the development of a person', such texts recall the close relationship between individual and culture that defines the Bildungsroman, while framing this relationship within a more political context (Armstrong 131). Like the war between Ethiopia and Somalia, the crisis in Uganda, Idi Amin's dictatorship, and the onset of HIV/AIDS disrupt the growth of Mugezi and other Ugandans who find themselves, like their nation, increasingly fragmented.

The Bildungsroman, that 'well-worn literary tool' described by Marc Redfield, has proven to be an especially effective tool for African writers to explore individuals, nations and traditions in crisis and transition, while working against the frustratingly resilient Western narrative of a dark continent. The African articulation of the Bildungsroman represents a vital contribution to the reconfiguring of the genre, as well as an active literary tradition in its own right. Its presence reminds us that genre can be malleable without losing meaning, and that genre, out of socio-historical necessity, is regularly reborn.

## Conclusion

Franco Moretti envisages the development of the Bildungsroman as 'not a straight line but a tree, with plenty of bifurcations for genres to branch off from each other' (234).[30] This is, I think, the best way to imagine the Bildungsroman itself. Moretti's tree offers a dynamic visual for the many branches of the Bildungsroman with which we are already familiar – the Entwicklungsroman, the Künstlerroman, and the Erziehungsroman – as well as the anti-Bildungsroman, the colonial Bildungsroman, the postcolonial Bildungsroman, and within the African postcolonial Bildungsroman the variants I describe above. To borrow Mpalive-Hangson Msiska's observation that the African novel 'was an imitation that exceeded the bounds of the object of imitation' (84), the postcolonial Bildungsroman has and by necessity must exceed 'the bounds' of the European Bildungsroman to assert its own identity and trajectory in the literary tradition. In turn, this recognises Maria Helena Lima's point that narrative forms 'require new topographies' as 'the world assumes different configurations' (432).

Finally, in formulating a definitional praxis of postcolonial and African postcolonial Bildungsromane, particular overlaps between the two genres highlight significant subversions of 'the object of imitation' the two genres share, but it is also important to view them as categorically distinct. As tempting as it may be to situate the African postcolonial Bildungsroman as a sub-genre of the postcolonial Bildungsroman, doing so would sublimate the particularities of those texts and work against Moretti's 'different geometrical pattern' that argues against the straight line by implying a hierarchical relationship between the postcolonial Bildungsroman and its many 'sub-genres' (234). Instead, the 'postcolonial Bildungsroman' should function as a basic embarkation point in our understanding of the Bildungsroman's translation and adaptation within postcolonial contexts in the genre's long and ongoing evolution. The African postcolonial Bildungsroman is a crucial point in that process.

# CHAPTER 10

# Lesbian, Gay and Trans Bildungsromane

## Meredith Miller

## Self and Social Scripts

For Mikhail Bakhtin, looking back across the development of the European novel during the Second World War, the Bildungsroman is a subset of a group of novelistic forms that mediate a relationship to the historical real. The Bildungsroman, for Bakhtin, is unique in its proper situation of individual emergence within historical time. Exemplified by Goethe in the fragment of Bakhtin's work that has survived, it presents the individual 'no longer within an epoch, but between two epochs, at the transition point from one to the other. The transition is accomplished in him and through him. He is forced to become a new, unprecedented human being.'[1] For Franco Moretti, the Bildungsroman mediates the relation between individual desires and socially determined identities, necessitated by the proliferating instabilities that characterise the bourgeois epoch: 'In all its diverse manifestations, the Bildungsroman has always held fast to the notion that *the biography of a young individual was the most meaningful viewpoint for the understanding and the evaluation of history.*'[2] These two related perspectives on the development of the European novel, though fifty years lie between them, share a common reduction. They idealise an individual for whom gendersex is not fully a component of social struggle.

This reduction becomes most obvious in Moretti's reading of Charlotte Brontë's *Jane Eyre*, a novel he determines to be 'infantile' and 'fairy-tale-like' (187). For Moretti, Jane's flight from Thornfield is not a stage on her journey to self, her experience of competing narratives of femininity and intellectual life, but a specifically English failure of the novelistic form. 'Any Bildungsroman worthy of the name would have had Jane remain among the needles of Thornfield . . . . facing the imperfect, debatable and perhaps incorrect nature of each fundamental ethical choice' (188). The implication is clear: 'fundamental ethical choices' do not include the preservation of self in the face of violent sexual power. For without Jane's flight, we would not see her refusal of St John Rivers and imperial evangelicalism, we would not see her absolute refusal to subordinate her own sexual fulfilment to manifest destiny.

And so, as feminist critics pointed out throughout the 1980s and 1990s, there is another framework for tracing the history of the European Bildungsroman, and that framework is gendersex. From the seventeenth century, the discursive formation of new, secularised nations requires the definition of individual citizens. These individuals are written from the start as subjects of will and desire.[3] Over the next hundred years, as the novel develops, both bodily and consumer desires form its central organising tensions. The European novel takes up ideas of self-development in precisely the historical period during which heterosexual gendering takes on an increasingly central importance in culture. In the later eighteenth century, as Michel Foucault has famously pointed out, economies and their organisation in the family are increasingly structured through sexuality.[4] Desire as a first principle in excess of organising structures becomes both the impetus to conformity and the threat to social complacency. Both of these are expressed through the novelistic romance plot which develops in this period. Lorna Ellis posits:

> an alternative genealogy for the *Bildungsroman* based on early eighteenth-century amatory fiction. Just as looking at the picaresque tradition emphasizes . . . independence and mobility . . . a consideration of amatory fiction and the romance tradition to which it belongs leads to a better understanding of the social strategies, including manipulation, that characterize the *Bildungsroman* heroine's negotiation with social expectations. In failing to recognize the links between the female *Bildungsroman* and the romance tradition, critics have also more easily missed the possible subversion in the *Bildungsroman* heroine's remaking of herself to fit societal expectations.[5]

Here, in allying the romance to the Bildungsroman, Ellis emphasises strategy, the subversive negotiation of the sexual self against the social machine. We could argue, following Foucault, that this emergence of self against social machine *is* modernity, and its primary site of negotiation is sexuality. For the centrality of sexual identity in modern culture arises from its very situation as the interface between individual desires and social structures. As Foucault points out in *History of Sexuality, Volume I*, the significance of the late eighteenth-century moment is that 'the natural laws of matrimony and the immanent rules of sexuality began to be recorded in two separate registers' (40). The sexual self within the body, travelling both inside and outside of family structures, was now the dynamic location of the modern individual.

In Bildungsromane from the eighteenth century forward, we see a focus on proper and improper gendering, on negotiations of femininity and masculinity both inside and outside the family. In women's Bildung, we see an explicit negotiation of the self as desiring body. It is this that Moretti misses in *Jane Eyre*, this primary expression, through gendersex, of the relation between the modern individual and the social scripts through which she must make meaning in her world. So, we ought to trace the queer Bildungsroman to its roots in the women's romance, that first articulation of the modern individual who traverses the social world in search of a way to make sense of her sexual desires. *Jane Eyre* is a founding text for the centuries-long focus on Anglo femininity as a location of emergence for the subject of will and desire, and thus a privileged site for the articulation of modernity.

We should also note *Jane Eyre*'s position specifically in the tradition of Gothic romance, to which it owes its striking mediation of the desiring body. Gothic romance should also have its place in the genealogy of queer Bildungsroman, for it is here that the problematics of the novelistic body make their first dramatic appearance. The desires and terrors of the female body are boldly expressed in the Gothic romance, from Mrs Radcliffe to Charlotte Brontë to its current articulations. At the same time, as *Northanger Abbey* famously warns us, the dangers of novel-reading lie not in the novel's relation to history, where it is superior to the dry productions of academics for its use of precisely those effects which Bakhtin and Moretti later celebrate. The danger of *certain* novels, for Austen and her fellow conservatives, lies in their excitement of bodily sensation. Gothic romance adventures represent the trembling sensibilities of the feminine body in startlingly direct language, but they also incite such responses in the bodies of readers. The Gothic body is both representational and direct.

Lesbian, gay and transgender Bildungsromane can be read through both critical strands laid out here. They quite clearly work to historicise the individual and her desires, posing the individual precisely 'between two epochs' (before and after sexual liberation) at the threshold of social recognition. They do this specifically by posing an essential, sexualised self against the social and familial structures of bourgeois modernity. The liberation of this self is constructed as the emergence of the new, modern relation between individual and state. Finally, they deploy those specific strategies for representing the desiring body and for hailing it which were developed in the Gothic romance.

So, the development of novelistic form in the eighteenth and nineteenth centuries reflects this context in which desire became a central attribute of the modern individual. It sat at the nexus of social order (the family), individual definition (emergence) and capital wealth (consumption), and it could unseat their ordered and stable relation. Franco Moretti links this increasing focus on desire to the effects of surplus production. Capitalism needs desiring individuals, individuals for whom desire is the primary location of self. 'No longer subject to a pre-existent need, for this very reason production begins to increase needs ... It transforms them from "needs" – a term which evokes the static image of an always identical reproduction – to "desires": which imply dynamism, change, novelty' (165). These latter attributes, characteristic of modernity and allied to desire, are also, throughout the nineteenth and twentieth centuries, linked to those counter-currents through which an aesthetic model of desire, as subjective response, places the individual in opposition to the social machine. Together, these sometimes contradictory effects make that form of the Bildungsroman which focuses specifically on the development of dissident sexual identity a signal, we might say inevitable, form for the modern novel. This chapter will examine queer Bildungsromane through this lens, that is, not simply as a minoritising expression of rights discourse, but as a central and inevitable component of Western culture across the twentieth century.

## The Modernist Moment

Bonnie Kime Scott's work has repositioned the modernist movement not as a radical engagement with form, but as a radical engagement with gender.[6] As Raymond Williams points out in *The Long Revolution*, the critical tradition which sees the early twentieth century as a specific moment of formal innovation in literature necessarily erases the majority of the novelistic fictions produced in that moment.[7] Many of the works elided in the selective critical tradition which defines modernism are new expressions of the sexual self, or reworked expressions deployed in new cultural registers. While some novels central to modernism's self-definition, such as Joyce's famous Küntslerroman, are journeys of self-development, those novels most central to the tradition of queer Bildungsroman sit uncomfortably at the limit of the modernist canon. Their articulation of the sexually dissident self is embedded in formal strategies which place them alternately in alignment with and in opposition to the orthodoxy of modernist 'literariness', posed self-consciously against nineteenth-century realism.

At the turn of the twentieth century, lesbian, gay and transgender writers strategically deployed existing discourses of sexology and psychoanalysis within the framework of the Bildungsroman specifically in order to pit the sexually dissident self against the social world. This strategy necessarily involved both a repositioning of the relation between self and social scripts which had typified the European Bildungsroman up to this point, and a renegotiation of the novel's relationship to grand historical narrative.

The realist project in the nineteenth century formulated characters specifically as types that could exemplify the effects of particular social relations. In order to produce the sexually dissident individual as an essential 'type', the techniques of realism were necessary. Products of their taxonomical age, social-realist novels created characters that sat illustratively within categories, as types sit within organic systems. In its first, early twentieth-century articulation, the narrative which produced the sexual self needed to negotiate such systems, social, medical and juridical. This was the available discursive material out of which the queer narrative self was made, and thus it could not participate fully in modernism's staged retreat from its referents. And yet, these sexually dissident types were not secondary, did not reflect or illustrate social relations. They were posed against those relations as essential and pre-existent. They staged a kind of triumph of the self without contingency, clearly allied to the modernist subject. At times, as in E. M. Forster's *Maurice* (1914; 1971), this essential self is formed through the radical subjectivity enabled by the Paterian aesthetic response. As such it rejects the systematising framework of sexology. One history of the queer Bildungsroman across the twentieth century might trace the ways in which novels of the lesbian, gay and transgender self variously deployed or refused those non-literary discourses which systematised the sexual subject.

If the queer Bildungsroman needed the realist type, it also needed those structures of time, both narrative and historical, which characterise the nineteenth-century novel. In order to pose an essential subject as progressively emergent, a novel needs a sense of historical landscape. In order to pose that subject as pre-eminent, stable and radically opposed to its context, it needs narrative time, the sense of progress and closure as well the sense of expansive, subjective time.

But what of a novel like Virginia Woolf's *Orlando* (1928)? It certainly produces a kind of journey centring on a sexually dissident self, and at the same time it refuses the bounds of historical time. In both characterisation

and narrative strategy, it refuses the unified individual. In doing this, it
necessarily removes itself from any manner of instrumentalisation beyond
the reproduction of its own position, which is performed by novels covering any manner of subject and aim, sharing only what Lukàcs terms
modernist form as a 'specific kind of content'.[8] The formal qualities of
queer Bildungsromane such as Forster's *Maurice* and Radclyffe Hall's
*The Well of Loneliness* (1928) mark them clearly as instrumental. They are
made for use (though *Maurice* may have waited a long time for its deployment), deliberately 'readerly' in Barthes sense, that is deliberately stabilising and productive of identity.[9]

So, at the moment when high modernism staged its radical formal
expression of the subjective turn, queer narrative reached at least halfway
back towards the established forms of nineteenth-century realism.
In projecting themselves as instruments for the sexually dissident self, novels
of lesbian, gay and transgender identity take, over and over across the
twentieth century, the form of the Bildungsroman. The designation 'coming
out novel' suggests all of those qualities of youth, instability and becoming
which typify the Bildungsroman, and which Moretti argues say more about
modernity itself than they do about the individual (5). Sexuality is itself the
inevitable and privileged substrate for this expression.

Both Radclyffe Hall's *The Well of Loneliness* and Forster's *Maurice*
produce sexual dissidence as the form and the meaning of their protagonists. Working in the early twentieth century, they necessarily engage with
sexual science as a structuring discourse for sexuality in their historical
moment. Jay Prosser, in *Second Skins: The Body Narratives of
Transsexuality*, points out that the continued reception of *The Well* as
'lesbian' involves a denial of its position as a transgender narrative.
Prosser discusses Hall's determined return to sexological narrative in
a decade when most of Western culture had turned towards psychoanaly-
tical narratives of sexual dissidence. For Hall, as other critics have noted,
this is part of an essentialist strategy, a plea for recognition on the basis of
innate bodily difference. Prosser argues that, because Hall modelled
Stephen's narrative specifically after case studies of 'inverts', '*The Well* is
not only thematically but concretely caught up in the inception of trans-
sexual history'.[10] Hall's narrator describes Stephen as an invert, and
Stephen herself (Hall uses the feminine pronoun for her protagonist
throughout the novel) finds her discursive reflection, identity and meaning, in a volume of Krafft-Ebing, found on her father's shelf. Throughout
the novel, we are provided with evidence of the bodily difference of

Stephen and other inverts, defined as biologically essential in sexological terms.

For Prosser what is at stake in discussion of *The Well* is the medicalisation of the transgender life narrative and the historical move towards operative transsexuality. In making these connections, he points to the connection between the narrative strategies of sexology and the form of the novel. We could add psychoanalysis to this, since its often-unremarked borrowing from sexology includes the case history method. The central medical formulations experienced by queer peoples in the twentieth century are predicated on novelistic forms of narrative, on the emergence of essential or contingent selves within the structures of the social world.

*The Well*, like its sexological sources, depends on both bodily evidence and life history narrative to produce its sexually dissident subjects. The biologically inflected idea of the natural plays a significant role in *The Well*'s characterisation and its plot structure. Being taken in to dinner by one Captain Ramsey, young Stephen reflects that 'if I were he I wouldn't be a bore, I could just be myself, I'd feel perfectly natural'.[11] The heterosexual pairing demanded by social decorum is rendered unnatural in the face of Stephen's 'natural' difference. This idea of natural/ unnaturalness returns at key moments throughout the novel. At times the narrative also gestures at a psychoanalytic aetiology for Stephen's difference. Her father had wanted a boy; her mother is cold and unloving, ultimately rejecting her. Her mother's womb is explicitly referred to as a hostile environment, a gesture at a notion of acquired characteristics which conflates a psychoanalytic narrative with a sexological one. Stephen's childish desire for a family servant provides a psychoanalytic origin narrative to which she returns in reverie at formative moments in her development.

As Stephen journeys through Europe, her narrative of development takes her through several relationships and provides views of a number of inverted characters, and those 'normal' (that is, feminine) women who desire them. As Prosser points out, the model here is sexological; to term Stephen a lesbian or a transgender person is to read her out of context. The notion of the invert is predicated on what Alan Sinfield terms the 'cross-sex grid'.[12] In a conflation of what Freud would later distinguish as aim and object-choice, nineteenth-century sexology often assumed that the desire for a person of the same sex was evidence of transgender movement. This immediately begged the question, what about the women who desired such inverts? This in turn led to a baroque taxonomy of degree and inclination. The novel sets out to classify Stephen and its other characters through both bodily difference and life history narrative.

Stephen's childhood identification with her father in the absence of motherly affection is dwelt on at length. Her experiences in war, family exile and various love affairs all provide the classic structure of Bildung, in which a radically continuous subject develops against a shifting array of encounters with 'the world' that form the narrative substrate of Stephen's emerging identity. Its context is the biologically determined type. In the Parisian salon of a character called Valérie Seymour, widely accepted as a depiction of Natalie Barney's home, Stephen encounters the 'types' with which she shares biological kinship. This forms one episode in her development. Here, the reader is pointed towards an array of specimens, and didactically taught to read clues which reveal inversion to the observant viewer:

> There was Pat who had lost her Arabella to the charms of Grigg and the Lido. Pat, who, originally hailing from Boston, still vaguely suggested a New England schoolmarm. Pat, whose libido apart from the flesh, flowed into entomological channels – one had to look twice to discern that her ankles were too strong and too heavy for those of a female . . . There was Jamie, very much more pronounced . . . (353–4)

We are instructed to read through the social surface here. Characters are made of both detailed superficial histories and of bodies. These bodies are significant in a manner which conflates characterisation with individuation, which moves inside the realist type and uses it as a reflector for the world.

In *Maurice*, written before *The Well* but revised and published long after, E. M. Forster is also at pains to render sexual dissidence as a bodily matter, directly physical before it is psychic. Forster opposes his protagonist specifically to the model of the Wildean aesthete, exemplified in Maurice's first, duplicitous lover, Clive. The two meet at Cambridge, where Maurice encounters characters such as Risley: 'dark, tall and affected. He made an exaggerated gesture when introduced, and when he spoke, which was continually, he used strong yet unmanly superlatives'.[13] Forster works to situate Maurice in opposition to such men, who are openly effeminate and associated with particular aesthetic tastes, with a Cambridge subculture made famous by the Wilde trial when Forster himself was sixteen years old. Maurice admits later that 'his interest in the classics had been slight and obscene' (99). He is defined purposely against effeminacy, having in maturity, 'a well-trained serviceable body and a face that contradicted it no longer. Virility had harmonized them and shaded either with dark hair' (102–3).

Though this is a clear rejection of the sexological narrative of inversion, which typically described male inverts as 'narrow-hipped', the invert is not rejected in favour of a purely psychic identity model. Maurice does not live as a consciousness inside his body, he is that body. The failure of his relationship with Clive is written specifically as a result of Clive's insistent separation of body and spirit and his cowardly desire to love Maurice 'spiritually'. Maurice's first 'crisis' of identity, his acceptance of his love for men, is followed by the realisation that he is 'neither body or soul, nor body and soul, but "he", working through both' (60). Despite his lack of aesthetic sensibility, the classical cultural model still defines him. He realises that he had 'always been like the Greeks and didn't know' (62). The cultural material of homosexual identity presented here is late Victorian – the mediation of aesthetic responses, the formative experience of the Oxbridge college, the articulation of commuter class identity against old families in their country seats and its concomitant new model for the family – but its narrative structure is that specifically twentieth-century form of Bildungsroman that would later be called the 'coming out' novel.

This twentieth-century version of the form involves an enhancement of the psychological fiction of the late Victorian age, an elevation of psychic interiority to mythic status. That is to say, it is to some degree modernist. While sometimes very frank about bodily desire, Forster works to situate Maurice's radically corporeal consciousness in an amorphous, redolent interiority, established early on in a fluid and highly metaphorical focalised narration: 'A trouble – nothing as beautiful as sorrow – rose to the surface of his mind, displayed its ungainliness and sank . . . he longed to be a little boy again, and to stroll half awake forever by the colourless sea' (30). By the end of the novel, this diffuse interiority will expand across the nation and the world, taking its characters outside of history.

It is a characteristic gesture of Forster's to allow his characters to escape from historical into mythic time. The final episode of *Maurice* bears a striking resemblance to Forster's feminist short story 'The Other Kingdom', first published in the *English Review* in 1909. It also echoes that valorisation of 'the holiness of direct desire' which Forster champions in *Where Angels Fear to Tread* (1907). Together with Alec, Maurice steps outside of culture, nation and history. Finally rejecting that 'speaking science' which dismisses his desires as rubbish, yet accepting that which defines him as a congenital homosexual, Maurice finds himself within a radical interiority, alienated from the social world around him:

when he stopped outside the park, because the King and Queen were
passing, he despised them at the moment he bared his head. It was as if
the barrier that kept him from his fellows had taken another aspect. He was
not afraid or ashamed any more. After all, the forests and the night were on
his side, not theirs; they, not he, were inside a ring fence. (187)

The triumphant queer self is mutually exclusive with national and social
belonging here. It is outside borders which are figured as national and as
'civilised'. Here, in London, the narrative foreshadows Maurice and Alec's
final disappearance from culture, nation and narrative itself. Their escape
from meaning is much like the disappearance of Forster's earlier heroine,
Evelyn, who literally, magically melts into the trees of her fenced-in forest
in 'The Other Kingdom'. The novel ends, not with Maurice and Alec
joining or escaping, but with Clive. Maurice and Alec have escaped the
novel itself. Maurice would rather 'close such a book than leave it lying
about to get dirtied . . . He could suffer no mixing of old and new . . .
Having finished his confession, he must disappear from the world that
brought him up' (213). Maurice and Alec act in sympathy with Forster's
own much-quoted assertion (in a letter to his friend Florence Barger) that
the novel was 'unpublishable until my death and England's'.[14] His characters exit the space of realism, which sits at the conjunction of the everyday and historical time, and disappear into mythos. Forster poses the
homosexual self as inconsistent with national history.

The Well, on the other hand, embraces historical time in a classic realist
manner, unproblematically. The fact that generations of readers have
taught each other to read Natalie Barney's 'real' home through Valérie
Seymour's fictional one, and to make other such equivalencies, has
mediated the novel's truth claims. Such readings through the real, like
the common practice of reading Bildungsromane from David Copperfield
to Zami autobiographically, render the novel consistent with its historical
context. Its bodies are real; we read the array of types in Seymour's salon as
coded references to real bodies which existed in time and place. Not just
any time and place, but a specifically, productively queer time and place –
Paris after the Great War.

The war itself provides The Well's other use of history. Stephen, as an
ambulance driver, finds scope for heroism in battle and there meets her
most significant lover, Mary Llewellyn. This episode situates the positions
of Mary and Stephen on a historical threshold. Women ambulance drivers
function as signs of historical change as sexual progress:

They were part of a universal convulsion and were being accepted as such, on their merits. And although their Sam Browne belts remained swordless, their hats and their caps without regimental badges, a battalion was formed in those terrible years that would never again be completely disbanded. War and death had given them a right to life, and life tasted sweet, very sweet to their palates. Later on would come bitterness, disillusion, but never again would such women submit to being driven back to their holes and corners. (275)

Here, historical upheaval, the constant change which characterises the experience of modernity, is in specific dialogue with this new kind of individual, the invert with a meaningful social place.

Finally, both *Maurice* and *The Well* are embedded in another kind of historical time. In the narrative canon formation of queer literature in English, they are placed as very specific markers. Each is instrumentalised in a way that Woolf's *Orlando*, to return to the earlier example, never has been. Whether and how *The Well* should be read, as a transgender or a lesbian novel, it held a central place in the reading histories of butch lesbians across several generations. *Maurice* is emblematic in another way, as the novel which spent six decades in the closet. Both *The Well* and *Maurice* partake of history through the middle twentieth century as emblems of subcultural identity. As productive, readerly narratives of queer desire they lend themselves to specific cultural use. This use depends on the structural elements of the Bildungsroman which they consciously deploy.

### Work, Sex and Meaning: Patricia Highsmith and Valerie Taylor

At the close of *The Way of the World*, Moretti makes a claim for the 'end of the century of the Bildungsroman' in the end of nineteenth-century realism. Following a fairly standard elucidation of this crisis of narrative realism through the late work of George Eliot, he argues:

> no convention outlives the fall of its foundations. And when the new psychology started to dismantle the unified image of the individual; when the social sciences turned to 'synchrony' and 'classification', thereby shattering the synthetic perception of history; when youth betrayed itself in its narcissistic desire to last forever; when in ideology after ideology the individual figured simply as a part of the whole – then the century of the *Bildungsroman* was truly at an end. (227–8)

Yet it was precisely these notions of 'synchrony' and 'classification', expressed as a continual dance of dissidence and inclusion, that enabled the development of lesbian, gay and transgender Bildungsromane across the first half of the twentieth century. We might argue that the Bildungsroman did not end, but moved into subculture, including gay subculture, which fostered its specific qualities and enabled that incubation of queer subjects through which Western national cultures now claim global ethical dominance.

Throughout the twentieth century, the differences in narrative structure and style which distinguish *The Well* from *Maurice* – realist type versus universalised subject; bodily evidence versus diffuse consciousness; historical versus mythic time – would continue to be written across class difference as cultural registers of the popular and the literary. In 1952, with the burgeoning paperback market already proliferating a kaleidoscopic array of narratives of lesbian development, Patricia Highsmith published *The Price of Salt* (titled *Carol* in the UK) under the pseudonym Claire Morgan. Much like a character from George Gissing, Highsmith's heroine, Therese, locates the modern self in an ambiguous class position which exists at an uneasy nexus of wage labour, aesthetic desire and sexual longing. These things trouble and overlap each other and in the tension among them Therese experiences her development. These forces are immediately evident in the novel's opening scene, where the impermanent, threshold context of Therese's life is established. She sits in the soul-destroying atmosphere of the cafeteria in the department store where she works for minimum wage, eating grey, unpleasant food and thinking of the paintings of Mondrian, of escaping birds and her vocation as a theatrical set designer. Throughout the first movement of the novel Therese is situated through images of entrapment. She is fascinated by a toy train, imprisoned on its tracks and forced to run by its 'tyrannical master': 'It was like something gone mad in its imprisonment, something already dead that would never wear out, like the dainty, springy-footed foxes in the Central Park Zoo, whose complex footwork repeated and repeated as they circled their cages.'[15] At the department store Therese meets Mrs Robichek, who stands throughout the novel for its class sympathies, and functions as the abject self of its heroine. Ageing, unattractive and alone, an immigrant victim of a fickle labour market, Mrs Robichek fascinates and repels Therese. She later signals her attainment of maturity by overcoming her repulsion and sending odd presents of kitschy packaged food back to Mrs Robichek from across America.

The novel's primary *mise en scène* established, Therese then experiences a dramatic and inexplicable cathexis towards a wealthy suburban mother. This scene is canonically placed in terms of the romance, in chapter three:

Their eyes met at the same instant, Therese glancing up from a box she was opening, and the woman turning her head so she looked directly at Therese. She was tall and fair, her long figure graceful in the loose fur coat that she held open with a hand on her waist. Her eyes were grey, colourless, yet dominant as light or fire, and, caught by them, Therese could not look away. (35–6)

Therese's body announces itself as her 'heart stumbles' and her 'face grows hot'. All of the signals of the romance are there, including the structural placement of the scene. It is also embedded in a context of consumer desire, proletarian alienation and aesthetic longing, all firmly established in the first two chapters. This moment of lesbian desire strikes without warning and the novel never seeks to explain it. Its narrative of development, centred on Therese, is a coming to terms with a pre-existing condition, rather than a becoming in the face of social forces. In a manner now become common to most queer Bildungsromane, the self is a radically constant measure of the social world around it. The narrative of emergence presented here depends on the myth of an essential core for the individual, outside of social context.

*The Price of Salt* does carefully establish itself within the form of the Bildungsroman, even as it alters it. Immediately before we see Therese's meeting with Carol, we find her reading Joyce's *A Portrait of the Artist as a Young Man* (34). Therese's hastily sketched back story shows her to be a kind of orphan, rejected by her mother. '"Child, child,"' the older Carol hails her at one point, '"where do you wander – all by yourself?"' (84). The novel's climactic episode takes the form of a journey west, the very substrate of the American Bildungsroman in the twentieth century.

But there are no worries here about sexological categorisations, and psychoanalytic histories are only very lightly sketched. As Therese's erstwhile boyfriend Richard tries to come to terms with her inexplicable distance, he asserts that lesbian desires '"don't just happen. There's always some reason in the background."' When Therese dutifully searches her life history for such a background she cannot find one. She compares herself reflectively to stories she has heard about 'girls falling in love, and she knew what kind of people they were and what they looked like. Neither she nor Carol had ever looked like that' (100). This reflection is key to an understanding of how Highsmith places her heroine and her novel within the social world of the immediate post-war era, in opposition to its developing queer subcultures. Therese spends a good deal of time in Greenwich Village among 'creatives'. She is aware of lesbian subculture, but rejects it.

Likewise, Highsmith herself, once the book was rejected by Random House, did not turn to the lively market for lesbian narrative existing in paperback houses nearby. She chose a respectable middlebrow publisher, Coward-McCann, and gained *The Price of Salt* a place on a list which included hardback reprints of classics and numerous volumes of what would today be called 'accessible literary' fiction. The novel earned a *New York Times* book review, in which Charles Rolo assured readers that Highsmith dealt with this 'explosive material' with 'sensitivity and good taste'.[16] The oppositions which structure both Therese's understanding of her own lesbian desires and the review of the novel itself provide hints at the context of production and reception for lesbian, gay and transgender narrative in post-war America.

Many paperback houses imposed narrative formulas on queer novels during the 1950s, and it is possible, though not certain, that Therese and Carol would not have been allowed to end their novel together in a pulp paperback context. As the decade drew to a close, these formulas were superseded. Some editors, most notably Leona Nevler at Fawcett Gold Medal, allowed lesbian-identified authors to write open-ended or affirming novels for a growing subcultural audience. These novels, especially at Fawcett, took the form of series which followed a character or characters through various relationships, deliberately undoing the romance plot and its sense of an ending. These series clearly deployed a progress narrative of individual development within a hostile social context, and they shared with *The Price of Salt* that pointed opposition between lesbian fulfilment and capitalist alienation which characterises the post-war period.

The signal difference, for writers such as Ann Bannon and Valerie Taylor, who both published with Fawcett Gold Medal from the late 1950s into the 1960s, was the positing of the housewife as the nascent being of lesbian narrative. Her alienation derives from the context of heterosexual marriage, from not engaging in meaningful or productive labour. The structural formula here is a remarkable foreshadowing of Betty Friedan's *The Feminine Mystique* (1963), with one radical difference. For Freidan 'over-sexualisation' is the problem of the housewife and the family; for Taylor and Bannon, sexualisation is the answer, the stabilising sense of an ending. We might say that these novels are written from the perspective of Carol, rather than Therese. Socially infantilised, these housewives function as threshold figures for realist narratives of queer development which illustrate those dominant structures of identity that imprison social actors in the bourgeois state. Like *The Price of Salt*, they follow the form of the

Bildungsroman in posing the emergent lesbian individual within and against the historical time frame of the nation.

Valerie Taylor's *Stranger on Lesbos* (1959) opens as its heroine Frances returns to university, positioning her quite clearly at the centre of Bildung. Her son is a teenager and her husband is preoccupied with work. In the opening paragraph Frances has 'a crazy feeling that the last twenty years had dissolved and she was fifteen again, hesitating on the threshold of County High'.[17] In class she meets her first lesbian partner, and they embark on a relationship doomed to failure. This novel closes on Frances repenting and her husband granting forgiveness, heterosexual marriage restabilised in its sense of an ending. Four years later, in the same year in which *The Feminine Mystique* was first published (1963), Taylor brought out *Return to Lesbos* with Midwood-Tower. Here, Frances continues her movement towards stable identity, ending this volume in a fulfilling lesbian relationship. Again, as at the outset of *Stranger*, the close of *Return to Lesbos* gestures knowingly both towards the narrative of development in which her heroines are formed and to the serial repetition of desire and fulfilment which their context of publication allowed. On the final page, Frances's new partner, Erika, leans 'her whole weight against Frances, a promise for the night that lay ahead. "It's a good beginning, though"', she says.[18] The series produced by Ann Bannon and Valerie Taylor in the late 1950s and 1960s clearly invoke the Bildungsroman's sense of journey and emergence, as well as its production of identity as essential type. Yet they also resist the stabilising closure of the marriage plot as they evoke serial monogamy through both formal structure and content.

Taylor, Bannon and Highsmith all share a structure of feeling in which work, alienation and consumer/sexual desire form the context for the lesbian self. These novels, posing alienating labour against lesbian desire, seek to separate desire from its consumer context and put it back in the body. They dissent from a heterosexuality posed as a signal component of the structure of the bourgeois nation. As Frances lies awake next to her husband in *Return to Lesbos*, she reflects despairingly that 'he even wanted to buy her a fur coat'. Her next thought is that '[t]o make love with a man seemed to her a kind of perversion' (57). These women, depicted as possessing essentialist lesbian bodies, occupy a standpoint of critique *vis-à-vis* the relation between capital, sex and nation. In *The Price of Salt*, Richard attempts to convince Therese to abandon her road trip with Carol and participate in a more 'healthy' kind of journey. He first proffers Paris and aesthetic fulfilment, which Therese rejects in favour of meaningful creative work in New York. Once Therese has headed west, Richard writes to her, 'I'll come out to you – and show you what America is really like' (212). Somehow, the America she sees with Carol is not real. It is, like Forster's mythic sylvan England, inside yet not inside the national space.

Highsmith and Taylor both position the desiring body through psychological prose. Frances reflects directly on bodily desire in internal monologue in *Return to Lesbos*: 'The body, she reminded herself – Do this, do that, and the fulfilled body moves and purrs like a stroked kitten. But she was unable to minimize it. Even her skin felt good' (105). The lesbian body is essential and exhaustive here, and Taylor's concern is to examine its consequences in a social world which is not structured to accommodate it. The same might be said of *The Price of Salt*, though its narrative strategies arguably exist in a difference cultural register. Therese and Carol do have sex, in a hotel room scene where it is rendered almost accidental. As Rolo's review puts it, in wonderfully deflected language, 'it is Therese who, with purblind innocence, causes them to become lovers'.[19] Highsmith renders sex as Forster does, as metaphorical, amorphous and transcendent, inside Therese's radical interiority: 'And now it was a pale blue distance and space, an expanding space in which she took flight suddenly like a long arrow. The arrow seemed to cross an impossibly wide distance with ease, seemed to arc on and on in space, and not quite to stop. Then she realised she still clung to Carol' (200). Presumably, this diffusion of the desiring body into abstract language constitutes what the reviewer calls 'sensitivity and good taste'. It also seems likely that it played a role in the novel's placement with a middlebrow publisher rather than a pulp paperback house.

There are two models for the lesbian body here, one produced through more direct language than the other, and this narrative difference defines, at least in part, the cultural register of the two novels. In terms of reception, it is always impossible to know who read what and how, specifically what work readers did in the interpretation of these novels. Kate Adams contrasts *The Price of Salt* and a 1952 paperback called *Women's Barracks*. She argues that Highsmith's message is 'radical' specifically because it is couched in conventional terms. *Women's Barracks* on the other hand, held up as the exemplum of lesbian pulp, does 'the dominant culture's work by representing lesbian sexuality and the independent woman as threats to bourgeois culture and to its ideals of normal womanhood'.[20] There is an implication regarding reception and cultural use here. To 'do the dominant culture's work' would be to stabilise this ideology in the minds of actual women and men. To be radical would be to destabilise, to make ideology visible to the reader. Yet this is not theorised, in Adams or in the work of other critics who damned pulp narrative, such as Bonnie Zimmerman and Julie Abraham. Abraham objects specifically to the romance plot, which she terms the 'heterosexual plot', reading lesbian love stories as 'mere' substitutions. Bonnie Zimmerman contrasts them to 'more serious' literature. The difference between Highsmith's work and Taylor's, and between the critical reception of each, is a repetition of more widely applied critical ideas of the damning popular and the ideological passivity of the mass of readers, who are, as usual, feminised.[21] Once again, these readings ignore the centrality of romance narrative to the development of the desiring self posed against the social world, the common origin of romance and Bildungsroman. They also fail to note that romance narrative, from its inception, has been a clear subversion of narratives which seek to instrumentalise sexuality in the realm of the rational, to place it in a subordinate relation to capital.

Yet even within these formulations which valorise *The Price of Salt* over contemporary pulp, Highsmith's narrative is posed falsely as structurally opposed to those of writers such as Taylor. Both deploy structures of Bildung, placing their heroines radically on the threshold of becoming in the face of a hostile social world. Both pose lesbian desire as disruptive to relations of work, capital and nation in the bourgeois state. Each novel, though its narrative strategy may be distinct, seeks to pose a desiring lesbian body as the foundation of its heroine's experience. Finally, Highsmith's narrative strategies do not place her outside of cultural authority, are not in that sense disruptive, but rather form her (limited) claim to it, in the form of literariness.

Critical arguments around the production and reception of lesbian and gay pulp narratives tend to position what is most often called 'dominant' or 'heterosexual' culture against a queer culture which would, ideally, disrupt, challenge or change it. This cultural model initially left the ability to do this, cultural agency, to the producers of such texts, rather than their readers. Two or three decades after the war, in the context of popular movements for sexual liberation, the question of queer author against publisher as representative of dominant culture, of art/truth versus capital, would be answered differently.

## Subculture and Small Presses

From the 1960s, identitarian liberation movements were subject to increasing definition and differentiation. Individuals existing at the nexus of various relations of class, race and sexuality expressed the impetus to choose between competing self-definitions and calls to political participation. This model of dissident groups defined by identity, as Alan Sinfield points out, creates space for recognition and community solidarity at the same time as it relies on a structure which positions such groups always as outsiders within the national space. Sinfield examines such texts as Larry Kramer's 1985 play *The Normal Heart* and David Wojnarowicz's collection of auto-biographical essays, *Close to the Knives* (1991), noting how each poses the gay male subject as an outsider petitioning for citizenship rights within his own nation. This outsider/insider formulation of the national space is the flip side of subcultural empowerment, Sinfield argues. Through this inevitable positioning we are always reincorporated into that ideological structure which posed us as outsiders in the first instance. At the same time, for Sinfield, subcultures do 'constitute *partially alternate subjectivities*' where we can think ourselves, and live ourselves, at least halfway out of ideology.[22]

In the 1980s and 1990s, on both sides of the Atlantic, small presses constituted specifically around feminist and queer communities proliferated. Many of the novels now recognised as classics of the coming out genre were originally published by such presses, which seemed at least partly to sidestep the questions of high and low culture, open expression of identity and damning ideology raised by the marketing and critical reception of Highsmith and Taylor in earlier decades. These novels pose a radically queer self against the social world, and yet also posit a new relation between queer self and national culture, one defined by the subcultural movements in which they were embedded. In the context of subcultural articulation, the queer Bildungsroman expresses a new formal reflexivity and a multiplicity of redeployments, challenging the relation between the individual and historical time and yet retaining its basic assumptions. The Bildungsroman as a novelistic form is clearly central to what Sinfield calls, 'the typically subcultural process of reinvesting an earlier textual moment' (285). It is the inevitable tool for the coming out novel fostered in this mid-twentieth-century small-press context, posing the queer subject which Sinfield argues is 'poised at the brink of perpetual emergence' (281). As such, the Bildungsroman is the inevitable form for queer subcultural articulation. This is not accidental, but reflects those relations between sexuality, desire, progress, individual life narrative and the rise of the bourgeois nation state discussed at the start of this chapter.

Three novels might serve to illustrate some reworkings of the Bildungsroman by lesbian and gay writers publishing with independent presses on either side of the Atlantic: Jeanette Winterson's *Oranges Are Not the Only Fruit* (1985), Neil Bartlett's *Ready to Catch Him Should He Fall* (1990) and Audre Lorde's *Zami: A New Spelling of My Name* (1982) were all published by independent presses and all knowingly rework the classic structure of the Bildungsroman. Winterson's *Oranges Are Not the Only Fruit*, originally published by the newly formed Pandora Press in 1985, details the emergence of a lesbian teenager in a small northern English town. In her introduction to the 1991 Vintage edition, Winterson is at pains to situate the novel on the progressive side of the imagined post-modern break which then dominated the critical landscape. She claims that, 'In structure and style *Oranges* wasn't like any other novel.' Specifically rejecting narratives of progress and development, she writes disingenuously: '*Oranges* is an experimental novel: its interests are anti-linear.'[23] The claim for unprecedented form erases the novel's own mod-ernist history. At a stroke, it discounts Nella Larsen, Gertrude Stein, Djuna Barnes and other sexually dissident writers who worked against realist unity of purpose and meaning. It also denies the novel's own structure, which clearly leads the reader from the oppression to the expression of an essentially lesbian self.

Winterson's (and her critics') claims for *Oranges* as non-linear and unprecedented are based on its magically real elements and its inserted fragments of fairy-tale narrative, which provide didactic parallels to the novel's realist action. These elements sometimes function as detours around expressions of desire and emotion, as in the scene where Jeanette first has sex with Katy. In place of the action here, in place of the expression of lesbian desire or the presence of the desiring lesbian body, we are given a quasi-biblical passage that evokes the *Song of Solomon*. Yet the *Old Testament* book itself produces more textual body than *Oranges*. In the aggregate these passages allow the novel to maintain its ironic distance, which breaks only once, in the romanticised depiction of Jeanette's inti-macy with Melanie. Immediately, the narrator asks, 'What is it about intimacy that makes it so very disturbing?' (101). We might see these narrative deflections as Winterson's refusal to place the lesbian self in a determining body, or to romanticise lesbian desire. The novel also refuses historical context and national narrative. Its action could be almost any-where in the twentieth-century West, and in place of historical time we get the shift back and forth from small-town community to the static time of myth.

Still, *Oranges* provides a very clear narration of individual development, upon which it does reflect. The novel's final movement, named after the *Book of Ruth*, shows Jeanette having moved, like Tom Jones or David

Copperfield, from country to city and a stable identity. Her reflective return home closes the novel. The narrator remarks on the threshold state, on moving forward and looking back, and in invoking Lot's wife, also invokes Highsmith's earlier lesbian Bildungsroman. 'Going back after a long time will make you mad, because the people you left behind do not like to think of you changed' (156). The structure of *Oranges* is clearly linear, and designed to produce the emergent queer self. Much as Winterson tries to sidestep the relation between narrative and identity, they cannot be written as separate effects.

In *Ready to Catch Him Should He Fall*, published by Serpent's Tail in 1990, Neil Bartlett playfully embraces the narrative of progress, providing its end point and its production of meaning in the safety of subcultural space. The novel's characters are rendered allegorical by names such as Boy, O and Madame and its narrator engages in a direct address which invites its readers into the sense of belonging and community Bartlett celebrates: 'if you don't know what that feeling is, if you don't know why it's like that then you know nothing, nothing, nothing. I'm sorry.'[24] Playing with the productive narrative form of the romance plot, the novel is divided into sections titled 'Single', 'Couple' and 'Family'. Gesturing at its historical relation to molly house culture, the 'Couple' section is divided into such chapters as 'Publishing the Banns', 'Robing the Bride' and 'Setting up Home'. Throughout the novel's first sequence its central character, Boy, walks obsessively around London, travelling countless miles without purpose, the subject of diffuse desire without context. In a deliberate use of the form developed as Bildungsroman, Bartlett places Boy as the young traveller on the threshold of emergence and identity.

Stumbling on 'the bar' gives Boy context and meaning, and the novel details his mentoring by Madame, his acquisition of queer history through directed reading of her library, and his social positioning at the centre of a dramatic romance in which the entire community voyeuristically participates. Primarily a dramatic writer, Bartlett creates a highly visual sense of enclosed, radically separate and almost timeless community in *Ready to Catch Him*, but it is a community stalked by history. At the edges of the narrative, sometimes graphically separated into chapters of only a paragraph or two, we see the violence done to gay men in the streets outside the bar. Minor characters arrive bruised or cut, or disappear into hospitals outside the story. These episodes take the form of Gothic hauntings, only just there, liminal and threatening but never fully incorporated. In this way, Bartlett creates the sense of subcultural enclosure within the broader and more hostile culture outside the bar and outside the narrative.

Gothic and other generic effects in Bartlett's novel allow the embedding of the queer self in both textual and national history while at the same time maintaining his radical separateness, his manifest dissent.

Audre Lorde's American novel *Zami: A New Spelling of My Name*, originally published by Persephone Press in 1982, places its protagonist at the centre of national history, used as the backdrop for the production of meaningful selfhood. Like *Ready to Catch Him, Zami* reflects both thematically and structurally on the effects of subculture. Towards the novel's close the narrator reflects on urban lesbian subculture in the years prior to popular gay liberation:

> Keeping ourselves together and on our own tracks, however wobbly, was like trying to play the Dinizulu War Chant or a Beethoven sonata on a tin dog whistle.
>
> The important message seemed to be that you had to have a place. Whether or not it did justice to whatever you felt you were about, there had to be some place to refuel and check your flaps.
>
> In times of need and great instability, the place sometimes became more a definition than the substance of why you needed it to begin with.[25]

This more critical formulation of subculture typifies Lorde's generally reflexive treatment of the relationship between the individual self and collective meaning. Ultimately, the narrator comes to realise that 'there was a piece of the real me bound in each place, and growing'. She is multiple and contingent, but multiply rooted. Subculture, with its many partial inclusions and contingencies, provides meaning in its very structure, rather than its content: 'It was a while before we came to realise that our place was the very house of difference rather than the security of any one particular difference' (226).

Throughout the novel, Lorde references the major historical events of the middle twentieth century – war, colonial nation-building and revolt, political execution and the emergence of identitarian resistance movements. At the same time, she often poses the narrative of its central character, Audre, as markedly oblique to these events. In a second subtitle the novel hails itself as the template for a new form, 'biomythography'. Like Winterson and Bartlett, Lorde recognises a crucial relation between narrative form and the production of identity. Where *David Copperfield* and *Jane Eyre* announced themselves as 'autobiographies' knowing that truth claim would be read as fiction, *Zami* announces her life story as myth knowing it will be read as the truth of experience and both embracing and subverting that reading. Biomythography purposefully sidesteps the opposition of objective and subjective truths. This, by extension, also disrupts the opposition between high modernism and realism and allows for a critical narrative which can usefully trace the history of the queer Bildungsroman across the twentieth century.

We might perhaps read *Zami* in the context of a queer Bildungsroman such as Edmund White's *A Boy's Own Story* (1982), which places its emergent queer white subject at the threshold of the racially organised map of the nation, as drawn in the American canon. Like Bartlett and Lorde, White plays pointedly with the structure of Bildungsroman, gesturing early on to English public school narratives, refusing linear plot development and concluding with a paradoxical sense of arrival and contingency. Yet this emergent subject produces a remarkably stable sense of national history. Like Carson McCullers, White uses the racial geography of the American city to produce sexuality as mystery and sexual emergence as a journey into the unknown. Having related his first sexual experience and his first exposure to the black neighbourhoods where his family's servants live, the narrator then waits to pick up a trick in a square full of 'hillbillies'. 'In my naïveté', he tells us, 'I imagined that all poor people, black and white, like each other and that here ... I might find my way back to the [black] street, that smell of burning honey, that blood as red as mine and that steady, colorless flare in the glass chimney ... '[26] Here and elsewhere in the novel, the mysterious black neighbourhood is directly conflated with the narrator's mysterious desires. White's queer narrator has internalised the racial geography of America. It is his psychic landscape, and thus the substance of a radically white queer subject. Like those subjects of the European Bildungsroman whom White invokes at the outset, he need not destabilise national narrative in order to stabilise himself. He is consistent with the canonical structure of modernity.

Lorde's *Zami* poses its narrator as oblique to history, allowing Lorde to present a historical margin from which the meaning of the national narrative changes. Initially, this off-centre history is formulated by the manner in which Audre's mother filters the reality of racism for her children. Her mother elaborately pretends that white people spit randomly in the street, not directly and purposefully on black children. Immediately, we as readers are invited to read through the official narrative, against the grain. Travelling from New York to the segregated south with her family, young Audre is told that the food served in train cars is unhealthy, not that it is forbidden. The charade falls apart when they are refused service at a lunch counter in Washington DC. Further on in the narrative and years later in Audre's life, the protest against the execution of the Rosenbergs is presented in the context of this memory of lunch counter segregation.

History, for Audre, is a determined and continuous narrative within which the lesbian self emerges, but this history does not run parallel to national hegemony. Roughly midway through the narrative Audre hears the name of Crispus Attucks for the first time. 'How was that possible? . . . I had been taught by some of the most highly respected historians in the country. Yet, I never once hear the name mentioned of the first man to fall in the american revolution' (132–3).

Often, those moments in the novel which structure Audre as an emergent individual are also written metaphorically through grand historical narrative. Describing her early teen years, the narrator tells us that, 'Relationships in my family came to resemble nothing so much as a West Indian version of the Second World War. Every conversation with my parents, particularly with my mother, was like a playback of the Battle of the Bulge in Black panorama with stereophonic sound. Blitzkrieg became my favourite symbol for home' (82–3). While queering national history by posing it through the specific individual standpoint of black experience, Lorde also subsumes its grand landscape into her own psychological one, transforming it in the process.

Like Forster, Lorde refuses the separation of psychic and physical selves. Throughout *Zami*, the desiring body is rendered palpable and seamlessly embedded in the development of consciousness. Early on, the narrator describes the onset of menstruation through a scene in which the pounding of her mother's souse for her favourite dinner becomes a profoundly sensual experience. Across nine pages of text, this simple preparation of food becomes not just the sign of cultural inheritance, but of desire for her mother's body, sexual awakening and physical change (71–80).

*Zami* also presents us with the consequences of the sexual body in a lengthy and graphic episode which poses illegal abortion as both a historically bounded social experience and a highly focalised experience of the textual body (107–15). This abortion is part of Audre's total lesbian experience, of living in a sexual body in a particular time and place. It situates her female body within the surrounding narrative of butch-femme subculture. Her early sexual experiences are both social, in their negotiation of the subcultural imperative to butch-femme role play, and essential: 'I never questioned where my knowledge of her body and her need came from. Loving Ginger that night was like coming home to a joy I was meant for, and I only wondered, silently, how I had not known it would be so' (139). This and other sexual encounters in the novel, including abortion, described in frank and sometimes rapturous detail, are presented specifically as stages on a journey to meaning and stable self-positioning.

Sex is the stuff of knowledge, and Audre must consume it to attain self-realisation: 'Until the very moment that our naked bodies touched ... I had no idea what I was doing there, nor what I wanted to do there' (138). The trajectory of Bildung here is towards a specific relation between the individual and history, one which reveals national history as contingent and constructed. At the same time, it is towards an essential lesbian identity grounded in the sexual/textual body of the poet Audre Lorde, conflated imperfectly with the author of the book. Lorde's use/subversion of the formal effects of Bildungsroman 'reinvests an earlier textual moment' in just the way Sinfield describes. It is possible because the movement of resistance and incorporation is the stuff of the Bildungsroman structure. Positioning its subjects as emerging into meaning against the national historical, Bildungsroman performs, at the level of meaning, a similar effect of resistance and incorporation to that which Sinfield describes as the substance of subculture.

## Vanishing Points

The turn of the twenty-first century has been characterised in part by a new and more centrally defining relationship between queer self and national identity in the West. Both Jasbir Puar and Rahul Rao have noted the new ideological positioning of the post-9/11 West as the site of queer freedom, opposed to Islamic nation states.[27] Puar argues in *Terrorist Assemblages: Homonationalism in Queer Times* that 'there is a transition underway in how queer subjects are relating to nation states' (xii). Lesbian, gay male and transgender identities now function simultaneously as signs of the progressive freedom of the West and as perversions which queer demonised members of Islamic states. We might think of Khaled Hosseini's *The Kite Runner* (2003) as an example of this formulation. Its evil characters are Taliban leaders with hidden paedophilic, gay desires and its protagonist ends this novel of development safely within a heterosexual American family, flying a kite in the arguably iconic queer space of Golden Gate Park. Focusing on the popular discourse of metrosexual identity, Puar argues that, 'As a counterpart to the age of U.S. imperialism, metrosexuality triumphantly hails American modernity as the space of sexual exceptionalism and promotes a union between queerness and patriotism' (69). Similar ideological oppositions between East and West, figured as sexual persecution and incorporation, arguably operate throughout Europe. We might say that the subject of queer Bildung now emerges on the global, rather than the national, stage. Queer identity now functions as a national border, rather than a marginal space within the nation. With queer subjects so intrinsic to national identity, can they still act as those semi-outsiders which Alan Sinfield describes? Can a central, radically queer and emergent figure pose the kind of cultural resistance and incorporation which has come to define queer Bildungsromane? Or can we follow Moretti's model and claim an end of the century of queer Bildungsroman?

Gay and transgender Bildungsromane are certainly alive and well, especially in the young adult fiction market, which is so hungry for structurally unified narratives of development.[28] Indeed, queer protagonists seem privileged subjects for young adult fiction in English in the second decade of the twenty-first century, where, produced by both queer- and straight-identified authors, they stand in for the alienation/incorporation dynamic more generally. Again, this is a further expression of the centrality of the queer self to current Western notions of ethical correctness. The new, closer relation between queer subjects and national identities means that subjects of queer Bildungsromane function much as the emergent young artist or entrepreneur did for the nineteenth-century Bildungsroman. They have been incorporated as new signifiers of the triumph of belonging over adversity which is the mythic relation between individual and nation state.

There are vanishing points for queer Bildungsromane, but it is likely they have been with us all along. Two such vanishing points, historical and linguistic, are exemplified by J. T. LeRoy's *Sarah* (2000) and Adam Mars-Jones's 'John Cromer' trilogy, which begins with *Pilcrow* (2008) and continues with *Cedilla* (2011). These narratives pose queer selves as threshold figures, as journeying forward, yet as inessential, contingent, outside of national space and history or constituted in linguistic instability. Once we call them Bildungsroman, have we stretched the definition beyond a useful meaning?

LeRoy's *Sarah*, which focuses on Cherry Vanilla, a twelve-year-old transgendered sex worker, opens by posing its central character on the edge of the attainment of meaningful work and identity. She will be gifted with the raccoon penis bone which stamps her as belonging to the pimp Glad, and to those in the know, as a special brand of sexual experience. We follow Cherry on an ill-conceived journey full of hazards as she makes a kind of sense of her world, but the novel quickly comes apart in terms of both genre and stable meaning. We find ourselves in a magically real world in which plastic icons hold magic power, truck stops serve elaborate gourmet meals and twelve-year-old sex workers have second sight.

The primary drive of the novel is Cherry's desire both to be and to have her mother. She derives sexual pleasure in being called by her mother's name, Sarah. She attempts to bath like Sarah, to dress like her, to make up like her and to do the same work. These desires are the one element of the novel presented as stable, as natural. At the culmination of her adventures, having achieved something like a stable sense of identity through her work, Cherry returns to her original 'lot', to the room in which she began the novel, living with Sarah: 'Every fiber in my body yearns for her, to tell her I am home. It feels like we are two magnets, separated by a loose-leaf sheet.'[29] Breaking into the room, pushing aside the inevitable, physically threatening male customer, Cherry climbs into the bed and experiences a blissful union with her mother's body. The following sentence finds her in jail, and we realise that the man and woman in the hotel room were strangers, that Sarah has been gone for months, and that all of the novel's repeated experiences of bodily, biological identity and desire have been falsely constructed. There is no sense of an ending for Cherry, no clicking into place. Its final assertions are undone as they are made.

Place, too, historical and national space, are rejected here, together with the conventions of realism. Though *Sarah* produces a more fluid and lyrical narrative than *Oranges Are Not the Only Fruit*, it performs a similar rejection of nation and history. The truck-stop worlds of *Sarah* are never permeated by any larger historical time or space. Occasional references outside of them, to Yankees or Paris, only enhance their radical separateness. The space is clearly southern and the novel partakes of all the 'queer' effects of the represented American South, but only as a national margin. *Sarah* speaks from the abject of national history, deliberately playing on associations of southern perversity, superstition and historical dissent. As such, its queer protagonist has no national history against which to appear, no hegemonic culture within which to emerge. By Sinfield's definition we might not even call it subcultural, since it provides no call for inclusion at all. We ought not to pose this as a 'postmodern' refusal of identity and stable meaning, however. This is not a break with modernity. All of the same claims might be made for Djuna Barnes's Robin, who sits uncomfortably at the centre of *Nightwood* (1936), and ends that canonically modernist novel in a specific retreat from identity and coherent meaning. *Sarah*'s primary meta-fictional effect was the scandal created around the revelation that its author was in fact a heterosexual woman named Laura Albert. In that moment our attachment to authenticity, to reading through character identity to real bodies, was starkly revealed.

In *Pilcrow* and *Cedilla*, Adam Mars-Jones makes a determined claim to postmodern narrative, reworking Proust to the point of absurdity. His protagonist is confined to bed, prey to hypersensitivity and morbid linguistic obsession, conveying all of the neuroses and none of the nostalgic affect of Proust's narrator. Mars-Jones produces a queer protagonist who, unable to use his body, retreats into language as pure abstraction. The body of John Cromer, protagonist of Mars-Jones's continuing trilogy, is rigid and unresponsive, disabled by improper treatment of his illness. John's body is the tight boundary of his experience, and as such is insistently present. In a manner common to narratives of immobilising disability, however, it is presented as radically separate from the self as mind. This mind is posed continually as the developing self of the protagonist. Its substrate is language.

At the outset the novel signifies its address to Bildungsroman by pointedly invoking both *Tristram Shandy* and *A Portrait of the Artist as a Young Man* as intertexts. It quickly settles on a Proustian formation, however, and this becomes its sustained mode. Confined for years to bed, and of course, precociously intelligent, John becomes minutely and pedantically obsessed with language. The narrator is at pains to point to the contingency of linguistic meaning and the ultimate arbitrariness of signifiers. In the section entitled 'The Twenty-Seventh Letter' John has a lengthy argument about the alphabet with his visiting tutor, who insists the alphabet has only 26 letters. John draws the 'æ', establishing both the contingency of systems of meaning and his own precocity at a stroke. Such meditations on signs continue throughout both *Pilcrow* and *Cedilla*. Eventually, the character begins to muse on the self, 'this mysterious sense of "I" . . . this entity which burned'.[30] Having established already the novel's linguistic distance from any such stable formulations, it now invites us to read this with heavy irony. The novel is divided into very short sections, each titled for a word play derived from its content, and such continued breaks and prolepses interrupt any attempt to form a continuity of meaning.

We are presented with John's same-sex object-choice, at first characteristically deflected from the sight of two men affectionately touching onto a linguistic meditation on the word 'mate', which the upper-class John has never before heard. This is quickly dismissed as a mechanical concern. The thoughts John had were not to do 'with touch and excitement, they were to do with understanding how the world worked. In a sense, they were scientific' (163). By how the world works, the confined John means, how language lies on top of reality and causes it to be interpreted. These self-consciously postmodernist gestures create, as advertised, a very particular, contingent relationship to the real. They pose a self inside language, rather than inside the social world. Yet selves inside the social-historical world, like selves inside language, are constructed by context. In refusing stability, such gestures also sidestep the dynamism of self against social circumstance which is another kind of contingency, in historical meaning.

Can the 'John Cromer' trilogy be called a Bildungsroman, then? Can *Sarah*, refusing the national historical space, produce the meaning of social individuals? E. M. Forster invoked the nation specifically in rejecting it. He constructed the nation as bounded, restrictive and radically opposed to an essential queer self. For LeRoy and Mars-Jones, the nation is not rejected, it is largely absent. It and history have little part in making the meaning of the individuals at the centre of these narratives. This despite the fact that *Pilcrow* and *Cedilla* are set very carefully within historical time. Mars-Jones's chosen treatment of language leaves his protagonist so tightly inside the subjective turn that the dynamic relationship to history, that relationship that is Bildung, cannot take effect.

We might follow Moretti in concluding that 'the coming out novel' says more about modernity than it does about sexually dissident individuals. Its positioning of the individual against the national historical, its blending of subjective and historical time and emergence, is inescapably realist. The centrality of sexual subjects to this narrative is not marginal; it is structural. It expresses the centrality of sexual subjects to modernity per se. New, twenty-first century positionings of queer Bildungsromane continue to pose the modern subject as the location of individual will and desire, emerging within history. The Bildungsroman is, and has been, an instru-mental form. Its enactment of narrative time is teleological, with an end point in stable identity. It does the work of situating subjects inside history and material life and has no structural resistance to cultural incorporation. Given the nature of its relationship to the historical real, Bildungsromane will necessarily evolve as relations of nation, capital and sexuality shift. We might argue that the later twentieth century and the beginning of the twenty-first is, in fact, the Bildungsroman's queer moment. But is that moment as transformative as we once hoped it would be?

# CHAPTER II

# Bildungsromane and Graphic Narratives

## Ian Gordon

Graphic narratives that we treat as Bildungsromane are so often not Bildungsromane at all, but rather autobiographical works. This of course is both a problem and not a problem for several reasons. First, autobiography is a field open to criticism for being loose with the process of questioning the sort of memories from which narratives are constructed. Second, many Bildungsromane are taken, rightly or wrongly, as belonging to the genre of *roman-à-clef*. Third, the term often applied to this form of comic art is 'graphic novel', which, although primarily a marketing term used in an effort to distinguish a supposedly more serious work from the commercial pap of superhero comic books, has become a descriptor for a range of work much of which falls more on the side of memoirs or autobiography than fiction. But yet because they are marketed with the word novel in the title, and probably because they are comics in form, somehow they seem to slip in to the world of fiction through the Bildungsroman door. All of this suggests a somewhat membrane-thin line between genres. Both Michael Chaney and Hillary Chute have pointed to the ways in which graphic narratives highlight 'the material process of making', something relevant to both fiction and autobiography. In this revelation of process graphic narratives inflect and challenge the closures of Bildungsromane that follow key narrative epiphanies. Graphic narratives then offer us a form of Bildungsromane in which process is more important than closure. One further wrinkle in my consideration is that graphic narratives build on comic strips and comic book storytelling techniques and methods, and both those comic forms also have traditions of very long-term serial narratives; something too that plays against closure.[1]

Although the boom in autobiographical graphic narratives can be attributed to Art Spiegelman's *Maus* (1986), the roots of Bildungsromane blossoming in comic art lie in the history of comic books and, in particular, superhero comic books.[2] The British academic Martin Flanagan, in making a case in 2007 for the similarity of the blockbuster 2002 *Spider-Man* film to the Marvel comic book and the indie 2001 *Ghost World* from the Daniel Clowes graphic novel of the same title (1997), addresses this issue. Comic books, he notes, almost from the outset, 'had the capacity to harness a powerful repertoire of images around adolescence, growth and the assumption of responsibility'. These tales appealed both to youthful readers and adults 'with an investment in how cultural representations of youth and growing up are organized'.[3]

*The Amazing Spider-Man* from the 1960s was certainly not the first superhero comic book to offer a form of Bildungsroman, but it was one of the clearest expressions of the form in comic books. Although designated 'Spider-Man', Peter Parker was a high school student when he obtained his powers after being bitten by a radioactive spider on a school field trip. From his origins in 1962 to his marriage in 1987, Spider-Man's superhero adventures went hand-in-hand with the classic development from callow youth to formed adult typical of the Bildungsroman. Already an orphan and living with an older uncle and aunt in the first Spider-Man story, as the tale unfolds his failure to stop a robber later results in the death of his Uncle Ben at the hands of that same thief. If the burden of this was not enough his frail Aunt May had scant resources and money was a constant worry. At school as Peter Parker he was constantly bullied and mocked by the sports jock and the cool kids. Initially in his part-time job at the *Daily Bugle* he mooned over Betty Brant, a secretary, but *Spider-Man*'s writers threw Mary Jane Watson, the daughter of a friend of his aunt, into this mix in late 1966. Later, in college, his love interest shifted to a fellow student, Gwen Stacey. In this process Peter Parker–Spider-Man developed greater depths of emotional and psychological fortitude. In 1971, the steadiness of the character was such that apparently the Nixon White House asked the publisher to do an anti-drugs story in which Spider-Man confronted and condemned the use of hard drugs. Although the Comics Code of the era banned the mention of drugs, Marvel produced a three-part story in May–July 1971.[4]

*Spider-Man*, though, was not alone in showing distinct traces of the Bildungsroman. Archie Andrews, the central character of the eponymous range of *Archie* comics, might seem the least likely of all comic book characters to be considered as having any connection to the Bildungsroman form. Stuck as he is in perpetual teenagehood Archie seemingly never develops at all and learns nothing that could be considered achieving an emotional depth or maturity. But as Bart Beaty perceptively demonstrates, one of the commonly perceived tenets of Archie's story, that it involves an unresolved competition between Veronica and Betty for Archie's affections, is misleading, or at least was so during the 1960s. He shows that Archie was very much in a relationship with Veronica, albeit a fraught one, and that Betty was in fact an interloper who maliciously sought to break up the pair due to her obsession with Archie. As Beaty points out, at times Betty's behaviour reached pathological levels.[5] In the 1960s Archie's preference for Veronica can be read as a sensible decision on the road to stability and adulthood with the only flaw in his choice being that Veronica had not yet reached such a level of maturity. That is, in the 1960s Archie progressed all the way up to the end point of teenagehood and obtaining a form of maturity, but clearly for what were commercial reasons, could never bring closure to that moment. Archie remains stuck in a never-ending tale of development.

These examples notwithstanding, the interest in comics as a form of Bildungsroman stems from the wave of graphic novels published in increasing numbers since the success of Art Spiegelman's *Maus*. To be sure, *Maus* is often thought of more for Spiegelman's representation strategies of using anthropomorphised animals to represent Jews, Germans and Poles, but as Joshua Brown notes it is a work of history and one that demonstrates how oral accounts can be used to shape historical narratives. He argues that *Maus* is 'a successful work of history because it fails to provide the reader with a catharsis, with the release of tension gained through the complacent construct of knowing all'.[6] Brown's vision of history then has a certain open-endedness and he sees historical works, at least those of merit, as not providing the catharsis so often present in Bildungsromane. As history, *Maus* slides into the realm of the Bildungsroman by in part being Spiegelman's tale of his own passage to adult awareness, something that one realises in reading the book that he only achieved through the creation of *Maus*. The second volume of *Maus* created a minor kerfuffle at the *New York Times* about whether it should be categorised as fiction or history/memoir. Although resolved in favour of history/memoir, the issue at hand seems to have been the form of representation and comic art traditions, more than the content per se.[7]

### Bildungsromane and the Autobiographical Graphic Narrative

Deciding to read autobiographical graphic novels as Bildungsromane requires some examination of the reasons for doing so. In the introduction to his edited collection of essays on autobiography and graphic novels, Michael A. Chaney draws on the work of Sidonie Smith and Julia Watson to remind readers that 'the pact negotiated between the generic clues of a text and a reader trained by convention to recognize them determines whether a text will be read as fiction . . . or as autobiography'. Thus, he says, 'the question of whether any given narrative belongs to fiction or auto-biography is ultimately one that readers must negotiate'.[8] In her *Autobiographical Comics*, Elisabeth El Refaie takes up this point. El Refaie argues that genres are now more porous and that writers' and readers' conventions and expectations have shifted. She ties autobiographical work to identity construction through stories, whether real or imagined. With regard to autobiographical comics the decision on whether to read the work as Bildungsroman again comes back to how readers situate the author; how loosely or tightly they connect the life being written about with the person doing the writing. El Refaie points to David Herman's work on narrative to explain the multiplicity of an author in autobiographical work: the real-life person, the person narrating, and the person being spoken about. As with *Maus*, the process of gathering the maturity gained in a Bildungsroman comes not just through the experience, but the reflection on that experience, through writing or reading, something that is always an engaged act. Furthermore, with at least some autobiographical comics, such as the work of Harvey Pekar, the writer and the artist are a separate entity, which complicates the notion of autobiography if the construction of that genre is taken to be an act of writing or creation of the text by a single individual.

Much of what separates autobiography from Bildungsroman is the notion that the former has a closer relationship to the truth or a verisimilitude that the latter lacks. But should this determine the way a work is analysed? Truth, or the reasonable approximation of what happened in the past, is the business of historians. Memoirs and autobiographies fall elsewhere on a scale of exactitude about the past. Art Spiegelman's insistence that *Maus* be classified as History stems from the very real concern about deniers of the Holocaust, something that drove him to the meticulous research that contextualises his father's tale. But to take a random example the same cannot be said for Alison's Bechdel's *Fun Home* (2006), similar in that it is a double narrative, but wildly dissimilar in that there are not deniers of her father's life and experiences. Rather than focus on the issue of 'truth', which in any case as Bart Beaty notes, 'fundamentally deadens the instrumentality of autobiographical study', perhaps it is best to sidestep the issue entirely except in so far as the rhetorical strategy of writing autobiography and memoir colours the narrative.[9] In other words, looking at the narrative itself rather than being preoccupied with genre concerns offers an entry point to examining what graphic novels bring to the concept of the Bildungsroman. It is the unique ways in which graphic texts can depict memory and time that defines their specific contribution to the Bildungsroman genre. In what follows I consider a number of texts for the ways in which they engage with what it means to move through time, or be stuck in it, and the implications of those two experiences for a sense of coming of age.

Many graphic novels that we read as Bildungsromane are memoirs. That is, the processes of development are shown from a present point of view. What these graphic novels add most to Bildungsromane is what the comic art form can achieve on the page. The first page of *Maus* is a useful example. The page and *Maus* begin by establishing the place and time: Rego Park, N.Y. c. 1958. This descriptor sits above a panel that extends across the whole page. In that panel two narrative boxes describe the scene: 'It was summer I remember I was ten or eleven . . . ' and ' . . . I was roller-skating with Howie and Steve'. The image in the panel is of three anthropomorphised mice roller-skating on a suburban sidewalk. In the next panel the narrator tells us ' . . . 'til my skate came loose' and within the panel an inset shows this happening and the remainder of the panel is a close-up of the mouse with the striped shirt from the first panel exclaiming 'Ow!' and in the process of falling. In the first panel the author is present both in the 1986 present of the book's publication in the form of the narrator, and as a skater in the circa 1958 of his memories. And right at the start, with the innocuous seeming 'c.' and the 'I was ten or eleven', Spiegelman directs the reader to the problems of memory. In the second panel Spiegelman as narrator is still present and also doubly present in 1958, or thereabouts, through a panel within a panel showing two moments depicting the cause and effect of his fall. Throughout *Maus* Spiegelman narrates and appears at different stages of his life. The whole story, then, is an act of memory. And supplemented as it is by research, the prime moving force of the book is Art recovering the memories of his father Vladek. Spiegelman showed the way that in the comic form the present can address the past with an immediacy not available in other printed forms. The graphic novel as Bildungsroman is not simply a story told but a story revealed through a medium that allows self-reflexive representation in a liminal space, often as tightly focused as a moment captured in a single panel. That is, the process of maturation and understanding is not just told or shown, but through the pages of the comic takes effect. Other mediums, including prose novels, can do this, but it is the immediacy of comic art that sets graphic novels apart. The achievements of graphic novels in this regard might be understood by examining how such effects are achieved in other mediums. In graphic novels, though, it is through a complex process including the history of the form itself.

Pat Grant's graphic novel *Blue* (2012) is a meditation on an Australian childhood at a beachside town. Everything in it is, he says, 'bullshit'. Bullshit as Grant uses it here is roughly the equivalent of the yarns (stories) Australians tell each other in pubs. There is a kernel of truth in them, but the spinner of the yarn does not let the truth get in the way of a good story. Life's events are told in a manner that the teller thinks they should have happened. For Americans, this is somewhat akin to Elwood saying to Jake in the 1980 film *The Blues Brothers*, 'It wasn't a *lie*, it was just *bullshit*.' Grant's bullshit veers very close to his own experience. Like his protagonists, Grant lived in a beachside town, wagged (cut) school to go surfing and once went to look at the remains of a body on a train track, before backing out at the last minute like his characters. Many Australians will recognise aspects of their own childhood and youth in this story and certainly those who grew up near beaches, even the non-surf suburban bay beaches of Melbourne, will connect with aspects of the story. Grant brings an appreciation of the role played by memory in so many comic stories to the telling of his narrative and to his understanding of the medium. In an essay in *Blue* he explains that Shaun Tan (*The Arrival*, 2006) told him that 'comics are almost always about memory about looking back, about making sense of the past'. Grant adds:

> It may be that all storytelling is about memory to some extent, but cartooning seems more powerfully linked to juvenile vocabularies of being and knowing than other kinds of writing. Sinking into the story space that comic art affords us – as cartoonists, but also as readers – is to step back into an adolescent or pre-adolescent state, bypassing the analytical and historical filters with which we, as adults, process sensory data. This leaves us exposed to raw, emotive readings of time, space and form. Comic art seems to be the key that many people need to access a chamber of their psyche that is otherwise locked away from the adult consciousness.

For Grant the history of comics 'consists of a thousand coming of age narratives tangled up together in an unruly lump'.[10]

Scholarship on comics tries to unpick this unruly lump into threads using different analytical approaches. Consider *Maus*, which gave rise to a boom in scholarly work on comics. Joseph (Rusty) Witek, the first academic to write at length about *Maus*, treated it as history in his *Comic Books as History*. In *Alternative Comics: An Emerging Literature* Charles Hatfield examined *Maus* and other works by artists and writers such as Gilbert

Hernandez and Harvey Pekar through their autobiographical aspects. Other scholars developed studies of trauma and memory around *Maus* including Marianne Hirsch's concept of post-memory, a powerful explanation of the way that the trauma of Holocaust survivors and their memories remain with their children as memory, but acquired through discursive frameworks and lived experience at one degree of removal from the events.[11] These graphic novels or narratives, then, are open to various methods of interpretation; approaching them as a means of meditating on the nature of the Bildungsroman is but one. Furthermore, the range and style of graphic novels is extensive and if one takes these to be just a form of comic art media, without taking into consideration superhero comics, Archie comics or indeed Disney comics, then the range of genres is still extensive. Trying to discuss *the* graphic novel, or even particular types of graphic novels, and Bildungsromane is then counterproductive and rather than doing so I examine several different graphic narratives and their relationship to the Bildungsroman as indicative of the sort of work being done in this medium.

## Fun Home

Alison Bechdel's *Fun Home* is a particularly useful work to show the strengths of graphic novels as Bildungsromane. Comparing Bechdel's narrative strategies in her book with the other telling of her story in the Tony-award-winning Broadway musical version of *Fun Home* (2015) reveals the ability of the form to represent negotiations of the past in a contemporaneous manner. Bechdel is present in the graphic *Fun Home* in three manners: as a young girl living at home, a college student, and, through the narrative voice of the text boxes, the adult author of the story. In the stage version three actresses play Bechdel at these different ages. Staged as theatre in the round the musical achieves a seamless interweaving of the different moments of Bechdel's narrative. The complexity of *Fun Home* in its book form becomes apparent by the presence of the adult Bechdel as narrator; that is, the only way to make the story work on stage was to have the book's narrative boxes represented by an actor as the author. The musical then draws out and highlights the importance of the narrator's voice. To put this another way: if a reader unfamiliar with comic conventions saw the musical first and then read the graphic novel she might search in vain for the adult Bechdel, not realising her presence is in the narrative text boxes. The presence of the narrator makes *Fun Home* an interaction with the past. The story is not simply being told, but represented as being created and the structure of the book draws the reader in to that conceit.

Bechdel uses comic art's capacities to literally show, not tell, her story to full advantage. As she unpacks the past and shows us her passage to adulthood she recreates in simulations of diaries, passages from books, maps, photographs, cartoons, and the array of flotsam and jetsam that are the souvenirs of life. The story has three key plot devices: Bechdel's growth into self-recognition as a lesbian, her father Bruce's hidden sexuality, and his suicide. In the book, only one of these is rock solid: Bechdel is a lesbian. Her father Bruce was most likely a closeted gay man, but Bechdel leaves open the possibility that he might have been bisexual or perhaps better described as queer and he certainly comes across as a queer fish. Likewise, in her telling, it is possible that his death, when he was hit by a truck, was an accident. Because the narrative is episodic, and not linear, *Fun Home*'s verisimilitude effect is in part achieved through mirroring the ways in which people remember their lives. Few people sit down and examine their life in a linear fashion. Sorting photographs or discovering forgotten diaries might bring back certain memories and most likely these do not immediately require contextualisation beyond the immediacy of the moment they capture. Likewise, hearing a song that triggers memories will not lead to a long reverie lining up songs that trigger memories in a linear fashion, but rather go to specific moments or episodes in a life. Bechdel presents herself as an unreliable witness because, for instance, the adult author tells us the young Bechdel stopped recording events in her diary, or if she did so, became somewhat opaque in her manner. At a meta level *Fun Home* is Bechdel's meditation on reaching maturity and like *Maus*, the act of creating the work, at least in the way this act of creation is represented in the book, is the moment of realising the maturation, the passage to which the book traces.

In his comic book *Ice Haven* (2005) Daniel Clowes created the character Harry Naybors, a comic book critic. Done partially tongue-in-cheek in response to what Clowes perceived as the ridiculousness of such an undertaking, some of what the character says has been described by Hillary Chute, an academic who specialises in graphic narratives, as 'a really articulate, apt description of comics'. Chute has a point: Clowes through Naybors posits that comics have endured:

> as a vital form [because] while prose tends toward pure 'interiority,' coming to life in the reader's mind, and cinema gravitates towards 'exteriority' of experiential spectacle, perhaps 'comics,' in its embrace of both the

interiority of the written word and the physicality of image, more closely replicates the true nature of human consciousness and the struggle between private self-definition and corporeal 'reality'.[12]

Such a way of regarding comics helps us understand the way in which we read comics, both in the formal sense of cognitive process, and in the ways that our reading produces recognition, appreciation and pleasure.

### American Born Chinese

Rocío Davis, a scholar with an interest in Asian American autobiography, has described Gene Luen Yang's *American Born Chinese* (2007) as a work that embodies 'an autobiographical perspective' in the way he 'draws the Asian American process of ethnic appreciation and self-acceptance'. As Davis notes, *American Born Chinese* comes in three parts: a retelling of the Monkey King story from *Journey to the West* with an added Christian twist to the Buddhist tale; a Bildungsroman in the story of Jin Wang, a Chinese American boy looking for his place in life; and in Yang's words, 'a sit-com on paper' that plays with racial stereotypes of Chinese and the infamous William Hung of *American Idol* fame.[13] Another multi-award-winning graphic narrative like *Fun Home*, Yang's work though is not so immediately obvious as a memoir and more closely fits a tight definition of the Bildungsroman, if for no other reason than the three-part arrangement places it firmly in the domain of fiction rather than memoir and autobiography. Yang interweaves the three parts, to create a coming-of-age story in which the parts of the self are eventually resolved in a holistic fashion. By reworking *Journey to the West* with a Christian theme Yang is able to use the Monkey King to represent a Chinese counterpoint to his character's American present. In the 'sit-com on paper' section of the novel Yang deploys a bucktoothed, queue-wearing, stereotyped depiction of a Chinese, Chin-Kee, to unsettle his Americanised character Danny. As the novel reaches its dénouement Yang reveals Chin-Kee as the Monkey King and Danny as a transmogrified Jin Wang. Danny is a false identity for Jin Wang and he needs Chin-Kee/the Monkey King to intercede to find his true self, and redemption (here we have a thinly disguised Christian theme) with his friend Wei-Chen.

*American Born Chinese* is, then, a Bildungsroman in which Jin Wang comes of age. What makes it distinctive and adds to the form is its manner of telling as a graphic narrative. The use of the stereotypical Chin-Kee is something that could only be done visually. As John Kuo-Wei Tchen showed in his book *New York before Chinatown* images of the Chinese in America were highly varied and the meaning attributed to an image, for instance of a man wearing Chinese garb and effecting a queue, was not fixed as a racist cliché until late in the nineteenth century.[14] The opprobrium heaped on Chinese in America coincided with the development of a rich visual culture in various illustrated magazines that mixed politics with humour, or what passed for humour. In particular on the West Coast, in San Francisco in the pages of *The Wasp*, a virulent anti-Chinese sentiment found its clearest expression in editorial cartoons with horrible racist caricatures.[15] These images swiftly moved across various printed forms of American culture including trade cards (small playing-card-sized advertisements for products), some of which spruiked the advantages of celluloid shirt collars because they would lead to the expulsion of Chinese both from laundry work and from the United States. The point here is that a Bildungsroman about coming to terms with identity and being an American-born person of Chinese origin has much to gain from the comics medium because the sort of stereotypes that need to be grappled with have long found expression visually. By introducing Chin-Kee, Yang takes on over a hundred years of racist images of Chinese. Just as *Maus* achieved some of its emotional power as a telling of the Holocaust by depicting Jews as mice, this direct confrontation with the racist imagery, and the shy admittance that such imagery creates self-doubt and self-hate and a desire to distance Chinese American identity from a Chinese past and a fresh-off-the-boat (FOB) present, is what makes *American Born Chinese* such a notable Bildungsroman. The graphic element of the book is key to Danny/Jin Wang's attainment of a new sense of self.

## The Diary of a Teenage Girl

Phoebe Gloeckner's *The Diary of a Teenage Girl* (2002) at first glance is closer to a classical Bildungsroman than other graphic narratives. In the introduction to the 2015 revised edition Gloeckner states firmly that the book is a novel. Moreover, she says the book is 'not history, or documentary or a confession, and memories will be altered or sacrificed, for factual truth has little significance in the pursuit of emotional truth'.[16] And yet it is no secret that Gloeckner is the source for her character, fifteen-year-old Minnie Goetze who has a sexual relationship with her mother's lover. The book is an equal mix of prose and comic art with much of the prose from Gloeckner's diary as a fifteen-year-old, some of the pages of which are reproduced in their original form as an appendix to the 2015 edition.

Hillary Chute describes the book as the rawest she has ever read.[17] The book is certainly bracing and reads as if one of Joan Didion's young subjects in her famous 1960s essay on the scene in San Francisco, 'Slouching Towards Bethlehem', had begun to chronicle her life without Didion's cool distance and whiff of moral disdain. And although *The Diary of a Teenage Girl* concludes with Minnie realising that she is better than the 'son-of-a bitch' she has been fucking (it is hard to think of the act having much to do with love) this could well be a temporary state of affairs, because throughout the book Minnie comes to crystal-clear realisations and certainties only to abandon them a day or two later, as is common enough for fifteen-year-olds. Moreover, Gloeckner in a 2015 interview with the AV Club describes this character (both in her book and the man himself) as 'not the type of person who's able to reflect on any of that'. And while *The Diary of a Teenage Girl* is a reflection on her circumstances, Gloeckner remains reluctant to close down the lived quality of the circumstances by labelling what occurred. Her exchange with the AV Club interviewer shows her state of mind:

AVC:   What term do you use to describe it yourself? Abuse, an affair, rape, a relationship?

PG:   Well, the thing is, I don't really judge it as simply as calling it one thing or another. If I did, I don't think I could have written the book the way I did. I was trying to just describe it exactly as it was for that girl. She wasn't thinking in those terms, because she wasn't able to, so I wasn't thinking in those terms. It is a relationship, it's a sexual relationship. To say it's abuse or rape is, again, qualifying it in a way that's in a sense simplifying it, and that wasn't my intent.[18]

Gloeckner's reluctance to label this act at the centre of her novel because that would simplify what occurred also means that there is none of the sort of closure that, say, Spiegelman, Bechdel and Yang achieve. The rawness of the book in many ways is because Gloeckner chooses to hold on to the trauma at its centre, whereas the aforementioned three tend to resolve it through their work. But perhaps Gloeckner's resolution, and the lesson she takes from Minnie, is to not latch on to certitudes that she will most likely abandon.

*The Diary of a Teenage Girl* also demonstrates one of the limits of the graphic form in representation. For Chute the book 'stands alone . . . for its brave, unabashed take on the complexities of life' at fifteen. But of course, as she says, that is 'just in the prose', although her 'just' is pointing to the other strengths of the book whereas my use here is pointing to a limit.[19]

Depicting sex between a minor and an adult visually over the course of a graphic narrative might, and in some countries almost certainly would, be considered child pornography. (In Australia, for instance, a man was put on a good behaviour bond for possessing child pornography in the form of a satirical take on *The Simpsons*.[20]) In prose the story, although haunting, passes somewhat more innocuously, even if one or two of the illustrated plates accompanying this portion of the novel might raise an eyebrow. Gloeckner's Minnie had a brutal entry into an adult world that no child or teenager should experience. But Bildungsromane so often deal with growing awareness of sexuality and its physical manifestations.

## This One Summer

Mariko Tamaki and her cousin Jillian Tamaki's *This One Summer* (2014) offers a lighter, if no less serious story of a girl coming of age. The context makes the difference: far from the contemptuous, self-loathing adults and the hedonistic San Francisco scene that Gloeckner's Minnie has to contend with, the Tamakis' characters Rose and Windy are surrounded by more grounded adults and the surface pleasantness of a lakeside holiday town. Whereas *The Diary of a Teenage Girl* is told from the perspective of an adult looking back *This One Summer* unfolds in a present with a young narrator. Gloeckner's narrative choice holds the significant traumas of the past at a distance as a way of containing them. There is just enough slippage between fiction and autobiography that this strategy lets a reader experience the struggles of a teenager surrounded by destructive adults but at a distance, where the author's ability to tell it provides some small reassurances of survival. *This One Summer*, told from the perspective of a pubescent girl, can afford to be more intimate so that moments that an adult might look back on, and understand as minor misunderstandings or confusion, capture the way that in the moment pubescence, in and of itself, is traumatic. The book moves from breezy light moments of summer to its darker storms. Windy is fascinated by the idea of developing 'boobs', but hers is a child's fascination with the idea of the body and its functions, innocent of the potential for trauma. The slightly older Rose is not as fascinated with the notion and as the story progresses she finds herself with a puzzling crush on Duncan, an older boy. The sense of a developing body and what accompanies it is more of a reality and hence more perplexing for Rose. Mariko Tamaki sets up a binary between Rose's mother Alice, who has lost a baby, and Jenny, one of the restless teenagers in town, who is pregnant, possibly by Duncan. The binary plays out in the penultimate pages of the book when Alice, who miscarried her baby while swimming the previous summer, and who has avoided the water all summer long, saves Jenny when the latter attempts to drown herself. The book hints strongly that this moment will cause both Alice and Jenny to overcome their depressive states.

The book ends with Rose's luggage noticeably heavier than when she arrived and this visual image seems to point to her coming of age. Stated bluntly like this the metaphor might seem forced, but the panel is easy enough to pass over and it may well be that only a reader looking for clues would associate it with the qualities suggesting a coming of age. Or perhaps the bag is heavy from the rocks she collected following a habit picked up from her father. It seems that she removes these rocks because two panels later her bag seems lighter. This might signal a reconciliation with her mother, possibly achieved in part by a shift from identification with her father to her mother, or simply leaving behind aspects of her childhood. Importantly, in the passage before, Windy signals her lack of development by passing Rose a packet of Twizzlers, Windy's snack of choice all summer long. Food, it seems, is Windy's subliminal defence against maturing before her time. Mariko's writing is more than supported by Jillian Tamaki's art that shifts effortlessly between brooding interiors in close-ups, to brilliantly lit sun-drenched expanses of beaches, from the lushness of woods, to the cool depth of water and more. She contrasts Rose's father Evan's somewhat contained exuberance listening to Rush with Windy's sheer uninhibited *joie de vivre* when listening to music. And by shifting from pages with multiple panels showing action close-up in very tight sequential time (174–5), to pages with relatively few panels that show a longer passage of time (178), and pages where the image is surrounded by blankness (245) the Tamakis convey the way in which the sense of time on any given day of a summer holiday can stretch out beyond its metaphysical bounds and achieve a timelessness and stillness. The choice to work in an indigo blue colour palette adds lushness to forest scenes, stillness to Tamaki's nights and a depth to her water.

As the novel ends, what weighs more on the reader is a departure from the liminal space of summer rather than Rose's coming of age (particularly since there is no physical evidence of that in breast development or menstruation) and what that might mean. The last pages show the detritus of summer (the aforementioned collected rocks) on Rose's bed and a clock is ticking. The final page is blank save for one more 'tick' and 'Boobs would be cool'.[21] The story ends on a melancholy note because summer is over. For the adult reader, this type of summer has probably long since passed and a certain type of wistful nostalgia creeps in and a longing for space and time when things just happen and time seems slowed down. The novel serves as a reminder that the things that happened were not always easy to deal with, but the time to let them unfold was precious. This is a useful redemptive nostalgia and reminds us that while it might be impossible to recreate such spaces the effort might be useful. And, of course, it reminds us of the importance of bodily changes in women's lives. The novel does not fully resolve what it is that Rose takes from the summer. Mariko Tamaki explained in an interview that, 'I think most people spend their whole lives trying to figure out how and what to be. As I understand it, it's not something that stops with adulthood. I think adolescence is interesting because it's the start of this process. Everything is just that much more on the surface than it is when you're an adult.'[22] Like Gloeckner's work, there is no hard and fast resolution and this underpins the importance of time and space for reflection and simply being, as *This One Summer* so wonderfully depicts.

## The Story of My Tits

Jennifer Hayden's title *The Story of My Tits* (2015) might seem to promise a coming-of-age story centred on a girl's anxiety about developing the bodily attributes of womanhood. And that story is indeed part of this book, but Hayden extends the story beyond this opening tale to her life with and without her tits. Diagnosed with breast cancer at forty-three Hayden had a double mastectomy and when recovering read a graphic novel. In this moment, she 'felt this deep stirring clarity. Certainty. The almost sexual heat of ignition'. The result was the decision to create her graphic novel, because it seemed that 'you can do anything with this format'.[23] Inspired by yoga Hayden tries to let go of her regrets and anxieties and to live in the present and *The Story of My Tits* is a manifestation of that effort, treating with humour the trauma of previous cancers in her family, overcoming the anxiety of what people will think about the stories she has to tell, and in the making of the graphic novel very much living in the present. Again, as in so many other graphic novels, the form of Hayden's spiritual education is the graphic novel in the reader's hand and this represents her hard-earned wisdom that 'we go on living with our uncertainties' and her expression that it is far easier to do so if we can remain humorous in the face of life's hardships (344). Does the genre require both an epiphany and closure? If both then Hayden's desire to live in the present and the acknowledgement of continued uncertainty might seem the point at which the notion of

Bildungsroman has been stretched too far and loses its analytical usefulness. But if an epiphany about one's course in life, and some sense of how to live it usefully, is the key to Bildungsromane then *The Story of My Tits* might stretch, but not break the genre.

## Here

Richard McGuire's *Here* might seem out of place among this collection of graphic works that deal with themes relevant to the Bildungsroman. Originally published as a six-page, thirty-six-panel comic in the Art Spiegelman and Françoise Mouly edited magazine *Raw* in 1989, *Here* plays with the formal properties of comics showing panels within panels that depict different eras in the same space, a living room in a house and the same space before and after the house's existence, a technique that expanded the number of panels to eighty-five, and more importantly in a deceptively simple idea revolutionised the depiction of time and space in comics. No less a figure than Chris Ware, author of such acclaimed graphic works as *Jimmy Corrigan, the Smartest Kid on Earth* (2000) and *Building Stories* (2012) has waxed lyrical on its impact in exploring the potential of comics to represent 'space and time ... in a way that's closer to real memory and experience than anything that had come before in comics'.[24] In 2014 Pantheon published a three-hundred-page colour version of *Here*, which was accompanied by an e-book version and an exhibition at the Morgan Museum in New York City that traced the development of the book from the 1989 comic strip. In the e-book version a linear sense of time is further diffused because the reader can shuffle scenes in what seem infinite combinations.

In the 2014 version, the setting in the New Jersey township of Perth Amboy becomes clear because that town's Proprietary House, the one-time residence of the colonial governor of New Jersey, is depicted as being opposite the living room space depicted. In a panel depicting 1984, a girl doing a splits handstand thinks Ben Franklin lived in the house. In other panels showing 1775, a man referred to as William awaits the arrival of his father who is bringing William's son whom he has not seen for some years. William and his father are somewhat at odds over the ongoing disputes between the British Crown and its American colonies. All of this makes it rather clear to a historian, or anyone who takes a minute to check Wikipedia, that Benjamin Franklin did indeed have a connection to the house since his bastard son, William Franklin, occupied the house as the last Royal Governor of New Jersey and Benjamin reunited his bastard son with his own bastard son. The house in question then is on Kearny Ave, and internal evidence in the story makes it clear this is a depiction of McGuire's own living room, as indeed property records confirm. McGuire's innovation in opening graphic narrative's story-telling techniques to another layer of temporal representation seems to flow from an engagement with history and his own place in such a history. The work is full of referents to events and people around Perth Amboy. For instance, McGuire alludes to George Inness, a mid-nineteenth-century landscape painter with a connection to Perth Amboy, and to anyone familiar with Inness's work the reference is immediately clear since McGuire has captured the colour tones of Inness's lush work in the 1870s. A panel labelled 2011 depicts floods that hit the area in that year. *Here* reminds us that we do not reach maturity or spiritual awareness in a vacuum. The places we live in and the way we think about them, the memories and history we choose to bring to considering our lives, and indeed the futures we imagine, all play a role in our development. *Here* is not only an innovative comic, but a plea for historical imagination and the use of memory in shaping ourselves. *Here* is a testament, a Bildungsroman of sorts, to the role of McGuire's home in his development. Not just his home, but also his memories of it, and his memories of what he imagined in it and of it.

If Archie is forever coming of age because of the commercial strictures of a teen-based comic book, *Here* reminds us that we are all always coming of age. Memories and reflections on memories and history shape who we are. If classic Bildungsromane show us the passage to maturity then the recent crop of graphic novels also have that effect. But because of the sort of narrative strategies available to their creators, through the distinctive forms of comics, which are not just a mix of text and image, but rather something unique beyond that mix, they can show us that maturing is a process that we make, rather than simply undertake or live through, and then remember. If the classical Bildungsroman tends to suggest narrative closure then the graphic novel holds moments open through a particular way of telling stories that involves showing how events and processes are lived and remembered.

# Notes

## Introduction

1. Marc Redfield contends that the Bildungsroman 'does not properly exist' but rather 'exemplifies the ideological construction of literature by criticism' (Marc Redfield, 'Preface' in *Phantom Formations: Aesthetic Ideology and the Bildungsroman* (Ithaca and London: Cornell University Press, 1996), n.p.).
2. Tobias Boes, 'Introduction' to Karl Morgenstern, 'On the Nature of the Bildungsroman', *PMLA* 'Criticism in Translation' 124.2 (2009), p. 647.
3. Jeffrey L. Sammons, 'The Mystery of the Missing *Bildungsroman*, or: What Happened to Wilhelm Meister's Legacy?', *Genre* 14.2 (1981), p. 230.
4. Marc Redfield, 'The Bildungsroman' in David Scott Kastan (ed.), *The Oxford Encyclopedia of British Literature* (Oxford: Oxford University Press, 2006), n. p. [online].
5. Jerome Buckley says that 'the *Entwicklungsroman* [is] a chronicle of a young man's general growth rather than his specific quest for self-culture; the *Erziehungsroman* [emphasises] the youth's training and formal education' (Buckley, *Season of Youth: The Bildungsroman from Dickens to Golding* (Cambridge, MA: Harvard University Press, 1974), p. 13). Michael Minden defines the Künstlerroman as a novel that depicts 'how its subject becomes an artist' (Minden, *The German Bildungsroman: Incest and Inheritance* (Cambridge: Cambridge University Press, 1997), p. 32).
6. Jed Esty defines the Antibildungsroman as 'the plot of degeneration' and the Metabildungsroman as one that 'lay[s] bare the contingent elements of a progressivist genre'. (Esty, *Unseasonable Youth: Modernism, Colonialism, and the Fiction of Development* (Oxford: Oxford University Press, 2011), p. 13).
7. Both Martin Swales (1978) and Michael Beddow (1982) include Wieland's work in their genealogies of the German Bildungsroman; many other critics agree with Esther Kleinbord Labovitz that Goethe's is 'the archetype of the genre' (*The Myth of the Heroine: The Female Bildungsroman in the Twentieth Century* (New York: Peter Lang, 1986), p. 1), including Minden (p. 5), who describes Goethe's novel as 'seminal'.

8. Franco Moretti, *The Way of the World: The Bildungsroman in European Culture* (London: Verso, 2000), p. 5. Further references to this edition appear parenthetically.

9. Mann, quoted in Sammons, p. 240.

10. Kelsey L. Bennett, *Principle and Propensity: Experience and Religion in the Nineteenth-century British and American Bildungsroman* (Columbia: University of South Carolina, 2014), p. 1.

11. Michael Beddow, *The Fiction of Humanity: Studies in the Bildungsroman from Wieland to Thomas Mann* (Cambridge: Cambridge University Press, 1982), p. 1.

12. Martin Swales, *The German Bildungsroman from Wieland to Hesse* (Princeton, NJ: Princeton University Press, 1978), p. 12.

13. M. M. Bakhtin, '*The Bildungsroman* and Its Significance in the History of Realism (Toward a Historical Typology of the Novel)' in Caryl Emerson and Michael Holquist (eds.), *Speech Genres & Other Late Essays* (Austin: University of Texas Press, 1986), p. 23.

14. Minden, *The German Bildungsroman*, p. 5.

15. Bennett, *Principle and Propensity*, p. 6.

16. John Marks, *Gilles Deleuze: Vitalism and Multiplicity* (London: Pluto Press, 1998), p. 45.

17. Colin Wilson, *The Outsider* (London: Indigo, 1997), p. 51.

18. See, for example, Helena Feder, *Ecocriticism and the Idea of Culture: Biology and the Bildungsroman* (Abingdon, Oxon. & New York: Routledge, 2014), and Jill R. Ehnenn, 'Reorienting the Bildungsroman: Progress Narratives, Queerness, and Disability in *The History of Sir Richard Calmady* and *Jude the Obscure*', *Journal of Literary and Cultural Disability Studies* 11.2 (2017), pp. 151–68.

## Chapter 1 The German Tradition of the Bildungsroman

1. Fritz Martini discovered in 1961 that Karl Morgenstern used the term *Bildungsroman* in a series of essays published between 1817 and 1824: 'Der Bildungsroman: Zur Geschichte des Wortes und der Theorie' in Rolf Selbmann (ed.), *Zur Geschichte des deutschen Bildungsromans* (Darmstadt: Wissenschaftliche Buchgesellschaft, 1988), pp. 239–64. The essays have been republished in Selbmann (ed.), *Zur Geschichte*, pp. 45–99, and partially translated into English by Tobias Boes, *PMLA*, 124.2 (2009), pp. 650–9, who also provides a 'Critical Introduction' to the texts: *PMLA*, 124.2 (2009), pp. 647–9.

2. M. M. Bakhtin, 'The *Bildungsroman* and Its Significance in the History of Realism (Toward a Historical Typology of the Novel)' in Caryl Emerson and Michael Holquist (eds.), *Speech Genres & Other Late Essays* (Austin: University of Texas Press, 1986), p. 23.

3. Franco Moretti, *The Way of the World: The Bildungsroman in European Culture* (London: Verso, 1987), p. 5.

4. Norbert Elias, *The Court Society*, trans. Edmund Jephcott (New York: Pantheon, 1983).

5. Jean-Jacques Rousseau, *The Confessions*, trans. J. M. Cohen (London: Penguin, 1953), p. 17.

6. Ian Watt, *The Rise of the Novel: Studies in Defoe, Richardson and Fielding* (Berkeley and Los Angeles: University of California Press, 1957). Jürgen Habermas, *The Structural Transformation of the Public Sphere: An Inquiry into a Category of Bourgeois Society*, trans. Thomas Burger (Cambridge, MA: MIT Press, 1991).

7. Robert Darnton, *The Literary Underground of the Old Regime* (Cambridge, MA: Harvard University Press, 1982). Benedict Anderson, *Imagined Communities: Reflections on the Origin and Spread of Nationalism* (London: Verso, 1991).

8. Todd Kontje, *Private Lives in the Public Sphere: The German Bildungsroman as Metafiction* (University Park, PA: Pennsylvania State University Press, 1992).

9. Erich Auerbach, *Mimesis: The Representation of Reality in Western Literature*, trans. Willard R. Trask (Princeton: Princeton University Press, 1968), p. 17.

10. Anthologies of religious autobiographies included Gottfried Arnold, *Vitae Patrum oder Das Leben der Altväter* (*Lives of the Patriarchs*) (1699) and Johann Henrich Reitz, *Historie der Wiedergebohrnen* (*History of the Reborn*) (1691–1701). Heinrich Jung-Stilling's *Lebensgeschichte* (*Autobiography*) (1777–1804) built on this tradition and inspired the sixth book of *Wilhelm Meister's Apprenticeship*, 'Bekenntnisse einer schönen Seele' ('Confessions of a Beautiful Soul'). Influential works of epistolary fiction include Richardson, *Pamela* (1740) and *Clarissa* (1749); Rousseau, *Julie, ou La Nouvelle Héloïse* (1762); and Goethe, *Die Leiden des jungen Werther* (*The Sufferings of Young Werther*) (1774).

11. Ernst Ludwig Stahl, 'Die Entstehung des deutschen Bildungsromans im achtzehnten Jahrhundert' in Selbmann (ed.), *Zur Geschichte*, p. 127.

12. René Girard, *Deceit, Desire, and the Novel: Self and Other in Literary Structure*, trans. Yvonne Freccero (Baltimore and London: Johns Hopkins University Press, 1965), pp. 1–4.

13. Joan B. Landes, *Women in the Public Sphere in the Age of the French Revolution* (Ithaca: Cornell University Press, 1988), p. 158, p. 12.

14. See for instance John Smith, 'Cultivating Gender: Sexual Difference, *Bildung*, and the *Bildungsroman*', *Michigan Germanic Studies* 13.2 (1987), p. 220.

15. Moretti, *The Way of the World*, p. 22; Jeannine L. Blackwell, 'Bildungsroman mit Dame: The Heroine in the German *Bildungsroman*', Dissertation, Indiana University, 1982. See also Todd Kontje, *The German Bildungsroman: History of a National Genre* (Columbia, SC: Camden House, 1993), pp. 102–9.

16. Todd Kontje, *Women, the Novel, and the German Nation 1771–1871: Domestic Fiction in the Fatherland* (Cambridge University Press, 1998), p. 194.

17. On the proximity of some definitions of the Bildungsroman to popular fiction, see Martin Swales, *The German Bildungsroman from Wieland to Hesse* (Princeton University Press, 1978), pp. 11–12; Rolf Selbmann, *Der deutsche Bildungsroman*, Sammlung Metzler 214 (Stuttgart: Metzler, 1984), p. 37; and Selbmann, 'Einleitung' in Selbmann (ed.), *Zur Geschichte*, pp. 18–19.

18. Cited from Kontje, *The German Bildungsroman*, p. 24.

19. Jeffrey L. Sammons, 'The Mystery of the Missing *Bildungsroman*, or: What Happened to Wilhelm Meister's Legacy?', *Genre*, 14.2 (1981), pp. 229–46; Marc Redfield, *Phantom Formations: Aesthetic Ideology and the Bildungsroman* (Ithaca and London: Cornell University Press, 1996).

20. Jürgen Jacobs pursues this strategy in his study of *Wilhelm Meister und seine Brüder: Untersuchungen zum deutschen Bildungsroman* (Munich: Fink, 1972), declaring that one canonical Bildungsroman after the next fails to conform to the generic standard and concluding that the Bildungsroman is an 'unfulfilled genre'.

21. Thus Frederick Amrine dismisses the concept of the Bildungsroman as the critical equivalent of phlogiston that should be retired as a relic of outmoded scholarship: 'Rethinking the *Bildungsroman*', *Michigan Germanic Studies*, 13 (1987), p. 134. Sammons underscores the generic variety of late nineteenth-century German fiction that has been obscured by the focus on the Bildungsroman ('The Mystery'). See also Sammons, 'The Bildungsroman for Nonspecialists: An Attempt at a Clarification' in James N. Hardin (ed.), *Reflection and Action: Essays on the Bildungsroman* (University of South Carolina Press, 1991), pp. 26–45.

22. Northrop Frye, *Anatomy of Criticism: Four Essays* (Princeton University Press, 1957), p. 140.

23. In German usage the term *Entwicklungsroman* (novel of development) generally refers to a work of any era that focuses primarily on the development of a central character, while the term *Bildungsroman* is restricted to modern novels written no earlier than the late eighteenth century. See Lothar Köhn, *Entwicklungs- und Bildungsroman: Ein Forschungsbericht* (Stuttgart: Metzler, 1969), pp. 1–19, Melitta Gerhard, *Der deutsche Entwicklungsroman bis zu Goethes 'Wilhelm Meister'*, new edition (Bern and Munich: Francke, 1968), and Jürgen Jacobs and Markus Krause (eds.), *Der Deutsche Bildungsroman: Gattungsgeschichte vom 18. bis zum 20. Jahrhundert* (Munich: Beck, 1989). The Bildungsroman, in turn, is often

distinguished from the *Erziehungsroman* (pedagogical novel). Boundaries are fluid, but the Bildungsroman tends to depict the open-ended development of the protagonist, whereas the *Erziehungsroman* features a mentor who leads his pupil to a predetermined goal in the manner of Rousseau's *Émile* (1762).

24. Tobias Boes, *Formative Fictions: Nationalism, Cosmopolitanism, and the Bildungsroman* (Ithaca: Cornell University Press, 2012), p. 3.

25. Kontje, *The German Bildungsroman*.

26. Thomas Mann, 'Der Entwicklungsroman' in Mann, *Essays*, Hermann Kurzke and Stephan Stachorski (eds.) (Frankfurt am Main: Fischer, 1993), vol. 1, p. 289.

27. Mann devoted much of the First World War to a long essay, *Betrachtungen eines Unpolitischen* (*Reflections of a Nonpolitical Man*, 1918).

28. Hans Schwerte, *Faust und das Faustische: Ein Kapitel deutscher Ideologie* (Stuttgart: Klett, 1962).

29. Richard J. Evans, *The Coming of the Third Reich* (New York: Penguin, 2003), p. xxv. See also W. H. Bruford on the political dangers of *The German Tradition of Self-Cultivation: 'Bildung' from Humboldt to Thomas Mann* (Cambridge University Press, 1975).

30. Rüdiger Safranski, *Romantik: Eine deutsche Affäre* (Munich: Hanser, 2007), pp. 370–1.

31. Wilhelm Dilthey, 'Der Bildungsroman' in Selbmann (ed.), *Zur Geschichte*, pp. 120–1.

32. On the 'emphatically devolved' character of Imperial Germany, see Christopher Clark, *Iron Kingdom: The Rise and Downfall of Prussia, 1600–1947* (Cambridge, MA: Harvard University Press, 2006), pp. 556–7. David Blackbourn also notes that 'the federal Empire resembled more closely the present-day European Union than it did contemporary federal (but republican) states such as the USA or Switzerland' in his *History of Germany 1780–1918: The Long Nineteenth Century* (Oxford: Blackwell, 1997), p. 200.

33. James J. Sheehan, *German History 1770–1866* (Oxford: Clarendon, 1989), p. 14. Further references to this edition appear parenthetically.

34. Reinhart Koselleck, *Kritik und Krise: Eine Studie zur Pathogenese der bürgerlichen Welt*, Suhrkamp Taschenbuch Wissenschaft 36 (Frankfurt am Main: Suhrkamp, 1976), p. 30.

35. Anderson, *Imagined Communities*, p. 7; see also Lynn Hunt, *The Family Romance of the French Revolution* (Berkeley: University of California Press, 1992).

36. Johann Wolfgang Goethe, *Gedichte 1756–1799* in Goethe, *Sämtliche Werke: Briefe, Tagebücher und Gespräche*, Karl Eibl (ed.) (Frankfurt am Main: Deutscher Klassiker Verlag, 1987), vol. 1, p. 507.

37. Klaus Epstein uses the term *Reform Conservative* to distinguish individuals such as Lothario from those who defended the status quo and others who wanted to turn back the clock to an earlier age: *The Genesis of German Conservatism* (Princeton University Press, 1966), pp. 7–22. See also Dieter Borchmeyer, *Höfische Gesellschaft und französische Revolution bei Goethe: Adliges und bürgerliches Wertsystem im Urteil der Weimarer Klassik* (Kronberg: Athenäum, 1977), pp. 164–70, and Rolf-Peter Janz, 'Zum sozialen Gehalt der *Lehrjahre*' in Helmut Arntzen (ed.), *Literaturwissenschaft und Geschichtsphilosophie: Festschrift für Wilhelm Emrich* (Berlin: de Gruyter, 1975), pp. 320–40.

38. Friedrich Schiller, *On the Aesthetic Education of Man in a Series of Letters*, trans. Reginald Snell (New York: Ungar, 1965), pp. 29–30.

39. Boes, *Formative Fictions*, pp. 38–42; see for instance Jacobs, *Wilhelm Meister und seine Brüder*, and Michael Minden, *The German* Bildungsroman: *Incest and Inheritance* (Cambridge University Press, 1997).

40. Cited from *Goethes Werke*, Erich Trunz (ed.) (Hamburg: Wegner, 1950), vol. 8, p. 571.

41. Franco Moretti, *Atlas of the European Novel 1800–1900* (London and New York: Verso, 1998), p. 66.

42. Although the novel has been translated as *Green Henry*, I use Heinrich to be consistent with the German spelling, as in Wilhelm, not William, Meister.

43. Gottfried Keller, *Der grüne Heinrich: Erste Fassung* in Keller, *Sämtliche Werke*, Thomas Böning and Gerhard Kaiser (eds.) (Frankfurt am Main: Deutscher Klassiker Verlag, 1954), vol. 2, p. 561.

44. Keller, 'Einkehr unterhalb des Rheinfalls' in *Sämtliche Werke*, vol. 1, p. 150. Keller made his controversial remarks about a potential pan-German federation in 1872, shortly after Imperial Germany had annexed Alsace. Keller refuted charges that he was advocating a similar German takeover of Switzerland in an open letter to the *Basler Nachrichten* on April 4, 1872 (*Sämtliche Werke*, vol. 7, pp. 287–9). On the public controversy caused by Keller's comments, see Emil Ermatinger, *Gottfried Kellers Leben* (Stuttgart: Cotta, 1918), pp. 435–7; and Adolf Muschg, *Gottfried Keller* (Munich: Kindler, 1977), pp. 276–7, as well as the detailed commentary in the critical edition, *Sämtliche Werke*, vol. 7, pp. 924–31.

45. Mann, 'Der Entwicklungsroman', *Essays*, vol. 1, p. 290.

46. Mann began *Felix Krull* before the First World War, but it remained a fragment for decades. He finally published part one of the novel in 1954, but died before he could complete the project.

47. Gerhart Mayer, 'Zum deutschen Antibildungsroman', *Jahrbuch der Raabe-Gesellschaft* (1974), pp. 41–64. In his subsequently published survey of the German Bildungsroman from Wieland to the present, Mayer examines

Bildungsromane and Antibildungsromane in successive eras of German literary history: *Der deutsche Bildungsroman: Von der Aufklärung bis zur Gegenwart* (Stuttgart: Metzler, 1992).

48. Moretti, *The Way of the World*, p. 63. In the immediate post-war period, Karl Schlechta wrote a withering critique of the authoritarian aspects of *Wilhelm Meister's Apprenticeship* and *Journeyman Years* that was largely ignored by other critics at the time but which anticipates Moretti's subsequent comments: *Goethes Wilhelm Meister* (Frankfurt am Main: Klostermann, 1953).

49. Thomas Mann, 'Einführung in den Zauberberg für Studenten der Universität Princeton' in Mann, *Gesammelte Werke in Zwölf Bänden* (Frankfurt am Main: Fischer, 1960), vol. 11, p. 616. On the place of *The Magic Mountain* in the German tradition of the Bildungsroman, see Russell A. Berman, 'Modernism and the *Bildungsroman*: Thomas Mann's *Magic Mountain*' in Graham Bartram (ed.), *The Cambridge Companion to the Modern German Novel* (Cambridge University Press, 2004), pp. 77–92.

50. Hermann J. Weigand, *Thomas Mann's Novel Der Zauberberg* (New York and London: Appleton-Century, 1933), p. 5.

51. Schiller to Goethe, November 28, 1796, in Emil Staiger (ed.), *Briefwechsel Schiller Goethe* (Frankfurt am Main: Insel, 1966), vol. 1, p. 319.

52. Friedrich Schlegel, 'Über Goethes Meister' in Ernst Behler (ed.), *Kritische Friedrich-Schlegel-Ausgabe* (Munich, Paderborn, Vienna: Thomas, 1967), vol. 2, p. 133.

53. David S. Luft, *Robert Musil and the Crisis of European Culture 1880–1942* (Berkeley: University of California Press, 1980), p. 18.

54. Thomas Mann, *The Magic Mountain*, trans. John E. Woods (New York: Vintage, 1995), p. 377. Further references to this edition appear parenthetically.

55. See the diary entries of October 7, 22, and November 19, 1918, and March 16, 1920. Thomas Mann, *Tagebücher 1918–1921*, Peter de Mendelssohn (ed.) (Frankfurt am Main: Fischer, 1979), p. 27, pp. 42–3, p. 86, p. 400.

56. Mann, *The Magic Mountain*, p. 487; italics in original. Further references to this edition appear parenthetically.

57. John Reddick, *The 'Danzig Trilogy' of Günter Grass: A Study of The Tin Drum, Cat and Mouse and Dog Years* (London: Secker and Warburg, 1975).

58. Günter Grass, 'To be continued …', trans. Michael Henry Heim, *PMLA* 115 (1999), p. 298.

59. P. Cornelius Tacitus, *Germania: Bericht über Germanien*, trans. Josef Lindauer (Munich: Deutscher Taschenbuch Verlag, 1977), section 2, p. 13.

60. Simon Schama, *Landscape and Memory* (New York: Knopf, 1995), pp. 75–134; Christopher B. Krebs, *A Most Dangerous Book: Tacitus's Germania from the Roman Empire to the Third Reich* (New York: Norton, 2011).

61. Celia Applegate, *A Nation of Provincials: The German Idea of Heimat* (Berkeley: University of California Press, 1990).

## Chapter 2  The French Bildungsroman

1. (No usages are listed for the plural Bildungsromane.) The authors and works concerned are Julien Gracq, *Préférences* (1961); Georges Perec, *La Disparition* (1969) and *Je suis né* (1990); Raymond Queneau, *Journaux 1914–65* (1996); François Nourissier, *À défaut de génie* (2000); Marcel Bénabou, *Écrire sur Tamara* (2002); Anne Garréta, *Pas un jour* (2002); Jacques Roubaud, *La Bibliothèque de Warburg: version mixte* (2002); Gérard Genette, *Bardadrac* (2006). FRANTEXT accessed 27 June 2016.

2. In Gracq, Perec (twice), Jean d'Ormesson, Régis Debray, Nourissier, Bénabou (three times).

3. François Jost, 'La tradition du Bildungsroman', *Comparative Literature*, 21.2 (1969), pp. 97–115; Jean-Marie Paul (ed.), *Images de l'homme dans le roman de formation ou Bildungsroman* (Nancy: Centre de Recherches Germaniques et Scandinaves, 1995); Philippe Chardin (ed.), *Roman de formation, roman d'éducation dans la littérature française et dans les littératures étrangères* (Paris: Kimé, 2007).

4. My arguments about differences between the 'French Bildungsroman' and those of other national cultures draw on a number of important analyses, in particular those of Franco Moretti, *The Way of the World: The Bildungsroman in European Culture* (London: Verso, 1987), and Chardin's edited collection of essays, *Roman de formation* (especially Chardin's own introduction, 'Avant-propos', pp. 7–20, and his chapter on Proust, 'Un genre se forme à tout âge: vieillissement et rajeunissement du roman de formation de Flaubert à Proust', pp. 135–48). See too Paul, who describes the mutation of the idea of 'formation' as more 'brutal' in France than elsewhere (Jean-Marie Paul, 'Avant-propos' in *Images de l'homme*, pp. 7–29 [p. 28 n. 2]). Also valuable here are Michael Beddow, *The Fiction of Humanity: Studies in the Bildungsroman from Wieland to Thomas Mann* (Cambridge University Press, 1982); Eric Downing, *After Images: Photography, Archaeology, and Psychoanalysis and the Tradition of Bildung* (Detroit: Wayne State University Press, 2006); Todd Kontje, *The German Bildungsroman: History of a National Genre* (Columbia, SC: Camden House, 1993); Michael Minden, *The German Bildungsroman: Incest and Inheritance* (Cambridge University Press, 1997); Lesley Sharpe (ed.), *The Cambridge Companion to Goethe* (Cambridge University Press, 2002); Martin Swales, *The German Bildungsroman from Wieland to Hesse* (Princeton University Press, 1978).

5. Moretti, *Way of the World*, p. 72.

6. See, for example, Régis Boyer, 'Peut-on considérer les sagas islandaises comme des romans de formation?' in Paul, *Images de l'homme*, pp. 33–47; Ellen McWilliams, *Margaret Atwood and the Female Bildungsroman* (Farnham, Surrey and Burlington, VT: Ashgate, 2009); Gregory Castle, *Reading the Modernist Bildungsroman* (Gainesville, FL: University Press of Florida, 2006).

7. The main text of this chapter henceforth normally refers simply to *Wilhelm Meister* rather than to *Wilhelm Meister's Apprenticeship*.

8. See Audrey Vermetten, 'La tradition du roman d'apprentissage dans l'œuvre de George Cukor' in Chardin, *Roman de formation*, pp. 109–18 (p. 111).

9. For the 'conformity/confirmation' narrative see, for example, Jean-Marie Paul, 'Avant-propos' in Paul, *Images de l'homme*, pp. 7–29 (p. 19).

10. *La Chanson de Roland* (n.p.: Librairie Générale Française, 1990), lines 4000–1. Unless otherwise stated, translations in this chapter are mine.

11. Michel de Montaigne, *Essays*, trans. J. M. Cohen (Harmondsworth: Penguin, 1958), p. 288 (from 'On the Art of Conversation', pp. 285–311).

12. *Critique of The School for Wives* (*La Critique de l'École des femmes*, 1663) (scene vi) in Molière, *Œuvres complètes*, vol. I (Paris: Gallimard, 1971).

13. Pierre Corneille, *Cinna* (Act V, scene iii, lines 1696–7) in *Œuvres complètes* (Paris: Seuil, 1963).

14. Marie-Madeleine de Lafayette, *La Princesse de Clèves* (Paris: Gallimard, 1972), p. 155.

15. On the dearth of siblings of the Bildungsroman hero see, for example, Minden, *German Bildungsroman*, p. 3.

16. Denis Diderot, *Le Neveu de Rameau* in *Œuvres romanesques* (Paris: Garnier, 1962), p. 492. The original manuscript was discovered at the end of the nineteenth century.

17. Johann Wolfgang von Goethe, *Wilhelm Meister's Apprenticeship*, ed. and trans. Eric A. Blackall in cooperation with Victor Lange (Princeton University Press, 1989). For the first statement ('Wilhelm was beginning to feel … '), see p. 105. For firmer ones: towards the end of the book Wilhelm is told that 'a man who drinks [error] to the dregs must recognise the error of his ways … '; he takes a proffered scroll, opens it and reads: *Certificate of Apprenticeship*. Later he objects that he is 'none the wiser', but is told that the Certificate's maxims 'have real solid foundation' (pp. 302–3, p. 336).

18. Minden describes it as a 'brilliant balance of randomness and regularity' and observes that it 'makes discontinuities appear, far from eradicating them' (*German Bildungsroman*, p. 22, p. 59).

19. See Gerhart Hoffmeister's essay 'Reception in Germany and abroad' in Sharpe, *Cambridge Companion to Goethe*, pp. 232–55. Goethe was, for example, seen as replacing classicist 'imitation' with creativity: this would contribute to key aesthetic manifestos by Stendhal and Hugo.

20. See John Isbell, *The Birth of European Romanticism: Truth and Propaganda in Staël's De l'Allemagne* (Cambridge University Press, 1994), p. 67, p. 81, p. 85, and especially pp. 86–9.

21. Marcel Proust, *In Search of Lost Time* (*À la recherche du temps perdu*, 1913–27), 4 vols. (Paris: Gallimard, 1987–9), IV 498. In the rest of this chapter, I shall refer to Proust's title as *À la recherche*, there being no satisfactory abbreviated form in English.

22. Terence Cave, *Mignon's Afterlives: Crossing Cultures from Goethe to the Twenty-First Century* (Oxford University Press, 2011), pp. 98–9.

23. Gérard de Nerval, *Les Chimères* (Geneva/Paris: Droz/Minard, 1966), p. 45.

24. See Cave's chapter three, 'Nineteenth-century French afterlives', pp. 87–124. As Cave suggests, Mignon's prominence was in part due to accidents of translation, her song being initially better known than *Wilhelm Meister* itself, but he shows that this is by no means the whole story.

25. See above, n. 17.

26. These aspects are emphasised by, for example, Castle, *Modernist Bildungsroman* (pp. 9–10, p. 19), and also by Swales, *German Bildungsroman* (p. 29, p. 32); by Kontje, *German Bildungsroman* (p. 88, p. 95); and by Moretti, *Way of the World*, p. 134, pp. 165–7, pp. 171–3, p. 199, p. 201.

27. Benjamin Constant, *Adolphe* (Paris: Garnier, 1968), p. 30.

28. René Girard, *Mensonge romantique et vérité romanesque* (Paris: Grasset, 1961).

29. Stendhal, *Le Rouge et le Noir* in Henri Martineau (ed.), *Romans et nouvelles*, vol. I (Paris: Gallimard, 1952), p. 252.

30. Moretti advances pertinent arguments for seeing French 'difference' in this area: see his chapters two and three, 'Waterloo Story' and 'The World of Prose'.

31. Critics have suggested that among the belief systems or ideologies contributing to an interest in personal or social improvement, hence helping to form the Bildungsroman, were (as mentioned) Christianity and the Enlightenment; 'Whiggishness' (faith in social progress); utopian socialism; later in the century, Darwinism; and eventually Fascism. See in particular Kontje's chapters two and three, 'Ideology and the German Bildungsroman (1848–1945)' and 'Postwar Critics and the German Bildungsroman', in his *German Bildungsroman* (also p. x for the 'Fascist appropriation' of the model and p. 21 for the 'politically conservative cultural élite' in whose hands the Bildungsroman long remained). Among other critics who make germane contributions in this area are Castle on the role of the Catholic Church (*Modernist Bildungsroman*, p. 29); Cave on humanism and 'enlightenment' (*Mignon*, p. 32, p. 245); McWilliams on socialism, the Nazi model, and feminism (*Margaret Atwood*, p. 8, p. 24, p. 28, p. 151); Chardin on the Enlightenment, religion, 'pre-Darwinism', pedagogy and 'Whiggishness' (for instance, the moralising, optimistic, 'progressist' tradition of

the Victorian Bildungsroman: *Roman de formation*, p. 18, p. 139, p. 143; see also, in the same volume, Florence Bancaud's and Didier Masseau's comments, p. 40, p. 41, p. 49, pp. 128–9); Paul on Christianity (*Images de l'homme*, p. 18); Minden on the Enlightenment (*German Bildungsroman*, p. 23); Downing on class, classical education and the 'brutal implications' of the Nazis' 'appropriation of Bildung' (*After Images*, p. 11, p. 274, p. 278). Finally, Hoffmeister refers to Goethe's 'anticipation' of both the Third Reich and socialist realism (in 'Reception', Sharpe, p. 246, pp. 248–9).

32. See Leo Bersani, *Balzac to Beckett: Center and Circumference in French Fiction* (New York: Oxford University Press, 1970); also Alison Finch on Balzac in 'The stylistic achievements of Flaubert's fiction' in Timothy Unwin (ed.), *The Cambridge Companion to Flaubert* (Cambridge University Press, 2004), pp. 145–64 (p. 148).

33. Honoré de Balzac, *Le Père Goriot* (Paris: Librairie Générale Française, 1961), pp. 434–5.

34. Honoré de Balzac, *La Cousine Bette* (Paris: Librairie Générale Française, 1963).

35. Gustave Flaubert, *Madame Bovary* (Paris: Bordas, 1990), pp. 41–2; trans. Geoffrey Wall, *Madame Bovary* (Harmondsworth: Penguin, 1992), p. 31. 'Free indirect style' is the indirect reporting of speech or, more often, thought without the indicators 'She supposed that', 'He wondered if', etc.

36. Jane Austen, *Emma* (London: Oxford University Press, 1966), p. 134, p. 136.

37. 'La bêtise consiste à vouloir conclure', letter of 4 September 1850 to Louis Bouilhet in Gustave Flaubert, *Correspondance*, 4 vols. (Paris: Gallimard, 1973–98), I, pp. 679–80.

38. Moretti states: 'With its lean and cold lucidity, *Sentimental Education* brings to an end a century of narrative attempts', and, still balder: 'The *Bildungsroman* is over' (*Way of the World*, p. 177).

39. See Jacques Suffel, 'Introduction' in Gustave Flaubert, *Trois Contes* (Paris: Garnier, 1969), pp. vi–vii.

40. However, Edmund Wilson's *Axel's Castle* (1931) tars all Western *fin de siècle* and early twentieth-century literature with the same brush: he claims that its foremost practitioners prefer the dream to the reality, the waiting to the event. But the work he deems quintessential is French (the one that supplies his title, Villiers de L'Isle-Adam's play *Axël*, 1886).

41. See Malcolm Bowie, 'The question of *Un coup de dés*' in Malcolm Bowie, Alison Fairlie, Alison Finch (eds.), *Baudelaire, Mallarmé, Valéry: New Essays in Honour of Lloyd Austin* (Cambridge University Press, 1982), pp. 142–50.

42. Arthur Rimbaud, *Œuvres* (Paris: Garnier, 1960), pp. 128–31.

43. See, for example, Christopher Prendergast, *Mirages and Mad Beliefs: Proust the Skeptic* (Princeton University Press, 2013), e.g. pp. 1–4.

44. Philippe Chardin, 'Un genre se forme à tout âge: vieillissement et rajeunissement du roman de formation de Flaubert à Proust' in Chardin, *Roman de formation*, pp. 135–48.

45. Some critics have doubted that *À la recherche* itself is the narrator's projected book; see, however, Jennifer Rushworth, 'Derrida, Proust, and the promise of writing', *French Studies*, 69.2 (2015), pp. 205–19.

46. Philip Kolb (ed.), Marcel Proust and Jacques Rivière, *Correspondance (1914–22)* (Paris: Plon, 1955), p. 3.

47. J. M. Cocking, *Proust: Collected Essays on the Writer and His Art* (Cambridge University Press, 1982), p. 25.

48. Both pieces are in Pierre Clarac and Yves Sandre (eds.), Marcel Proust, *Contre Sainte-Beuve, précédé de Pastiches et mélanges et suivi de Essais et articles* (Paris: Gallimard, 1971), pp. 478–81 and pp. 647–50.

## Chapter 3 The Bildungsroman and Nineteenth-Century British Fiction

1. See Kelsey L. Bennett, *Principle and Propensity: Experience and Religion in the Nineteenth-Century British and American Bildungsroman* (Columbia: University of South Carolina Press, 2014), p. 8.

2. Susan Fraiman, *Unbecoming Women: British Women Writers and the Novel of Development* (New York: Columbia University Press, 1993), p. 4.

3. Lorna Ellis, *Appearing to Diminish: Female Development and the British Bildungsroman, 1750–1850* (Lewisburg: Bucknell University Press, 1999).

4. Franco Moretti, *The Way of the World: The* Bildungsroman *in European Culture* (London: Verso, 2000), p. 12.

5. M. M. Bakhtin, 'The *Bildungsroman* and Its Significance in the History of Realism (Toward a Historical Typology of the Novel)' in Caryl Emerson and Michael Holquist (eds.), *Speech Genres & Other Late Essays* (Austin: University of Texas Press, 1986), pp. 16–18.

6. See Georg Lukács, *The Historical Novel*, trans. Hannah and Stanley Mitchell (London: Merlin Press, 1962), pp. 30–63.

7. Thomas L. Jeffers, *Apprenticeships: The Bildungsroman from Goethe to Santayana* (New York and Houndmills: Palgrave Macmillan, 2005), p. 109.

8. Laura Green, *Literary Identification from Charlotte Brontë to Tsitsi Dangaremba* (Columbus: Ohio State University Press, 2012), pp. 2–5.

9. See Gerlinde Röder-Bolton, *George Eliot and Goethe: An Elective Affinity* (Amsterdam: Rodopi, 1998), pp. 12–14.

10. See, for example, Rosemary Ashton, *The German Idea: Four English Writers and the Reception of German Thought 1800–1860* (London: Libris, 1994), p. 80; and G. B. Tennyson, 'The Bildungsroman in Nineteenth-Century English

Literature' in Rosario Armato and John M. Spalek (eds.), *Medieval Epic to the Epic Theater of Brecht* (University of South Carolina Press, 1968), p. 139.

11. Thomas Carlyle, 'Translator's Preface to the First Edition of Meister's Apprenticeship' in *Wilhelm Meister's Apprenticeship and Travels: Translated from the German of Goethe*, 3 vols. (London: Chapman & Hall, 1888), p. vi.

12. Thomas Carlyle, 'Death of Goethe' in *Critical and Miscellaneous Essays* (London: Chapman & Hall, 1888), vol. 3, p. III.

13. Charles Eliot Norton (ed.), *Correspondence between Goethe and Carlyle* (London: Macmillan, 1887), p. 7.

14. See Barry V. Qualls, *The Secular Pilgrims of Victorian Fiction: The Novel as Book of Life* (Cambridge: Cambridge University Press, 1982), pp. 10–11.

15. Tennyson, 'The Bildungsroman in Nineteenth-Century English Literature', p. 143.

16. Thomas Carlyle, *Sartor Resartus* (Oxford and New York: Oxford University Press, 1987), p. 70, p. 89, p. 76. Further references to this edition occur parenthetically.

17. See, for example, Charles Frederick Harrold, *Carlyle and German Thought: 1819–1834* (Hamden and London: Archon Books, 1963), p. 6, pp. 204–7.

18. Wilhelm Dilthey, '*Sartor Resartus*: Philosophical Conflict, Positive and Negative Eras, and Personal Resolution', *Clio*, 1.3, 1972, p. 60.

19. Ashton, *The German Idea*, p. 22.

20. Susanne Howe, *Wilhelm Meister and His English Kinsmen: Apprentices to Life* (New York: Columbia University Press, 1930), p. 10. Further references to this edition appear parenthetically.

21. Benjamin Disraeli, *Contarini Fleming: A Psychological Romance* (London: Peter Davies, 1927), p. ix, p. 361.

22. Lord Lytton, *Ernest Maltravers* (London: Routledge, 1873), pp. 7–8. Further references to this edition occur parenthetically.

23. Lord Lytton, *Alice; or, The Mysteries* (London: Routledge, 1873), p. 265.

24. See Richard Salmon, *The Formation of the Victorian Literary Profession* (Cambridge University Press, 2013).

25. Geraldine Jewsbury, *The Half Sisters* (Oxford and New York: Oxford University Press, 1994), p. 186. Further references to this edition appear parenthetically.

26. Samuel Smiles, *Self-Help; With Illustrations of Character, Conduct, and Perseverance* (Oxford and New York: Oxford University Press, 2002), p. 17. Further references to this edition appear parenthetically.

27. Jerome Buckley, *Season of Youth: The Bildungsroman from Dickens to Golding* (Cambridge, MA: Harvard University Press, 1974), p. 23, p. 42.

28. Charles Dickens, *David Copperfield* (Harmondsworth: Penguin, 1996), p. 560. Further references to this edition occur parenthetically.

29. Robin Gilmour, 'Memory in *David Copperfield*', *Dickensian*, 75, 1975, p. 30, p. 39.
30. See Buckley, *Season of Youth*, p. 42; and Moretti, *The Way of the World*, pp. 189–92.
31. Charles Dickens, *Great Expectations* (Harmondsworth: Penguin, 1996), pp. 74–5, p. 60, p. 319. Further references to this edition occur parenthetically.
32. Tennyson, 'The Bildungsroman in Nineteenth-Century English Literature', p. 144.
33. Moretti, *The Way of the World*, p. 4.
34. Moretti, p. 5. I would argue that David Copperfield exhibits another side of modernity in his commitment to rationalised labour and autonomous self-formation.
35. Ellis, *Appearing to Diminish*, p. 161.
36. See Fraiman, *Unbecoming Women*, p. 13; and Elizabeth Abel, Marianne Hirsch, and Elizabeth Langland (eds.), *The Voyage In: Fictions of Female Development* (Hanover and London: University Press of New England, 1983), p. 19.
37. Karen E. Rowe, '"Fairy-born and human-bred": Jane Eyre's Education in Romance' in *The Voyage In*, Abel et al. (eds.), p. 76; and Fraiman, *Unbecoming Women*, p. 118.
38. See Qualls, *The Secular Pilgrims of Victorian Fiction*, p. 83.
39. See, especially, *The History of Pendennis* (1848–50) and *The Adventures of Philip* (1861–2).
40. Qualls, *The Secular Pilgrims of Victorian Fiction*, p. 43, p. 83.
41. Bennett, *Principle and Propensity*, p. 71.
42. See Qualls, *The Secular Pilgrims of Victorian Fiction*, p. 83.
43. Charlotte Brontë, *Villette* (Harmondsworth: Penguin, 1988), p. 95. Further references to this edition occur parenthetically.
44. Charles Kingsley, *Alton Locke, Tailor and Poet* (Oxford and New York: Oxford University Press, 1983), p. 38.
45. Moretti, 'Preface' in *The Way of the World*, p. vii.
46. The phrases in quotation are taken from Jed Esty, 'The Colonial Bildungsroman: *The Story of an African Farm* and the Ghost of Goethe', *Victorian Studies*, 49.3, 2007, p. 410, but the specific groupings of early and late nineteenth-century authors are based on my own sense of how these writers are generally positioned.
47. George Eliot is chronologically the last English (and European) writer to be discussed in detail by Moretti before an Appendix which briefly covers the period 1898 to 1914.

48. See Georg Lukács, *The Theory of the Novel: A Historico-philosophical essay on the forms of great epic literature*, trans. Anna Bostock (London: Merlin Press, 1971), pp. 112–31.

49. See Marianne Hirsch, 'Spiritual *Bildung*: The Beautiful Soul as Paradigm' in *The Voyage In*, Abel et al. (eds.), p. 33, p. 37.

50. Fraiman, *Unbecoming Women*, p. 31, p. 141; see also Buckley, *Season of Youth*, p. 97.

51. Buckley, *Season of Youth*, p. 181.

52. George Meredith, *The Ordeal of Richard Feverel* (Harmondsworth: Penguin, 1998), p. 492. Further references to this edition appear parenthetically.

53. Tennyson, 'The Bildungsroman in Nineteenth-Century English Literature', p. 142.

54. Dorothea Barrett, *Vocation and Desire: George Eliot's Heroines* (London and New York: Routledge, 1989), p. 18.

55. Alan Mintz, *George Eliot and the Novel of Vocation* (Cambridge, MA: Harvard University Press, 1978), p. 6.

56. George Eliot, *Daniel Deronda*, ed. Barbara Hardy (Harmondsworth: Penguin, 1967), p. 171. Further references to this edition occur parenthetically.

57. See G. H. Lewes, 'The Apprenticeship of Life', *The Leader*, 1 (1), March 1850–(2), June 1850.

58. See James Hardin (ed.), *Reflection and Action: Essays on the Bildungsroman* (Columbia: University of South Carolina Press, 1991).

59. See Georg Wilhelm Friedrich Hegel, *The Philosophy of History*, trans. J. Sibree (New York: Dover Publications, 1956), pp. 29–33.

60. George Meredith, *Beauchamp's Career* (Oxford and New York: Oxford University Press, 1988), p. 18, p. 33. Further references to this edition appear parenthetically.

61. See Margaret Harris, 'Introduction' to *Beauchamp's Career*, p. xvii.

62. Matthew Arnold, *Culture and Anarchy and Other Writings* (Cambridge University Press, 1993), p. 62.

63. Walter Pater, *The Renaissance: Studies in Art and Poetry* (Oxford and New York: Oxford University Press, 1986), p. 153.

64. Walter Pater, *Marius the Epicurean* (London: Penguin, 1985), p. 49, p. 106. Further references to this edition appear parenthetically.

65. Gregory Castle argues that the revival of interest in aesthetic education during this period heralds a specifically 'Modernist' recuperation of the eighteenth-century ideal of Bildung: see *Reading the Modernist Bildungsroman* (Gainesville: University Press of Florida, 2006), pp. 1–4.

66. Henry James, *The Princess Casamassima* (Harmondsworth: Penguin, 1986), p. 157. Further references to this edition appear parenthetically.

67. George Levine, *How to Read the Victorian Novel* (Oxford: Blackwell Publishing, 2008), p. 88.

68. See Castle, *Reading the Modernist Bildungsroman* for an account of *Jude the Obscure* from the opposite historical perspective (pp. 77–100).

69. Thomas Hardy, *Jude the Obscure* (Peterborough, ON: Broadview, 1999), p. 116. Further references to this edition appear parenthetically.

70. Charlotte Riddell, *A Struggle for Fame: A Novel*, 3 vols. (London: Richard Bentley, 1883), I, p. 225. Sarah Grand's *The Beth Book* (1897), another important example of the 'New Woman' Bildungsroman, also belongs in this group, though its ending somewhat complicates its emphasis on autonomous female self-development.

71. Ella Hepworth Dixon, *The Story of a Modern Woman* (Peterborough, ON: Broadview, 2004), p. 80. Further references to this edition appear parenthetically.

72. Moretti, *The Way of the World*, p. 5.

## Chapter 4  The Bildungsroman in Imperial Russia and the Soviet Union

1. Kristin Gjesdal, '*Bildung*' in Michael N. Forster and Kristin Gjesdal (eds.), *The Oxford Handbook of German Philosophy in the Nineteenth-Century* (Oxford: Oxford University Press, 2015), pp. 695–719.

2. Franco Moretti, *The Way of the World: The Bildungsroman in European Culture* (London: Verso, 2000).

3. Mikhail Bakhtin, 'The *Bildungsroman* and Its Significance in the History of Realism (Toward a Historical Typology of the Novel)' in Caryl Emerson and Michael Holquist (eds.), *Speech Genres & Other Late Essays* (Austin: University of Texas Press, 1986), pp. 10–59.

4. Karl Morgenstern, 'On the Nature of the Bildungsroman', trans. Tobias Boes, PMLA, 124:2 (2009), pp. 647–59. Further references to this edition appear parenthetically.

5. Friedrich von Blackenburg, *Versuch über den Roman* (Stuttgart: J.B. Metzlerische Verlagsbuchhandlung, 1774), pp. 145–7. Further references to this edition appear parenthetically.

6. V. V. Vinogradov, *Istoriia slov* (Moscow: Akademiia Nauk RF, 1999), p. 792.

7. Andrzej Walicki, *A History of Russian Thought from the Enlightenment to Marxism*, trans. Hilda Andrews-Rusiecka (Oxford: Clarendon Press, 1980), pp. 74–80.

8. J. G. Herder, *Journal meiner Reise im Jahr 1769* (Leipzig: Reklam, 1972), p. 24.

9. I. V. Kireevskii, 'Deviatnadsatyi vek' in *Polnoe sobranie sochinenii*. 3 vols. (Moscow: Moskovskii Universitet, 1911), vol. I, pp. 85–108. Further references to this edition appear parenthetically.

10. P. Ia. Chaadaev's influence on Kireevskii has been much debated. For an overview of this discussion see Abbot Gleason, *European and Moscovite: Ivan Kireevsky and the Origins of Slavophilism* (Cambridge, MA: Harvard University Press, 1972), pp. 112–14.

11. V. G. Belinskii, *Polnoe sobranie sochinenii*, 30 vols. (Moscow, 1953–9), vol. 7, pp. 428–35.

12. N. I. Pirogov, 'Voprosy Zhizni' in *Izbrannye pedagogicheskie sochineniia* (Moscow: Academia, 1953), pp. 47–72.

13. Apollon Grigor'ev, 'Razvitie idei narodnosti v russkoi literature so smerti Pushkina' in *Apologiia pochvennichestva* (Moscow: Institut russkoi tsivilizatsii, 2008), pp. 184–607.

14. Boris Eikhenbaum, *Lermontov. Opyt istoriko-literaturnoi otsenki* (Leningrad: Gosizdat, 1924), p. 139.

15. A. N. Veselovskii, *Istoricheskaia poetika* (Leningrad: Khudozhestvennaia literatura, 1940), p. 66.

16. V. F. Shishmarev, *Aleksandr Veselovskii i russkaia literatura* (Leningrad: Izdatel'stvo LGU, 1946), pp. 17–24. See also Kate Holland, 'From the Prehistory of Russian Novel Theory: Alexander Veselovsky and Fyodor Dostoevsky on the Modern Novel's Roots in Folklore and Legend' in Boris Maslov and Ilya Kliger (eds.), *Persistent Forms: Explorations in Historical Poetics* (New York: Fordham University Press, 2015), pp. 440–66.

17. The term became popular after the publication of Dilthey's *Poetry and Experience* (1906), though he had already used it in his *Life of Schleiermacher* (1870).

18. The main products of this period are 'Discourse in the Novel' (1934–5), 'From the Prehistory of Novelistic Discourse' (1940), 'Epic and Novel' (1941), and the Bildungsroman book.

19. See note 3. Another text that was probably part of Bakhtin's Bildungsroman study and which was eventually published as a free-standing essay is 'Forms of Time and of the Chronotope in the Novel'. Written in 1937–9, it was significantly revised in 1973. For an up-to-date discussion of this text's history, see the commentary in Bakhtin's *Sobranie sochinenii v semi tomakh*, vol. VI, pp. 797–800.

20. M. M. Bakhtin, 'Roman kak literaturnyi zhanr' in *Sobranie sochinenii*, vol. III, pp. 608–43.

21. 'Forms of Time and of the Chronotope in the Novel' (1937–8), as well as the book on the Bildungsroman.

22. M. M. Bakhtin, 'Roman vospitaniia i ego znachenie v istorii realizma' in *Sobranie sochinenii*, vol. III, pp. 181–217.

23. 'The *Bildungsroman* and Its Significance in the History of Realism,' pp. 42–3. On the similarity between Bakhtin's view of the Bildungsroman and Schlegel's theory of the novel see Galin Tihanov, *The Master and the Slave: Lukács, Bakhtin, and the Ideas of Their Time* (Oxford: Clarendon Press, 2000), p. 145.

24. See note 7.

25. A. N. Radischev, *Polnoe sobranie sochinenii* (Moscow-Leningrad: Akademia Nauk SSSR, 1938), vol. I, pp. 153–212. Further references to this edition appear parenthetically.

26. A. N. Radischev, 'O cheloveke, ego smertnosti i bessmertii' in *Polnoe sobranie sochinenii*. 3. vols. (Moscow-Leningrad: Akademia, 1938–54), vol. II, pp. 37–142.

27. N. M. Karamzin, *Pis'ma russkogo puteshestvennika, 'Literatrnye pamiatniki'* (Leningrad: Akademia, 1984).

28. N. M. Karamzin, *Izbrannye sochineniia v dvukh tomakh*, 2 vols. (Moscow-Leningrad: Khudozhestvennaia literatura, 1964), vol. I, pp. 755–81.

29. A. S. Pushkin, *Sobranie sochinenii v desiati tomakh*. 10 vols. (Moscow: Khudozhestvennaia literatura, 1960), vol. V, pp. 286–411. Further references to this edition appear parenthetically.

30. D. S. Mirsky, *A History of Russian Literature* (New York: Knopf, 1927), p. 228.

31. Ivan Turgenev, 'Hamlet and Don Quixote', trans. Moshe Spiegel, in *Chicago Review*, 17.4 (1965), pp. 92–109.

32. Another common, but less accurate, translation of this title is *Fathers and Sons*.

33. On the generic proximity of Herzen's memoir to the Bildungsroman see Lydia Ginzburg, *O psikhologicheskoi proze* (Leningrad: Khudozhestvennaia literatura, 1977), p. 252. See also Sofya Gurvich-Lischiner, *Tvorchestvo Aleksandra Gercena i nemetskaia literatura* (Frankfurt a. Main: Peter Lang, 2001), p. 79.

34. Scholars continue to debate the precise dating of Herzen's drafts. For a thorough discussion of the textological issue see Irina Paperno, 'Introduction: Intimacy and History. The Gercen Family Drama Reconsidered' in Russian Literature 61.1 (2007), pp. 1–65.

35. The most illuminating Western account of Herzen's work is by Isaiah Berlin. See his 'Herzen and His Memoirs' in *Against the Current: Essays in the History of Ideas* (Princeton: Princeton University Press, 2013), pp. 188–212. The family drama has been subject to several studies, including E. H. Carr, *The Romantic Exiles: A Nineteenth-Century Portrait Gallery* (Boston: MIT Press, 1981).

36. The English translation of this text is available in Alexander Herzen, *Ends and Beginnings*, trans. Constance Garnett, Aileen Kelly (ed.) (Oxford: Oxford University Press, 1968).

37. N. G. Chernyshevsky, 'L.N. Tolstoy's *Childhood* and *Boyhood* and *Military Tales*' in Ralph E. Matlaw (ed.), *Belinsky, Chernyshevsky and Dobrolyubov: Selected Criticism* (Bloomington: Indiana University Press, 1962), pp. 95–107.

38. A major influence on Tolstoy's trilogy was Rousseau. For an illuminating discussion of Tolstoy's debts to Rousseau see Donna Tussing Orwin, *Tolstoy's Art and Thought: 1847–1880* (Princeton, NJ: Princeton University Press, 1993).

39. I provide a detailed interpretation of *War and Peace* as a Bildungsroman in my monograph *For Humanity's Sake: The Bildungsroman in Russian Culture* (Toronto and London: University of Toronto Press, 2011). See chapter six, pp. 91–134.

40. M. M. Bakhtin, 'Formy vremeni i khronotopa v romane' in *Sobranie sochinenii*, vol. III, pp. 472–89.

41. Ilya Kliger, *The Narrative Shape of Truth: Veridiction in Modern European Literature* (University Park: Pennsylvania State University Press, 2011), pp. 145–76.

42. Donna Orwin, *Consequences of Consciousness* (Stanford: Stanford University Press, 2007), p. 141.

43. Konstantin Mochul'skii, *Dostoevsky: His Life and Work*, trans. Michael A. Minihan (Princeton: Princeton University Press, 1967), p. 182.

44. M. M. Bakhtin, *Problems of Dostoevsky's Poetics*, Caryl Emerson (ed.), trans. William Booth (Minneapolis: University of Minnesota Press, 1984), p. 28.

45. Lev Shestov, 'Dostoevsky and Nietzsche: The Philosophy of Tragedy' in Lev Shestov, *Dostoevsky, Tolstoy, and Nietzsche*, trans. Spencer Roberts (Columbus: Ohio University Press, 1978).

46. I discuss Dostoevsky's attempt to write a Bildungsroman in chapter seven of *For Humanity's Sake*, pp. 135–73.

47. F. M. Dostoevsky, *Polnoe sobranie sochinenii v tridtsati tomakh*, V. G. Bazanov et al. (eds.), 30 vols. (Leningrad: Nauka, 1972–90), vol. 18, p. 69.

48. Dostoevsky, *Polnoe sobranie sochinenii v tridtsati tomakh*, vol. 11, p. 193.

49. For an intriguing discussion of the projected sequel to *The Brothers Karamazov* see Igor Volgin, *Poslednii god Dostoevskogo* (Moscow: Sovetskii pisatel', 1986).

50. L. N. Tolstoy, *Polnoe sobraie sochinenii v devianosta tomakh*, V.G. Chertkov et al. (eds.), 90 vols. (Moscow: Khudozhestvennaia literatura, 1928–58), vol. 32, p. 433.

51. Tolstoy, *Polnoe sobraie sochinenii v devianosta tomakh*, vol. 55, p. 243.

52. Ivan Bunin, *Zhizn' Arsen'eva* (Moscow: Eksmo, 2014).

53. Katerina Clark, *The Soviet Novel: History as Ritual* (Chicago: University of Chicago Press, 1981), p. 57.
54. Bulgakov's novel was published for the first time in the journal *Moscow* in 1966–7. The first uncensored publication in the USSR was in 1973.
55. The novel's first Russian edition was published in Milan in 1957. For an overview of the translation and publication history see Angela Livingstone, *Pasternak's Doctor Zhivago*. In *Landmarks of World Literature* (Cambridge: Cambridge University Press, 1989).
56. An English translation of Ehrenburg's speech is published at www.sovlit.net.
57. Vassily Aksenov, *A Ticket to the Stars*, trans. Andrew MacAndrew. (New York: New American Library, 1963).
58. It was published in the journal *Novyi Mir* in 1986.
59. Andrei Bitov, *Pushkin House*, trans. Susan Brownsberger (Normal, IL: Dalkey Archive Press, 1987), pp. 286–319.
60. This scene, which alludes to Pushkin's *The Bronze Horseman*, concludes the third (and last) Epilogue, pp. 328–39.
61. Viktor Pelevin, *Omon Ra* (New York: New Directions, 1998).

## Chapter 5  The American Bildungsroman

1. For discussion of the Bildungsroman in Canada and Latin America, see Ellen McWilliams, *Margaret Atwood and the Female Bildungsroman* (Farnham: Ashgate, 2009) and Yolanda A. Doub, *Journeys of Formation: The Spanish American Bildungsroman* (New York and Oxford: Peter Lang, 2010).
2. A substantial number of Bildungsromane have been published in the US: W. Tasker Witham estimates that six hundred novels for adult readers 'dealing with problems of adolescence' appeared between 1920 and 1960; Mary Jean DeMarr identifies another six hundred published between 1960 and 1982. See W. Tasker Witham, *The Adolescent in the American Novel 1920–1960* (New York: Frederick Ungar, 1964) and Mary Jean DeMarr and Jane S. Bakerman, *The Adolescent in the American Novel Since 1960* (New York: Ungar, 1986).
3. 'In Congress, July 4, 1776. The unanimous Declaration of the thirteen united States of America. … We hold these truths to be self-evident, that all men are created equal, that they are endowed by their Creator with certain unalienable Rights, that among these are Life, Liberty and the pursuit of Happiness', www.archives.gov/founding-docs/declaration-transcript. Francis Scott Key, 'The Star-Spangled Banner' in Geoffrey Moore (ed.), *The Penguin Book of American Verse* (London: Penguin, 2011), p. 66.
4. 'The Pledge of Allegiance to the Flag: "I pledge allegiance to the Flag of the United States of America, and to the Republic for which it stands, one Nation

under God, indivisible, with liberty and justice for all.", should be rendered by standing at attention facing the flag with the right hand over the heart' www.law.cornell.edu/uscode/text/4/4.

5. https://obamawhitehouse.archives.gov/blog/2009/01/21/president-barack-ob amas-inaugural-address

6. Frederic Carpenter, 'The Adolescent in American Fiction', *The English Journal* 46.6 (1957), p. 319.

7. See, for example, Stella Bolaki, *Unsettling the Bildungsroman: Reading Contemporary Ethnic American Women's Fiction* (Amsterdam: Rodopi, 2011); Jennifer Ho, *Consumption and Identity in Asian American Coming-of-Age Novels* (New York and London: Routledge, 2013); Geta LeSeur, *Ten Is the Age of Darkness: The Black Bildungsroman* (Columbia, MO: University of Missouri Press, 1995); Christy Rishoi, *From Girl to Woman: American Women's Coming-of-Age Narratives* (Albany, NY: State University of New York Press, 2003).

8. Kenneth Millard, *Coming of Age in Contemporary American Fiction* (Edinburgh: Edinburgh University Press, 2007), p. 5.

9. Barton C. Friedberg, 'The Cult of Adolescence in American Fiction', *The Nassau Review* 1.1 (1964), pp. 34–35.

10. *Encyclopædia Britannica* identifies Goethe's novel as 'the classic example of the genre' (www.britannica.com/art/bildungsroman), and confirms the novel's relationship with the German Enlightenment: it 'sets forth the 18th-century humanistic ideal of self-education and the development of intellect' (www.britannica.com/topic/Wilhelm-Meisters-Apprenticeship).

11. Franco Moretti, *The Way of the World: The Bildungsroman in European Culture*, new edition (London: Verso, 2000). Moretti argues that at the turn of the eighteenth century 'youth … achieves its symbolic centrality' in society, and the Bildungsroman emerges because European culture requires a strategy for understanding modernity (Moretti, *Way of the World*, p. 5). Moretti excludes American fiction from his study on the grounds that it, like Russia, has a 'marked religious dimension', unlike 'secularized' Western Europe. He further argues that a specifically American concept of nature, alien to the 'urban thematics of the European novel' and the fact that, in American narratives, 'the hero's decisive experience, unlike in Europe, is not an encounter with the "unknown", but with an "alien" – usually an Indian or a Black' sets it apart from the European form of the genre (Moretti, note 1, p. 247). Moretti's assessment, especially the final point, is not borne out by this chapter.

12. Brigid Lowe, 'The Bildungsroman' in Robert L. Caserio and Clement Hawes (eds.), *The Cambridge History of the English Novel* (Cambridge: Cambridge University Press, 2012), p. 406.

13. Moretti, *Way of the World*, p. 26. Further references to this edition appear parenthetically.

14. M. M. Bakhtin, 'The *Bildungsroman* and Its Significance in the History of Realism (Toward a Historical Typology of the Novel)' in Caryl Emerson and Michael Holquist (eds.), *Speech Genres & Other Late Essays* (Austin: University of Texas Press, 1986), p. 22.

15. Bakhtin, '*Bildungsroman*', p. 22.

16. Canonical examples of the European Bildungsroman bear out Moretti's contention: Wilhelm Meister's association with the theatre takes him outside normal society; Werther kills himself; Jane Eyre, Emma Woodhouse, Elizabeth Bennett, David Copperfield and Pip all marry.

17. Ralph Waldo Emerson, 'Self-Reliance' in Stephen E. Whicher (ed.), *Selections from Ralph Waldo Emerson: An Organic Anthology* (Boston: Houghton Mifflin, 1960), p. 148.

18. This expression was first used as the title of a pacifist Quaker publication: American Friends Service Committee, *Speak Truth to Power: A Quaker Search for an Alternative to Violence*, 1955.

19. Moretti proposes that Napoleon's 'restless ambiguity makes him the natural representative of an age in which existence truly becomes … "problematic"' (Moretti, *Way of the World*, p. 76).

20. David Reynolds, *America: Empire of Liberty* (London: Penguin, 2010), p. 93.

21. 'Traditionally, historians have put war deaths at about 360,000 for the Union and 260,000 for the Confederates. In the second decade of the 21st century, however, a demographer used better data and more sophisticated tools to convincingly revise the total death toll upward to 752,000 and indicated that it could be as high as 851,000', according to *Encyclopædia Britannica* (www.britannica.com/event/American-Civil-War/The-cost-and-significance-of-the-Civil-War).

22. Lowe, 'Bildungsroman' in *Cambridge History of the English Novel*, p. 413.

23. Joan Didion, 'One Week after 9/11: Jon Wiener interviews Joan Didion', *Los Angeles Review of Books*, September 11, 2013, https://lareviewofbooks.org/article/one-week-after-911/

24. Hildegard Hoeller, 'Preface' in Horatio Alger, Jr., *Ragged Dick or, Street Life in New York with Boot Blacks* (New York and London: W. W. Norton & Co., 2008), p. x.

25. Alger, *Ragged Dick*, p. 6. Further references to this edition appear parenthetically.

26. Gary Scharnhorst, 'Demythologizing Alger' in Alger, *Ragged Dick*, p. 182.

27. 'Congressional Record, V. 144, Pt. 5, April 21, 1998 to April 30, 1998', Congress, 1998, p. 6696.

28. Carol Nackenoff, *Fictional Republic: Horatio Alger and American Political Discourse* (Oxford: Oxford University Press, 1994), p. 5.

29. Sarah Waxman, 'History of Central Park, New York', www.ny.com/articles/centralpark.html

30. Scharnhorst, 'Demythologizing Alger' in Alger, *Ragged Dick*, pp. 184–5. Scharnhorst notes that Alger was criticised and satirised by contemporaries including Louisa May Alcott, W. D. Howells and Stephen Crane.

31. Hoeller, 'Preface' in Alger, *Ragged Dick*, p. ix.

32. Mark Twain, *Adventures of Huckleberry Finn*, Norton Critical Edition, third edition (New York: Norton, 1999), p. 13. Further references to this edition appear parenthetically.

33. Marc Redfield, 'The Bildungsroman' in Joseph Slaughter, *Human Rights, Inc: The World Novel, Narrative Form, and International Law* (New York: Fordham University Press, 2007), p. 86.

34. Stephen Crane, *The Red Badge of Courage* in Stephen Crane, *Prose and Poetry*, College Edition (New York: Library of America, 1996), p. 83. Further references to this edition appear parenthetically.

35. Jack London, *Martin Eden* (London: Penguin, 1985), p. 40, p. 34. Further references to this edition appear parenthetically.

36. R. W. B. Lewis, *The American Adam: Innocence, Tragedy and Tradition in the Nineteenth Century* (Chicago and London: University of Chicago Press, 1968), p. 1.

37. R. Baird Shuman, 'Initiation Rites in Steinbeck's "The Red Pony"', *The English Journal* 59.9 (1970), p. 1255.

38. Larry McMurtry, *The Last Picture Show* (London: Penguin, 2011), p. 3, p. 228.

39. Todd Womble, 'Windswept and Scattered: Place and Identity in Larry McMurtry's *The Last Picture Show*' in Paul Varner (ed.), *New Wests and Post-Wests: Literature and Film of the American West* (Newcastle upon Tyne: Cambridge Scholars Publishing, 2013), p. 94.

40. Cormac McCarthy, *The Border Trilogy* (London: Picador, 2002), p. 17. Further references to this edition appear parenthetically.

41. Philipp Meyer, *American Rust* (London and New York: Simon & Schuster, 2009), p. 133. Further references to this edition appear parenthetically.

42. 'President Barack Obama's Inaugural Address', January 21, 2009. https://obamawhitehouse.archives.gov/blog/2009/01/21/president-barack-obamas-inaugural-address

43. Elizabeth Abel, Marianne Hirsch, and Elizabeth Langland (eds.), *The Voyage In: Fictions of Female Development* (Hanover and London: University Press of New England, 1983), p. 5.

44. Kathleen M. Therrien, '"Why Do They Have To … To … Say Things … ?": Poverty, Class, and Gender in Betty Smith's *A Tree Grows in Brooklyn*', *Legacy* 16.1 (1999), p. 93.

45. Betty Smith, *A Tree Grows in Brooklyn* (London: Arrow, 2000), p. 249, p. 250. Further references to this edition appear parenthetically.

46. Barbara White, *Growing Up Female: Adolescent Girlhood in American Fiction* (Westport, CT: Greenwood Press, 1985), p. 19.

47. Dorothy Allison, *Bastard out of Carolina* (New York: Plume, 1993), p. 3. Further references to this edition appear parenthetically.

48. Millard, *Coming of Age*, p. 156.

49. James Richard Giles, *The Spaces of Violence* (Tuscaloosa: University of Alabama Press, 2006), p. 75

50. Millard, *Coming of Age*, p. 161.

51. Matt Wray and Annalee Newitz in J. Brooks Bouson, '"You Nothing but Trash": White Trash Shame in Dorothy Allison's *Bastard out of Carolina*', *The Southern Literary Journal* 34.1 (2001), p. 101.

52. Louisa May Alcott, *Little Women* (Ontario: Broadview, 2001), p. 45. Further references to this edition appear parenthetically.

53. Henry James, *What Maisie Knew* (Oxford and New York: Oxford University Press, 1992), p. 22. Further references to this edition appear parenthetically.

54. Alfred Habegger, '"What Maisie Knew": Henry James's Bildungsroman of the Artist as Queer Moralist' in Gert Buelens (ed.), *Enacting History in Henry James: Narrative, Power, and Ethics* (Cambridge: Cambridge University Press, 1997), p. 93.

55. Edith Wharton, *Summer* (New York and London: Penguin, 1993), p. 47. Further references to this edition appear parenthetically.

56. Karen Weingarten, 'Between the Town and the Mountain: Abortion and the Politics of Life in Edith Wharton's *Summer*', *Canadian Review of American Studies* 40.3 (2010), p. 359.

57. Harper Lee, *To Kill a Mockingbird* (London: Arrow, 2010), p. 98. Further references to this edition appear parenthetically.

58. Rachael McLennan, *Adolescence, America, and Postwar Fiction: Developing Figures* (Basingstoke: Palgrave Macmillan, 2009), p. 101.

59. Sylvia Plath, *The Bell Jar* (London: Faber and Faber, 1999), p. 81. Further references to this edition appear parenthetically.

60. Claudine Raynaud, 'Coming of Age in the African American Novel' in Maryemma Graham (ed.), *The Cambridge Companion to the African American Novel* (Cambridge: Cambridge University Press, 2006), p. 109.

61. Geta LeSeur, *Ten Is the Age of Darkness: The Black Bildungsroman* (Columbia and London: University of Missouri Press, 1995), p. 4.

62. James Baldwin, *Go Tell It on the Mountain* (New York: Delta, 2000), p. 226.

63. Paule Marshall, *Brown Girl, Brownstones*, new edition (London: Virago, 1982), p. 307.

64. D'Arcy McNickle, *The Surrounded* (New York: Quality Paper Book Club, 1998), p. 2, p. 15.

65. Enrique Lima, 'The Uneven Development of the "Bildungsroman": D'Arcy McNickle and Native American Modernity', *Comparative Literature* 63.3 (2011), p. 299.

66. Jude Todd, 'Knotted Bellies and Fragile Webs: Untangling and Re-Spinning in Tayo's Healing Journey', *American Indian Quarterly* 19.2 (1995), p. 157.

67. Derek Parker Royal, 'Plotting a Way Home: The Jewish American Novel' in Alfred Bendixen (ed.), *A Companion to the American Novel, Genres and Traditions* (Oxford: Wiley-Blackwell, 2012), p. 244.

68. Abraham Cahan, *The Rise of David Levinsky* (New York: Penguin, 1993), p. 526. Further references to this edition appear parenthetically.

69. Alice Kessler-Harris, 'Foreword: Finding *Bread Givers*' in Anzia Yezierska, *Bread Givers: A Novel* (New York: Persea, 2003), p. xxxiv. Further references to this edition appear parenthetically.

70. Carol B. Schoen, *Anzia Yezierska* (Boston: Twayne, 1982), p. 61.

71. Martin Japtok, *Growing Up Ethnic: Nationalism and the Bildungsroman in African American and Jewish American Fiction* (Iowa City: University of Iowa Press, 2005), p. 107.

72. Jewish Canadian Mordecai Richler employs a similar strategy in his Bildungsroman, *The Apprenticeship of Duddy Kravitz* (1959), the title of which evokes Goethe's *The Apprenticeship of Wilhelm Meister*.

73. Saul Bellow, *The Adventures of Augie March* (London: Everyman's Library, 1995), p. 5.

74. Nicholas Nardini, 'A Fresh-Start Doctrine: The Marshall Plan, *The Adventures of Augie March*, and the Bildungsroman after Nationalism', *Arizona Quarterly: A Journal of American Literature, Culture, and Theory* 71.2 (2015), p. 15.

75. Maxine Hong Kingston, *The Woman Warrior: Memoirs of a Girlhood Among Ghosts* (London: Picador Classic, 2015), p. 24.

76. Christy Rishoi, *From Girl to Woman: American Women's Coming-of-Age Narratives* (Albany: State University of New York Press, 2003), p. 153.

77. Deborah L. Madsen, 'Chinese American Writers of the Real and the Fake: Authenticity and the Twin Traditions of Life Writing', *Canadian Review of American Studies/Revue Canadienne d'Etudes Américaines* 36.3 (2006), p. 269.

78. Sandra Cisneros, *The House on Mango Street* (London: Bloomsbury, 2004), p. 110.

79. Gerald Clarke, *Capote: A Biography*, Kindle edition (New York: Rosetta Books, 2013), n.p.
80. Truman Capote, *Other Voices, Other Rooms* (London: Pan, 1988), p. 85.
81. Gary Richards, *Lovers and Beloveds: Sexual Otherness in Southern Fiction, 1936–1961* (Baton Rouge: LSU Press, 2007), p. 37.
82. Edmund White, 'On the Line' in *A Boy's Own Story* (London: Picador, 1983), n.p.
83. Larry Duplechan, *Blackbird* (Vancouver: Arsenal Pulp Press, 2006), p. 222.
84. J. D. Salinger, *The Catcher in the Rye* (London: Penguin, 1994), p. 1. Further references to this edition appear parenthetically.

## Chapter 6  The Modernist Bildungsroman

1. Franco Moretti, *The Way of the World: The Bildungsroman in European Culture* (London: Verso, 2000).
2. Tobias Boes, *Formative Fictions: Nationalism, Cosmopolitanism and the Bildungsroman* (Ithaca: Sginale-Cornell University Press and Cornell University Library, 2012), pp. 3–7, p. 28.
3. Jed Esty, *Unseasonable Youth: Modernism, Colonialism and the Fiction of Development* (Oxford and New York: Oxford University Press, 2012), p. 2, p. 15.
4. In the phrase 'classical Bildung', the word 'classical' refers to the aesthetico-spiritual form of Bildung developed by Johann von Goethe, Friedrich Schiller and Wilhelm von Humboldt in the late eighteenth century. Opposed to this classical form are socially pragmatic or instrumental variants (for example, the 'coming of age' motif, which has a strong juridico-legal component). When used in the phrase 'classical Bildungsroman', the word 'classical' refers to the eighteenth- and nineteenth-century traditions of realist Bildungsromane, both the aesthetico-spiritual and socially pragmatic varieties. See my *Reading the Modernist Bildungsroman* (Gainesville: University Press of Florida, 2006), chapters one and two.
5. Wilhelm von Humboldt, *The Limits of State Action*, J. W. Barrow (ed.) (1850; repr. Cambridge: Cambridge University Press, 1969), p. 16.
6. Humboldt writes, 'in as much as the State, in its positive care for the external and physical well-being of the citizen (which are closely connected with his inner being), cannot avoid creating hindrances to the development of individuality, we find another reason why it should not be permitted to exercise such interference except in the case of the most absolute necessity' (*The Limits of State Action*, pp. 38–47).
7. Johann Wolfgang von Goethe, *Wilhelm Meister's Apprenticeship* [*Wilhelm Meisters Lehrjahre*] 1795–6, vol. 9 of *Goethe: The Collected Works*, trans. Eric

A. Blackall (ed.) (Princeton: Princeton University Press, 1995). Bildungsheld is the hero or protagonist of Bildung.

8. On the temporality of inner life, see my 'Destinies of *Bildung*: Belatedness and the Modernist Novel', in *A History of the Modernist Novel*, Gregory Castle (ed.) (New York: Cambridge University Press, 2015), pp. 483–507.

9. Max Saunders, *Self Impression: Life-Writing, Autobiografiction and the Forms of Modern Literature* (Oxford: Oxford University Press, 2010), p. 58. Jaime Hovey, in *A Thousand Words: Portraiture, Style, and Queer Modernism* (Columbus: The Ohio State University Press, 2006), describes a similar quality in the 'queer modernist portrait', which focuses 'on dynamic aspects of style and personality, presenting both the sitter's style and personality and the personality of the artist who renders her', p. 7.

10. Saunders, *Self Impression*, pp. 40–1. According to Saunders, *auto/biography* is a term for works 'that fuse together autobiography and biography'.

11. I follow Mikel Dufrenne, who holds that the 'represented world' is that part of the work (the 'aesthetic object') that relies on a mimetic relation to the concrete social world; the 'expressed world' is that which belongs solely to the work. The two are engaged in a dialectical relation that constitutes the 'world of the work'. Depending on the alignment of this relation in the text, the result is conventional novelistic realism or experimental anti-mimeticism. See Dufrenne, *The Phenomenology of Aesthetic Experience*, trans. E. S. Casey (Evanston: Northwestern University Press, 1966), especially pp. 166–98.

12. G. W. F. Hegel, *Hegel's Aesthetics: Lectures on Fine Art*, trans. T. M. Knox (Oxford: Clarendon Press, 1975), I, p. 593.

13. On contradiction and Bildung, see Marc Redfield, *Phantom Formations: Aesthetic Ideology and the Bildungsroman* (Ithaca: Cornell University Press, 1996), especially chapters one and two.

14. Oscar Wilde, 'The English Renaissance of Art', in *Miscellanies*, Robert Ross (ed.), vol. 14 of *The Collected Works of Oscar Wilde* (London: Methuen, 1908), p. 294. This was the inaugural lecture for Wilde's American Tour, held on January 9, 1882, at Chickering Hall in New York.

15. Oscar Wilde, 'House Decoration,' in *Miscellanies*, 294. 'Nothing is so ignoble that art cannot sanctify it' (ibid., p. 290).

16. Oscar Wilde, 'Art and the Handicraftsman,' *Miscellanies*, p. 301.

17. Friedrich Schiller, *On the Aesthetic Education of Man in a Series of Letters*, trans. Elizabeth M. Wilkinson and L. A. Willoughby (eds.) (Oxford: Clarendon Press, 1967), p. 313, p. 9.

18. Humboldt formed just such a group, a *Tugendbund* ('league of virtue') devoted to the free expression of thoughts and feelings, with a view towards 'mutual self-improvement' (W. H. Bruford, *The German Tradition of Self-*

*Cultivation: 'Bildung' from Humboldt to Thomas Mann* (London: Cambridge University Press, 1975), p. 5).

19. Walter Pater, *The Renaissance: Studies in Art and Poetry: The 1893 Text*, D. L. Hill (ed.) (Berkeley: University of California Press, 1980), pp. 183–4.

20. Pater, *Renaissance*, p. 188.

21. Pater, in *Imaginary Portraits*, offers another variation of life writing 'in the form of non-fictional biography, which he encourages us to read as fiction and autobiography. Put neologistically, auto/biography has become auto/biografiction' (*Self Impression*, p. 40). On the history of literary portraiture up through Pater, see pp. 62–70.

22. Walter Pater, *Imaginary Portraits* (1887; rpt. London and New York: Macmillan, 1914), p. 18. Subsequent references to this edition will be cited in the text as *IP*.

23. Oscar Wilde, quoted in Richard Ellmann, *Oscar Wilde* (New York: Vintage, 1987), p. 311.

24. Quoted in Wilde, 'English Renaissance', p. 272.

25. Oscar Wilde, *The Picture of Dorian Gray*, Michael Patrick Gillespie (ed.), second edition (New York: Norton, 2007), p. 111. Subsequent references to this edition will be cited in the text as *DG*. My remarks in this chapter on Wilde, Joyce and Woolf augment and refine my chapters on each in *Reading the Modernist Bildungsroman*.

26. Wilde, quoted in Ellmann, *Oscar Wilde*, p. 319.

27. Mikel Dufrenne, *In the Presence of the Sensuous: Essays on Aesthetics*, trans. Mark S. Roberts and Dennis Gallagher (eds.) (Atlantic Highlands, NJ: Humanities Press International, 1987), p. 7.

28. Dorrit Cohn's *Transparent Minds: Narrative Modes for Presenting Consciousness in Fiction* (Princeton: Princeton University Press, 1978) remains an important source on free-indirect style and narrated monologue. On Joyce's use of both, see John Paul Riquelme, *The Teller and Tale in Joyce's Fiction: Oscillating Perspectives* (Baltimore and London: Johns Hopkins University Press, 1983), pp. 52–8.

29. James Joyce, *A Portrait of the Artist as a Young Man*, John Paul Riquelme (ed.) (New York: Norton, 2007), p. 145. Subsequent references to this edition will be cited in the text as *P*.

30. Boes, *Formative Fictions*, p. 134.

31. On the implications for genre and narrative form of Joyce's use of autobiography in *Portrait*, see Riquelme, *Teller and Tale*, chapter two. There are many specialised studies of Joyce's use of his own biography, and the best starting point is Richard Ellmann's biography *James Joyce*, new and revised edition (New York: Oxford University Press, 1983). See also the Viking Critical edition of *Portrait*, edited by Chester G. Anderson (New York:

Viking Press, 1964), which includes a table of correspondences between Joyce's and Stephen's life history.

32. On the complex and coded inscription of the autobiographical real in Forster, see Tony Brown, 'Edward Carpenter, Forster and the Evolution of *A Room with a View*', *ELT* 30.3 (1987), pp. 279–301.

33. On novels of development featuring women, see Elizabeth Abel, Marianne Hirsch and Elizabeth Langland (eds.), *The Voyage In: Fictions of Female Development* (Hanover and London: University Press of New England, 1983) and Susan Fraiman, *Unbecoming Women: British Women Writers and the Novel of Development* (New York: Columbia University Press, 1993).

34. E. M. Forster, *A Room with a View* (London: E. Arnold, 1919), p. 33. Subsequent references to this edition will be cited in the text as *R*.

35. Under the general title of *Pilgrimage*, Richardson published thirteen 'chapter volumes', as she called them, between 1915 and 1938 tracing the life of her fictional avatar, Miriam Henderson. The first three volumes – *Pointed Roofs, Backwater* and *Honeycomb*, usually published together as *Pilgrimage I* – contain the inaugural Bildung-plot of the series, which thereafter traces the *long durée* of Miriam's adult life, which is more or less in line with Richardson's.

36. Virginia Woolf, *The Voyage Out* (1915; rpt. Oxford: Oxford University Press, 2001), p. 197, pp. 138–9. Subsequent references to this edition will be cited in the text as *VO*.

37. Richardson, *Honeycomb*, in *Pilgrimage I*, Gill Hanscombe (ed.) (Urbana and Chicago: University of Illinois Press, 1979), p. 45. Subsequent references to this edition of the first three volumes of *Pilgrimage – Pointed Roofs, Backwater, Honeycomb* – will be cited in the text as *PR, B* and *H*, respectively. Please note: because Richardson made liberal use of ellipses (...), my own will be in square brackets [...].

38. Gillian Hanscombe, 'Introduction', in *Pilgrimage I*, 1. On the relation between Richardson's autobiography and her fiction, see Hanscombe's *The Art of Life: Dorothy Richardson and the Development of Feminist Consciousness* (Columbus: Ohio University Press, 1983).

39. Dufrenne, *The Phenomenology of Aesthetic Experience*, p. 98.

40. Dorothy Richardson, 'Foreword', *Pilgrimage I*, p. 9. She notes further that realist novels by 1911 were 'largely explicit satire and protest, and every form of conventionalized human association [was] arraigned by biographical and autobiographical novelists', p. 9.

41. On the use of autobiography, and the extent to which it was not necessary for readers to know it to grasp the 'integrity and coherence' of *Pilgrimage* as fiction, see the 'General Introduction' to *Windows on Modernism: Selected*

*Letters of Dorothy Richardson*, Gloria G. Fromm (ed.) (Athens and London: University of Georgia Press, 1995), pp. xviii–xx, p. 3.

42. I do not describe her style as 'stream of consciousness', a phrase that Richardson abjured, calling it a 'formula devised to meet the exigencies of literary criticism'. She did not believe one could 'compar[e] consciousness to a stream' ('Foreword', *Pilgrimage I*, p. 11).

43. Virginia Woolf, 'The Fiction of Dorothy Richardson', in *Essays of Virginia Woolf*, vol. 3: 1919–1924, Andrew McNeillie (ed.) (London: Hogarth Press, 1986. San Diego: Harcourt, Brace Jovanovich, 1986), p. 12. Richardson notes sardonically that '[F]eminine prose', as in Dickens and Joyce, 'should properly be unpunctuated' ('Foreword', *Pilgrimage I*, p. 12).

44. Virginia Woolf, *The Diary of Virginia Woolf*, vol. 2: 1920–1924, Anne Olivier Bell and Andrew McNeillie (eds.) (New York: Harcourt Brace Jovanovich, 1978), p. 14.

45. Richardson, letter to E. B. C. Jones, May 12, 1921, in *Windows on Modernism*, p. 50.

46. On world-making as a cognitive process that produces 'metaworlds', see Elisabeth Bronfen, *Dorothy Richardson's Art of Memory: Space, Identity, Text*, trans. Victoria Appelbe (Manchester and New York: Manchester University Press, 1999), especially chapter five.

47. *HERmione* and *Asphodel* were not published in the author's lifetime. H. D. intended these texts to form what she called the Madrigal cycle. Two other texts are either part of this cycle or revisions of it: *Bid Me to Live (A Madrigal)*, which was drafted in the late 1930s and recasts the material in *Asphodel* (ca. 1912–19), and *Paint It Today* (1960), which focuses on H. D.'s relationship with Frances Josepha Gregg. On these textual issues, see Robert Spoo, 'H. D.'s Dating of *Asphodel*: A Reassessment,' *The H. D. Newsletter* 4.2 (Winter 1991), pp. 31–40. Spoo rightly calls *Asphodel* an 'autobiographical Bildungsroman', but I see no reason why we cannot extend this judgement to include *HERmione*.

48. Sean Latham, *The Art of Scandal: Modernism, Libel Law, and the Roman à Clef* (Oxford: Oxford University Press, 2009), p. 9. Robert Spoo's edition of *Asphodel* contains the 'key' to both novels in the form of an appendix that describes the historical counterparts of all major and some minor characters (H. D., *Asphodel*, Robert Spoo (ed.) (Durham: Duke University Press, 1992)).

49. Virginia Woolf, *Mrs Dalloway*, Mark Hussey (ed.) (1925; rpt. New York: Harcourt, 2005), p. 35.

50. H. D., *HERmione* (New York: New Directions, 1981), pp. 3–4. Subsequent references to this edition will be made in the text as *HER*.

51. H. D., *Asphodel*, p. 53. Subsequent references to this edition will be made in the text as *A*.

52. Two of Pound's most important early works in the classical style, *Personae* and *Exultations*, came out in 1909.
53. Pater, *The Renaissance*, p. 187.
54. Elsewhere Hermione speaks of art as 'the discriminating and selecting and bringing odd distorted images into right perspective' (*HER* 139).
55. Elizabeth Bowen, *The Last September* (1929; rpt. New York: Anchor Books, 2000), p. 41. Subsequent references to this edition will be cited in the texts as *LS*.
56. Esty, *Unseasonable Youth*, p. 166.

## Chapter 7 Bildungsromane for Children and Young Adults

1. James Eli Adams, *A History of Victorian Literature* (Oxford: Blackwell Publishing, 2012), pp. 123–4.
2. Maureen Moran, *Victorian Literature and Culture* (London and New York: Continuum, 2011), pp. 81–2.
3. Ellen McWilliams, *Margaret Atwood and the Female Bildungsroman* (Farnham, Surrey & Burlington, VT: Ashgate Publishing, 2009), p. 28.
4. See, for instance, Jacqueline Rose, *The Case of Peter Pan or the Impossibility of Children's Fiction* (London: Macmillan, 1984).
5. Deborah Cogan Thacker and Jean Webb, *Introducing Children's Literature: From Romanticism to Postmodernism* (London and New York: Routledge 2002), p. 3.
6. Margaret Meek and Victor Watson, *Coming of Age in Children's Literature* (London and New York: Continuum, 2003), p. 25.
7. Giovanna Summerfield and Lisa Downward, *New Perspectives on the European Bildungsroman* (London and New York: Continuum, 2012), p. 3.
8. Maureen Moran, *Catholic Sensationalism and Victorian Literature* (Liverpool University Press, 2007), p. 177.
9. Rosi Braidotti, *Transpositions* (Cambridge and Malden: Polity Press, 2008), p. 43, p. 35.
10. See Fiona McCulloch, '"No Longer Just Human": The Posthuman Child in Beth Revis's *Across the Universe* Trilogy' in *Children's Literature Association Quarterly* 41.1 (Spring 2016), pp. 74–92.
11. Rachel Falconer, 'Young adult fiction and the crossover phenomenon' in David Rudd, *The Routledge Companion to Children's Literature* (ed.) (New York and London: 2010), p. 89.
12. Rosi Braidotti, 'Becoming-world' in Rosi Braidotti, Patrick Hanafin and Bolette Blaagaard (eds.), *After Cosmopolitanism* (Abingdon and New York: Routledge, 2013), p. 8.

13. Tobias Boes, *Formative Fictions: Nationalism, Cosmopolitanism, and the Bildungsroman* (New York: Cornell University Press, 2012), p. 181.

14. See Fiona McCulloch, *Contemporary British Children's Fiction and Cosmopolitanism* (New York and London: Routledge, 2017), pp. 98–114, pp. 83–97.

15. See Fiona McCulloch, 'Dis-membering "Patriotism"': Cosmopolitan Haunting in Theresa Breslin's *Remembrance*' in *The Lion and the Unicorn*, 38.3 (Sept. 2014), pp. 342–59.

16. Charles Kingsley, 'Human Soot' in Mrs Kingsley (ed.), *Charles Kingsley: His Letters and Memories of His Life*, Vol. II, seventh abridged edition (London: C. Kegan Paul and Co., 1880), pp. 242–3.

17. Charles Kingsley, *The Water-Babies* (Oxford and New York: Oxford University Press, 1995), p. 33, p. 17. Further references to this edition appear parenthetically.

18. See Fiona McCulloch, *The Fictional Role of Childhood in Victorian and Early Twentieth-Century Children's Literature* (New York and Ontario: Edwin Mellen Press, 2004), pp. 117–48.

19. Mike Cadden, 'Home Is Matter of Blood, Time, and Genre: Essentialism in Burnett and McKinley' in *Ariel: A Review of International English Literature*, 28.1 (1997), p. 55.

20. Frances Hodgson Burnett, *The Secret Garden* (London and New York: Puffin Books 1994), p. 1. Further references to this edition appear parenthetically.

21. Jerry Phillips, 'The Mem Sahib, the Worthy, the Rajah and His Minions: Some Reflections on the Class Politics of *The Secret Garden*' in *The Lion and the Unicorn*, 17.2 (1993), p. 182.

22. Shirley Foster and Judy Simmons, *What Katy Read: Feminist Re-Readings of 'Classic' Stories for Girls* (Hampshire and London, MacMillan Press, 1995), p. 189.

23. Heather Murray, 'Frances Hodgson Burnett's *The Secret Garden*: The Organ (ic)ized World', in Perry Nodelman (ed.), *Touchstones: Reflections on the Best in Children's Literature Vol. 1* (West Lafayette, IN: Purdue University, 1985), pp. 40–1.

24. See McCulloch, *The Fictional Role of Childhood in Victorian and Early Twentieth-Century Children's Literature*, pp. 149–73.

25. Alison Lurie, *Boys and Girls Forever: Children's Classics from Cinderella to Harry Potter* (London: Vintage, 2004), p. 31.

26. Gail S. Murray, *American Children's Literature and the Construction of Childhood* (New York: Twayne Publishers, 1998), pp. 103–4.

27. L. Frank Baum, *The Wizard of Oz* (London: Diamond Books, 1993), p. 5. Further references to this edition appear parenthetically.

28. Yoshido Junko, 'Uneasy men in the land of Oz' in Roderick McGillis (ed.), *Children's Literature and the Fin de Siècle* (Connecticut and London: Praeger, 2003), p. 161.

29. Sarah Gilead, 'Magic abdured: closure in children's fantasy fiction' in Peter Hunt (ed.), *Literature for Children: Contemporary Criticism* (London and New York: Routledge, 1992), p. 83. Further references to this edition appear parenthetically.

30. See Fiona McCulloch, *Children's Literature in Context* (London and New York: Continuum, 2011), pp. 72–80.

31. Ursula K. Le Guin, *A Wizard of Earthsea* (London: Penguin Books, 1991), p. 12. Further references to this edition appear parenthetically.

32. Briony Lipton and Elizabeth Mackinlay, *We Only Talk Feminist Here: Feminist Academics, Voice and Agency in the Neoliberal University* (Palgrave Macmillan, 2017), p. 96.

33. Millicent Lenz, 'Ursula K. Le Guin' in Peter Hunt and Millicent Lenz, *Alternative Worlds in Fantasy Fiction* (London and New York: Continuum, 2001), p. 47. Further references to this edition appear parenthetically.

34. Ursula. K. Le Guin interview, 'Chronicles of Earthsea', *The Guardian*, 9 February 2004, www.theguardian.com/books/2004/feb/09/sciencefictionfantasyandhorror.ursulakleguin

35. J. K. Rowling, *Harry Potter and the Philosopher's Stone* (London: Bloomsbury, 1997), p. 7.

36. J. K. Rowling, *Harry Potter and the Deathly Hallows* (London: Bloomsbury, 2007), p. 569.

37. J. K. Rowling, *Harry Potter and the Goblet of Fire* (London: Bloomsbury, 2000), p. 627.

38. J. K. Rowling, *Harry Potter and the Order of the Phoenix* (London: Bloomsbury, 2003), p. 155.

39. See McCulloch, *Contemporary British Children's Fiction and Cosmopolitanism*, pp. 1–62.

40. Roberta Seelinger Trites, *Disturbing the Universe: Power and Repression in Adolescent Literature* (University of Iowa Press, 2000), pp. 18–19.

41. Philip Pullman, *The Amber Spyglass* (London: Scholastic, 2001), p. 386. Further references to this edition appear parenthetically.

42. Julie Bertagna, *Exodus* (London: Young Picador, 2003), p. 178. Further references to this edition appear parenthetically.

43. See McCulloch, *Contemporary British Children's Fiction and Cosmopolitanism*, pp. 150–74.

44. Gillian Cross, *Where I Belong* (Oxford University Press, 2010), p. 340. Further references to this edition appear parenthetically.

45. Beth Revis, *Across the Universe* (London: Penguin Books, 2011), pp. 100–1. Further references to this edition appear parenthetically.
46. Saci Lloyd, *Momentum* (London: Hodder Children's Books, 2011), p. 125.
47. See McCulloch, *Contemporary British Children's Fiction and Cosmopolitanism*, pp. 135–49.
48. Louise O'Neill, *Only Ever Yours* (London: Quercus, 2014), p. 133. Further references to this edition appear parenthetically.

## Chapter 8 The Female Bildungsroman in the Twentieth Century

1. Lorna Ellis, *Appearing to Diminish: Female Development and the British Bildungsroman, 1750–1850* (Lewisburg: Bucknell University Press, 1999), p. 22.
2. Franco Moretti, *The Way of the World: The Bildungsroman in European Culture* (London: Verso, 1987), p. 24.
3. Terence Cave, *Mignon's Afterlives* (Oxford: Oxford University Press, 2011), p. 243.
4. Georgia Christinidis, 'Radical transformation: Angela Carter's adaptation of the Bildungsroman', *Textual Practice* 26.3 (2012), pp. 467–87, p. 473, www.tandfon line.com/author/Christinidis%2C+Georgia
5. Angela Carter, *Heroes and Villains* (Harmondsworth: Penguin, 1981), p. 100. Further references to this edition appear parenthetically.
6. Angela Carter, *Nights at the Circus* (London: Vintage, 2006), p. 133. Further references to this edition appear parenthetically.
7. Joseph Campbell, *The Hero with a Thousand Faces*, second edition (Princeton, New Jersey: Princeton University Press, 1968), p. 30.
8. Elizabeth Abel, Marianne Hirsch and Elizabeth Langland (eds.), *The Voyage In: Fictions of Female Development* (Hanover and London: University Press of New England, 1983), p. 4. Further references to this edition appear parenthetically.
9. Penny Brown, *Poison at the Source: The Female Novel of Self-Development in the Early Twentieth Century* (Basingstoke: Macmillan, 1992), p. 8.
10. Charlotte Brontë, *Jane Eyre* (Oxford: Oxford University Press, 1969), pp. 372–3. Further references to this edition appear parenthetically.
11. George Eliot, *The Mill on the Floss* (Oxford: Oxford University Press, 1913), p. 9. Further references to this edition appear parenthetically.
12. Gayatri Chakravorty Spivak, 'Three women's texts and a critique of imperialism', *Critical Inquiry*, Autumn 1985, pp. 243–61, p. 251.
13. Letter from Jean Rhys to Diana Athill dated 20 February 1966, in Francis Wyndham and Diana Melly (eds.), *Jean Rhys Letters 1931–66* (Harmondsworth: Penguin, 1984), pp. 296–8, p. 297.

14. Jed Esty, *Unseasonable Youth: Modernism, Colonialism and the Fiction of Development* (Oxford: Oxford University Press, 2011), p. 3. Further references to this edition appear parenthetically.

15. Mark Stein, *Black British Literature: Novels of Transformation* (Columbus: The Ohio University Press, 2004), p. 30, p. 23. Further references to this edition appear parenthetically.

16. Andrea Levy, *Every Light in the House Burnin'* (London: Review, 1994), p. 213. Further references to this edition appear parenthetically.

17. Dave Gunning, 'Unhappy Bildungsromane' in Jeannette Baxter and David James (eds.), *Andrea Levy* (London: Bloomsbury, 2014), pp. 9–22, p. 22.

18. Meera Syal, *Anita and Me* (London: HarperCollins, 1997), p. 296. Further references to this edition appear parenthetically.

19. Susan Fraiman, *Unbecoming Women: British Women Writers and the Novel of Development* (New York: Columbia University Press, 1993), p. 129.

20. Jane Eldridge Miller, *Rebel Women: Feminism, Modernism and the Edwardian Novel* (London: Virago, 1994), p. 4. Further references to this edition appear parenthetically.

21. Esther Kleinbord Labovitz, *The Myth of the Heroine: The Female Bildungsroman in the Twentieth Century* (New York: Peter Lang, 1986), p. 7.

22. May Sinclair, 'Clinical Lectures on Symbolism and Sublimation', 1, Medical Press (August 89, 1916), pp. 118–22, p. 120, quoted in Suzanne Raitt, *May Sinclair: A Modern Victorian* (Oxford: Clarendon Press, 2000), p. 254. Further references to this edition appear parenthetically.

23. Dorothy Richardson, *Honeycomb* (London: Duckworth, 1917), p. 100.

24. Jean Radford, introduction to *The Life and Death of Harriett Frean* (London: Virago, 1980), n.p.

25. May Sinclair, *The Life and Death of Harriett Frean* (London: Collins, 1922), pp. 14–15. Further references to this edition appear parenthetically.

26. Winifred Holtby, *The Crowded Street* (London: John Lane, 1924), p. 24. Further references to this edition appear parenthetically.

27. Zoe Fairbairn, introduction to Radclyffe Hall, *The Unlit Lamp* (London: Virago, 1980), p. 5.

28. Radclyffe Hall, *The Unlit Lamp* (London: Cassell, 1924), p. 263. Further references to this edition appear parenthetically.

29. Doris Lessing, *Martha Quest* (London: Michael Joseph, 1952), p. 22, p. 23.

30. Paulina Palmer, '"She began to show me the words she had written, one by one": Lesbian Reading and Writing Practices in the Fiction of Sarah Waters', *Women: A Cultural Review*, 19.1, spring, 2008, pp. 69–86, p. 70.

31. Moretti, *The Way of the World*, p. 24.

32. Rita Felski, *Beyond Feminist Aesthetics: Feminist Literature and Social Change* (Cambridge: Harvard University Press, 1989), p. 139.

33. Ellen Morgan, 'Humanbecoming: Form and Focus in the Neo-Feminist Novel' in Susan Koppelman Cornillon (ed.), *Images of Women in Fiction: Feminist Perspectives* (Bowling Green, Ohio: Bowling Green University Popular Press, 1972), pp. 183–205, p. 185.

## Chapter 9  The Postcolonial Bildungsroman

1. Nuruddin Farah, *Maps* (New York and London: Penguin, 1986), p. 14, emphasis original. Further references to this edition appear parenthetically.
2. Derek Wright, 'Mapping Farah's Fiction: The Postmodern Landscapes', in *Emerging Perspectives on Nuruddin Farah*, Derek Wright (ed.) (Trenton: Africa World Press, 2002), p. 96. Further references to this edition appear parenthetically.
3. Charles Dickens, *Our Mutual Friend* (White, Stokes, and Allen: 1885). 'No children for me. Give me grownups,' professes Dickens's strange 'person of the house', the dolls' dressmaker Jenny Wren, who states that she 'can't bear children' (Dickens p. 229). For Askar, 'it was the visceral dislike of children's babble or the infantile rattle of their mechanical contrivances and the noise of their demands', that he finds so displeasing (Farah p. 14). Not only does Askar's criticism about children recall Jenny Wren's own words – 'Always running about and screeching, always playing and fighting, always skip-skip-skipping on the pavement and chalking it for their games!' (Dickens p. 229) – both characters' allegiance to adults rather than children can be tied to their respective strangeness. Jenny's physical difference – she is a dwarf and a cripple – has separated her from the world of children, and she has come to hate the neighbour children who peek through keyholes, calling her names, and mocking her bowed legs. Though still a child (twelve years old) when the reader meets her, the responsibilities of caring for her drunken father and supporting the family, and a lifetime of torment at the hands of other children, have led her to develop an affinity for adults, who she finds more sensible and quiet (p. 230). Askar's strangeness is more complex, rooted not in any physical difference, but in his unnerving stare and blunt observations about the world, as well as his intensely intimate relationship with Misra. That relationship, coupled with his distaste for the few children he knows when he is younger, makes his preference for adults practically inevitable though no less striking.
4. Francesca Kazan, 'Recalling the Other Third World: Nuruddin Farah's *Maps*' in Wright (ed.), *Emerging Perspectives on Nuruddin Farah's Maps*, p. 256.
5. José Santiago Fernández Vásquez, 'Recharting the Geography of Genre: Ben Okri's *The Famished Road* as a Postcolonial Bildungsroman,' *Journal of*

*Commonwealth Literature* 27.2 (2002), p. 86. Further references to this article appear parenthetically.

6. Maria Helena Lima, 'Decolonizing Genre: Jamaica Kincaid and the Bildungsroman', *Genre* 26.4 (1993), p. 434. Further references to this article appear parenthetically.

7. Pheng Cheah, *Spectral Nationality: Passages of Freedom from Kant to Postcolonial Literatures of Liberation* (New York: Columbia, 2003), p. 242. Further references to this edition appear parenthetically.

8. Alioune Sow, 'Political Intuition and African Autobiographies of Childhood', *Biography: An Interdisciplinary Quarterly* 33.3 (2010), pp. 498–517, p. 502. Further references to this article appear parenthetically.

9. Franco Moretti, *The Way of the World: The Bildungsroman in European Culture* (London: Verso, 2000), p. 15. Further references to this edition appear parenthetically.

10. Simon Hays, '*Nervous Conditions*, Lukacs, and the Postcolonial Bildungsroman', *Genre: Forms of Discourse and Culture* 46.3 (2013), pp. 317–34, p. 319. Further references to this article appear parenthetically.

11. Ralph Austen, 'Struggling with the African Bildungsroman,' *Research in African Literatures*, 46.3 (2015), p. 217. Further references to this article appear parenthetically.

12. Marc Redfield, *Phantom Formations: Aesthetic Ideology and the Bildungsroman* (Ithaca and London: Cornell University Press, 1996), p. vii. Further references to this edition appear parenthetically.

13. Mpalive-Hangson Msiska, 'Genre: Fidelity and Transgression in the Post-Colonial African Novel' in Walter Goebel and Saskia Schabio (eds.), *Locating Postcolonial Narratives and Genres* (New York: Routledge, 2012), p. 85. Further references to this edition appear parenthetically.

14. Jed Esty, *Unseasonable Youth: Modernism, Colonialism, and the Fiction of Development* (Oxford: Oxford University Press, 2011), p. 18. Further references to this edition appear parenthetically.

15. M. M. Bakhtin, 'The *Bildungsroman* and Its Significance in the History of Realism (Toward a Historical Typology of the Novel)' in Caryl Emerson and Michael Holquist (eds.), *Speech Genres & Other Late Essays* (Austin: University of Texas Press, 1986), p. 20–1, emphasis original. Further references to this edition appear parenthetically.

16. Jed Esty, 'The Colonial Bildungsroman: *The Story of an African Farm* and the Ghost of Goethe', *Victorian Studies* 49.3 (2007), p. 411. Further references to this article appear parenthetically.

17. Apollo Amoko, 'Autobiography and Bildungsroman in African Literature' in F. Abiola Irele (ed.), *The Cambridge Companion to the African Novel*

(Cambridge: Cambridge University Press, 2009), p. 201. Further references to this edition appear parenthetically.

18. Esty, 'The Colonial Bildungsroman', p. 408.

19. Moretti, *The Way of the World*, p. 5, emphasis original.

20. Msiska, 'Genre: Fidelity and Transgression in the Post-Colonial African Novel,' p. 76.

21. Msiska argues that though there were authors, such as Cyprian Ekwensi and the Onitsha Market writers who wrote for an African audience and focused on 'the lived experience of African subjects', such writing was still highly imitative, and not particularly critical of colonialism. Chinua Achebe's work broke from these problems, helping to usher in what Msiska refers to a '*post-colonial counter discourse*' (emphasis original, p. 80). Msiska argues that a hybrid of realism and modernism was used by writers like Achebe and Ngũgĩ wa Thiong'o, who also 'inserted an indigenous aesthetic', thus 'starting the process of decolonizing the novel as a genre in Africa' (p. 83).

22. Sow later states that childhood in African letters is expected to have a 'politics' (Smith and Watson, qtd in Sow p. 502), and 'a narrative of childhood during colonization that *does not* expose major conflicts is considered an anomaly, and the experience of that childhood is perceived as little relevant for understanding colonialism or the resistance to it' (Sow p. 502; my emphasis). These words remain applicable to both the postcolonial and African Bildungsroman, in which so frequently the vestiges of colonialism stubbornly cling to the postcolonial nation and subject.

23. Camara Laye, *The Dark Child: The Autobiography of an African Boy*, trans. James Kirkup and Ernest Jones (New York: Farrar, Straus and Giroux, 1994), p. 19. Further references to this edition appear parenthetically.

24. David J. Mickelson, 'The *Bildungsroman* in Africa: The Case of *Mission terminée*', *The French Review* 59.3 (1986), p. 427. Further references to this article appear parenthetically.

25. Chimamanda Ngozi Adichie, *Purple Hibiscus* (Chapel Hill: Algonquin, 2012), p. 47. Further references to this edition appear parenthetically.

26. Emmanuel Dongala, *Johnny Mad Dog*, trans. Maria Louise Ascher (New York: Picador, 2006), p. 44. Further references to this edition appear parenthetically.

27. Maria Kruger, *Women's Literature in Kenya and Uganda: The Trouble with Modernity* (New York: Palgrave Macmillan, 2010), p. 158.

28. Andrew H. Armstrong, 'Narrative and the Re-Cor(d)ing of Cultural Memory in Moses Isegawa's *Abyssinian Chronicles* and *Snakepit*', *Journal of African Cultural Studies* 21.2 (2009), pp. 127–43. Further references to this article appear parenthetically.

29. Derek Wright, 'Parenting the Nation: Some Observations on Nuruddin Farah's *Maps*', *College Literature* 19.3 (1992), pp. 176–84, p. 176. Further references to this article appear parenthetically.

30. Moretti argues for this pattern in the light of what he argues were the 'opposite directions' taken by the late Bildungsroman and modernism as the 'nineteenth-century episode fell apart' under the weight of war, modernisation, and the collapse of the insular nation state. 'Narratives', Moretti states, 'could concentrate *either* on kernels *or* on satellites: the late Bildungsroman chose the former and modernism the latter' (emphasis original, p. 234). 'Kernels' and 'satellites' are two types of narrative episode: the first focuses on 'abrupt, irreversible choices among widely different options' while in the second, 'slower, subordinate events [that] qualify and enrich the chosen course' (p. 233). For the late Bildungsroman, kernels that once were 'produced *by* the hero as turning points of his free growth' are now produced '*against* him, by a world that is thoroughly indifferent to his personal development' (p. 233). This is the direct consequence, Moretti argues, of the rise of institutions in social relations over relations between individuals (p. 230).

## Chapter 10 Lesbian, Gay and Trans Bildungsromane

1. Mikhail Bakhtin, 'The *Bildungsroman* and Its Significance in the History of Realism (Towards a Historical Typology of the Novel)' in Caryl Emerson and Michael Holquist (eds.), *Speech Genres and Other Late Essays*, trans. Vern W. McGee (Austin: University of Texas Press, 1986), pp. 10–59 (p. 22).

2. Franco Moretti, *The Way of the World: The Bildungsroman in European Culture* (London: Verso, 1987), p. 227 (italics original). Further references to this edition appear parenthetically.

3. See, for example, the discussion of will and desire as markers of the individual in John Locke, *An Essay Concerning Human Understanding* (1689), (Oxford: Clarendon Press, 1979).

4. See Michel Foucault, 'Domain' in *The Will to Knowledge: The History of Sexuality, Volume I*, trans. Robert Hurley (London: Penguin, 1998), pp. 103–14. Further references to this edition appear parenthetically.

5. Lorna Ellis, *Appearing to Diminish: Female Development and the British Bildungsroman, 1780–1950* (Lewisburg: Bucknell University Press, 1999), pp. 42–3.

6. See Bonnie Kime Scott's two critical anthologies, *The Gender of Modernism: A Critical Anthology* (Bloomington: Indiana University Press, 1990) and *Gender in Modernism: New Geographies, Complex Intersections* (Urbana: University of Illinois Press, 2006). For an analysis of the ideological role of femininity as a

structuring frame for the idea of modernity in this period, see Rita Felski's *The Gender of Modernity* (Cambridge, MA: Harvard University Press, 1995).

7. Raymond Williams (1961), *The Long Revolution* (London: Hogarth Press, 1992).

8. Georg Lukàcs, *The Meaning of Contemporary Realism*, trans. Hannah and Stanley Mitchell (London: Merlin, 1956), p. 19.

9. See Roland Barthes, *S/Z*, trans. Richard Miller (Oxford: Blackwell, 1990) pp. 7–8.

10. Jay Prosser, '"Some Primitive Thing Conceived in a Turbulent Age of Transition": The Invert, *The Well of Loneliness* and the Narrative Origins of Transsexuality' in *Second Skins: The Body Narratives of Transsexuality* (New York: Columbia University Press, 1998), p. 140.

11. Radclyffe Hall, *The Well of Loneliness* (London: Virago, 1982) pp. 353–4. Further references to this edition appear parenthetically.

12. See Alan Sinfield, *The Wilde Century: Effeminacy, Oscar Wilde and the Queer Moment* (London: Cassell, 1994) pp. 42–7

13. E. M. Forster, *Maurice* (London: Penguin, 1972) p. 32. Further references to this edition appear parenthetically.

14. Philip Gardner, 'The Evolution of E.M. Forster's *Maurice*' in Judith Scherer Herz and Robert K. Martin (eds.), *E. M. Forster: Centenary Revaluations* (Basingstoke: Palgrave Macmillan, 1982), p. 207.

15. Patricia Highsmith *Carol* (*The Price of Salt*) (London: Bloomsbury, 2010) p. 9. Further references to this edition appear parenthetically.

16. Charles J. Rolo, 'Carol and Therese: *The Price of Salt* by Claire Morgan', *New York Times*, 18 May 1952, BR23.

17. Valerie Taylor, *Stranger on Lesbos* (London: New English Library, 1970) p. 5.

18. Valerie Taylor, *Return to Lesbos* (Tallahassee: Naiad Press, 1982) p. 189. Further references to this edition appear parenthetically.

19. Rolo, 'Carol and Therese'.

20. Kate Adams, 'Making the World Safe for the Missionary Position: Images of the Lesbian in Post-World War II America', in Karla Jay and Joanne Glasgow (eds.), *Lesbian Texts and Contexts: Radical Revisions* (London: Onlywomen Press, 1992), p. 257.

21. See Julie Abraham, 'Introduction' in *Are Girls Necessary? Lesbian Writing and Modern Histories* (New York: Routledge, 1996) and Bonnie Zimmerman, *The Safe Sea of Women: Lesbian Fiction, 1969–1989* (London: Onlywomen Press, 1992).

22. Alan Sinfield, 'Diaspora and Hybridity: Queer Identity and the Ethnicity Model', *Textual Practice* 10.2 (1996), p. 287 (italics original). Further references to this edition appear parenthetically.

23. Jeanette Winterson, 'Introduction' in *Oranges Are Not the Only Fruit* (London: Vintage, 1991), pp. xii–xiii. Further references to this edition appear parenthetically.

24. Neil Bartlett, *Ready to Catch Him Should He Fall* (London: Serpent's Tail, 1990), p. 113.

25. Audre Lorde, *Zami: A New Spelling of My Name* (New York: Crossing Press, 1982) p. 225. Further references to this edition appear parenthetically.

26. Edmund White, *A Boy's Own Story* (London: Picador, 1982) p. 50.

27. See Jasbir K. Puar, *Terrorist Assemblages: Homonationalism in Queer Times* (Durham: Duke University Press, 2007). Further references to this edition appear parenthetically. Rahul Rao, *Third World Protest: Between Home and the World* (Oxford University Press, 2012).

28. See, for example: Meredith Russo, *If I Was Your Girl* (New York: Flatiron Books, 2016); Becky Albertalli, *Simon vs. the Homo Sapiens Agenda* (New York: Balzer and Bray, 2015); and Lisa Williamson, *The Art of Being Normal* (London: David Fickling, 2016).

29. J. T. LeRoy (Laura Albert), *Sarah* (London: Bloomsbury, 2000) pp. 164–5.

30. Adam Mars-Jones, *Pilcrow* (London: Faber and Faber, 2008), p. 146. Further references to this edition appear parenthetically.

## Chapter 11 Bildungsromane and Graphic Narratives

1. Hillary L. Chute, *Graphic Women: Life Narrative and Contemporary Comics* (New York: Columbia University Press, 2010), p. 109, cited by Michael Chaney, *Reading Lessons in Seeing: Mirrors, Masks and Mazes in the Autobiographical Novel* (Jackson: University Press of Mississippi, 2016), p. 9.

2. Ian Gordon, 'Making Comics Respectable: How *Maus* helped Redefine a Medium' in Paul Williams and James Lyons (eds.), *The Rise of the American Comics Artist: Creators and Contexts* (Jackson: University Press of Mississippi, 2010), pp. 160–7.

3. Martin Flanagan, 'Teen Trajectories in *Spider-Man* and *Ghost World*', in Ian Gordon, Matthew P. McAllister, and Mark Jancovich (eds.), *Film and Comic Books* (Jackson: University Press of Mississippi, 2007), pp. 147–8.

4. Bradford W. Wright, *Comic Book Nation: The Transformation of Youth Culture in America* (Baltimore: Johns Hopkins University Press, 2001), p. 239.

5. Bart Beaty, *12 Cent Archie* (New Brunswick: Rutgers University Press, 2015), pp. 38–41, pp. 49–52.

6. Joshua Brown, 'Of Mice and Memory', *The Oral History Review* 16.1 (1988), p. 98; Gordon, 'Making Comics Respectable', pp. 160–7.

7. Ruth Franklin, 'Art Spiegelman's Genre-Defying Holocaust Work, Revisited', *New Republic* (October 5, 2011), https://newrepublic.com/article/95758/art-spiegelman-metamaus-holocaust-memoir-graphic-novel

8. Michael Chaney, 'Introduction', in *Graphic Subjects: Critical Essays on Autobiography and the Graphic Novel* (Madison: University of Wisconsin Press, 2011), pp. 3–4.

9. Bart Beaty, *Unpopular Culture: Transforming the European Comic Book in the 1990s* (Toronto: University of Toronto Press, 2007), p. 143. And again *Maus* would be an exception to this sidestepping.

10. Pat Grant, 'Genealogy of the Boofhead: Image, Memory and Australian Surf Comics', in *Blue* (Marietta, GA: Top Shelf, 2012), n.p.

11. Joseph Witek, *Comic Books as History: The Narrative Art of Jack Jackson, Art Spiegelman, and Harvey Pekar* (Jackson: University Press of Mississippi, 1989); Charles Hatfield, *Alternative Comics: An Emerging Literature* (Jackson: University Press of Mississippi, 2005); Marianne Hirsch, 'Family Pictures: Maus, Mourning, and Post-Memory', *Discourse* 15.2 (Winter 1992–3), pp. 3–29.

12. Hillary Chute, *Outside the Box: Interviews with Contemporary Cartoonists* (Chicago: University of Chicago Press, 2014), pp. 112–13.

13. Rocío Davis, '*American Born Chinese*: Challenging the Stereotype' in Michael Chaney (ed.), *Graphic Subjects: Critical Essays on Autobiography and the Graphic Novel* (Madison: University of Wisconsin Press, 2011), p. 279. See also Gene Luen Yang, 'Why Comics?', lecture at Penn State University, December 10, 2008, www.youtube.com/watch?v=xYA3HNbc7Rs

14. John Kuo-Wei Tchen, *New York before Chinatown: Orientalism and the Shaping of American Culture, 1776–1882* (Baltimore: Johns Hopkins University Press, 2001).

15. Philip P. Choy, Marlon K. Hom, and Lorraine Dong, *Coming Man: Nineteenth Century American Perceptions of the Chinese* (Seattle: University of Washington Press, 1995); Richard Samuel West, *The San Francisco Wasp: An Illustrated History* (Northampton, MA: Periodyssey Press, 2004).

16. Phoebe Gloeckner, *The Diary of a Teenage Girl: An Account in Words and Pictures* (Berkeley: North Atlantic Books, 2015), p. xv.

17. Hillary Chute, 'Foreword', *The Diary of a Teenage Girl*, p. xiii.

18. Sean T. Collins, 'Phoebe Gloeckner on reopening *The Diary of a Teenage Girl*', *AV Club* (August 13, 2015), www.avclub.com/article/phoebe-gloeckner-reopening-diary-teenage-girl-223696

19. Chute, 'Foreword', p. xiii.

20. 'Fake Simpsons cartoon is child porn, judge rules', *ABC News* (December 9, 2008), www.abc.net.au/news/2008–12-08/fake-simpsons-cartoon-is-child-porn-judge-rules/233562

21. Jillian Tamaki and Mariko Tamaki, *This One Summer* (New York: First Second, 2014), p. 319.

22. Harper Harris, 'Mariko and Jillian Tamaki on This One Summer winning the Caldecott and Printz Honors', *The Beat* (February 13, 2015), www.comicsbeat .com/mariko-and-jillian-tamaki-on-winning-the-caldecott-and-printz-honors-and-this-one-summer/

23. Jennifer Hayden, *The Story of My Tits* (Marietta, GA: Top Shelf Productions, 2015), p. 296. Further references to this edition appear parenthetically.

24. Chris Ware, 'Richard McGuire and "Here": A Grateful Appreciation', *Comic Art* 8 (2008), p. 6.

# Bibliography

## Primary

Adichie, Chimamanda Ngozi, *Purple Hibiscus* (Chapel Hill: Algonquin, 2012).

Aksenov, Vassily, *A Ticket to the Stars*, trans. Andrew MacAndrew (New York: New American Library, 1963).

Albertalli, Becky, *Simon vs. the Homo Sapiens Agenda* (New York: Balzer and Bray, 2015).

Alcott, Louisa May, *Little Women* (Ontario: Broadview, 2001).

Alger, Jr., Horatio, *Ragged Dick or, Street Life in New York with Boot Blacks* (New York and London: W. W. Norton & Co., 2008).

Allison, Dorothy, *Bastard out of Carolina* (New York: Plume, 1993).

American Friends Service Committee, *Speak Truth to Power: A Quaker Search for an Alternative to Violence*, 1955.

Austen, Jane, *Emma* (London: Oxford University Press, 1966).

Baldwin, James, *Go Tell It on the Mountain* (New York: Delta, 2000).

Balzac, Honoré de, *La Cousine Bette* (Paris: Librairie Générale Française, 1963).

Balzac, Honoré de, *Le Père Goriot* (Paris: Librairie Générale Française, 1961).

Bartlett, Neil, *Ready to Catch Him Should He Fall* (London: Serpent's Tail, 1990).

Baum, L. Frank, *The Wizard of Oz* (London: Diamond Books, 1993).

Bechdel, Alison, *Fun Home: A Family Tragicomic* (Boston: Houghton Mifflin, 2006).

Bellow, Saul, *The Adventures of Augie March* (London: Everyman's Library, 1995).

Bertagna, Julie, *Exodus* (London: Young Picador, 2003).

Bitov, Andrei, *Pushkin House*, trans. Susan Brownsberger (Normal, IL: Dalkey Archive Press, 1987).

Bowen, Elizabeth, *The Last September* (New York: Anchor Books, 2000).

Brontë, Charlotte, *Jane Eyre* (Oxford: Oxford University Press, 1969).

Brontë, Charlotte, *Villette* (Harmondsworth: Penguin, 1988).

Bunin, Ivan, *Zhizn' Arsen'eva* (Moscow: Eksmo, 2014).

Burnett, Frances Hodgson, *The Secret Garden* (London and New York: Puffin Books, 1994).

Cahan, Abraham, *The Rise of David Levinsky* (New York: Penguin, 1993).

Capote, Truman, *Other Voices, Other Rooms* (London: Pan, 1988).

Carlyle, Thomas, *Sartor Resartus* (Oxford and New York: Oxford University Press, 1987).

Carter, Angela, *Heroes and Villains* (Harmondsworth: Penguin, 1981).

Carter, Angela, *Nights at the Circus* (London: Vintage, 2006).

*Chanson de Roland, La* (n.p.: Librairie Générale Française, 1990).

Cisneros, Sandra, *The House on Mango Street* (London: Bloomsbury, 2004).

*Congressional Record* 144.5, 21 April 1998–30 April 1998, p. 6696.

Constant, Benjamin, *Adolphe* (Paris: Garnier, 1968).

Corneille, Pierre, *Cinna*, in *Œuvres complètes* (Paris: Seuil, 1963).

Crane, Stephen, *The Red Badge of Courage* in Stephen Crane, *Prose and Poetry*, College Edition (New York: Library of America, 1996).

Cross, Gillian, *Where I Belong* (Oxford University Press, 2010).

Dangarembga, Tsitsi, *Nervous Conditions* (Boulder, CO: Lynne Reinner, 2004).

Dickens, Charles, *David Copperfield* (Harmondsworth: Penguin, 1996).

Dickens, Charles, *Great Expectations* (Harmondsworth: Penguin, 1996).

Dickens, Charles, *Our Mutual Friend* (White, Stokes and Allen, 1885).

Diderot, Denis, *Le Neveu de Rameau* in *Œuvres romanesques* (Paris: Garnier, 1962).

Didion, Joan, 'One Week after 9/11: Jon Wiener interviews Joan Didion', *Los Angeles Review of Books*, 11 September 2013, https://lareviewofbooks.org/article/one-week-after-911/

Disraeli, Benjamin, *Contarini Fleming: A Psychological Romance* (London: Peter Davies, 1927).

Dixon, Ella Hepworth, *The Story of a Modern Woman* (Peterborough, ON: Broadview, 2004).

Dongala, Emmanuel, *Johnny Mad Dog*, trans. Maria Louise Ascher (New York: Picador, 2006).

Dostoevsky, Fyodor Mikhailovich, *Polnoe sobranie sochinenii v tridtsati tomakh*, V. G. Bazanov et al. (eds.), 30 vols. (Leningrad: Nauka, 1972–90).

Duplechan, Larry, *Blackbird* (Vancouver: Arsenal Pulp Press, 2006).

Eliot, George, *Daniel Deronda* (Harmondsworth: Penguin, 1967).

Eliot, George, *The Mill on the Floss* (Oxford: Oxford University Press, 1913).

Emerson, Ralph Waldo, 'Self-Reliance' in Stephen E. Whicher (ed.), *Selections from Ralph Waldo Emerson: An Organic Anthology* (Boston: Houghton Mifflin, 1960).

Farah, Nuruddin, *Maps* (New York & London: Penguin, 1986).

Flaubert, Gustave, *Correspondance*, 4 vols. (Paris: Gallimard, 1973–98).

Flaubert, Gustave, *Madame Bovary* (Paris: Bordas, 1990).

Flaubert, Gustave, *Madame Bovary*, trans. Geoffrey Wall (Harmondsworth: Penguin, 1992).

Flaubert, Gustave, *Trois Contes* (Paris: Garnier, 1969).

Forster, E. M., *A Room with a View* (London: Edward Arnold, 1919).

Forster, E. M., *Maurice* (London: Penguin, 1972).

Gloeckner, Phoebe, *The Diary of a Teenage Girl: An Account in Words and Pictures* (Berkeley: North Atlantic Books, 2015).

Goethe, Johann Wolfgang von, *Wilhelm Meister's Apprenticeship*, ed. and trans. Eric A. Blackall in cooperation with Victor Lange (Princeton: Princeton University Press, 1989).

Grass, Günter, 'To be continued . . . ', trans. Michael Henry Heim, *PMLA* 115 (1999), p. 298.

Hall, Radclyffe, *The Unlit Lamp* (London: Cassell, 1924).

Hall, Radclyffe, *The Unlit Lamp* (London: Virago, 1980).

Hall, Radclyffe, *The Well of Loneliness* (London: Virago, 1982).

Hardy, Thomas, *Jude the Obscure* (Peterborough, ON: Broadview, 1999).

Hayden, Jennifer, *The Story of My Tits* (Marietta, GA: Top Shelf Productions, 2015).

H. D., *HERmione* (New York: New Directions, 1981).

H. D., *Asphodel* (Durham: Duke University Press, 1992).

Herzen, Alexander, *Ends and Beginnings*, trans. Constance Garnett (Oxford: Oxford University Press, 1968).

Highsmith, Patricia, *Carol* (London: Bloomsbury, 2010).

Holtby, Winifred, *The Crowded Street* (London: John Lane, 1924).

James, Henry, *The Princess Casamassima* (Harmondsworth: Penguin, 1986).

James, Henry, *What Maisie Knew* (Oxford and New York: Oxford University Press, 1992).

Jewsbury, Geraldine, *The Half Sisters* (Oxford and New York: Oxford University Press, 1994).

Joyce, James, *A Portrait of the Artist as a Young Man* (New York: Viking Press, 1964).

Joyce, James, *A Portrait of the Artist as a Young Man* (New York: Norton, 2007).

Keller, Gottfried, *Der grüne Heinrich: Erste Fassung* in Keller, *Sämtliche Werke*, vol. 2, (Frankfurt am Main: Deutscher Klassiker Verlag, 1954).

Key, Francis Scott, 'The Star-Spangled Banner' in Geoffrey Moore (ed.), *The Penguin Book of American Verse* (London: Penguin, 2011).

Kingsley, Charles, *Alton Locke, Tailor and Poet* (Oxford and New York: Oxford University Press, 1983).

Kingsley, Charles, *The Water-Babies* (Oxford University Press, 1995).

Kingston, Maxine Hong, *The Woman Warrior: Memoirs of a Girlhood Among Ghosts* (London: Picador Classic, 2015).

Lafayette, Marie-Madeleine de, *La Princesse de Clèves* (Paris: Gallimard, 1972).

Laye, Camara, *The Dark Child: The Autobiography of an African Boy*, trans. James Kirkup and Ernest Jones (New York: Farrar, Straus and Giroux, 1994).

Lee, Harper, *To Kill a Mockingbird* (London: Arrow, 2010).

Le Guin, Ursula K., *A Wizard of Earthsea* (London: Penguin Books, 1991).

Le Guin, Ursula K., 'Chronicles of Earthsea', *Guardian*, 9 February 2004, www.theguardian.com/books/2004/feb/09/sciencefictionfantasyandhorror.ursulakleguin

LeRoy, J. T. [Laura Albert] *Sarah* (London: Bloomsbury, 2000).

Lessing, Doris, *Martha Quest* (London: Michael Joseph, 1952).

Levy, Andrea, *Every Light in the House Burnin'* (London: Review, 1994).

Lewes, G. H., 'The Apprenticeship of Life', *Leader and Saturday Analyst*, 7 January–30 June 1850, I.II, pp. 260–1.

Lloyd, Saci, *Momentum* (London: Hodder Children's Books, 2011).

London, Jack, *Martin Eden* (London: Penguin, 1985).

Lorde, Audre, *Zami: A New Spelling of My Name* (New York: Crossing Press, 1982).

Lytton, Lord, *Alice; or, The Mysteries* (London: Routledge, 1873).

Lytton, Lord, *Ernest Maltravers* (London: Routledge, 1873).

Mann, Thomas, *The Magic Mountain*, trans. John E. Woods (New York: Vintage, 1995).

Marshall, Paule, *Brown Girl, Brownstones*, new edition (London: Virago, 1982).

Mars-Jones, Adam, *Pilcrow* (London: Faber and Faber, 2008).

McCarthy, Cormac, *The Border Trilogy* (London: Picador, 2002).

McGuire, Richard, *Here* (New York: Pantheon, 2014).

McMurtry, Larry, *The Last Picture Show* (London: Penguin, 2011).

McNickle, D'Arcy, *The Surrounded* (New York: Quality Paper Book Club, 1998).

Meredith, George, *Beauchamp's Career* (Oxford and New York: Oxford University Press, 1988).

Meredith, George, *The Ordeal of Richard Feverel* (Harmondsworth: Penguin, 1998).

Meyer, Philipp, *American Rust* (London and New York: Simon & Schuster, 2009).

Molière, *Œuvres complètes* (Paris: Gallimard, 1971), vol. I.

Montaigne, Michel de, *Essays*, trans. J. M. Cohen (Harmondsworth: Penguin, 1958).

Nerval, Gérard de, *Les Chimères* (Geneva/Paris: Droz/Minard, 1966).

O'Neill, Louise, *Only Ever Yours* (London: Quercus, 2014).

Pater, Walter, *Marius the Epicurean* (London: Penguin, 1985).

Pelevin, Viktor, *Omon Ra* (New York: New Directions, 1998).

Plath, Sylvia, *The Bell Jar* (London: Faber and Faber, 1999).

Proust, Marcel, *À la recherche du temps perdu*, 4 vols. (Paris: Gallimard, 1987–9).

Pater, Walter, *Marius the Epicurean* (London: Penguin, 1985).

Proust, Marcel, *Contre Sainte-Beuve, précédé de Pastiches et mélanges et suivi de Essais et articles*, Pierre Clarac and Yves Sandre (eds.), (Paris: Gallimard, 1971).

Proust, Marcel, and Jacques Rivière, *Correspondance (1914–22)*, Philip Kolb, (ed.), (Paris: Plon, 1955).

Pushkin, Alexander S., *Sobranie sochinenii v desiati tomakh*, 10 vols. (Moscow: Khudozhestvennaia literatura, 1960).

Revis, Beth, *Across the Universe* (London: Penguin Books, 2011).

Richardson, Dorothy, *Honeycomb* (London: Duckworth, 1917).

Richardson, Dorothy, *Pilgrimage I* (Urbana and Chicago: University of Illinois Press, 1979).

Riddell, Charlotte, *A Struggle for Fame: A Novel*, 3 vols. (London: Richard Bentley, 1883).

Rimbaud, Arthur, *Œuvres* (Paris: Garnier, 1960).

Rousseau, Jean-Jacques, *The Confessions*, trans. J. M. Cohen (London: Penguin, 1953).

Rowling, J. K., *Harry Potter and the Deathly Hallows* (London: Bloomsbury, 2007).

Rowling, J. K., *Harry Potter and the Goblet of Fire* (London: Bloomsbury, 2000).

Rowling, J. K., *Harry Potter and the Order of the Phoenix* (London: Bloomsbury, 2003).

Rowling, J. K., *Harry Potter and the Philosopher's Stone* (London: Bloomsbury, 1997).

Russo, Meredith, *If I Was Your Girl* (New York: Flatiron Books, 2016).

Salinger, J. D., *The Catcher in the Rye* (London: Penguin, 1994).

Schiller, Friedrich, *On the Aesthetic Education of Man in a Series of Letters*, ed. and trans. Elizabeth M. Wilkinson and L. A. Willoughby (Oxford: Clarendon Press, 1967).

Sinclair, May, *The Life and Death of Harriett Frean* (London: Collins, 1922).

Sinclair, May, *The Life and Death of Harriett Frean* (London: Virago, 1980).

Smiles, Samuel, *Self-Help; With Illustrations of Character, Conduct, and Perseverance* (Oxford and New York: Oxford University Press, 2002).

Smith, Betty, *A Tree Grows in Brooklyn* (London: Arrow, 2000).

Stendhal, *Le Rouge et le Noir* in Henri Martineau (ed.), *Romans et nouvelles* (Paris: Gallimard, 1952), vol. I.

Syal, Meera, *Anita and Me* (London: HarperCollins, 1997).

Tamaki, Jillian and Mariko Tamaki, *This One Summer* (New York: First Second, 2014).

Taylor, Valerie, *Return to Lesbos* (Tallahassee: Naiad Press, 1982).

Taylor, Valerie, *Stranger on Lesbos* (London: New English Library, 1970).

Tolstoy, L. N., *Polnoe sobraie sochinenii v devianosta tomakh*, V.G. Chertkov et al. (eds.), 90 vols. (Moscow: Khudozhestvennaia literatura, 1928–58), vol. XXXII.

Twain, Mark, *Adventures of Huckleberry Finn*, Norton Critical Edition, third edition (New York: Norton, 1999).

Wilde, Oscar, *Miscellanies*, Robert Ross (ed.), *The Collected Works of Oscar Wilde* (London: Methuen, 1908), vol. XIV.

Wilde, Oscar, *The Picture of Dorian Gray*, second edition (New York: Norton, 2007).

Williamson, Lisa, *The Art of Being Normal* (London: David Fickling, 2016).

Winterson, Jeanette, *Oranges Are Not the Only Fruit* (London: Vintage, 1991).

Wharton, Edith, *Summer* (New York and London: Penguin, 1993).

White, Edmund, *A Boy's Own Story* (London: Picador, 1982).

Woolf, Virginia, *Mrs Dalloway* (New York: Harcourt, 2005).

Woolf, Virginia, *The Voyage Out* (Oxford: Oxford University Press, 2001).

Yang, Gene Luen, *American born Chinese* (New York : First Second, 2006).

Yezierska, Anzia, *Bread Givers: A Novel* (New York: Persea, 2003).

## Secondary

*ABC News*, 'Fake Simpsons cartoon is child porn, judge rules' (9 December 2008), www.abc.net.au/news/2008–12-08/fake-simpsons-cartoon-is-child-porn-judge-rules/233562

Abel, Elizabeth, Marianne Hirsch, and Elizabeth Langland (eds.), *The Voyage In: Fictions of Female Development* (Hanover and London: University Press of New England, 1983).

Abraham, Julie, *'Are Girls Necessary?' Lesbian Writing and Modern Histories* (New York: Routledge, 1996).

Adams, James Eli, *A History of Victorian Literature* (Oxford, Blackwell Publishing, 2012).

Amrine, Frederick, 'Rethinking the *Bildungsroman*', *Michigan Germanic Studies* 13 (1987), pp. 119–39.

Anderson, Benedict, *Imagined Communities: Reflections on the Origin and Spread of Nationalism* (London: Verso, 1991).

Applegate, Celia, *A Nation of Provincials: The German Idea of Heimat* (Berkeley: University of California Press, 1990).

Armstrong, Andrew H., 'Narrative and the Re-Cor(d)ing of Cultural Memory in Moses Isegawa's *Abyssinian Chronicles* and *Snakepit*', *Journal of African Cultural Studies* 21.2 (2009), pp. 127–43.

Arnold, Matthew, *Culture and Anarchy and Other Writings* (Cambridge University Press, 1993).

Ashton, Rosemary, *The German Idea: Four English Writers and the Reception of German Thought 1800–1860* (London: Libris, 1994).

Auerbach, Erich, *Mimesis: The Representation of Reality in Western Literature*, trans. Willard R. Trask (Princeton: Princeton University Press, 1968).

Austen, Ralph A., 'Struggling with the African Bildungsroman', *Research in African Literatures* 46.3 (2015), pp. 214–31.

Bakhtin, M. M., 'The *Bildungsroman* and Its Significance in the History of Realism (Toward a Historical Typology of the Novel)' in Caryl Emerson and Michael Holquist (eds.), *Speech Genres & Other Late Essays*, trans. Vern W. McGee (Austin: University of Texas Press, 1986).

Bakhtin, M. M., 'Formy vremeni i khronotopa v romane' in *Sobranie sochinenii*, vol. III, pp. 472–89.

Bakhtin, M. M., *Problems of Dostoevsky's Poetics*, trans. William Booth, Caryl Emerson (ed.) (Minneapolis: University of Minnesota Press, 1984).

Bakhtin, M. M., 'Roman vospitaniia i ego znachenie v istorii realizma' in *Sobranie sochinenii*, vol. III, pp. 181–217.

Bakhtin, M. M., 'Roman kak literaturnyi zhanr' in *Sobranie sochinenii*, vol. III, pp. 608–43.

Bakhtin, M. M., *Sobranie sochinenii v semi tomakh*, vol. VI, pp. 797–800.

Barrett, Dorothea, *Vocation and Desire: George Eliot's Heroines* (London and New York: Routledge, 1989).

Barthes, Roland, *S/Z*, trans. Richard Miller (Oxford: Blackwell, 1990).

Baxter, Jeannette, and David James (eds.), *Andrea Levy* (London: Bloomsbury, 2014).

Beaty, Bart, *12 Cent Archie* (New Brunswick: Rutgers University Press, 2015).

Beaty, Bart, *Unpopular Culture: Transforming the European Comic Book in the 1990s* (Toronto: University of Toronto Press, 2007).

Beddow, Michael, *The Fiction of Humanity: Studies in the Bildungsroman from Wieland to Thomas Mann* (Cambridge: Cambridge University Press, 1982).

Belinskii, V. G., *Polnoe sobranie sochinenii*, 30 vols. (Moscow, 1953–9), vol. 7, pp. 428–35.

Bell, Anne Olivier, and Andrew McNeillie (eds.), *The Diary of Virginia Woolf*, vol. 2: 1920–1924 (New York: Harcourt Brace Jovanovich, 1978).

Bennett, Kelsey L., *Principle and Propensity: Experience and Religion in the Nineteenth-Century British and American Bildungsroman* (Columbia: University of South Carolina, 2014).

Blackenburg, Friedrich von, Versuch über den Roman (Stuttgart: J.B. Metzlerische Verlagsbuchhandlung, 1774).

Berlin, Isaiah, 'Herzen and His Memoirs' in *Against the Current: Essays in the History of Ideas* (Princeton: Princeton University Press, 2013), pp. 188–212.

Berman, Russell A., 'Modernism and the *Bildungsroman*: Thomas Mann's *Magic Mountain*' in Graham Bartram (ed.), *The Cambridge Companion to the Modern German Novel* (Cambridge University Press, 2004), pp. 77–92.

Bersani, Leo, *Balzac to Beckett: Center and Circumference in French Fiction* (New York: Oxford University Press, 1970).

Blackbourn, David, *History of Germany 1780–1918: The Long Nineteenth Century* (Oxford: Blackwell, 1997).

Blackwell, L. Jeannine, 'Bildungsroman mit Dame: The Heroine in the German *Bildungsroman* from 1770 to 1900', Dissertation, Indiana University, 1983.

Boes, Tobias, *Formative Fictions: Nationalism, Cosmopolitanism, and the Bildungsroman* (Ithaca: Cornell University Press, 2012).

Bolaki, Stella, *Unsettling the Bildungsroman: Reading Contemporary Ethnic American Women's Fiction* (Amsterdam: Rodopi, 2011).

Borchmeyer, Dieter, *Höfische Gesellschaft und französische Revolution bei Goethe: Adliges und bürgerliches Wertsystem im Urteil der Weimarer Klassik* (Kronberg: Athenäum, 1977).

Bouson, J. Brooks, '"You Nothing but Trash": White Trash Shame in Dorothy Allison's *Bastard out of Carolina*', *The Southern Literary Journal* 34.1 (2001), pp. 101–23.

Bowie, Malcolm, Alison Fairlie, Alison Finch (eds.), *Baudelaire, Mallarmé, Valéry: New Essays in Honour of Lloyd Austin* (Cambridge: Cambridge University Press, 1982).

Braidotti, Rosi, *Transpositions* (Cambridge and Malden: Polity Press, 2008).

Braidotti, Rosi, Patrick, Hanafin, Bolette Blaagaard (eds.), *After Cosmopolitanism* (Abingdon and New York, Routledge, 2013).

Bronfen, Elisabeth, *Dorothy Richardson's Art of Memory: Space, Identity, Text*, trans. Victoria Appelbe (Manchester and New York: Manchester University Press, 1999).

Brown, Joshua, 'Review Essay: Of Mice and Memory', *The Oral History Review* 16.1 (1988), pp. 91–109.

Brown, Penny, *Poison at the Source: The Female Novel of Self-Development in the Early Twentieth Century* (Basingstoke: Macmillan, 1992).

Brown, Tony, 'Edward Carpenter, Forster and the Evolution of *A Room with a View*,' *ELT* 30.3 (1987), pp. 279–301.

Bruford, W. H., *The German Tradition of Self-Cultivation: 'Bildung' from Humboldt to Thomas Mann* (Cambridge University Press, 1975).

Buckley, Jerome, *Season of Youth: The Bildungsroman from Dickens to Golding* (Cambridge, MA: Harvard University Press, 1974).

Cadden, Mike, 'Home Is a Matter of Blood, Time, and Genre: Essentialism in Burnett and McKinley' in *Ariel: A Review of International English Literature* 28.1 (1997), pp. 53–67.

Campbell, Joseph, *The Hero with a Thousand Faces*, second edition (Princeton, NJ: Princeton University Press, 1968).

Carlyle, Thomas, 'Death of Goethe' in *Critical and Miscellaneous Essays* (London: Chapman & Hall, 1888), vol. 3.

Carlyle, Thomas, 'Translator's Preface to the First Edition of Meister's Apprenticeship' in *Wilhelm Meister's Apprenticeship and Travels: Translated from the German of Goethe*, 3 vols. (London: Chapman & Hall, 1888).

Carpenter, Frederic, 'The Adolescent in American Fiction', *The English Journal* 46.6 (1957), pp. 313–19.

Carr, E. H., *The Romantic Exiles: A Nineteenth-Century Portrait Gallery* (Boston: MIT Press, 1981).

Castle, Gregory, *Reading the Modernist Bildungsroman* (Gainesville, FL: University Press of Florida, 2006).

Castle, Gregory, (ed.), *A History of the Modernist Novel* (New York: Cambridge University Press, 2015).

Cave, Terence, *Mignon's Afterlives: Crossing Cultures from Goethe to the Twenty-First Century* (Oxford: Oxford University Press, 2011).

Chaney, Michael, *Graphic Subjects: Critical Essays on Autobiography and the Graphic Novel* (Madison: University of Wisconsin Press, 2011).

Chaney, Michael, *Reading Lessons in Seeing: Mirrors, Masks and Mazes in the Autobiographical Novel* (Jackson: University Press of Mississippi, 2016).

Chardin, Philippe, (ed.), *Roman de formation, roman d'éducation dans la littérature française et dans les littératures étrangères* (Paris: Kimé, 2007).

Cheah, Pheng, *Spectral Nationality: Passages of Freedom from Kant to Postcolonial Literatures of Liberation* (New York: Columbia, 2003).

Chernyshevsky, N. G., 'L. N. Tolstoy's *Childhood* and *Boyhood* and *Military Tales*' in Ralph E. Matlaw (ed.), *Belinsky, Chernyshevsky and Dobrolyubov: Selected Criticism* (Bloomington: Indiana University Press, 1962), pp. 95–107.

Choy, Philip P., Marlon K. Hom, and Lorraine Dong, *Coming Man: Nineteenth Century American Perceptions of the Chinese* (Seattle: University of Washington Press, 1995).

Christinidis, Georgia, 'Radical transformation: Angela Carter's adaptation of the *Bildungsroman*', *Textual Practice* 26.3 (2012), pp. 467–87, www.tandfonline.co m/author/Christinidis%2C+Georgia

Chute, Hillary L., *Graphic Women: Life Narrative and Contemporary Comics* (New York: Columbia University Press, 2010).

Chute, Hillary L., *Outside the Box: Interviews with Contemporary Cartoonists* (Chicago: University of Chicago Press, 2014).

Clark, Christopher, *Iron Kingdom: The Rise and Downfall of Prussia, 1600–1947* (Cambridge, MA: Harvard University Press, 2006).

Clark, Katerina, *The Soviet Novel: History as Ritual* (Chicago: University of Chicago Press, 1981).

Clarke, Gerald, *Capote: A Biography*, Kindle edition (New York: Rosetta Books, 2013).

Cocking, J. M., *Proust: Collected Essays on the Writer and His Art* (Cambridge: Cambridge University Press, 1982).

Cohn, Dorrit, *Transparent Minds: Narrative Modes for Presenting Consciousness in Fiction* (Princeton, NJ: Princeton University Press, 1978).

Collins, Sean T., 'Phoebe Gloeckner on reopening *The Diary of a Teenage Girl*', *AV Club* (13 August 2015), www.avclub.com/article/phoebe-gloeckner-reopening-diary-teenage-girl-223696

Cornillon, Susan Koppelman, (ed.), *Images of Women in Fiction: Feminist Perspectives* (Bowling Green, OH: Bowling Green University Popular Press, 1972).

Darnton, Robert, *The Literary Underground of the Old Regime* (Cambridge, MA: Harvard University Press, 1982).

DeMarr, Mary Jean, and Jane S. Bakerman, *The Adolescent in the American Novel Since 1960* (New York: Ungar, 1986).

Dilthey, Wilhelm, '*Sartor Resartus*: Philosophical Conflict, Positive and Negative Eras, and Personal Resolution', *Clio* 1.3 (1972), pp. 40–60.

Doub, Yolanda A., *Journeys of Formation: The Spanish American Bildungsroman* (New York and Oxford: Peter Lang, 2010).

Downing, Eric, *After Images: Photography, Archaeology, and Psychoanalysis and the Tradition of Bildung* (Detroit: Wayne State University Press, 2006).

Dufrenne, Mikel, *In the Presence of the Sensuous: Essays on Aesthetics*, ed. and trans. Mark S. Roberts and Dennis Gallagher (Atlantic Highlands, NJ: Humanities Press International, 1987).

Dufrenne, Mikel, *The Phenomenology of Aesthetic Experience*, trans. E. S. Casey (Evanston: Northwestern University Press, 1966).

Ehnenn, Jill R., 'Reorienting the Bildungsroman: Progress Narratives, Queerness, and Disability in *The History of Sir Richard Calmady* and *Jude the Obscure*', *Journal of Literary and Cultural Disability Studies* 11.2 (2017), pp. 151–68.

Eikhenbaum, Boris, *Lermontov. Opyt istoriko-literaturnoi otsenki* (Leningrad: Gosizdat, 1924).

El Refaie, Elisabeth, *Autobiographical Comics: Life Writing in Pictures* (Jackson: University Press of Mississippi, 2015).

Elias, Norbert, *The Court Society*, trans. Edmund Jephcott (New York: Pantheon, 1983).

Ellis, Lorna, *Appearing to Diminish: Female Development and the British Bildungsroman, 1750–1850* (Lewisburg: Bucknell University Press, 1999).

Ellmann, Richard, *James Joyce*, new and revised edition (New York: Oxford University Press, 1983).

Ellmann, Richard, *Oscar Wilde* (New York: Vintage, 1987).

Epstein, Klaus, *The Genesis of German Conservatism* (Princeton University Press, 1966).

Ermatinger, Emil, *Gottfried Kellers Leben* (Stuttgart: Cotta, 1918).

Esty, Jed, 'The Colonial Bildungsroman: *The Story of an African Farm* and the Ghost of Goethe', *Victorian Studies* 49.3 (2007), pp. 407–30.

Esty, Jed, *Unseasonable Youth: Modernism, Colonialism, and the Fiction of Development* (Oxford: Oxford University Press, 2011).

Evans, Richard J., *The Coming of the Third Reich* (New York: Penguin, 2003).

Falconer, Rachel, 'Young adult fiction and the crossover phenomenon' in David Rudd (ed.), *The Routledge Companion to Children's Literature* (New York and London, 2010).

Feder, Helena, *Ecocriticism and the Idea of Culture: Biology and the Bildungsroman* (Abingdon, Oxon. and New York: Routledge, 2014).

Felski, Rita, *Beyond Feminist Aesthetics: Feminist Literature and Social Change* (Cambridge: Harvard University Press, 1989).

Felski, Rita, *The Gender of Modernity* (Cambridge, MA: Harvard University Press, 1995).

Foster, Shirley, and Judy Simmons, *What Katy Read: Feminist Re-Readings of 'Classic' Stories for Girls* (Hampshire and London: MacMillan Press, 1995).

Foucault, Michel, *The Will to Knowledge: The History of Sexuality, Volume I*, trans. Robert Hurley (London: Penguin, 1998).

Fraiman, Susan, *Unbecoming Women: British Women Writers and the Novel of Development* (New York: Columbia University Press, 1993).

Franklin, Ruth, 'Art Spiegelman's Genre-Defying Holocaust Work, Revisited', *New Republic* (5 October 2011), https://newrepublic.com/article/95758/art-spiegelman-metamaus-holocaust-memoir-graphic-novel

Friedberg, Barton C., 'The Cult of Adolescence in American Fiction', *The Nassau Review* 1.1 (1964), pp. 26–35.

Fromm, Gloria G., (ed.), *Windows on Modernism: Selected Letters of Dorothy Richardson* (Athens and London: University of Georgia Press, 1995).

Frye, Northrop, *Anatomy of Criticism: Four Essays* (Princeton University Press, 1957).

Gerhard, Melitta, *Der deutsche Entwicklungsroman bis zu Goethes 'Wilhelm Meister'*, new edition (Bern and Munich: Francke, 1968).

Gilead, Sarah, 'Magic abdured: Closure in children's fantasy fiction' in Peter Hunt (ed.), *Literature for Children: Contemporary Criticism* (London and New York: Routledge, 1992).

Giles, James Richard, *The Spaces of Violence* (Tuscaloosa: University of Alabama Press, 2006).

Gilmour, Robin, 'Memory in *David Copperfield*', *Dickensian* 71 (1975), pp. 30–42.

Ginzburg, Lydia, *O psikhologicheskoi proze* (Leningrad: Khudozhestvennaia literatura, 1977).

Girard, René, *Deceit, Desire, and the Novel: Self and Other in Literary Structure*, trans. Yvonne Freccero (Baltimore and London: Johns Hopkins University Press, 1965).

Gjesdal, Kristin, '*Bildung*' in Michael N. Forster and Kristin Gjesdal (eds.), *The Oxford Handbook of German Philosophy in the Nineteenth-Century* (Oxford: Oxford University Press, 2015), pp. 695–719.

Gleason, Abbot, *European and Moscovite: Ivan Kireevsky and the Origins of Slavophilism* (Cambridge, MA: Harvard University Press, 1972).

Goebel, Walter, and Saskia Schabio (eds.), *Locating Postcolonial Narratives and Genres* (New York: Routledge, 2012).

Goethe, Johann Wolfgang, *Gedichte 1756–1799* in Karl Eibl (ed.), *Sämtliche Werke: Briefe, Tagebücher und Gespräche* (Frankfurt am Main: Deutscher Klassiker Verlag, 1987), vol. 1.

Gordon, Ian, Matthew P. McAllister, and Mark Jancovich (eds.), *Film and Comic Books* (Jackson: University Press of Mississippi, 2007).

Grant, Pat, 'Genealogy of the Boofhead: Image, Memory and Australian Surf Comics' in *Blue* (Marietta, GA: Top Shelf, 2012).

Green, Laura, *Literary Identification from Charlotte Brontë to Tsitsi Dangaremba* (Columbus: Ohio State University Press, 2012).

Grigor'ev, Apollon, 'Razvitie idei narodnosti v russkoi literature so smerti Pushkina' in *Apologiia pochvennichestva* (Moscow: Institut russkoi tsivilizatsii, 2008), pp. 184–607.

Gurvich-Lischiner, Sofya, *Tvorchestvo Aleksandra Gercena i nemetskaia literatura* (Frankfurt a. Main: Peter Lang, 2001).

Habegger, Alfred, '"What Maisie Knew": Henry James's Bildungsroman of the Artist as Queer Moralist' in Gert Buelens (ed.), *Enacting History in Henry James: Narrative, Power, and Ethics* (Cambridge: Cambridge University Press, 1997).

Habermas, Jürgen, *The Structural Transformation of the Public Sphere: An Inquiry into a Category of Bourgeois Society*, trans. Thomas Burger (Cambridge, MA: MIT Press, 1991).

Hanscombe, Gillian, *The Art of Life: Dorothy Richardson and the Development of Feminist Consciousness* (Columbus: Ohio University Press, 1983).

Hardin, James N., (ed.), *Reflection and Action: Essays on the Bildungsroman* (University of South Carolina Press, 1991).

Harris, Harper, 'Mariko and Jillian Tamaki on This One Summer winning the Caldecott and Printz Honors', *The Beat* (13 February 2015), www.comicsbeat .com/mariko-and-jillian-tamaki-on-winning-the-caldecott-and-printz-honors- and-this-one-su

Harrold, Charles Frederick, *Carlyle and German Thought: 1819–1834* (Hamden and London: Archon Books, 1963).

Hatfield, Charles, *Alternative Comics: An Emerging Literature* (Jackson: University Press of Mississippi, 2005).

Hays, Simon, '*Nervous Conditions*, Lukacs, and the Postcolonial Bildungsroman', *Genre: Forms of Discourse and Culture* 46.3 (2013), pp. 317–34.

Hegel, G. W. F., *Hegel's Aesthetics: Lectures on Fine Art*, trans. T. M. Knox (Oxford: Clarendon Press, 1975), vol. I.

Hegel, G. W. F., *The Philosophy of History*, trans. J. Sibree (New York: Dover Publications, 1956).

Herder, J. G., *Journal meiner Reise im Jahr 1769* (Leipzig: Reklam, 1972).

Herz, Judith Scherer and Robert K. Martin (eds.), *E. M. Forster: Centenary Revaluations* (Basingstoke: Palgrave Macmillan, 1982).

Hirsch, Marianne, 'Family Pictures: Maus, Mourning, and Post-Memory', *Discourse* 15.2 (Winter 1992–3), pp. 3–29.

Ho, Jennifer, *Consumption and Identity in Asian American Coming-of-Age Novels* (New York and London: Routledge, 2013).

Hovey, Jaime, *A Thousand Words: Portraiture, Style, and Queer Modernism* (Columbus: The Ohio State University Press, 2006).

Howe, Susanne, *Wilhelm Meister and His English Kinsmen: Apprentices to Life* (New York: Columbia University Press, 1930).

Humboldt, Wilhelm von, The Limits of State Action, J. W. Barrow (ed.) (Cambridge: Cambridge University Press, 1969).

Hunt, Lynn, *The Family Romance of the French Revolution* (Berkeley: University of California Press, 1992).

Irele, F. Abiola (ed.), *The Cambridge Companion to the African Novel* (Cambridge: Cambridge University Press, 2009).

Isbell, John, *The Birth of European Romanticism: Truth and Propaganda in Staël's De l'Allemagne* (Cambridge: Cambridge University Press, 1994).

Jacobs, Jürgen, *Wilhelm Meister und seine Brüder: Untersuchungen zum deutschen Bildungsroman* (Munich: Fink, 1972).

Jacobs, Jürgen and Markus Krause (eds.), *Der Deutsche Bildungsroman: Gattungsgeschichte vom 18. Bis zum 20. Jahrhundert* (Munich: Beck, 1989).

Janz, Rolf-Peter, 'Zum sozialen Gehalt der *Lehrjahre*' in Helmut Arntzen (ed.), *Literaturwissenschaft und Geschichtsphilosophie: Festschrift für Wilhelm Emrich* (Berlin: de Gruyter, 1975), pp. 320–40.

Japtok, Martin, *Growing Up Ethnic: Nationalism and the Bildungsroman in African American and Jewish American Fiction* (Iowa City: University of Iowa Press, 2005).

Jay, Karla and JoAnne Glasgow (eds.), *Lesbian Texts and Contexts: Radical Revisions* (London: Onlywomen Press, 1992).

Jeffers, Thomas L., *Apprenticeships: The Bildungsroman from Goethe to Santayana* (New York and Basingstoke: Palgrave Macmillan, 2005).

Jost, François, 'La tradition du Bildungsroman', *Comparative Literature*, 21.2 (1969), pp. 97–115.

Junko, Yoshido, 'Uneasy men in the land of Oz' in Roderick McGillis (ed.), *Children's Literature and the Fin de Siècle* (Connecticut and London: Praeger, 2003).

Karamzin, N. M., *Izbrannye sochineniia v dvukh tomakh*, 2 vols. (Moscow-Leningrad: Khudozhestvennaia literatura, 1964).

Karamzin, N. M., *Pis'ma russkogo puteshestvennika, 'Literatrnye pamiatniki'* (Leningrad: Akademia, 1984).

Keller, Gottfried, 'Einkehr unterhalb des Rheinfalls' in *Sämtliche Werke*, vol. 1, p. 150.

Keller, Gottfried, Open letter to the *Basler Nachrichten* on 4 April 1872 in *Sämtliche Werke* vol. 7, pp. 287–9.

Kingsley, Charles, 'Human Soot' in Mrs Kingsley (ed.), *Charles Kingsley: His Letters and Memories of His Life*, seventh abridged edition (London: C. Kegan Paul and Co., 1880), vol. 2, pp. 242–3.

Kireevskii, I. V., 'Deviatnadsatyi vek' in *Polnoe sobranie sochinenii*, 3 vols. (Moscow: Moskovskii Universitet, 1911), vol. I, pp. 85–108.

Kliger, Ilya, *The Narrative Shape of Truth: Veridiction in Modern European Literature* (University Park: Pennsylvania State University Press, 2011).

Köhn, Lothar, *Entwicklungs- und Bildungsroman: Ein Forschungsbericht* (Stuttgart: Metzler, 1969).

Kontje, Todd, *The German Bildungsroman: History of a National Genre* (Columbia, SC: Camden House, 1993).

Kontje, Todd, *Private Lives in the Public Sphere: The German Bildungsroman as Metafiction* (University Park, PA: Pennsylvania State University Press, 1992).

Kontje, Todd, *Women, the Novel, and the German Nation 1771–1871: Domestic Fiction in the Fatherland* (Cambridge: Cambridge University Press, 1998).

Koselleck, Reinhart, *Kritik und Krise: Eine Studie zur Pathogenese der bürgerlichen Welt*, Suhrkamp Taschenbuch Wissenschaft 36 (Frankfurt am Main: Suhrkamp, 1976).

Krebs, Christopher B., *A Most Dangerous Book: Tacitus's Germania from the Roman Empire to the Third Reich* (New York: Norton, 2011).

Kruger, Maria, *Women's Literature in Kenya and Uganda: The Trouble with Modernity* (New York: Palgrave Macmillan, 2010).

Labovitz, Esther Kleinbord, *The Myth of the Heroine: The Female Bildungsroman in the Twentieth Century* (New York: Peter Lang, 1986).

Landes, Joan B., *Women in the Public Sphere in the Age of the French Revolution* (Ithaca: Cornell University Press, 1988).

Latham, Sean, *The Art of Scandal: Modernism, Libel Law, and the Roman à Clef* (Oxford: Oxford University Press, 2009).

Lenz, Millicent, 'Ursula K. Le Guin' in Peter Hunt and Millicent Lenz, *Alternative Worlds in Fantasy Fiction* (London and New York, Continuum, 2001).

LeSeur, Geta, *Ten Is the Age of Darkness: The Black Bildungsroman* (Columbia, MO: University of Missouri Press, 1995).

Levine, George, *How to Read the Victorian Novel* (Oxford: Blackwell Publishing, 2008).

Lewis, R. W. B., *The American Adam: Innocence, Tragedy and Tradition in the Nineteenth Century* (Chicago and London: University of Chicago Press, 1968).

Lima, Enrique, 'The Uneven Development of the "Bildungsroman": D'Arcy McNickle and Native American Modernity', *Comparative Literature* 63.3 (2011), pp. 291–306.

Lima, Maria Helena, 'Decolonizing Genre: Jamaica Kincaid and the Bildungsroman', *Genre: Forms of Discourse and Culture* 26.4 (1993), pp. 431–59.

Lipton, Briony and Elizabeth Mackinlay, *We Only Talk Feminist Here: Feminist Academics, Voice and Agency in the Neoliberal University* (London: Palgrave Macmillan, 2017).

Livingstone, Angela, *Pasternak's Doctor Zhivago. In Landmarks of World Literature* (Cambridge: Cambridge University Press, 1989).

Locke, John, *An Essay Concerning Human Understanding* (1689) (Oxford: Clarendon Press, 1979).

Lowe, Brigid, 'The Bildungsroman' in Robert L. Caserio and Clement Hawes (eds.), *The Cambridge History of the English Novel* (Cambridge: Cambridge University Press, 2012).

Luft, David S., *Robert Musil and the Crisis of European Culture 1880–1942* (Berkeley: University of California Press, 1980).

Lukács, Georg, *The Historical Novel*, trans. Hannah Mitchell and Stanley Mitchell (London: Merlin Press, 1962).

Lukács, Georg, *The Meaning of Contemporary Realism*, trans. Hannah Mitchell and Stanley Mitchell (London: Merlin, 1956).

Lukács, Georg, *The Theory of the Novel: A Historico-Philosophical Essay on the Forms of Great Epic Literature*, trans. Anna Bostock (London: Merlin Press, 1971).

Lurie, Alison, *Boys and Girls Forever: Children's Classics from Cinderella to Harry Potter* (London, Vintage, 2004).

Madsen, Deborah L., 'Chinese American Writers of the Real and the Fake: Authenticity and the Twin Traditions of Life Writing', *Canadian Review of American Studies/Revue Canadienne d'Etudes Américaines* 36.3 (2006), pp. 257–71.

Mann, Thomas, *Betrachtungen eines Unpolitischen [Reflections of a Nonpolitical Man]* (Berlin: S. Fischer, 1918).

Mann, Thomas, 'Einführung in den Zauberberg für Studenten der Universität Princeton' in Mann, *Gesammelte Werke in Zwölf Bänden* (Frankfurt am Main: Fischer, 1960).

Mann, Thomas, *Essays*, Hermann Kurzke and Stephan Stachorski (eds.), vol. 1 (Frankfurt am Main: Fischer, 1993).

Mann, Thomas, *Tagebücher 1918–1921* (Frankfurt am Main: Fischer, 1979).

Marks, John, *Gilles Deleuze: Vitalism and Multiplicity* (London: Pluto Press, 1998).

Maslov, Boris and Ilya Kliger (eds.), *Persistent Forms: Explorations in Historical Poetics* (New York: Fordham University Press, 2015).

Mayer, Gerhart, *Der deutsche Bildungsroman: Von der Aufklärung bis zur Gegenwart* (Stuttgart: Metzler, 1992).

Mayer, Gerhart, 'Zum deutschen Antibildungsroman', *Jahrbuch der Raabe-Gesellschaft* (1974), pp. 41–64.

McCulloch, Fiona, *Children's Literature in Context* (London and New York: Continuum, 2011).

McCulloch, Fiona, *Contemporary British Children's Fiction and Cosmopolitanism* (New York and London: Routledge, 2017).

McCulloch, Fiona, 'Dis-membering "Patriotism": Cosmopolitan Haunting in Theresa Breslin's *Remembrance*' in *The Lion and the Unicorn* 38.3 (September 2014), pp. 342–59.

McCulloch, Fiona, *The Fictional Role of Childhood in Victorian and Early Twentieth-Century Children's Literature* (New York and Ontario: Edwin Mellen Press, 2004).

McCulloch, Fiona, '"No Longer Just Human": The Posthuman Child in Beth Revis's *Across the Universe* Trilogy' in *Children's Literature Association Quarterly* 41.1 (Spring 2016), pp. 74–92.

McLennan, Rachael, *Adolescence, America, and Postwar Fiction: Developing Figures* (Basingstoke: Palgrave Macmillan, 2009).

McNeillie, Andrew (ed.), *Essays of Virginia Woolf, vol. 3: 1919–1924* (London: Hogarth Press, 1986; San Diego: Harcourt Brace Jovanovich, 1986).

McWilliams, Ellen, *Margaret Atwood and the Female Bildungsroman* (Farnham, Surrey and Burlington, VT: Ashgate, 2009).

Meek, Margaret and Victor Watson, *Coming of Age in Children's Literature* (London and New York: Continuum, 2003).

Mickelson, David J., 'The *Bildungsroman* in Africa: The Case of *Mission terminée*', *The French Review* 59.3 (1986), pp. 418–27.

Millard, Kenneth, *Coming of Age in Contemporary American Fiction* (Edinburgh: Edinburgh University Press, 2007).

Miller, Jane Eldridge, *Rebel Women: Feminism, Modernism and the Edwardian Novel* (London: Virago, 1994).

Minden, Michael, *The German Bildungsroman: Incest and Inheritance* (Cambridge: Cambridge University Press, 1997).

Mintz, Alan, *George Eliot and the Novel of Vocation* (Cambridge, MA: Harvard University Press, 1978).

Mirsky, D. S., *A History of Russian Literature* (New York: Knopf, 1927).

Mochul'skii, Konstantin, *Dostoevsky: His Life and Work*, trans. Michael A. Minihan (Princeton: Princeton University Press, 1967).

Moran, Maureen, *Catholic Sensationalism and Victorian Literature* (Liverpool University Press, 2007).

Moran, Maureen, *Victorian Literature and Culture* (London and New York: Continuum, 2011).

Moretti, Franco, *Atlas of the European Novel 1800–1900* (London and New York: Verso, 1998).

Moretti, Franco, *The Way of the World: The Bildungsroman in European Culture* (London: Verso, 1987/2000).

Morgenstern, Karl, 'On the Nature of the Bildungsroman', *PMLA* 'Criticism in Translation', 124.2 (2009), pp. 647–59.

Murray, Gail Schmunk, *American Children's Literature and the Construction of Childhood* (New York: Twayne Publishers, 1998).

Murray, Heather, 'Frances Hodgson Burnett's *The Secret Garden*: The Organ(ic) ized World' in Perry Nodelman (ed.), *Touchstones: Reflections on the Best in Children's Literature Vol. 1* (West Lafayette, IN: Purdue University, 1985).

Muschg, Adolf, *Gottfried Keller* (Munich: Kindler, 1977).

Nackenoff, Carol, *Fictional Republic: Horatio Alger and American Political Discourse* (Oxford: Oxford University Press, 1994).

Nardini, Nicholas, 'A Fresh-Start Doctrine: The Marshall Plan, *The Adventures of Augie March*, and the Bildungsroman after Nationalism', *Arizona Quarterly: A Journal of American Literature, Culture, and Theory* 71.2 (2015), pp. 149–74.

Norton, Charles Eliot, (ed.), *Correspondence between Goethe and Carlyle* (London: Macmillan, 1887).

Orwin, Donna, *Consequences of Consciousness* (Stanford: Stanford University Press, 2007.

Orwin, Donna Tussing, *Tolstoy's Art and Thought: 1847–1880* (Princeton, NJ: Princeton University Press, 1993).

Palmer, Paulina, '"She began to show me the words she had written, one by one": Lesbian Reading and Writing Practices in the Fiction of Sarah Waters', *Women: A Cultural Review* 19.1 (2008), pp. 69–86.

Paperno, Irina, 'Introduction: Intimacy and History. The Gercen Family Drama Reconsidered' in *Russian Literature* 61.1 (2007), pp.1–65.

Pater, Walter, *The Renaissance: Studies in Art and Poetry* (Oxford and New York: Oxford University Press, 1986).

Pater, Walter, *The Renaissance: Studies in Art and Poetry: The 1893 Text*, D. L. Hill (ed.) (Berkeley: University of California Press, 1980).

Paul, Jean-Marie, (ed.), *Images de l'homme dans le roman de formation ou Bildungsroman* (Nancy: Centre de Recherches Germaniques et Scandinaves, 1995).

Phillips, Jerry, 'The Mem Sahib, the Worthy, the Rajah and His Minions: Some Reflections on the Class Politics of *The Secret Garden*' in *The Lion and the Unicorn* 17.2 (1993), pp. 168–94.

Pirogov, N. I., '*Voprosy Zhizni*' in *Izbrannye pedagogicheskie sochineniia* (Moscow: Academia, 1953), pp. 47–72.

Prendergast, Christopher, *Mirages and Mad Beliefs: Proust the Skeptic* (Princeton, NJ: Princeton University Press, 2013).

Prosser, Jay, *Second Skins: The Body Narratives of Transsexuality* (New York: Columbia University Press, 1998).

Puar, Jasbir K., *Terrorist Assemblages: Homonationalism in Queer Times* (Durham: Duke University Press, 2007).

Qualls, Barry V., *The Secular Pilgrims of Victorian Fiction: The Novel as Book of Life* (Cambridge: Cambridge University Press, 1982).

Radischev, A. N., 'O cheloveke, ego smertnosti i bessmertii' in *Polnoe sobranie sochinenii* (Moscow-Leningrad: Akademia, 1938–54), vol. 2, pp. 37–142.

Radischev, A. N., *Polnoe sobranie sochinenii* (Moscow-Leningrad: Akademia Nauk SSSR, 1938), vol. 1.

Raitt, Suzanne, *May Sinclair: A Modern Victorian* (Oxford: Clarendon Press, 2000).

Rao, Rahul, *Third World Protest: Between Home and the World* (Oxford: Oxford University Press, 2012).

Raynaud, Claudine, 'Coming of Age in the African American Novel' in Maryemma Graham (ed.), *The Cambridge Companion to the African American Novel* (Cambridge: Cambridge University Press, 2006).

Reddick, John, *The 'Danzig Trilogy' of Günter Grass: A Study of the Tin Drum, Cat and Mouse and Dog Years* (London: Secker and Warburg, 1975).

Redfield, Marc, 'The Bildungsroman' in David Scott Kastan (ed.), *The Oxford Encyclopedia of British Literature* (Oxford: Oxford University Press, 2006).

Redfield, Marc, 'The Bildungsroman' in Joseph Slaughter, *Human Rights, Inc: The World Novel, Narrative Form, and International Law* (New York: Fordham University Press, 2007).

Redfield, Marc, *Phantom Formations: Aesthetic Ideology and the Bildungsroman* (Ithaca and London: Cornell University Press, 1996).

Reynolds, David, *America: Empire of Liberty* (London: Penguin, 2010).

Richards, Gary, *Lovers and Beloveds: Sexual Otherness in Southern Fiction, 1936–1961* (Baton Rouge: LSU Press, 2007).

Riquelme, John Paul, *The Teller and Tale in Joyce's Fiction: Oscillating Perspectives* (Baltimore and London: Johns Hopkins University Press, 1983).

Rishoi, Christy, *From Girl to Woman: American Women's Coming-of-Age Narratives* (Albany, NY: State University of New York Press, 2003).

Röder-Bolton, Gerlinde, *George Eliot and Goethe: An Elective Affinity* (Amsterdam: Rodopi, 1998).

Rolo, Charles J., 'Carol and Therese: *The Price of Salt* by Claire Morgan', *New York Times* 18 May 1952, BR23.

Rose, Jacqueline, *The Case of Peter Pan or the Impossibility of Children's Fiction*, (London: Macmillan, 1984).

Royal, Derek Parker, 'Plotting a Way Home: The Jewish American Novel' in Alfred Bendixen (ed.), *A Companion to the American Novel, Genres and Traditions* (Oxford: Wiley-Blackwell, 2012).

Rushworth, Jennifer, 'Derrida, Proust, and the promise of writing', *French Studies* 69.2 (2015), pp. 205–19.

Safranski, Rüdiger, *Romantik: Eine deutsche Affäre* (Munich: Hanser, 2007).

Salmon, Richard, *The Formation of the Victorian Literary Profession* (Cambridge: Cambridge University Press, 2013).

Sammons, Jeffrey L., 'The Mystery of the Missing *Bildungsroman*, or: What happened to Wilhelm Meister's Legacy?', *Genre* 14.2 (1981), pp. 229–46.

Saunders, Max, *Self Impression: Life-Writing, Autobiografiction and the Forms of Modern Literature* (Oxford: Oxford University Press, 2010).

Schama, Simon, *Landscape and Memory* (New York: Knopf, 1995).

Scharnhorst, Gary, 'Demythologizing Alger' in Horatio Alger, Jr., *Ragged Dick or, Street Life in New York with Boot Blacks* (New York and London: W. W. Norton & Co., 2008), pp. 182–98.

Schlechta, Karl, *Goethes Wilhelm Meister* (Frankfurt am Main: Klostermann, 1953).

Schlegel, Friedrich, 'Über Goethes Meister' in Ernst Behler (ed.), *Kritische Friedrich-Schlegel-Ausgabe* (Munich, Paderborn, Vienna: Thomas, 1967), vol. 2.

Schoen, Carol B., *Anzia Yezierska* (Boston: Twayne, 1982).

Schwerte, Hans, *Faust und das Faustische: Ein Kapitel deutscher Ideologie* (Stuttgart: Klett, 1962).

Scott, Bonnie Kime, *Gender in Modernism: New Geographies, Complex Intersections* (Urbana: University of Illinois Press, 2006).

Scott, Bonnie Kime, *The Gender of Modernism: A Critical Anthology* (Bloomington: Indiana University Press, 1990).

Selbmann, Rolf, *Der deutsche Bildungsroman*, Sammlung Metzler 214 (Stuttgart: Metzler, 1984).

Selbmann, Rolf (ed.), *Zur Geschichte des deutschen Bildungsromans* (Darmstadt: Wissenschaftliche Buchgesellschaft, 1988).

Sharpe, Lesley, (ed.), *The Cambridge Companion to Goethe* (Cambridge: Cambridge University Press, 2002).

Sheehan, James J., *German History 1770–1866* (Oxford: Clarendon, 1989).

Shestov, Lev, *Dostoevsky, Tolstoy, and Nietzsche*, trans. Spencer Roberts, (Columbus: Ohio University Press, 1978).

Shishmarev, V. F., *Aleksandr Veselovskii i russkaia literatura* (Leningrad: Izdatel'stvo LGU, 1946).

Shuman, R. Baird, 'Initiation Rites in Steinbeck's "The Red Pony"', *The English Journal* 59.9 (1970), pp. 1252–5.

Sinfield, Alan, 'Diaspora and Hybridity: Queer Identity and the Ethnicity Model', *Textual Practice* 10.2 (1996), pp. 271–93.

Sinfield, Alan, *The Wilde Century: Effeminacy, Oscar Wilde and the Queer Moment* (London: Cassell, 1994).

Smith, John, 'Cultivating Gender: Sexual Difference, *Bildung*, and the *Bildungsroman*', *Michigan Germanic Studies* 13.2 (1987), pp. 206–25.

Sow, Alioune, 'Political Intuition and African Autobiographies of Childhood', *Biography: An Interdisciplinary Quarterly* 33.3 (2010), pp. 498–517.

Spivak, Gayatri Chakravorty, 'Three Women's Texts and a Critique of Imperialism', *Critical Inquiry* (1985), pp. 243–61.

Spoo, Robert, 'H. D.'s Dating of *Asphodel*: A Reassessment', *The H. D. Newsletter* 4.2 (Winter 1991), pp. 31–40.

Staiger, Emil, (ed.), *Briefwechsel Schiller Goethe* (Frankfurt am Main: Insel, 1966), vol. 1.

Stein, Mark, *Black British Literature: Novels of Transformation* (Columbus: The Ohio University Press, 2004).

Steiner, Lina, *For Humanity's Sake: The Bildungsroman in Russian Culture* (Toronto and London: University of Toronto Press, 2011).

Summerfield, Giovanna and Lisa Downward, *New Perspectives on the European Bildungsroman* (London and New York, Continuum, 2012).

Swales, Martin, *The German Bildungsroman from Wieland to Hesse* (Princeton, NJ: Princeton University Press, 1978).

Tacitus, P. Cornelius, *Germania: Bericht über Germanien*, trans. Josef Lindauer (Munich: Deutscher Taschenbuch Verlag, 1977).

Tchen, John Kuo-Wei, *New York before Chinatown: Orientalism and the Shaping of American Culture, 1776–1882* (Baltimore: Johns Hopkins University Press, 2001).

Tennyson, G. B., 'The Bildungsroman in Nineteenth-Century English Literature' in Rosario Armato and John M. Spalek (eds.), *Medieval Epic to the Epic Theater of Brecht* (University of South Carolina Press, 1968), pp. 135–46.

Thacker, Deborah Cogan and Jean Webb, *Introducing Children's Literature: From Romanticism to Postmodernism* (London and New York: Routledge 2002).

Therrien, Kathleen M., '"Why Do They Have To . . . To . . . Say Things . . . ?": Poverty, Class, and Gender in Betty Smith's *A Tree Grows in Brooklyn*', *Legacy: A Journal of American Women Writers* 16.1 (1999), pp. 93–105.

Tihanov, Galin, *The Master and the Slave: Lukács, Bakhtin, and the Ideas of Their Time* (Oxford: Clarendon Press, 2000).

Todd, Jude, 'Knotted Bellies and Fragile Webs: Untangling and Re-Spinning in Tayo's Healing Journey', *American Indian Quarterly* 19.2 (1995), pp. 155–70.

Trites, Roberta Seelinger, *Disturbing the Universe: Power and Repression in Adolescent Literature* (University of Iowa Press, 2000).

Trunz, Erich, (ed.), *Goethes Werke* (Hamburg: Wegner, 1950), vol. VIII.

Turgenev, Ivan 'Hamlet and Don Quixote', trans. Moshe Spiegel, *Chicago Review* 17.4 (1965), pp. 92–109.

Unwin, Timothy, (ed.), *The Cambridge Companion to Flaubert* (Cambridge: Cambridge University Press, 2004).

Vásquez, José Santiago Fernández, 'Recharting the Geography of Genre: Ben Okri's *The Famished Road* as a Postcolonial Bildungsroman', *Journal of Commonwealth Literature* 37.2 (2002), pp. 85–106.

Veselovskii, A. N., *Istoricheskaia poetika* (Leningrad: Khudozhestvennaia literatura, 1940).

Vinogradov, V. V., *Istoriia slov* (Moscow: Akademiia Nauk RF, 1999).

Volgin, Igor, *Poslednii god Dostoevskogo* (Moscow: Sovetskii pisatel', 1986).

Walicki, Andrzej, *A History of Russian Thought from the Enlightenment to Marxism*, trans. Hilda Andrews-Rusiecka (Oxford: Clarendon Press, 1980).

Ware, Chris, 'Richard McGuire and "Here": A Grateful Appreciation', *Comic Art* 8 (2006), pp. 5–7.

Watt, Ian, *The Rise of the Novel: Studies in Defoe, Richardson and Fielding* (Berkeley and Los Angeles: University of California Press, 1957).

Waxman, Sarah, 'History of Central Park, New York', www.ny.com/articles/centralpark.html

Weigand, Hermann J., *Thomas Mann's Novel Der Zauberberg* (New York and London: Appleton-Century, 1933).

Weingarten, Karen, 'Between the Town and the Mountain: Abortion and the Politics of Life in Edith Wharton's *Summer*', *Canadian Review of American Studies/Revue Canadienne d'Etudes Américaines* 40.3 (2010), pp. 351–72.

West, Richard Samuel, *The San Francisco Wasp: An Illustrated History* (Northampton, MA: Periodyssey Press, 2004).

White, Barbara, *Growing Up Female: Adolescent Girlhood in American Fiction* (Westport, CT: Greenwood Press, 1985).

Williams, Paul, and James Lyons (eds.), *The Rise of the American Comics Artist: Creators and Contexts* (Jackson: University Press of Mississippi, 2010).

Williams, Raymond, *The Long Revolution* (London: Hogarth Press, 1992).

Wilson, Colin, *The Outsider* (London: Indigo, 1997).

Wilson, Edmund, *Axel's Castle* (New York and London: Charles Scribner's Sons, 1931).

Witek, Joseph, *Comic Books as History: The Narrative Art of Jack Jackson, Art Spiegelman, and Harvey Pekar* (Jackson: University Press of Mississippi, 1989).

Witham, W. Tasker, *The Adolescent in the American Novel 1920–1960* (New York: Frederick Ungar, 1964).

Womble, Todd, 'Windswept and Scattered: Place and Identity in Larry McMurtry's *The Last Picture Show*' in Paul Varner (ed.), *New Wests and Post-Wests: Literature and Film of the American West* (Newcastle upon Tyne: Cambridge Scholars Publishing, 2013).

Wright, Bradford W., *Comic Book Nation: The Transformation of Youth Culture in America* (Baltimore: Johns Hopkins University Press, 2001).

Wright, Derek, 'Parenting the Nation: Some Observations on Nuruddin Farah's *Maps*', *College Literature* 19.3 (1992), pp. 176–84.

Wright, Derek, (ed.), *Emerging Perspectives on Nuruddin Farah* (Trenton: Africa World Press, 2002).

Wyndham, Francis, and Diana Melly (eds.), *Jean Rhys Letters 1931–66* (Harmondsworth: Penguin, 1984).

Yang, Gene Luen, 'Why Comics?', lecture at Penn State University, 10 December 2008, www.youtube.com/watch?v=xYA3HNbc7Rs

Zimmerman, Bonnie, *The Safe Sea of Women: Lesbian Fiction, 1969–1989* (London: Onlywomen Press, 1992).

## Online Sources

www.archives.gov/founding-docs/declaration-transcript

www.britannica.com/art/bildungsroman

www.britannica.com/event/American-Civil-War/The-cost-and-significance-of-the-Civil-War

www.britannica.com/topic/Wilhelm-Meisters-Apprenticeship

www.law.cornell.edu/uscode/text/4/4.

www.sovlit.net

https://obamawhitehouse.archives.gov/blog/2009/01/21/president-barack-obamas-inaugural-address

# Index

Printed in Great Britain
by Amazon

67187870R00210